Fergus Fleming is the author of the bestselling *Killing Dragons*. His most recent book *Ninety Degrees North – The Quest for the North Pole* is also published by Granta Books. He lives near Gloucester.

BARROW'S BOYS

Fergus Fleming

Granta Books
London

Granta Publications, 2/3 Hanover Yard, London N1 8BE

First published in Great Britain by Granta Books 1998
Published in paperback by Granta Books 1999
This edition published by Granta Books 2001

A CIP catalogue record for this book is available
from the British Library.

1 3 5 7 9 10 8 6 4 2

Typeset by M Rules
Printed and bound in Great Britain by
Mackays of Chatham plc

CONTENTS

Preface and Acknowledgements		ix
Chronology of Major Expeditions		xiii
Maps		xvii

1	THE MAN AT THE ADMIRALTY	1
2	DEATH ON THE CONGO	13
3	THE MIRAGE OF LANCASTER SOUND	29
4	BUCHAN'S RETREAT	52
5	FURTHEST WEST	62
6	WINTER AT MELVILLE ISLAND	73
7	VICE-CONSULS OF MURZOUK	92
8	FAILURE AT FOXE BASIN	107
9	THE MAN WHO ATE HIS BOOTS	124
10	LYON'S DEPARTURE	154
11	SQUABBLES IN THE SAHARA	177
12	THE MADMAN OF TIMBUCTOO	201
13	THE ROAD FROM BADAGRY	215
14	PARRY TO THE POLE	233
15	ROSS RESURGENT	242

16	THE RIDDLE OF THE NIGER	253
17	SECOND SINGAPORES	274
18	ORDEAL OF THE *VICTORY*	281
19	'ANY ANIMAL WILL DO FOR A LION'	305
20	THE OVERLANDERS	318
21	THE BOTTOM OF THE WORLD	331
22	'YOU SEE HOW OUR HANDS SHAKE?'	348
23	THE LAST POST	363
24	*EREBUS* AND *TERROR*	372
25	THE ARCTIC COUNCIL	380
26	*INVESTIGATOR*	392
27	FRANKLIN'S FATE	405
28	RIDING THE GLOBE	420
	EPILOGUE	426
	Sources and References	446
	Bibliography	474
	Index	479

PREFACE AND
ACKNOWLEDGEMENTS

B ritish exploration in the first half of the nineteenth century is a
well-documented subject: the explorers themselves have been
written about, as have the areas they visited, but to my knowledge,
the people and places have never before been brought together in a
single volume. The reason for doing so now is John Barrow, a shadowy
figure who stalks the bibliography of the period but whose role as a
father of exploration, fully recognized during his time, seems to have
been forgotten. This book attempts to rectify that oversight. It is a
narrative rather than a biography and Barrow inevitably plays second
fiddle to his explorers. Yet he remains the driving force behind his
minions' more thrilling exploits and I hope that, in dusting down
these adventures, I have also managed to reposition him on the shelf –
shaky though his pedestal may sometimes seem.

In bringing Barrow and his men to life I have drawn wherever possible on primary sources – of which there are a multitude. Every
explorer kept a journal; many of them wrote memoirs. In addition
there are literally thousands of letters, diaries, memos and related
documents scattered throughout archives in England, Scotland,
Ireland, America, Canada and Australia. Digging through this mass of

paper would, however, have been an interminable task were it not for the spadework of previous authors, and in this respect I am indebted to Pierre Berton (his *Arctic Grail* is required reading for polar enthusiasts), Ernest Dodge, Kathleen Fitzpatrick, G. F. Lamb, Christopher Lloyd, Mercedes Mackay, Ann Parry and Francis Woodward, whose life of Lady Franklin is breathtaking given the illegibility of the source material. Thanks must also be given to A. G. E. Jones for his research on John and James Ross, which has been much used but little acknowledged – to judge, at least, from a slightly annoyed note preserved in the Royal Geographical Society archives. And last but not least there is A. Adu Boahen whose heavily footnoted study of Saharan history should be carried by anyone who wishes to explore the PRO's impenetrable Colonial Office microfilms.

In quoting from original letters, I have retained idiosyncracies of punctuation and spelling; they add flavour and also give a small insight into the authors' personalities. In similar vein, I realize that the Inuit peoples should properly not be called Eskimos, but as Barrow's explorers called them Eskimos – or Esquimaux, which some rhymed with 'saw' – I have followed the convention of the time. As regards African place-names, they were spelled in so many different ways, with many of the towns no longer existing or if they do exist being called something else entirely, that I have aimed only for consistency.

One omission in this book is the large part played by America in the search for Franklin – the aftermath of Barrow's final, disastrous attempt to discover the North-West Passage. Henry Grinell, a New York philanthropist, was a major contributor. He spent an estimated $100,000 in kitting out ships for Arctic service. His men endured hardships equal to any suffered by the British, and their characters and conflicts are just as involving. But they were not sent out by Barrow and therefore have been touched upon only fleetingly in this book. In any case, they were not so much searching for Franklin as trying for the North Pole – which is another book in itself.

I would like to express my gratitude to the following institutions for their help and, where appropriate, for permission to reproduce material in their possession: the Bodleian Library, Oxford; the British Library, London; the Colindale Newspaper Library, London; the Derbyshire Record Office, Matlock; the Dumfries Archive Centre; the Kensington and Chelsea Library, London; the London Library; the Museum of the History of Science, Oxford; the National Maritime Museum, Greenwich; the National Portrait Gallery, London; the National Portrait Gallery of Scotland, Edinburgh; the National Record of Archives, London; the Natural History Museum, London; the Plymouth Central Library; the Public Records Office, Kew; the Public Records Office of Northern Ireland, Belfast; the Royal Botanic Gardens Library and Archive, Kew; the Royal Geographical Society, London; the Royal Society, London; the Scott Polar Research Institute, Cambridge; and the Somerset Archive and Record Service, Taunton.

I would further like to thank my agent Gillon Aitken and his assistant Emma Parry; my editor Neil Belton; John and Phoebe Fortescue; Becky Hardie and Isobel Rorison at Granta; Jane Robertson for her copy-editing; Andrew Tatham for overseeing my access to the Royal Geographical Society archives; Rachel Rowe and Janet Turner, also of the RGS, for hauling an endless procession of tomes from the back gallery; Robert Headland and Philippa Smith at the Scott Polar Research Institute; and Hugo Vickers. I would also like to mention Claudia Broadhead, Elizabeth Burzacott, Rachel Keating, Sam Lebus and Matilda Simpson.

Finally, for her resolute endurance, sanguine attitude and steadfast forbearance – to use a few phrases from the period – I would like to thank, and dedicate this book to, Elizabeth Hodgson.

CHRONOLOGY OF MAJOR EXPEDITIONS

1816   James Tuckey sails to the Congo; none of his officers and few of his crew return alive.

1818   John Ross sails to Baffin Bay; he turns back at Lancaster Sound without finding an entrance to the North-West Passage.

1818   David Buchan fails to find a sea route to the North Pole via Spitsbergen.

1818–20   George Lyon and Joseph Ritchie try unsuccessfully to find the Niger by journeying down through the Sahara. After Ritchie's death Lyon is forced to return, having achieved little.

1819–20   William Edward Parry sails through Lancaster Sound and overwinters at Melville Island.

1819–22   John Franklin leads a disastrous overland expedition to

Canada's northern coastline in an attempt to link up with Parry's ships. More than half his party starve to death.

1821–3   Parry's second stab at the North-West Passage is halted at Fury and Hecla Strait.

1822–4   Hugh Clapperton, Dixon Denham and Walter Oudney embark on a rancorous journey through the Sahara. They discover Lake Chad but fail to reach the Niger.

1824   Lyon leads a futile expedition to Repulse Bay.

1824–5   Parry's final go at the North-West Passage ends with the wreck of the *Fury* and the abandonment of its stores in Prince Regent Inlet.

1825–6   Gordon Laing travels to Timbuctoo and becomes the first European to enter the town. He is murdered before he can return home.

1825–7   Franklin leads a second overland mission which manages to map more than 1,000 miles of new coastline.

1825–8   Clapperton attacks the Niger from the south. He and his three accompanying officers all die. They are survived only by Clapperton's servant, Richard Lander.

1827   Parry makes a doomed attempt to reach the North Pole across the polar ice cap. He is forced to turn back at 82° 45'.

1829–33   John Ross takes a small steam ship into Prince Regent Inlet and is beset for four winters. His nephew James discovers the North Magnetic Pole in 1831.

1830–1   Richard Lander and his brother John successfully trace the Niger to its mouth.

1833–5   George Back travels down the Great Fish River in an abortive attempt to rescue John Ross.

1836–7   Back sails disastrously to Wager Bay.

1837–9   Hudson's Bay Company overlanders Peter Dease and Thomas Simpson successfully map large stretches of Canada's Arctic coast.

1839–43   James Ross journeys to Antarctica with the *Erebus* and *Terror*. He charts large areas of undiscovered coastline and discovers the live volcano, Mt. Erebus.

1845–7   John Franklin takes the *Erebus* and *Terror* in search of the North-West Passage. He and the crews of both ships perish.

1848–9   James Ross takes two ships to find Franklin. He returns empty-handed.

1848–51   John Richardson and John Rae seek Franklin overland. They too fail.

1850–1   Horatio Austin leads a four-ship rescue mission to the eastern Arctic. He is accompanied by William Penny with two ships sponsored by Lady Franklin; by John Ross on his own, privately financed yacht; and by two American ships paid for by US philanthropist Henry Grinell.

1850–4   Robert McClure attacks from the west on board the *Investigator*. Trapped in the ice he is forced to abandon ship. Trekking east to meet up with Belcher's squadron (see below) he becomes the first man to cross *a* north-west passage.

1850–5   Richard Collinson penetrates via Bering Strait and comes within a few miles of finding Franklin's expedition.

1851–2   William Kennedy and Joseph-René Bellot lead Lady Franklin's second private expedition in search of her husband.

1852–4   Edward Belcher takes five ships into Lancaster Sound. He returns with only one.

1853–4   John Rae discovers relics of the Franklin expedition and hears reports of its demise.

1857–9   Leopold McClintock confirms Rae's story by finding three corpses and other detritus of Franklin's expedition. A note in a cairn confirms the death of Franklin and many of his men from unknown causes.

The search for the North-West Passage 1818-1827

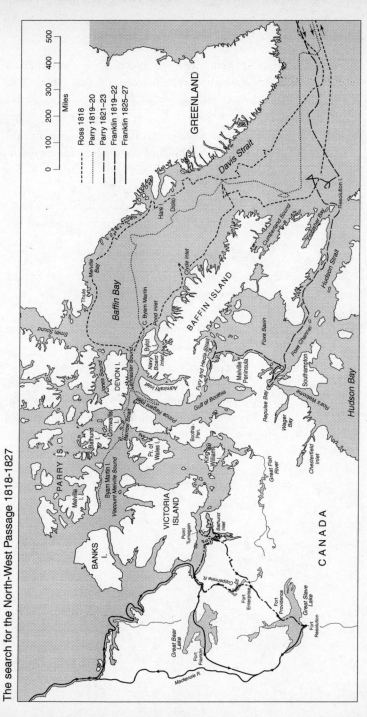

Miles
0   100   200   300   400   500

- - - - - Ross 1818
········· Parry 1819-20
- · - · - Parry 1821-23
- - - - - Franklin 1819-22
─────── Franklin 1825-27

GREENLAND

Davis Strait

Hare I.
Disko I.
Clyde Inlet
Cumberland Sound
Resolution I.
Frobisher Bay
Hudson Strait

BAFFIN ISLAND

Smith Sound
Thule
Melville Bay
Baffin Bay
C. Byam Martin
Pond Inlet
Bylot
Navy Board Inlet
Admiralty Inlet
Fury and Hecla Strait
Foxe Basin
Foxe Channel

DEVON I.
Lancaster Sound
Jones Sound
Barrow Strait

PARRY IS.
Melville I.
Bathurst
Cornwallis I.

Byam Martin I.
Viscount Melville Sound

Prince Regent Inlet
Gulf of Boothia
Melville Peninsula
Repulse Bay
Wager Bay
Southampton
Roe's Welcome
Chesterfield Inlet
Hudson Bay

BANKS I.

VICTORIA ISLAND
Pt. of Wales
Boothia Pen.
King Wm. I.
Great Fish River

Point Turnagain
Bathurst Inlet
Coppermine R.

CANADA

Great Bear Lake
Fort Franklin
Mackenzie R.
Fort Enterprise
Fort Providence
Fort Resolution
Great Slave Lake

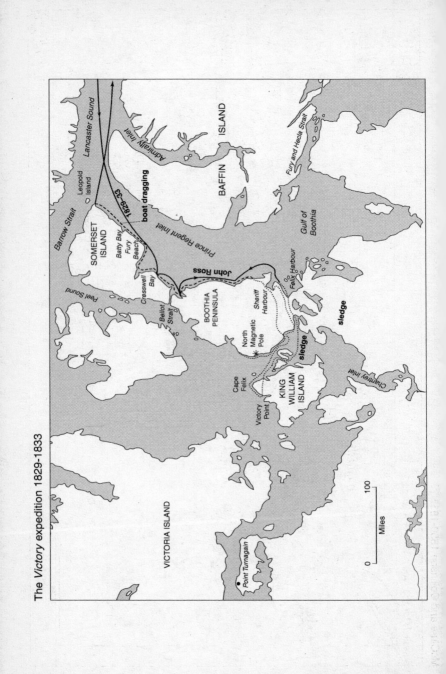

The *Victory* expedition 1829-1833

McClure and Collinson 1850-1855

Beaufort Sea

DEVON ISLAND
Lancaster Sound
BEECHEY
BAFFIN ISLAND
Melville Peninsula
Gulf of Boothia
CORNWALLIS I.
SOMERSET ISLAND
BATHURST
Barrow Strait
Peel Sound
BOOTHIA FELIX
MELVILLE I.
Sledge
King William I.
Winter Harbour
Franklin 1845-47
Viscount Melville Sound
VICTORIA ISLAND
Mercy Bay
BANKS ISLAND
PRINCE ALBERT PENINSULA
Prince of Wales Strait
Point Turnagain
Bathurst Inlet
Nelson Head
McClure 1850-54
Cape Bathurst
COLLINSON 1850-55
Mackenzie R.
Mackenzie Delta

0   200
Miles

The quest for Timbuctoo and the Niger 1822-1831

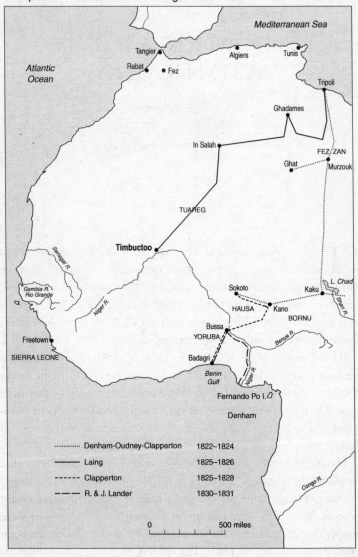

Mediterranean Sea

Atlantic Ocean

Tangier
Rabat • Fez
Algiers
Tunis
Tripoli

Ghadames

In Salah
FEZ-ZAN
Ghat
Murzouk

TUAREG

Timbuctoo

Senegal R.
Gambia R.
Rio Grande

Niger R.

Freetown
SIERRA LEONE

Sokoto
Kaku
L. Chad
HAUSA
Kano
BORNU
Shari R.

Bussa
YORUBA
Benue R.

Badagri
Niger R.

Benin Gulf

Fernando Po I.

Denham

....	Denham-Oudney-Clapperton	1822–1824
———	Laing	1825–1826
- - - -	Clapperton	1825–1828
— — —	R. & J. Lander	1830–1831

Congo R.

0   500 miles

1

THE MAN AT THE
ADMIRALTY

'To what purpose could a portion of our naval force be, at any time, but more especially in time of profound peace, more honourably or more usefully employed than in completing those details of geographical and hydrographical science of which the grand outlines have been boldly and broadly sketched by Cook, Vancouver and Flinders, and others of our countrymen?'[1]

These words were written in 1816 by John Barrow, Second Secretary to the Admiralty, in the introduction to Captain James Kingston Tuckey's journal of his expedition to the Congo of that same year. They were read by few but their swords-to-ploughshares sentiment was shared by many, particularly by the officers of the Royal Navy.

Having swelled during the Napoleonic Wars to proportions that would not be equalled for a century, the Royal Navy was in the throes of massive disarmament. On the whole it was a straightforward process. The ships were laid up 'in ordinary' and the seamen were simply thrown back onto the streets from which they had often been press-ganged in the first place. The officers, however, were a different matter. They were career men, they had political clout and they could not be dismissed so easily. In fact, their numbers increased until the navy, reduced to a rump of some 23,000 men from a peak of more than 130,000, had one officer for every four men. But 90 per cent of these officers had nothing to do. Mothballed on half-pay they yearned for something – a war would have been good – to get them back into service. But a war was unlikely. Their only hope of advancement was if someone higher up the Navy List died. Alas, such deaths proved rare in peace. Thirty years on, the navy was still feeling the effects of the Napoleonic Wars. The average age of an Admiral was seventy-six. Below them on the list hundreds of grey-haired captains drew their half-pay with autumnal melancholy. In 1846, of 1,151 officers, only 172 were in full employment.

Half-pay was not a happy prospect, amounting to little more than subsistence. So when Barrow asked the question 'to what purpose' the response was enthusiastic. To what purpose indeed?

Captain James Kingston Tuckey could have told them. But, alas, he was dead.

The Admiralty Board Room, situated on the first floor of Admiralty House, Whitehall, was the nerve centre of the world's largest and mightiest navy. On one wall, surmounting a pair of globes and flanked by bookshelves, was fixed a powder-blue wind clock whose indicator, linked to a vane on the roof, swung through the points of the compass. On another wall, charts hung in rolls nine-deep waiting to reveal the coastline of any given point in the known world. In the middle of the room, flanked by coal fires, the Lords of the Admiralty dispensed power from a mahogany table, seating ten, in the Sheraton-style, with fluted pilaster legs, the surface of light-green leather.

In this room, in 1804, John Barrow took his place as Second Secretary to the Admiralty. With the exception of a brief hiatus between 1806 and 1807, he was to remain there, through Whig and Tory administrations, for the next forty-one years. Although seemingly inferior, the position of Second Secretary was far from being so. The Admiralty Board, which took the navy's executive decisions – as opposed to the Navy Board which concerned itself with supplies and other administrative housekeeping – was overseen by a group of seven lords and two secretaries. The lords were political appointees to a man. They had little knowledge of the navy and, usually, not much interest in it either. They were, however, the men in charge and so, to assist them in their decisions, they called upon the services of the secretaries. The First Secretary was, like the lords, a Member of Parliament. His job was to deal with all political aspects of the navy. The Second Secretary, an apolitical civil servant, was charged with putting his superiors' decisions into practice and keeping the administration running smoothly.

To an outsider who observed proceedings at the green-topped table it would have been obvious where power lay. It lay with the lords – especially the First Lord – with their fine clothes, languid airs and high-toned political opinions. The First Secretary might have talked quite a bit, but he still showed deference. And the Second Secretary? He was the man who kept quiet and took the minutes. A look at the pay of these men would have told a different story. The ordinary lords received £1,000 per year. The First Secretary received four times that amount and the Second Secretary, on £2,000, was on level pegging with the First Lord himself. Between them the First and Second Secretaries were easily the most influential people in the Admiralty.

When Barrow joined this exalted company he was a dark-haired, moon-faced man of forty and was very much the *second* secretary. Born in 1764 near the town of Ulverston, north Lancashire, he could claim not the slightest drop of blue blood. His parents lived in a small cottage from which his father worked two fields. Socially and economically Barrow Senior was only one step up from a farmhand. John Barrow, however, proved to be a very intelligent child. He attended Ulverston's Tower Bank School until the age of thirteen by which time he could read and write Latin and Greek and was conversant with Shakespeare. A period as private tutor to a midshipman (older than himself) taught him confidence as well as a smattering of navigation. He was hungry for knowledge and had an insatiable appetite for work. Even 'at this early period of life,' he later wrote, 'I

had an inherent and inveterate hatred of idleness.'[2] A smug statement. But then he did have cause for smugness.

In quick succession he learned mathematics and astronomy from a
reclusive 'wise man', kept the accounts of a local iron foundry, spent
a summer whaling off Spitsbergen, attended the Astronomer Royal at
Greenwich, and at the age of twenty became tutor to a child prodigy,
Thomas Staunton, who was fluent in five languages and from whom
Barrow learned how to speak and write Chinese.

Barrow was intelligent. But intelligence alone got a man nowhere
in eighteenth-century England. What counted was patronage.
Fortunately for Barrow, the child prodigy's father was a baronet. The
baronet had the ear of Lord Macartney who, in turn, had the ears of
various political dukes and earls. When Macartney was proposed as
Ambassador for Britain's notoriously unsuccessful attempt to represent itself at the Chinese court in 1795, the process of patronage
trickled downhill. The earls and dukes asked Lord Macartney if he
could speak Chinese. He could not, so he asked the Baronet if he
knew anybody who could. The Baronet recommended John Barrow,
who was thus appointed official interpreter to Lord Macartney's
mission.

The embassy was a magnificent failure. Arriving at Peking with
gifts which included all the wonders of Western civilization – artillery,
telescopes, a coach-and-four, a balloon and pilot – Macartney was
treated with hospitable disgust before being dismissed with polite
contempt. According to the Chinese Emperor, the presence of a
British Ambassador was 'not in harmony with the regulations of the
Celestial Empire, we also feel very much that it is of no advantage to
your country'. In addition, 'we have never valued ingenious articles,
nor do we have the slightest need of your country's manufactures'.
And to underline it, 'This is a special edict.'[3]

As interpreter, Barrow must to some extent have been a bearer of
bad news. Yet somehow, during this hopeless visit, he managed to
ingratiate himself with Macartney. When Macartney was appointed
Governor of Cape Colony in South Africa, only a few months after his
return from China, he chose Barrow to accompany him.

The farmer's son who spoke Chinese excelled himself. He conducted the first Cape Colony census, mapped parts of the interior as far as the River Orange, in Namibia, made a few amateur geological surveys, and even contrived an interview with Shaka, King of the Zulus, whose impis would soon throw southern Africa into disarray. (A man of 'much good sense and prudence',[4] wrote Barrow, a little hastily.) In 1799, aged thirty-three, he married the daughter of a Stellenbosch judge and settled in a cottage at the foot of Table Mountain before returning to Britain four years later.

Whilst in Africa Barrow had managed to find another patron. General Francis Dundas, who had taken over the Governorship from Macartney in 1798, was part of the vast and influential Dundas clan whose members permeated the navy, military and parliament. His uncle was Lord Melville, a brutal and hard-nosed politician who was appointed First Lord of the Admiralty in May 1803. The day after his appointment, on the advice of Macartney and Dundas, Melville called Barrow to the Admiralty and informed him that he was to be Second Secretary.

Melville had chosen well. The post required somebody who was a bureaucrat, who knew what he was doing, and who respected rank. Barrow fulfilled all these criteria. He was a bureaucrat *par excellence*, who proved capable of reading and answering up to 40,000 letters per year; he had a passing acquaintance with life aboard ship, had experience of international affairs and had written two very well-received books on China and South Africa. Above all, he was a farmer's son from Lancashire who venerated the system which had got him so far.

The First Lord, however, whom Barrow duly praised for his 'urbanity, the kind and friendly manner in which his Lordship received all officers of the Navy, his invariable good humour, and above all his admitted impartiality',[5] was impeached two years later for granting contracts to his friends, peculation, and misappropriation of government funds. He fell with a thunder that even Napoleon noticed.

But Barrow survived. He was too junior to be involved with such shenanigans. Moreover, as he argued, he had a job to do and would do it under any administration. Having achieved office, he was damned if he would let it go, come Whig or Tory, and remained at the Admiralty until the age of eighty-one, thus establishing himself as Britain's first true civil servant.

On the surface, Barrow was a humble, unassuming clerk. He ate and drank in moderation – plain food and the occasional glass of port – and rarely took any exercise. Religiously, every summer, he took a month's holiday in the English countryside. He never went abroad – 'except twice or thrice I had a run on the Continent'.[6] He never fell ill, never took any medicine – in 1846 he had his pulse taken for the first time in fifty-three years – and his weight never varied from ten to eleven stone. As he liked to say, 'much may be ascribed to a regular and systematic course of life, to moderation in eating and drinking, and avoiding excess in both'.[7] His daily routine was unwavering. He did his work, came home, had dinner with his family, and then did a bit more work. He was so wedded to his Admiralty desk that it was presented to him as a retirement present. All in all, he appeared the model of dullness.

Now and again Barrow ventured into the limelight. He made no secret of the fact that he had been the last Admiralty official to see Nelson before his death at Trafalgar – the cult of Nelson, and the prestige associated with anybody who knew him, can only be guessed at nowadays – and it was he who suggested in 1816 that Napoleon be exiled to St Helena. But in the main he distanced himself from Admiralty policy-making. To have interfered overmuch might have led him into a dangerously partisan situation. In this respect he was very happy to be merely the man who took the minutes.

Yet behind this unassuming exterior lurked a man of ambition, intellect and remorseless application. Barrow would not jeopardize his post by interfering in decisions, but he was determined to make his name somehow. The route he chose was exploration. His efforts in South Africa had been praised highly: 'I do believe that no person, whether native or foreigner, has seen so much of the country, or seen it so well, and to such good purpose, as he has done,' wrote Lord Macartney. 'I imagine his travels will be a great acquisition to the world. His map must be particularly valuable, as it is the only one that can at all be depended upon.'[8] Barrow was proud of this praise and decided to build on it.

While the Napoleonic Wars dragged on, Barrow carved a niche for himself as a geographer. His books on South Africa and China – four volumes in all – had shed at least some light on those mysterious realms and had been well received, being reprinted in at least one foreign language. Thus encouraged, he had no trouble finding a post as geographical reviewer on the *Quarterly Review*, a journal designed to counter the influence of the left-leaning *Edinburgh Review*. When first approached in 1809 by William Gifford, the *Quarterly*'s founder, Barrow was reluctant to submit his 'crude observations' to the public eye – particularly as it had been stipulated that he must understand the subject he was writing about. After cutting his teeth on a few articles about China, however, he soon got into the swing of it. He took care not to overstep himself: 'In all my critical labours I avoided touching upon politics, almost, I might say, altogether,'[9] but even without mentioning politics he found enough to keep him busy. He wrote about China, Africa and America, about naval timber, 'dry-rot doctors and quackery in general',[10] about steam power, canals and railways. He examined the geography, history and customs of countries 'little or not at all known' until there was, by his own admission, 'scarcely a corner of the world left unscrutinised'.[11] His main interest, however, was exploration.

Exploration was an ideal topic for Barrow; it dealt with the unknown and by its nature required no particular understanding of the subject. All that was needed was a deft and inquiring mind; a reviewer could declaim as stridently and controversially as he liked without fear of retribution. With increasing confidence Barrow contributed more and more articles. Luckily, at that time, people were hungry for news about the unknown. Soon Barrow was the *Quarterly*'s most sought-after contributor. He wore his laurels lightly. The reviews 'were written off hand as an amusement',[12] he wrote modestly. 'It was to me a relaxation, after dinner, and a relief from the dry labours of the day.'[13] Nevertheless, an article by Barrow could add 1,000 to the

Quarterly's subscription list – an 8 per cent increase on circulation. His
reputation grew to the extent that he was soon being asked to write
for the *Encyclopedia Britannica*.

The *Quarterly*'s publisher was John Murray, a youngster whom
Walter Scott described as a man of 'more good sense and propriety of
sentiment than fall to the share of most of the trade'.[14] Barrow got on
well with Murray and the two men maintained a close friendship for
the rest of their lives. Barrow saw to it that Murray became the
Admiralty's official publisher and in later years he asked him to publish his own works that included five biographies – Anson, Howe,
Bligh, Macartney and Peter the Great – plus three volumes on geography. Given his long hours at the Admiralty this was an enormous
undertaking and Barrow himself was astonished when towards the
end of his life he 'found a parcel from Mr. Murray, enclosing eleven
thick octavo volumes, neatly bound in red Russia, and containing the
whole of the articles [in the *Quarterly*] that I had supplied up to that
time'.[15] In all, he had written 195 reviews.

Meanwhile, if Barrow truly wanted to make his mark in his chosen
field he needed official recognition and in 1806 was elected a Fellow
of the Royal Society. The Royal Society was supposedly formed for scientific purposes but in fact only a third of its members were scientists.
The rest were dubbed, optimistically, 'natural philosophers'. Barrow,
who was elected on account of his books, fell into the latter category.
(Even had his books been concerned solely with geography he would
still have been a lay member; the Royal Society did not consider geography a science.) The weekly meetings of the Royal Society were dull
beyond belief, but there was the Royal Society Club which provided
dinner on Thursdays (1s 6d, wine extra) in the company of such luminaries as Sir Humphry Davy, Nevil Maskeleyne, John Rennie and
'Phenomenon' Young, of whom Davy wrote, 'he knew so much that it
was difficult to say what he did not know'.[16] And on Sunday evenings
Barrow found stimulating company at 32 Soho Square, the home of the
Society's President, Sir Joseph Banks. Here they discussed the more
pressing concerns of natural philosophy, such as who had eaten the
most unlikely fish or animal. (Barrow won with hippo.)

Joseph Banks was a formative influence in Barrow's life. In his day, he had been one of Britain's most energetic and most vociferous exponents of exploration. He had circumnavigated the world with Captain Cook, had made his name as an explorer and botanist, and had ruled the Royal Society with despotic benevolence since 1778. By the time of Barrow's election he was a gouty, wheelchair-ridden sexuagenarian who barely had the strength to leave London. But for all his age and incapacity he was still a man to be reckoned with. He was wealthy, influential, and had experience of an age of scientific inquiry which had been all but forgotten in the turmoil of the Napoleonic Wars. He was a Great National Treasure, who did not really belong in the emerging, commercial world of the nineteenth century. Yet there he was. And when he spoke people listened.

Barrow listened more than most. Banks was, as Davy said, 'always ready to promote the objects of men of science, but he required to be regarded as a patron and readily swallowed gross flattery'.[17] Barrow was an old hand at the patronage game but, far from using Banks as a stepping stone to his own advancement, Barrow found himself overwhelmed by the older man's experience. Banks was a gifted individual, whose contribution to science was enormous, but he was also opinionated, didactic and, in his old age, often mistaken. Nevertheless, he became the man Barrow wished to emulate. The more he worshipped at his altar the more Barrow developed the mix of precise views and vague speculation that would characterize his tenure as Second Secretary. Before them both was spread the atlas. So many areas of it were blank. What lay at the North Pole? Did Antarctica exist? Was there a North-West Passage? Where was Timbuctoo? What lay at the heart of Africa? Barrow was not an imaginative man. On his visit to China's fabled Summer Palace he had been impressed by one thing: the brickwork in a garden wall. He was, however, a dreamer. His dream was that he could fill those blanks.

Helping him – or, more precisely, not hindering him – in his goal was the First Secretary (1809–30), the famously unpleasant John Wilson Croker. Croker was a talented but vituperative self-server who was loathed universally by his enemies and held in fearful respect by his right-wing political supporters. Publicly he was acknowledged as the best debater in Parliament. Privately, he was described as taste-less, shameless, malevolent and unscrupulous, a man who 'would go a hundred miles through sleet and snow, in a December night, to search a parish register, for the sake of showing that a man was ille-gitimate or a woman older than she said she was'.[18] The author Thomas Macaulay detested him 'more than cold boiled veal'.[19] To which Croker replied sneeringly of Macaulay, 'I disliked him at first sight before I even heard him open his mouth; his very person and countenance displeased me.'[20] Rumour had it that Croker was the model for Rigsby in Benjamin Disraeli's *Coningsby*, a man 'who pos-sessed, in a very remarkable degree, a restless instinct for adroit baseness'.[21] Disraeli did not deny it – to the delight of Macaulay, who had fostered the idea in the first place.

Croker was an avowedly political animal, who saw his Admiralty post as simply a rung on the parliamentary ladder. This was fortunate because, had he deigned to apply his mind to his job, he would have ruined not only Barrow's plans but the entire hydrographical section of the navy. His oft-stated opinion – which conformed with his almost fanatical detestation of anything modern, such as democracy – was that Britain had done very well with its old charts so why bother making new ones? He did everything in his power to hinder the chart-makers and it was only through the efforts of a few die-hards such as Captain Francis Beaufort – of wind scale fame – that anything was achieved in that direction at all. Logically, he should have been at log-gerheads with Barrow. But Barrow was a man who managed never to be at loggerheads with his superiors. Moreover, he was personally connected to Croker in that his eldest son, George, had married Croker's adopted daughter Nony. The two families even lived together in the same house for a while.

Both men used the *Quarterly Review* as a propaganda tool to further their own ends. And both shared the same conservative values, though Barrow's fear of the new was not as inclusive as Croker's and restricted itself to vehement attacks on the 'projectors', as he called them, who were always pestering the Admiralty with oddball ideas. One such project, which seems to have especially outraged him, was the notion that the navy scrap its sailing ships in favour of a steam-powered fleet. To the end of his life, when just such a development was underway, he was still deriding 'a fleet of iron steam vessels [as being] altogether useless . . . as ships of war'.[22]

Barrow has been called the father of Arctic exploration. In fact he was the father of global exploration, for which he has never been given due credit. He was also, though, a geographical 'projector' of the worst kind. He had no original views, receiving what he did from other sources – Banks, mostly – but thanks to his position he was able to make things happen. And like any true 'projector' he was a fanatic. Outwardly his 'project' had no chance of success. In the post-war climate of austerity, exploration came low on the Admiralty's list of priorities. Its budget was tight and there was little to spare for unnecessary fripperies. At a pinch it was willing to pay for the proper charting of strategic coastlines, such as those of the Mediterranean, but that was all. It was not interested in the unknown precisely because it was unknown. But Barrow made sure his project would suc-ceed. He argued that exploration would increase scientific knowledge, that it would be a boon to national commerce, and above all that it would be a terrible blow to national pride if other countries should open up a globe over which Britain ruled supreme. All Barrow's points had superficial merit, but it was the last one that struck home. There was also the fact that Barrow was such a serious, *moderate*, unobtrusive and respectful man. Surely he would not suggest anything to the Admiralty's detriment? Moreover, he was supported by Sir Joseph Banks. And above all, he was very persuasive.

Reluctantly, but unable to explain their reluctance, the Admiralty Lords let Barrow have his way. Between 1816 and 1845, therefore, the Second Secretary despatched volleys of expeditions – one ship, two ships, one man, three men, one a year, none a year, sometimes four a year – to every blank on the map that caught his fancy. Throughout it all, Barrow kept a cool, analytical head. Not until the end did he over-reach himself. Unfortunately, for all his cool analysis, Barrow was

never quite right. When he had a geographical opinion it was frequently the wrong one. And when he had no opinion he formed one
on the wildest of conjectures suggested by others. Sometimes he hit
the spot; more often he missed it. The Treasury dogged him remorselessly; in many expeditions the auditors' reports far exceeded in
volume those of the explorers themselves. Even the Admiralty Lords
were roused on occasion from their reveries to query the point of it all.

Barrow weathered the criticism with the same stubborn perseverance he brought to everything he did. He wanted to chart the
unknown; and he knew for certain that the public was on his side.
This was the age of Romanticism, where crags of ice, tempestuous
seas and tribes of undiscovered savages were far more interesting
than the dry perspectives of eighteenth-century Enlightenment. As
the journals of each expedition rolled off John Murray's presses, to be
snatched up by an eager readership, Barrow was well aware that he
was in tune with the times. It was apt, therefore, that he chose for his
first venture into the field one of the most popular, most glowingly
Romantic of all endeavours: the search for the Niger.

2

DEATH ON THE CONGO

Where did the Niger go? In 1816 this was a burning question for anyone who studied the available maps of Africa. Its existence had been first noted by a group of Phoenicians who circumnavigated Africa in the sixth century BC and was confirmed a century later by a party that travelled overland from Egypt. The latter reported a red, muddy river more than a mile wide which flowed east towards the Nile. It was filled with alluvial gold and the nearest large town was a place called Timbuctoo. Such was the power of the Nile and its civilization that it was only a few centuries before an African ruler suggested that its western equivalent flowed underground to enter the Nile via some undiscovered subterranean passage. The ruler gave the river a name, 'N'ger-ngereo', River of Rivers, or as we know it, the Niger.

In the second century AD the geographer Ptolemy admitted that the Niger existed but found no reason to suggest it joined the Nile. A compromise was reached by the Arab historian Edusi, one thousand years later, who proposed that the Nile and the Niger both emanated from a central lake in East Africa. But this had to be set against reports in the sixteenth century from the explorer Leo Africanus who actually reached the river and told the world that it flowed west-wards.

The controversy raged through the centuries, fuelled mostly by the dream of gold. In 1412 King John I of Portugal sent an expedition to West Africa which returned in fear that they might be boiled alive if they overstepped the equator – a fear that had been first put about by the Ancient Greeks. But King John's more intrepid son, Henry the Navigator, sent other crews who came back, unboiled, with news of a land which offered limitless quantities if not of gold then of slaves.

West Africa had long been targeted by Muslim slavers from the north and east. Now their European counterparts began to make their presence felt. As the slave trade settled into its grisly triangle of suffering between Europe, Africa and America, large, stone fortresses mushroomed on the West African coast, complete with dungeons and manned by whoever was willing. Massive barracoons were built to hold the human cargo; and they were built to last – they were still in use, as dwellings, in the 1950s.

But the rumours of gold did not go away. Nor were they just rumours. West Africa did contain a lot of gold. When the Emperor Mansa Musa of Mali passed through Cairo on his way to Mecca in 1324 his spending injected so much gold into the economy that Cairo's currency was depressed for years afterwards. However, although the gold mines of Ghana were being exploited by Portugal as early as the sixteenth century, there was a niggling suspicion that there was a lot more to be found somewhere else. That somewhere was Timbuctoo.

By the nineteenth century Timbuctoo had swelled in popular imagination from the dirt town it was into a seat of power and learning and thence into a grail of cupidity, whose roof tiles were even made of gold. In 1809 James G. Jackson, an English merchant in Morocco, published *An Accurate and Interesting Account of Timbuctoo, the Great Emporium of Central Africa*, in which the city became not just a repository of wealth but the dream of every red-blooded male adventurer. Its ruler 'possessed an immense quantity of gold . . . it is said that the massive bolts in his different palaces were of pure gold, as well as the utensils of his kitchen'.[1] Here, libidos raged without check. 'The climate of Timbuctoo is much extolled as being salutary and extremely invigorating, insomuch that it is impossible for the sexes to exist without intermarriage; accordingly it is said that there is no man of the age of eighteen who has not his wives or concubines . . . it is even a disgrace for a man who has reached the age of puberty to be unmarried.'[2] And as for trade, not only were the residents noted for their elegance and suavity but the banks of the Niger – which Jackson called the Nile – 'are as populous as those of any river in China'.[3] This was the voice of prurient capitalism. It made Jackson's book a best-seller which would be reprinted twice in ten years.

Even before Jackson's book came out, however, Timbuctoo was on Sir Joseph Banks's agenda. Slavery was abolished in Britain in 1797, and though it would be eight years before participation in the trade was outlawed (Britain made a lot of noise but did not, as has often been claimed, the abolition crusade*). Banks had his eye on West Africa's wealth. He took the gold, if not Timbuctoo itself, as granted. And in his practical way he wanted to know how the gold was to be brought out of Africa. The Niger was the answer.

On 8 June 1799 Banks wrote a letter to a parliamentary friend suggesting an effort be made to seize control of the area.

Please recommend to the Cabinet:
As the trade with the Negroes for manufactured goods is
already firmly established and as Gold, the main investment,
is found abundantly in all the torrents which fall into the
[Niger], I confess I feel strongly impressed with the hope of
success, should the project be fairly tried . . . science has never
yet been applied to the search for gold carried down by
torrents . . .

* Slave-trading was banned first by Denmark in 1802, by Britain and America in 1808, by Sweden in 1813, by the Netherlands a year later, by France in 1818 and by Spain in 1820 followed by Portugal in 1836. But under-the-counter trading to the Americas went on well into the 1850s.

Should the undertaking be fully resolved upon, the first step of the British Government must be to secure to the British throne, either by conquest or by treaty, the whole of the Coast of Africa from Arguin to Sierra Leone; or at least to procure the cession of the River Senegal, as the river will always afford an easy passage to any rival nation who means to molest the Countries on the banks of the [Niger].

Should the experiment be made, I have very little doubt that in a very few years a trading company might be established under the immediate control of the Government who would take upon themselves the whole expense of the measure, would govern the Negroes far more mildly and make them far more happy than they are now under the tyranny of their arbitrary princes, would become popular at home by converting them to the Christian religion, by inculcating in their rough minds the mild morality which is engrafted in the tenets of our faith, and by effecting the greatest practicable diminution of the Slavery of Mankind, upon the principles of natural justice and commercial benefit.[4]

Banks's proposal, which was not acted upon, sums up very accurately Britain's relationship with Africa in the century to come.

Already, as President of the African Association, Banks had authorized a number of expeditions to the Niger. There was the American John Ledyard, the Irishman Daniel Houghton and the 'Moor' Ben Ali. The first two died in the attempt without getting anywhere and the last vanished in London without even bothering to try. Then came Mungo Park, an intrepid Scot who was to become a legend in the annals of exploration. He went out twice, in 1795 and then again in 1805. His first journey was under the auspices of the African Association and was funded accordingly: he was given two days' provisions. He did, however, reach the Niger after many vicissitudes and was rewarded by the sight of the river 'glittering to the morning sun, as broad as the Thames at Westminster, and flowing slowly to the eastward'.[5] His second was sponsored by the government – to the tune of £60,000 – and saw him leading a band of forty-four British red-coats to find the rest of the river. One by one the soldiers died. By the time Park reached the Niger at the town of Bussa only five of his original contingent were alive. Then, on some undetermined date in 1805, he was attacked on the river and the entire expedition was wiped out. As soon as the disaster became common knowledge, Park was revered as a hero. Where was his journal? Where were his effects? What had he discovered? And where did the Niger go?

This was the state of things when Barrow entered the fray in 1816. By now the idea of colonizing Africa had been put on hold. The Napoleonic Wars had seen to that. But still the question remained: where *did* the Niger go?

Speculation was rife. Some had it going westward to connect with the Rivers Gambia or Senegal. Others said it disappeared into a massive swamp called Wangara. Still others insisted that it joined the Nile. Park himself – who died trying to find out – had been of the opinion that it flowed into the Congo. And a number of fence-sitters decided it went nowhere, but simply evaporated under the blazing African sun. There were a few who got it right, but in Barrow's view, 'The hypothesis of Mr. Reichard, a German geographer of some eminence, which makes the Niger pour its waters into the Gulf of Benin, is entitled to very little attention.'[6] Barrow was a Congo man. And so it was that Captain James Kingston Tuckey left Britain in 1816 to explore the Congo.

James Kingston Tuckey is a man about whom little is known. He had conducted the first survey of Sydney Harbour, had subsequently been captured by the French and during his imprisonment in Verdun had written four weighty volumes on maritime geography. He had followed Captain Matthew Flinders in the first-ever circumnavigation of Australia – and like him had been stranded and captured. Physically, he was serviceable rather than fit. 'His health appeared delicate,' Barrow wrote, 'he was, however, so confident that his constitution would improve by the voyage, and in a warm climate . . . that the Lords of the Admiralty conferred on him the appointment.'[7] A capable and competent officer, no doubt, but hardly the stuff of legend. One wonders why Barrow chose him. He may have had surveying experience but so had many others. Indeed, Barrow could have called upon Captain Francis Beaufort who had just returned from a surveying expedition to the eastern Mediterranean.

Beaufort, an exceptionally capable officer, is perhaps best known today for his invention of the Beaufort Scale to classify wind strength. In naval circles, though, he is famous for being one of the best hydrographers in history. His charts of Turkey, which he had just completed in 1816, were still the most definitive 160 years later. His journal of the survey was described by Barrow as 'superior to any of its kind in whatever language'[8] and the Second Secretary took pride in announcing that he, personally, had selected Beaufort 'out of the whole Mediterranean fleet'[9] for the task. Why, then, was he not selected for the Congo expedition? The answer was that Beaufort had fallen foul of First Secretary Croker. And for once in his life, Croker was not to blame. It started with a disagreement about his pay for the expedition. Beaufort believed, wrongly, that other officers had received some £2,000 more than he. Croker was conciliatory. Beaufort was petulant. The closer Croker came to middle ground the further Beaufort retreated. Finally, he refused to accept any pay at all. Amazingly, given his disposition and his opinion that surveying was a waste of time, Croker offered Beaufort in 1816 the job of surveying the coast of Ireland. Beaufort, partly from pique and partly for professional reasons, demurred.

For all that Barrow was Croker's friend, he knew that one went only so far with such a man. Beaufort had gone further. Therefore, he was not perhaps the most suitable candidate. There was one other reason, perhaps, for choosing Tuckey. He had sailed with Flinders. Although no qualification on its own, in Barrow's mind it may have been a necessary link with Banks's glory days of exploration.

The expedition was a mish-mash of surreal romanticism, high hopes and much ignorance. There was the place itself – 'almost a blank on our charts',[10] as Barrow enthused. Then there was the calibre of the explorers – the Royal Navy was, without any doubt, the most practised and most professional entity on the globe; its men were ideally placed to conduct such a venture. 'I am willing to put my trust in the professional and practical skill of the seamen who are to be entrusted with the charge of it,'[11] wrote Banks. And finally there was the territory, prey to every disease from river-blindness and malaria to bilharzia and dengue fever. Of this, nothing was said.

Banks, who had initially given the expedition his blessing, was one of the few people to realize the potential for disaster. The firmer Barrow's plans became the more Banks distanced himself from them. He wished to have nothing more to do with the project, he told Barrow, and limited his responsibility to finding a naturalist for the expedition. Barrow scoffed at his fears. Banks retorted, irritated at his protégé's inexperience. 'My Dear Sir, When I was 25 years old . . .'[12] began his lengthy, slightly condescending reply. But Barrow was not to be thwarted and Banks finally gave in.

In a burst of unlikely enthusiasm for new technology, the Admiralty decided that Tuckey's expedition should travel in a steam-powered vessel. Traditionally hide-bound, the navy had never commissioned a steam vessel before. But in this instance there were good reasons for doing so. Steam-boats had a shallower draught than sail, they were not dependent on fair winds, and were thus perfectly suited to river navigation – as had already been proved in America. Despite Barrow's objections an order was placed with Messrs Boulton and Watt for a thirty-ton twenty-horsepower engine which, with its accompanying paddles, was to be installed in a small, 100-ton sloop called the *Congo*. The total cost came to £1,700 and included the services of two 'engine men'.

The *Congo* splashed into the water at Deptford on 11 January 1816 and was immediately subject to criticism. The chief 'engine man', a Scot by the name of Murdoch, pointed out that the *Congo*'s draught was too deep for the paddles to operate. Ballast was duly removed to lift it out of the water. But even then the *Congo* could only make three knots as opposed to the eight achieved by American steamers. Nobody liked it, not Murdoch, not Tuckey and not even the engine's manufacturer, James Watt Jnr, who agreed that the *Congo* was quite

unseaworthy. Even a scientific enthusiast such as Rear-Admiral Sir
Home Popham, who had been responsible for such innovations as
the Congreve rocket and the torpedo, conceded that the ship 'is very
crank and I do not, by a more intimate acquaintance, improve my
opinion of her'.[13]

Barrow, on hearing these verdicts, was delighted. Dismissing out of
hand 'a shoal of projectors, every one ready with his infallible
remedy',[14] he wrote sternly to his superiors that steam power was
'useless and pernicious'[15] for the task in hand, that he had always
said so, that he had been constantly overruled, and now that he had
been proved right would the Admiralty please remove the engine –
Plymouth dock was in need of just such a device for pumping water –
and refit the Congo with sails.

His advice was taken, to the relief of everybody save Rear-Admiral
Popham who argued that 'no alteration will make her good for anything'.[16] And so the Royal Navy's first experiment with steam power
came to an inglorious end.

It had been an expensive experiment, but there were still more
expenses to be borne. The Congo had to be altered for sail instead of
steam, and kitted out with guns, provisions and all the usual trinketry
for distributing to the 'natives': beads, knives, mirrors, twenty-four
silk umbrellas and twenty 'plated pint tankards, fashionable'.[17]
(Tawdry as they were, the gifts alone cost £1,386.) A support ship – a
350-ton whaler called the Dorothea – had to be hired and manned. And
scientists had to be enrolled.

The remodelling of the Congo proved surprisingly successful.
Despite Popham's comments on what was, as Barrow admitted, a ship
whose shape 'pretty nearly resembles that of a horse-trough',[18] it
sailed well and when the trials were over Tuckey 'had no hesitation in
saying, that she was, in every respect, fit for the business'.[19] To make
the Congo yet more fit it was equipped with double-boats – light
rowing boats which, when joined by a canvas-roofed platform, could
hold twenty to thirty men and three months' supplies, and could pass
over any shallows that might obstruct the mother-ship.

The scientists, however, were something of a Hobson's Choice.

They comprised Professor Christian Smith, a Norwegian botanist; a Mr Cranch, an ex-bootmaker in the pay of the British Museum, who came aboard as 'Collector of Objects of Natural History'; Mr Tudor, a young and enthusiastic 'Comparative Anatomist'; and one Mr Galwey, 'Volunteer', who had no qualifications other than he had been born in Tuckey's home town and was a very persistent friend. There was also Mr Lockhart, a diligent gardener from Kew about whom little, unfortunately, is known because Barrow did not consider him a gentleman.

James Kingston Tuckey (actually his middle name was Hingston rather than Kingston, but it seems churlish to rectify a spelling mistake that has survived for so long) was a tall, stooping Irishman aged thirty who hailed from Mallow, in Cork. He had had a ghastly war, spending nine years as a captive in France during which time he had married a fellow prisoner, one Miss Stuart, and had produced a number of children. In 1814, as the British pressed in, he had been force-marched away from the front line, during which time he lost his youngest son, and on rescue and repatriation his seven-year-old daughter had died in excruciating pain when her clothes caught fire. These experiences, combined with long service in India and the Middle East during which he had contracted a liver disease, had reduced him to premature old age. His hair had mostly gone, and what remained was grey. His face was fixed in an expression of pensive despair. But he retained a dry and ironic humour that sustained him through life's hardships.

Tuckey's orders were simple: to explore the Congo as far upstream as he could. Barrow added a lengthy memorandum containing his views of African geography; he hoped, optimistically, that not only would the 'main trunk'[20] of the Congo be connected to the Niger but that 'a very considerable branch'[21] of it would lead to South Africa, thereby providing 'corroboration of the existence of some easy water communication'[22] through the continent. Another branch of it might also lead to the south-west, he counselled. And there was undoubtedly a third branch fed by a lake called Aquelunda as well as a fourth which went east. Any of these branches might also be a trunk, in which case Tuckey was to prosecute its course with vigour. By the

time Barrow finished, he had conjured up an aquatic growth which
spread its tendrils to every point of the compass and occupied most of
Africa. It takes two or three readings of this confusing document, thirteen pages long, to divine that Tuckey was, basically, being told to do
as he thought fit.

Tuckey's private opinion was that the Niger and the Congo were
separate rivers. In Barrow's eyes this rated as much attention as the
ridiculous notion that the Niger flowed into the Gulf of Benin. But
just in case, if by some unforeseen circumstance Tuckey was unable
to penetrate the Congo, he was to have a look around the Gulf if only
to dispel the myth put about by 'continental geographers',[23] as Barrow
disparagingly called them.

Barrow waxed eloquent on Tuckey's subsidiary duties. As he journeyed up the river he was to collect information on everything he
encountered: the state of the weather; the lie of the land; the look, the
depth and the taste of the water; he was to bring back samples of
birds, fish, trees, animals and fossils; he was to take mineral samples –
'The size of a common watch is sufficiently large for each specimen;
shape is of little consequence; that of a cube split in two is perhaps the
most convenient'[24] – and he was to look out for wood that could be
used as fuel or for making ships; he was to compile vocabularies of
every dialect, to note the presence of Muslim traders, to record
indigenous religions, to ascertain whether the locals had a written
history and to investigate the 'genius and disposition of the people, as
to talent, mental and bodily energy, habits of industry or idleness,
love, hatred, hospitality etc.'[25] On top of this he was given a list of
questions to which the African Association would be obliged if he
could provide answers. Envisaging an equatorial equivalent of France
or England they wanted to know the precise nature of the Congo
nation. What were its boundaries? How was it administered? Did it
have a monarch? Was his power absolute? Or did it have a Civil Code?
If so, how was it administered?

The little 100-ton *Congo*, which contained barely enough space for
its fifty-six crew and supplies, became on paper a veritable factoryship
of research. It was granted the unheard-of quota of four carpenters –

two were usually sufficient for a ship three times the size – whose days were to be spent constructing cases to hold the scientists' specimens. Where these cases were to be stored, like much else, was not precisely specified.

The *Congo*'s departure from Deptford on 26 February 1816 was less than optimistic. Professor Smith recorded dismally that 'people who were nearly strangers to me, here bade me farewell with tears in their eyes, and looks that expressed their doubt of seeing me any more'.[26] Mr Cranch, the genial cobbler-made-good, was burdened by a 'presentiment that he should never return, and . . . the expectation of such an event became weaker and weaker as his country faded from view'.[27] Tuckey himself was already sick from impending liver failure, though denying this to the surgeon.

A few days later the *Congo* passed Plymouth and Tuckey took the opportunity to send a letter informing Barrow that 'the scientific gentlemen were all horribly seasick'.[28] This done, he sailed sardonically for one of the most fever-ridden rivers in the world. At the mouth of the Congo he sent the *Dorothea* home and readied himself for the voyage to come. He looked through Barrow's memorandum once again. 'That a river of such magnitude,' wrote the Second Secretary, 'should not be known with any degree of certainty beyond 200 miles from its mouth, is incompatible with the present advanced state of geographical science, and little creditable to those Europeans who, for three centuries nearly, have occupied various parts of the coast near to which it empties itself into the sea.'[29]

With this admonishment in mind, Tuckey entered the River Congo. Initially it was like a nursery vision of Africa – crystal-clear water above a smooth, red clay bed; smoke rising from happy villages; parrots flying in streams at dawn and dusk across the mangrove swamps to feed off the cornfields on the opposite bank; comfortable temperatures which never rose above 76 °F; and, to provide the necessary touch of mystery, a huge, natural pillar of stone near the river's mouth surrounded by whirlpools and carved with innumerable symbols, which was a fetish of Seembi, the river's protective deity. As they sailed upriver, however, the reality became apparent. Down-at-heel

despots wearing cheap tiaras, cast-off uniforms, beadle's cloaks, and
displaying horrible skin conditions, came aboard to demand gifts and
rum – one man stayed five days to make sure the cask was empty.
Poverty was endemic, as was warfare. Poisoning was so commonplace
that every man of importance employed a food-taster – not that there
was much food to be tasted in most places. Once having purchased a
sheep and skinned it for dinner, Tuckey was horrified to find a man
chewing its hide, wool and all, that had been roasted to lukewarm on
a fire. Even where the land was capable of producing food, agriculture
was pursued in a half-hearted, apathetic fashion, cattle being left to
roam indiscriminately, never milked and often slaughtered in calf.

The cause of this economic ruin was slavery, which had been practised so relentlessly over the last 300 years that it was now a fact of
life. Few people dared venture a day's walk from their village lest they
be kidnapped by marauding gangs. Being sold as a slave had even
entered the penal code as punishment for adultery with a chief's wife.
Warfare was conducted for no other purpose than the capture of
slaves. Human beings had become the region's major product, the
sole currency with which chieftains could buy the shoddy wonders of
European civilization. The price of a man was fixed with all the exactitude of foreign exchange. The rate, in Tuckey's time, was two
muskets, two casks of gunpowder, fifty-two yards of cloth, one fancy
sash, two jars of brandy, five knives, five strings of beads, one razor,
one looking-glass, one cap, one iron bar, one pair of 'scizzars' and a
padlock. Now and then Tuckey caught glimpses of the trade. Hard-
bitten slavers carrying British and American crews and sailing under
Spanish or Portuguese colours flitted by night past the *Congo*, sending
an occasional cannon-ball its way, as they went about the business of
lifting what Tuckey estimated to be 2,000 slaves per year from the
Congo River – a relatively modest haul compared to other areas.

Tuckey took a lop-sided glee at the disappointment of his men
who had left England with the prospect of 'melting under an equinoc-
tial sun in the lightest cloathing'[30] and disporting freely with 'the
sable Venuses which they were to find on the banks of the Congo'.[31]
This ravaged paradise offered no such solaces.

On 2 August they reached Embomma, the river's major port. From here it was only eighteen days' sailing until they came to what they had been warned were impassable and torrential cataracts called Yellala. When they reached Yellala, they were pleasantly surprised. It was 'not a second Niagara', wrote Tuckey, 'which the description of the natives, and their horror of it had given us reason to expect [but] a comparative brook bubbling over its stony bed'.[32] But the cataract was enough to stop the *Congo*. Here Tuckey had to leave ship and travel overland, taking with him a few seamen, all the scientists and a group of locally hired Africans to act as porters and guides. Everything went wrong from this point.

Tuckey's nemesis was a particularly unpleasant strain of yellow fever, transmitted by mosquito, which manifested itself initially with a chill and a fierce headache. The sufferer's eyes became pearly and his tongue turned white. Lassitude and tremors followed, and the salivary ducts dried. The tongue went from yellow to brown, being finally coated with a black crust. The skin became jaundiced and, more often than not, the patient was in extreme pain. There was no cure. Death came within three and twenty days.

The first to fall ill was young Mr Tudor, whose eyes pearled over on 17 August, three days before the march began. Unaware of the nature of the disease that Tudor harboured – the others complained only of blisters and fatigue – Tuckey continued wryly on, dragging his stretcher-bound invalid up hills that needed 'fly's legs'[33] and over passes that were 'absolutely impassable to anything other than a goat'.[34] The country became rougher and food scarcer. Their interpreter, a freed slave who had been brought over from London, vanished quietly on 22 August, exchanging his given name Simmons for the one he had been born with, Prince Schi. Essential cooking equipment was 'dropped' by weary porters and tumbled downhill into the river. Meanwhile, the fever took its steady toll.

One by one the scientists fell ill and were sent back to the *Congo* to their inevitable fate. Tudor died on 29 August, Mr Cranch on 4 September and Galwey, the 'Volunteer', on 9 September. As the casualties mounted, Tuckey had no option but to retreat. The march back was a nightmare. Their African guides fled into the bush; supplies dwindled and were stolen. The remaining porters demanded ever more money to continue and left in droves when Tuckey could not supply it. As Tuckey struggled back to the ship his journal deteriorated into brief, tantalizing snapshots: 'Horrible face with leprosy . . .';[35] 'Size of their canoes . . .';[36] 'Natives extremely abstemious . . .';[37] 'Terrible march; worse to us than the retreat from Moscow . . .'[38]

When Tuckey finally reached the *Congo* on 16 September his diary became even more elliptic: 'Terrible report of the state on board: coffins . . .'[39] Yellow fever had struck the *Congo* too. Professor Smith went on the 22nd, and Mr Eyre the purser – 'a young man of a corpulent and bloated habit'[40] – followed him eight days later. By the beginning of October Tuckey and his second-in-command, Lt. Hawkey, were the only officers left alive. Hawkey was shuddering and sweating, already in the second stages of the disease, and Tuckey too was sick – though not from yellow fever but from malaria, which had begun to attack his ailing liver. Tuckey succumbed on 4 October. Lt. Hawkey lived two days longer before he, too, died.

By now everyone was ill. Only Lockhart, the Kew gardener, seemed untouched by disease. The survivors buried their dead at Embomma and fled swiftly under the command of Mr Fitzmaurice the mate. They arrived back in England, drastically diminished, bringing with them Lockhart's seeds and sprouts, neatly wrapped in muslin bags, Smith's cuttings – which Lockhart had packed – and a writhing mass of insect life that had once been the natural history specimens collected by Cranch and Tudor.

Tuckey had sailed 200 miles up the Congo and had penetrated only a few miles further on foot. His discoveries, as summarized depressingly by the *Naval Chronicle*, were that the river had too many rapids and the natives possessed a cruel and listless nature. Nothing could have been a greater failure.

In hindsight, given the ignorance of tropical conditions and the lack of even the most basic medicines, such an outcome was inevitable. Yet to Barrow the fatality was 'almost inexplicable'.[41] He had had every hope of success yet, he wrote in bewilderment, 'never were the results of an expedition more melancholy and disastrous'.[42] He wrote up Tuckey's journal as optimistically as he could and shelved it. Its last, wistful entry of 18 September read:

> Flocks of flamingoes going to the south denote the approach of rains.[43]

Barrow was disheartened, but soon a new goal beckoned – the North-West Passage. For centuries, ever since it had become a seafaring power, Britain had been searching for the 'vent' – to use an Elizabethan term – that linked the Atlantic and the Pacific Oceans. It lay, according to theory, to the north of the Americas, and if only it could be found, Europe – by which was meant Britain – could reach the treasures of Asia without having to undergo the long and stormy passages via the Cape of Good Hope or Cape Horn. It was a navigator's Eldorado and the map was littered with the names of those who had tried and failed to find it: Frobisher, Hudson, Baffin, Cabot, Foxe and others. Of all these, William Baffin had been the most successful, charting in 1616 the bay to the west of Greenland which still bears his name. But over the years, as ship after ship disappeared into the Arctic, most of them never to return, people grew weary of the Passage. All that had been discovered was a labyrinth of islands and ice-choked channels. It was a useless business; so useless that by 1815 most of the early mapping had been forgotten, with the exception of that great fur depot, Hudson Bay. Baffin Bay, charted so carefully, had dwindled to a chimera which in most eyes – those of Barrow included – did not exist. Even as late as 1824 it did not appear in the *Encyclopedia Britannica*, to which Barrow contributed on all matters pertaining to the Arctic.

But by 1817, prospects were different. Britain now had stronger ships, more professional seamen and, thanks to the Industrial Revolution, a great deal of money to spend. So much money, in fact, that despite popular disinterest the Board of Longitude was willing to open its purse to whoever made major inroads into the North-West

Passage. There was £5,000 for the first ship to reach 110° west, twice
that for 130° west, £15,000 for 150° west and £20,000 – about a million
pounds today – for reaching the Pacific.

'To what purpose . . .?' The phrase rang as splendidly in 1817 as it
had done a year before. Barrow decided to tip his cap at the North-
West Passage. And as if by magic, it opened before him.

3

THE MIRAGE OF
LANCASTER SOUND

An extraordinary thing was happening in the north. The great mass of ice which stretched from the coast of Greenland to the island of Spitsbergen, and which had hitherto prevented sailors from penetrating further north than 80° 48′, began to break up. What caused this phenomenon remains unknown. It would be nice to conjecture that this was the first hint of the greenhouse effect. More likely, it was just one of those unfathomable, meteorological hiccoughs to which the world is prone. Whatever the cause, the effect was obvious. Eighteen thousand square miles of ice had broken free from the polar cap and were gradually drifting southwards into the Atlantic. Their presence was palpable. European summers became noticeably cooler. In North America, Bostonians were puzzled to find that their maize crops failed to ripen. Iceland was virtually stranded, its bays, ports and inlets clogged by ice. Even in Britain, with its unpredictable weather, people spoke 'in the common vague way, that the seasons have altered lately'.[1]

Sir Joseph Banks, President of the Royal Society, made his own observation. According to one visitor, writing in December 1817, 'Another very curious fact which he mentioned to me, and the no less curious speculation he has formed upon it, are worthy of remark. The oil of whales is so constituted by nature, that they are suited to a warm temperature, and freeze at a very high degree of the thermometer. That of the Greenland whale, on the other hand, requires a very low temperature to freeze it. Now, Sir J. has observed that the Greenland oil which he uses in his own lamp will never burn of late, (and *that*, without any great degree of cold) from which he thinks it possible that the constitution of the animal may have been so far changed by a change in the temperature in the elements in which he lives, as, by warming his blood &c, to have affected a change in the nature of the oil he produces. The alteration in the temperature of the water he attributes to the clearing away of the mass of ice attached to the shores of Greenland.'[2]

Banks had first been alerted to the polar break-up by a whaler from Whitby, William Scoresby (whose father had invented the crow's nest), who had written of his 1817 voyages that he observed 'about two thousand square leagues of the surface of the Greenland seas, included between the parallels 74° and 80°, perfectly void of all ice, all of which had disappeared within the last two years'.[3] Scoresby went on to press his opinion that there was a vast polar sea, frozen on the surface but with free water beneath. He cited in evidence Atlantic whales taken with stone lance-heads from Russia embedded in their flesh, and whales caught in the Bering Strait that carried Greenland harpoons.

It would never be possible to sail over this sea, he reckoned, but a passage might possibly be found at its southern fringes in the Canadian Arctic. His sailing experience told him that such a passage would be navigable for only a few weeks at intervals of several years. 'Hence, as affording a navigation to the Pacific Ocean, the discovery of a north-west passage could be of no service.'[4] But he appealed to Banks's sense of discovery. Both from a scientific and patriotic stand there was much to be gained, as Banks saw it, from exploring this hitherto unknown wilderness.

For two decades at the beginning of the nineteenth century William Scoresby was the most successful whaler in Britain, scouring the

Arctic to bring back catches that were consistently greater – vastly greater – than those of his competitors. He went further into the ice than others, took more risks, lost fewer men and made more money: where an ordinary whaling ship could give a return of 25 per cent per annum over an average life of six years, a Scoresby ship returned 33.5 per cent. He himself noted that the inhabitants of Whitby, his home port, regarded his success with superstitious awe.

Physically, he was striking, even sinister-looking. Although slight he was enormously strong, and possessed of a stamina that seems unimaginable nowadays. Once, when his keel was ripped off by ice, and unable to staunch the leak by the usual method of fothering (wrapping a packed sail around and under the ship), he ordered his men to remove the ship's contents, haul it onto a floe and turn it over. During the 120 hours it took to make the repair, Scoresby slept for twelve. His face was that of a gypsy: high cheekbones, dark skin, pointed nose and chin, thin lips, black curly hair. His eyes held a force that even he did not understand. Once, as an experiment, he decided to outstare a ship's guard dog. The beast, reckoned to be the most savage of its kind, ran back and forth snarling in panic as Scoresby approached, before finally jumping overboard and drowning. The same power enabled him to tame polar bears, which he brought back from the Arctic as pets for his friends in Whitby. When at home, and not supervising the blubber vats, he would rescue the same bears from the coppices into which they inevitably escaped. The constabulary cheered, nervously, from a distance.

He was a self-taught scientist. To prove the insulating power of snow under the Arctic sun he grabbed several handfuls and packed them together to form a lens with which he successfully melted lead. He invented what he called 'ice shoes' – remarkably like skis, which he had never seen – for crossing thin ice. He devised a 'marine diver' with which he calculated that the sea was warmer at the bottom than the top. He was the first to notice that differences in sea colour were caused by plankton. On one whaling expedition he went up the coast of Greenland to reach a latitude of 82° 30′, a northernmost record that would stand until 1827. He wrote a book, published in 1820 under the title *An Account of the Arctic Regions*, that has been described as 'the foundation stone of Arctic science'.[5]

Despite being something of a wonder, Scoresby was at the same time a shy, retiring man and a devout Christian, who refused to fish on Sundays. Although perfectly suited for anything to do with the Arctic he was ill-equipped to navigate the social and political straits of the Admiralty. For most of his life he was to be the establishment's willing dupe.

It was he who first suggested to Banks that the Admiralty might undertake an expedition to settle the North-West Passage question once and for all. As he pointed out, if overseen by a whaling captain – he had himself in mind – 'the fishery might occasionally be prosecuted without detriment to the other object of the voyage [and] the expenses would be proportionately reduced and might possibly be altogether defrayed'.[6] Banks was interested, and thanked him for his 'very intelligent letter'.[7] But he had one query. If such a thing was possible, why had no whaler yet tried for the government's prize? And if the prize was too difficult, 'allow me to ask your opinion whether an act offering a thousand pounds for the reaching of every degree of latitude from 82° to the Pole would be likely to induce the masters of ships to make a trial to reach at least some of the unknown degrees of Latitude?'[8]

Scoresby's reply could be paraphrased in terms of expense and self-interest. But it is so uncompromisingly practical that it is worth repeating in full.

I am aware of the premiums offered by the Legislature for the attainment of certain situations on the polar regions, but am not surprised that they have not produced a single attempt, neither do I believe they ever will. Several reasons operate against them.

    1st Few of the commanders of Greenland ships have either a taste for discovery or sufficient nautical knowledge for effecting them.

    2nd The expenses of a fishing ship are so considerable that no owner considers himself justifiable in sinking these expenses and foregoing the advantages which may reasonably be expected of the fishing, to pursue objects of discovery in contemplation of a reward, the conditions of which are not known to be even possible. Besides, if we view the so called NW or NE Passage as practicable, we shall find the expense of outfit, trials, insurance, hire of ship and wages of the crew and Captain, would swallow up at least half of the premium offered. Now it is evident to those who visit the Greenland seas that were such a passage once accomplished it might not again be practicable in ten or even twenty years – it is evident that no premium could be adequate to the expense.

I do not mean to imply that there is no such thing as a northern passage to India, for I do not think the point has been satisfactorily determined; yet I firmly believe that if such a passage does exist, it will be found only at intervals of some years; this I deduce from attentive observation of the nature, drift and general outline of the polar ice.[9]

In all the years spent searching for the North-West Passage, past and future, no advice was crisper than that given by Scoresby. Banks was duly impressed and suggested – following Scoresby's between-the-lines reasoning – that Scoresby lead any proposed expedition.

Barrow liked the idea very much. Although he was not yet fin-ished with Africa, Tuckey's disaster had been a blow. What more glorious alternative could there be than the discovery of a polar route to the Orient?

Barrow's opinions on the Arctic were as intransigent as the ones he held on Africa. He not only believed that the North-West Passage existed and was perfectly navigable – whatever the evidence other-wise – but that the North Pole was open water. This was not as silly as it sounded; it was an incontrovertible fact that ice flowed south and the only obvious reason for it to do so was pressure from above. Theorists conjured a huge cistern of temperate water that forced its surrounding ring of ice down into the Atlantic and the Pacific. As for the North Pole, the same theorists imagined it to be a rocky outcrop – a little nipple of basalt perhaps – that poked from the earth's northern axis. Barrow was a believer in both the solid Pole and the 'Open Polar Sea' that surrounded it. When he despatched his first missions to the Arctic he expected them to prove his every conjecture.

The only stumbling block then was that Scoresby was not a naval man. When Scoresby came with his father from Whitby to meet him, Barrow was at first duplicitous and then rude. Scoresby's diary told the story. 'I found Mr. Barrow was particularly anxious that my Father or I, or both of us, should go in the proposed expedition; yet to my surprise he evaded conversation on the subject and generally avoided me in the room until, provoked by his conduct I watched an opportunity and put the question plainly to him – was it decided that I should have an employment in either of the expeditions, and if so, what situation was it that I might expect? He answered shortly and indirectly that if I *wished* to go I must call the next day at the Navy Board and give in my proposals, and then turning sharply he left the room.'[10]

Bewildered, Scoresby approached Banks who told him with some embarrassment that if the expedition went ahead it would be under naval control but that, should he be interested as 'they very much wished',[11] he would be welcomed as a pilot. Scoresby went home disappointed and out of pocket. '[From my interview] it clearly appeared that I had undertaken a journey to Town for nothing, and had been called upon in such a way that I could have no claim for my expenses.'[12]

On 29 November 1817, Banks wrote – on Barrow's insistence – to Lord Melville, First Lord of the Admiralty, urging him to seize the opportunity the change in conditions offered. Now was the time 'to endeavour to correct and amend the very defective geography of the Arctic Regions more especially on the side of America. To attempt the Circumnavigation of old Greenland, if an island or islands as there is reason to suppose. To prove the existence or non-existence of Baffin's Bay; and to endeavour to ascertain the practicability of a Passage from the Atlantic to the Pacific Ocean, along the Northern Coast of North America. These are objects which may be considered as peculiarly interesting to Great Britain not only from their proximity and the national advantages which they involve but also for the marked attention they called forth and the Discoveries made in consequence thereof in the very earliest periods of our foreign navigation.'[13]

Barrow waited a year before triumphantly publishing Scoresby's plans as his (anonymous) own in the *Quarterly Review*. And in 1818 he secured permission for two naval expeditions. The first, under Commander John Ross and Lieutenant William Edward Parry, was to try for the North-West Passage. The second, under Captain David Buchan and Lieutenant John Franklin, was to try for the North Pole. All the officers, Barrow crowed, were hand-picked and certain to succeed. Their orders confirmed his confidence: Buchan and Franklin were to cross the Pole and meet up with Ross and Parry after they had traversed the North-West Passage. The enterprise was to take a matter of months.

The men who inspired such confidence were all different, but shared three things in common: none of them had been anywhere near the Arctic; they were only going now for the chance of employment; and, secretly, they all hoped it might lead to promotion. Nobody even considered the first. The second was so obvious as to be not worth mentioning. And the third was so presumptuous that it dared not be spoken aloud – save by John Ross who, commendably, demanded it from the start.

His Royal Highness the Prince Regent having signified his pleasure to Viscount Melville, that an attempt should be made to discover a Northern Passage, by sea, from the Atlantic to the Pacific Ocean; We have, in consequence thereof, caused four ships or vessels to be fitted out and appropriated for that purpose, two of which, the *Isabella* and the *Alexander*, are intended to proceed together by the north-westward through Davis' Strait; and two, the *Dorothea* and *Trent*, in a direction as due north as may be found practicable through the Spitsbergen seas.[14]

Thus began Ross's orders. Whether John Ross was the right man to
lead this first expedition into the Arctic has long been a matter of
debate. Born in West Galloway on 24 June 1777, he had joined the
navy at the early age of nine and by the end of the Napoleonic Wars
had risen to the rank of lieutenant. His had been an eventful war,
ranging from the West Indies to the Mediterranean to the Baltic. He
was resourceful, without doubt – in Stockholm he was present at the
armed deposition of the mad King Gustavus IV Adolphus, and was
forced to flee the country in disguise. He was brave too – at the bat-
teries of Bilbao he survived terrible injuries: both legs and one arm
were broken, he was spitted by a bayonet, and received three sabre
wounds to the head. He was short, red-haired and quick-tempered.
He was stubborn and vain; during his lifetime he had his portrait
painted at least four times. Yet somehow he was appealing. Like
Scoresby he was self-taught and was forever tinkering with new ideas.
He had no hesitation in crossing the establishment, and while refusing to admit his mistakes, was willing to learn from them.

Ross was clearly capable. Of the 900 commanders who served
between 1814 and 1818 only nine were constantly employed and Ross
was one of them. As further proof of his ability, he had risen thus far
without any patronage other than that of his fellow officers, one of
whom, Sir George Hope, had pressed for his appointment to lead the
current expedition. However, Ross was not Barrow's first choice. The
man whom the Second Secretary would have liked to see in charge
was William Edward Parry.

Born in 1790, Parry was a young man on the make, whose war service had been spent mostly in placid blockades of the Baltic and
America. Pious, ambitious, with a good nose for what to say, when to
say it, and most important, who to say it to, he was Barrow's favourite.
His father was a society doctor in Bath and he knew all the right
people – a vital qualification in Barrow's eyes. Parry was a networker.
As he enthused after one visit to Banks's house at 22 Soho Square,
'This is an instance, out of many, of the incalculable advantage of
being on the spot. I always like to meet people face to face.'[15] Rather
annoyingly, Parry was also very good at his job. In the words of a later

historian and explorer, Sir Clements Markham, he was 'the beau ideal of an Arctic officer'.[16]

Ironically, Parry had never particularly wanted to go to the Arctic. His heart had been set on joining the Congo mission under Tuckey. But he was not too worried where he was sent so long as he was sent somewhere. As he wrote, 'hot or cold was all one to him, Africa or the Pole'.[17]

If Barrow could not have his way with the command of the mission, he could at least choose the remaining officers. He put Parry in charge of the second ship and when John Ross arrived in London he found there was space for only one more officer in the whole expedition. Ross chose his nephew James. A darker, taller version of his uncle, James Clark Ross shared the same temper, arrogance and vanity (five portraits). Unlike John Ross, however, he was politically astute and had the knack of making himself popular. He had served with his uncle ever since joining the navy in 1812, aged eleven, and was now a midshipman. In time he would become the navy's most experienced Arctic officer.

Descending on the *Isabella* – which, at 385 tons as opposed to the *Alexander*'s 252½, he judged 'the most proper ship for the senior officer'[18] – John Ross oversaw the ships' conversion to Arctic service. Everything was done to prepare for the icy conditions ahead. Both ships were double-planked, their interiors braced with extra timbers and their bows sharpened and reinforced with three-quarter-inch iron plates. Spare rudders and capstans were installed. Ice anchors, ice poles and ice saws were stowed, and a canvas roof was packed against the eventuality of a winter aboard ship. Beds, as opposed to bunks, were provided in case they had to be moved ashore in the event of shipwreck. The crews – mostly whalermen who had been tempted by the Admiralty's offer of double pay – were issued with cold-weather clothing and fur blankets. The officers, meanwhile, were supplied with a twenty-five-volume library of Arctic reference books, to which the Naval and Military Bible Society added ninety uplifting tracts to be shared between both ships. Against the possibility of wreck or repair they were given more than 3,000 feet of timber and 56,000 nails ranging in weight from six pounds to twenty-two ounces.

To justify the expedition's scientific aims the Admiralty and the Royal Society donated chronometers and compasses – the *Isabella* carried seven different models of each – plus a number of other instruments, among them Henry Kater's Pendulum for measuring the ellipticity of the globe, Mr Plentty's Cork Life Boat, Englefield's Mountain Barometer and Companion, Burt's Buoy and Knipper, Trengrouse's Apparatus for Saving Lives, and Troughton's Whirling Horizon. John Ross would later contribute to the array with a dredging device of his own invention which he whimsically christened 'the Deep Sea Clamm'.

There were the usual trinkets for distribution to the natives: 129 gallons of gin and brandy, 102 pounds of snuff, 40 umbrellas and other essentials. Should the recipients prove hostile there were a number of muskets and shotguns as well as nine eighteen-pounder carronades.

Ross recorded every detail scrupulously, right down to the pay which each man could expect. He himself would receive £46 per month and Parry £23. Midshipmen, including James Ross, would be paid £6 2s 8d. Able-bodied seamen got £3, the cook £4 and the carpenter £6. The plutocrat of the crew was the *Isabella*'s surgeon who almost touched Ross with £39 4s 6d. The marine privates who were supposed to keep order and quell mutinies were the lowest-paid, receiving a dismissive £1 14s 10d for not being proper sailors. The roster also included two supernumeraries: Captain Edward Sabine of the Royal Artillery who was to be the expedition's expert on natural history and magnetic observations (he had some experience of the latter but little of the former); and an Eskimo called John Sackheuse who was enlisted at £3 to act as interpreter. Sackheuse was the joker in the Admiralty pack. A native of southern Greenland, he had somehow made his way to Britain – as a stowaway on a whaler according to his more practised accounts which, it must be said, tended to vary. He declared himself to be a committed Christian whose one aim was to return home and convert his fellow countrymen.

Preparations started at Deptford in January 1818, and for the next three months created a good deal of excitement. As the grandest and most ambitious naval adventure to date it caught the public fancy. People swarmed from London on day excursions to Deptford, checking on progress as eagerly as did Ross and Parry. Despite windy weather, the crowds swelled to a peak on 31 March when His Royal Highness the Duke of Clarence, Lord Melville, the First Lord of the Admiralty, and Sir Thomas Byam Martin, Comptroller of the Navy, arrived in the stately red-and-gold Admiralty barge to give the ships their final inspection.

The *Dorothea* and *Trent* had undergone similar preparations and when a favourable south-easterly wind came on 25 April, all four vessels sailed out of the Thames and up the east coast of Britain. By the end of the month they were off Lerwick and on 1 May the two expeditions parted company.

By 3 June, Ross was in Davis Strait off the west coast of Greenland. Seven days later the two ships were sailing up a ten-mile-wide channel between the coast and the central ice pack of Baffin Bay. This was by no means uncharted territory, as was underlined when they rounded a corner and discovered the whaling fleet, 'between thirty and forty British ships at anchor, giving to this frozen and desolate region the appearance of a flourishing seaport . . . Every ship cheered us as we passed.'[19] But for Ross, Parry and the others who had never visited the Arctic before, it was like entering a new world. The sea jostled with icebergs of fantastic shapes and colours, the cliffs screamed with sea birds and the sun shone for twenty-four hours of the day. 'It is hardly possible,' wrote Ross of the massed bergs, 'to imagine anything more exquisite . . . by night as well as day they glitter with a vividness of colour beyond the power of art to represent.'[20] Everything was weird and new. Even vision was distorted. Ross reported that at a distance of only a few miles ships appeared to be of 'monstrous height'[21] – a phenomenon which he was unable to explain but which was caused by atmospheric refraction.

Parry too was awed by their surroundings. 'The weather was beautifully fine and clear,' he wrote on one calm night, 'and nothing could exceed the serenity, and at the same time the grandeur, of the whole scene around us. The water was glassy smooth, and the ships glided gently among the numberless masses of ice . . . The land of Greenland, rugged, high, and almost entirely covered with snow, filled up the eastern horizon, and Disko Island was now more plainly visible to the Northward, its hills reflecting the bright redness of the midnight sun.'[22]

It was early in the season – a month early, according to the whalers – and the ice had yet to be broken by bad weather. Ross tried and failed to find a way through the central pack before following what leads he could closer to the shore. At times both crews were forced to disembark and haul their ships through narrow channels in the ice, heaving to the rhythm set by the *Isabella*'s fiddler.

In these early days the expedition had a carnival-like air. The men climbed bergs and tobogganed down snow shutes. The officers set up observatories, meticulously recorded their findings and toasted their successes. Even when the *Isabella*'s fiddler fell through the ice into sub-zero waters he emerged unscathed and, after a change of clothes, was soon back at his post, scraping away cheerfully.

But if the journey was a carnival it was a Dantesque one, tinged at times with madness and surreal images. They sailed past the Whale Islands, whose governor, a Norwegian named Flushe who had lived there for the last eleven years with his wife, children, six Danes and 100 Eskimos, paddled out to inform them that last year had been so hard they had had to eat their dogs, and this year was even harder. Then he plashed gloomily back to his lonely existence. Past Love Bay, on Disko Island, they saw a Danish whale factory which had been set alight by rival whalers. Later, venturing ashore at Four Island Point, they encountered a British surgeon buying skulls from an Eskimo cemetery. This world was as detached as it could be from their own.

For a while they kept company with three whalers, among them the *Three Brothers* of Hull, a famous old ship which would be lost later in the season. Those of Ross's men who had never before seen whales were amazed at the sight. *En masse* the sound of their blowing resembled distant artillery; their spouts rose into the air like smoke from a village. James Ross was given the chance of killing a forty-six-foot black-and-white specimen, which his uncle found a distasteful sight. He recorded, with a sympathy unusual for the time, the whale's spout turning red with blood, and the harpooners' boats withdrawing to avoid their quarry, 'rolling and writhing in dreadful agony, lashing the sea from side to side with his tail and fins, till he expired'.[23] But he was grateful for the whale's nine tons of blubber, which was divided 5:4 between the two ships to provide fuel and light should they have to overwinter. They sailed on, leaving behind the carcase, or *krang* as whalers called it, a stinking hulk at which seabirds would peck till the skeleton sank to the bottom.

By the end of July the whales and the whalers had gone and the two naval vessels were on their own. They were now in uncharted waters and the weather was turning. The ice was breaking up, the men were back on board, and heavy gales became commonplace. They were near the top of Baffin Bay and had long passed the furthest recorded north for this area of 75° 12′. Icebergs were everywhere – Parry counted 1,000 before giving up – and the weather was harsh. Even experienced men were cowed by the conditions. During one gale the two ships were forced against each other by the ice and it seemed as if they were going to be crushed. At the last moment, however, the wind changed and the ice backed off. The *Isabella* and the *Alexander* parted reluctantly, their entangled anchors stretching out until the *Alexander*'s hawser snapped. All agreed that they owed their lives to the reinforcements installed by the Deptford gangs. 'Neither the masters, the mates, nor those who had been all their lives in the Greenland service, had ever experienced such imminent peril,' Ross wrote, 'and they declared a common whaler must have been crushed to atoms.'[24]

In search of a safe haven, Ross ordered a harbour to be cut in the ice of what he called Melville Bay. It was good, solid ice, unlike the vagrant bergs and uncertain young ice which filled the sea. Normally it would have been a good decision. The ice in Baffin Bay comprises three kinds: sea ice, quickly formed, quickly disintegrated; land ice, solid the year round; and the central pack, which is fed by the Arctic

Ocean and accumulates into a mass of bergs wavering between the safety of cold seas and the prevailing pressure of a north wind. Normally the central pack moves southwards. But when a strong wind blows up Baffin Bay the ice changes direction. When this happens, seasoned sailors do as Ross did – they cut a harbour in the firm, land ice, and hope that it will protect them.

Ross, the first man ever to try this trick in this spot, was unlucky. His harbour was hardly ready when the wind changed and the central pack came piling in. He barely escaped it. In a huge surge the pack slammed against the land ice, concertinaing it into fifty-foot-high ridges. The harbour, so laboriously cut with the nine-foot ice saws, disappeared in an instant. This area of the Arctic would become known as a deathtrap. In 1819 the central pack smashed fourteen whalers; in 1821, eleven; another seven in 1822; in 1830 nineteen ships were crushed, leaving several thousand men stranded on the ice. All in all, Ross got off lightly.

By 8 August the seas were calm again. And the following day they saw a small group of men gesticulating from the shore to the east. At first Ross thought they were shipwrecked sailors; but when the ships tacked, and the men 'set up a simultaneous shout, accompanied with many strange gesticulations, and went off in their sledges with amazing velocity',[25] he realized they must be Eskimos.

The Eskimos had good reason to be shy. They had never seen a white man before. In fact, they had never seen other Eskimos either. They were Polar Eskimos, who had split from the main group of Greenland Eskimos in about 1450, and had wandered northwards during a period known as the Little Ice Age, adapting to the cold and the available food supply to such a degree that they had lost most of the usual Arctic skills. When southern Greenlanders finally made contact in 1856 – when the Little Ice Age was coming to a close – the Polar Eskimos had to be taught such essentials as how to use a kayak, how to fire a bow and arrow, how to hunt caribou and how to net migrating char. Little wonder then, that they avoided Ross. As far as they knew, they were the only people in the world.

Ross spent an unfruitful day trying to make contact with the elusive

Eskimos. He placed gifts on a four-foot-high stool; they went untouched. He released a dog with beads around its neck; the dog was later found asleep on the ice by the stool, its beads as undisturbed as the gifts. He erected a flag, displaying the sun and the moon over a sprig of Arctic shrub, the only plant he had found in the region. Like the gifts, and like the dog, it was ignored. Finally, Ross hung a bag of presents on the pole, painted it with a large hand pointing towards the ships, and waited. The following morning, at about 10 a.m., eight sledges hove into view and halted on the shore, giving the flag and the hand a wide berth. An advance party of four men disembarked, walked across the ice and hovered nervously behind a strip of open water. John Sackheuse was sent to greet them and soon established that they spoke a recognizable dialect of his own language. They had come this far south in order to hunt narwhals, he translated, and they were terrified that the strangers intended to kill them.

Clad in his Western finery, including a beaver-skin hat, Sackheuse reassured them that it was safe.

'Come on!' he shouted.

'Go away!' the Eskimos shouted back.[26]

Sackheuse returned to the ship and came back with two men carrying a plank which was laid across the channel. Crossing to the other side, he offered gifts: beads, a shirt and a knife. The first two failed to tempt but the knife was irresistible. A man snatched it up. Sackheuse held out his hand. Tentatively, the man touched it.

In the history of European exploration this contact stands out as one of the most benign and bizarre. Descending from their ships in full naval regalia – cocked hats, dress swords, tailcoats and buckled shoes – Ross and Parry advanced across the ice towards the fur-clad Eskimos. They handed over gifts of mirrors and knives, which were received with rapture. Meanwhile they pulled hard on their noses, on Sackheuse's sombre instruction that this was the accepted mode of greeting. By this time the initial four Eskimos had been joined by the remaining four who had stayed on the sleds, and the entire company, talking, shouting and thrashing their dogs with whips to shut them up, were invited aboard the *Isabella*. This was not exploitation, or conquest, merely a meeting. Neither side had any design on the other. They were simply curious about each other.

The Eskimos learned about the strangers. They learned that their ships did not come from the moon or the sun, despite the peculiar flag which had been displayed. They learned, too, that the ships were inanimate objects. 'Who are you? What are you? Where do you come from?'[27] one Eskimo yelled at a boat. It took a full display of launching and landing, with men aboard, to persuade him that it was nothing more than a vessel that floated on water. They learned that the strangers kept pigs – frightening – and a terrier – despicably small – and possessed more iron than they could have believed possible. In the metal-free Arctic, iron was prized more than anything: one man tried valiantly to heave the ironsmith's anvil away but made do in the end with a big hammer that was later recovered from a snowdrift. They learned that the strangers could paint: three of them had their portraits done by Lt. Hoppner and Midshipmen Skene and Bushnan. They also learned, after an odd display by Mr Beverley, Ross's surgeon, that the strangers could juggle, but at this 'they became uneasy, and expressed a wish to go on deck'.[28]

The Eskimos asked interminable questions. What kind of ice were the *Isabella*'s skylights made from? Were watches good to eat? What skin did the strangers make their cables from? Was there anyone on the other side of a mirror? Were the ships *really* inanimate (after all, they had seen their wings move)? And how could they be made of wood, when the only source in the Arctic was a little willow whose trunk was no thicker than a finger? More importantly, were the newcomers a race of men, or did they have any women? On being shown 'a miniature I had of Mrs. Ross'[29] they departed *en masse* for the *Alexander*, which they presumed must contain the *Isabella*'s female contingent. They returned very quickly.

On that day and others, as they gradually crept around this unexplored part of Baffin Bay, the white men learned in turn about the Eskimos. They learned that they were a new and undiscovered people – Ross called them Arctic Highlanders – and had 'no knowledge of any thing but what originates, or is found, in their own country'. In fact, the Arctic Highlanders were so isolated that they had even lost their mythology: 'nor have they any tradition how they came to this spot,' wrote Ross, 'or from whence they came; having until the moment of our arrival, believed themselves to be the only inhabitants of the universe'.[30] They did not even have any interest in the afterlife, saying only that long ago a wise man had suggested they might go to the moon when they were dead but that the idea was now generally rejected. To Ross's very great credit he did not proselytize, but merely recorded.

The Arctic Highlanders were as pristine as a people could be. They could count no higher than five, and had no expression for a quantity greater than two fives, ten – which simply became 'a lot'. They had no laws of possession, so dear to the European mind, and would walk off happily with anything that took their fancy. They could play football, put on a fine display of dog-sledging, make spears from narwhal tusks and hunt foxes that came in three colours: black, red and white. They danced in an embarrassingly familiar manner – 'The gestures and actions were not wanting,' as a later, very Victorian commentator put it, 'in that reprehensible element, for which the Nautch of India and the Can-can of the most polished nation in the world are notorious.'[31] The Arctic Highlanders also had iron of their own. This last was a discovery of tremendous importance. Eskimos were nomads, not miners; and besides, there was no iron in the Arctic to be mined. Yet, as Ross noticed, their knives were edged with flattened strips of the metal. At first he assumed these little strips had been made from the detritus of Western civilization – washed-up barrel-hoops or nails. On closer inquiry, however, he learned that the Arctic Highlanders had their own mother lode in the Sowallik, or Iron Mountains. Having questioned a man as to its source Ross discovered that, within a few days' travel, there was a place where iron lay scattered above the ground: little bits here and there, but a lump about four feet long from which the Eskimos chipped shards using a hard green stone. As a final favour, before the Eskimos left, Ross asked for a piece of this iron. He suspected it might be from a meteorite. Sure enough, when it was analysed, it was found to be of extra-terrestrial origin.

On the 16th, Ross made another unique find. Rounding a headland which he named Cape York, he encountered a 600-foot cliff covered in crimson snow. A party was sent ashore and discovered that the colour was no mere surface bloom, but penetrated the snow down to the very rock, in places at depths of twelve feet. Under a microscope, magnified 110 times, the snow was seen to be riddled with minute, round, red particles. The general opinion was that it was some form of plant life, perhaps seeds which had drifted from the russet-tinted vegetation which lined the top of the cliffs.

They were wrong to suppose the particles were seeds. But they were right to say it was of vegetable origin. The startling phenomenon of red snow, now an accepted part of Arctic geography, is caused by a rapidly multiplying, unicellular plant called *Protococcus nivalis*.

So far, Ross's expedition had been a success. He had mapped the eastern side of Baffin Bay, and had made two important scientific finds – a new race of Eskimos and the crimson snow. He would dearly have liked to spend more time with the Arctic Highlanders. But he had already made his tentative farewells in order to fulfil the main thrust of his orders – to ascertain the existence of a North-West Passage. In this he was to be astonishingly, perversely, incompetent.

At the northern tip of Baffin Bay is a seaway – normally clogged with ice, but a seaway nonetheless – called Smith Sound, which leads up the north-western coast of Greenland. Ross reached the mouth of Smith Sound on 19 August, surveyed it from a distance of twelve leagues, and declared it a bay. There was no way north out of Baffin Bay, Ross said. To the south-west of Smith Sound lies Jones Sound, a similarly ice-clogged passage which leads west to the Arctic Ocean. At midnight on 23 August, Ross saw that it ended in a 'ridge of very high mountains'.[32] Without bothering to investigate further, he announced that Jones Sound, too, was a bay.

To the south of Jones Sound is Lancaster Sound. If any North-West Passage existed, this was judged its most likely entrance, and as the two ships approached it on 30 August, their rigging was crowded with sailors peering for signs of an open strait. In the morning of 1 September, Ross sailed into Lancaster Sound with the slower

Alexander lagging behind. It was 4 a.m. and foggy. But even in such poor visibility, Ross determined that Lancaster Sound, too, was a bay. He described the moment at length in his journal.

The land which I then saw was a high ridge of mountains, extending directly across the bottom of the inlet. This chain appeared high in the centre, and those towards the north had, at times the appearance of islands, being insulated by fog at their bases. Although a passage in this direction appeared hopeless, I was determined completely to explore it, as the wind was favourable; and, therefore, continued all sail. At eight the wind fell a little, and the Alexander being far astern I sounded and found six hundred and seventy-four fathoms, with a soft muddy bottom. There was, however, no current, [Ross's orders had stated very specifically that he was to find and follow the current which, it was presumed, must carry the ice from the open polar sea] and the temperature of the mud was 29½° . . . The weather now variable, being cloud and clear at intervals. Mr. Beverley, who was most sanguine, went up to the crow's nest; and at twelve, reported to me, that before it became very thick, he had seen the land across the bay, except for a very short space.

Although all hopes were given up, even by the most sanguine, that a passage existed, and the weather continued thick, I determined to stand higher up, and put into any harbour I might discover, for the purpose of making magnetical observations. Here I felt the want of a consort, which I could employ to explore a coast, or discover a harbour; but the *Alexander* sailed so badly, and was so leewardly, that she could not be safely employed on such a service. During this day we shortened sail several times, to prevent our losing sight of her altogether.

About one, the *Alexander* being nearly out of sight to the eastward, we hove to for half an hour, to let her come up a little; and at half-past one, she being within six or seven miles

of us, we again made all sail . . . At half-past two, (when I went
off deck to dinner) there were some hopes of its clearing, and
I left orders to be called on the appearance of land or ice a-
head. At three, the officer of the watch, who was relieved to
his dinner by Mr. Lewis, reported, on his coming into the
cabin, that there was some appearance of its clearing at the
bottom of the bay; I immediately, therefore, went on deck,
and soon after it completely cleared for about ten minutes,
and I distinctly saw the land, round the bottom of the bay,
forming a connected chain of montains with those which
extended along the north and south sides. This land appeared
to be at the distance of eight leagues; and Mr. Lewis, the
master, and James Haig, leading man, being sent for, they
took its bearings, which were inserted in the log; the water on
the surface was at temperature 34°. At this moment I also saw
a continuity of ice, at the distance of seven miles, extending
from one side of the bay to the other . . . At a quarter past
three, the weather again became thick and unsettled; and
being now perfectly satisfied that there was no passage in this
direction, nor any harbour into which I could enter, for the
purpose of making magnetical observations, I tacked to join
the *Alexander*, which was at the distance of eight miles; and
having joined her a little after four, we stood to the south-
eastward.[33]

Before he turned south, Ross named the new features on his chart.
The range he had seen at the end of Lancaster Sound became the
'Croker Mountains' and the bay before them 'Barrow Bay'.

If Ross's journal sounds like a statement for the defence, it is
because it was precisely that. He was utterly mistaken. Lancaster
Sound was, and is, the one open seaway into the North-West Passage.
And had he looked harder he would have found this out.

Why didn't he look harder? The question would bedevil his career
much as it bedevilled Arctic historians for more than a century afterwards. As a puzzled study of 1880 put it, Ross was 'an excellent and

accomplished navigator, a man of considerable intellectual power, a Scotchman, and not one given to accept his facts on the endorsement of his imagination'.[34] So why?

Was he scared, perhaps? Was he, as Barrow would later suggest, running away from the prospect of a winter in the ice? This is unlikely. His war record proved his bravery and he was not only willing but expecting to overwinter. As he wrote on 9 July, should he be unable to explore Lancaster Sound he hoped to be far enough south to 'make our winter quarters tolerable'.[35]

One possible answer lies in the Arctic weather patterns, which become particularly confusing in August. Generally it is sunny and warm; the landscape is one of dry boulders or boggy marshland rather than the preconceived notion of eternal ice. Occasionally, however, freezing fogs can descend. In Ross's time, these fogs arrived in a cloud of white, freezing everything with which they came in contact. Each change of tack was signalled by a shower of ice from the ropes. Meanwhile, although forward visibility was nil, the skies above remained blue. When the fog cleared, visibility improved. But it was a deceptive clarity, obscured by mirages. Objects wobbled and shimmered in the air. A flat ice-field could appear on one side as a towering forest and on the other as a low-lying island. Distant ships swelled to towering castles, and shrank to blobby sausages in the course of an hour. But weather on its own was no excuse. Ross could handle fog. And although he marvelled at the mirages, he knew them for what they were. As he himself said, 'We were often able to see land at an immense distance, and we have certain proof that the power of vision was extended beyond one hundred and fifty miles.'[36]

While aware of refraction, Ross was nevertheless unaware of all the tricks it could play. He knew that it could distort visible objects but he did not know that it could create seemingly visible objects where none lay. The effect – like crimson snow, now a matter of Arctic fact – is caused by light penetrating the atmosphere and being reflected back by the ice. On its way up it is distorted by turbulence and by progressively warmer bands of air. To this is added the curve of the earth's atmosphere which lends a natural vertical bias to any image. The result is a chain of sharp peaks, shaded in grey, with dark ridge lines. It looks exactly like a mountain range.

It was undoubtedly this phenomenon that caused Ross to turn back from Lancaster Sound. It may also have caused his retreat from Smith Sound and Jones Sound. But in all three cases there was an added factor: someone, Parry or one of the other officers, maybe even James Ross, had suggested on each occasion that the Sounds be explored further. If there was one thing guaranteed to ensure Ross clung to a bad decision it was someone questioning it. In this instance Ross's natural stubbornness was exacerbated by insecurity. It was his first solo command and he was not going to let his authority be undermined by presumptuous whipper-snappers who lacked his experience – at forty-one, Ross was thirteen years older than Parry, the next in seniority.

Thus, a combination of natural and human factors caused Ross to make such a mess of the mission. But he cannot take the blame entirely. He had been set certain objectives and wanted to complete them as quickly and efficiently as possible. He was a practical man, who wanted to do the job according to instructions, within the price. He wanted his crew to return safely – which they did; not a single man contracted scurvy, not a single man died.

His fault, as his detractors would point out, was that he had lacked imagination. But Ross was not being paid to be imaginative. He was being paid to follow orders. The gist of Ross's orders had been to explore Baffin Bay and to ascertain the possibilities of a North-West Passage leading from it. He had done that. His orders also stated that in case the North-West Passage proved non-existent, Ross was to avoid being caught in the ice. He was to be out of Davis Strait by mid-September or 1 October at the latest. From Lancaster Sound he had 400 miles to cover before he was out of Davis Strait. He obeyed his orders almost to the letter. Having in his own mind ascertained the non-existence of a North-West Passage he sailed south, charting as he went. On 1 October he was off Cumberland Sound, the last of the possible westward entries mapped by Baffin. This, too, was an inlet, and a genuine one in this case. Then he left Davis Strait and headed for home. On 14 November the ships had reached the Thames and two days later Ross was handing in his papers at the Admiralty. Uncannily, Buchan had stepped through the Admiralty doors only fifteen minutes earlier.

4

BUCHAN'S RETREAT

While Ross had been battling controversially around Baffin Bay, the *Dorothea* and the *Trent* had endured a hair-raising series of near disasters. Initially, all had gone well. On entering the Arctic Circle, the crews had been amazed and delighted by their first sight of icebergs. They had marvelled at a shower of snow, each flake as hard as a hailstone, which tinkled onto their decks. They had stayed up all night to gape at a sun that never set. But after the novelty came the nightmare. Unlike Ross, who had sailed into a relatively protected zone, Buchan and Franklin had to contend with unadulterated foul weather. Gales blew, coating both ships with several tons of ice which built up so fast on the bows that the men had to continually hack it off with axes. At the same time they had to beat the ropes with sticks in order to maintain a semblance of manoeuvrability. By the time they reached their appointed rendezvous at Magdalena Bay, a dark and dreary fjord on the island of Spitsbergen, they were weary to the bone. The sight to the north of the polar ice pack, stretching 'in one vast unbroken plain' from the shore to the horizon, did little to convince them that their voyage would be successful. Nor did the four great glaciers of Magdalena Bay, the largest of which, the 1,000-foot-long 'Waggon Way', frowned down on them with all the force of its 300-foot vertical face, oozing forth icebergs relentlessly.

On the other hand, the pack was not as dense as they had been led to believe. Although it was unnavigable, comprising chunks that were too large to be forced aside by the ships' bows and too thick to be cut with ice saws, it was nevertheless riddled with narrow passages of open water. If open water existed here it might exist elsewhere, and in greater quantity. This was the one thought which cheered them through the nights, whose silence was punctuated by the boom of bursting icebergs and the thump of rock slabs tumbling from the cliffs.

They left Magdalena Bay on 7 June and set out along the westward margin of the pack. The pack curved northwards, a promising sign. But around the pack they found brash ice – a paste of tiny floes, five feet thick, which extended for miles. A ship could force its way through brash ice but, as Franklin discovered when he did so, it could freeze in an instant. He spent an uncomfortable night marooned in the brash until daylight thawed him free and he was able to rejoin the *Dorothea*.

On 12 June they passed the northernmost tip of Spitsbergen and could go no further. Their way was blocked by impenetrable pack ice. And as icebergs began to close around them, they found themselves trapped. A party tried to walk to shore over the ice but were overtaken by fog, got lost and had to be rescued by another party. Back at the ships, meanwhile, the men amused themselves with a bit of lamping, which consisted of lighting a fire of walrus fat and shooting whatever animal came to investigate. Their only trophy was a small polar bear, six feet long and three and a half feet high, whose stomach was perfectly empty save for one grisly relic – a garter of the type used by Greenland whalers.

The ice finally cleared on 6 July and by the following day Buchan was sailing up a promising lead of open water. By the same evening the lead had begun to ice over, and the ships had to be warped forward, a method which involves attaching an anchor to a distant block

of ice, and winching the ship towards it. In this manner Buchan
dragged his expedition to its most northerly position of 80° 37′.

It was as if they were climbing a hill. From that point everything
began to slide backwards. A northerly wind arose, driving ships and
ice before it. Despite two days' continual warping, Buchan was unable
to make any real progress. In fact, after they had warped forwards
three miles, they had lost two in real terms. Both ships were nipped
badly by encroaching ice, and the *Trent* had begun to leak.

Undeterred by his lack of progress, Buchan tried some scientific
experiments. On 19 July he lowered the lead and found 300 fathoms.
To his amazement, the lead came up with not only several living
specimens of starfish and a lobster, but also a branch of dead coral.
Darwin had yet to do his ground-breaking research on coral, but even
without it Britain's navy was well-educated enough to know that coral
grew mainly in warm waters. Did this mean that the Arctic climate
had once been much warmer? Or did it mean that Barrow's temperate
polar ocean was within reach?

The discovery marked the end of the expedition. Having warped
his way into the pack, Buchan now decided to warp his way out of it.
The weather had grown colder and ice had formed behind him. He
had thirty miles to cover before he reached open sea. Five hours
later that distance had dropped to twenty-nine miles. It took another
216 hours, working day and night, before the two ships were free.
Buchan must be given all credit for persistence. Instead of heading
for home, he continued west towards Greenland. But within a day
the ships were being beaten against the pack by a ferocious gale that
tipped the ships so violently that their bells rang. Four hours later,
when the gale died down, both ships were wrecks. There was no
choice now but to concede defeat. They returned to Spitsbergen for
repairs.

It was a gloomy sojourn, enlivened only by a man named Spink,
who climbed a 1,000-foot glacier and took the short cut home by sliding down its forty-foot face. They watched with panic as he sheered
his way through the snow, steering by his heels, until he crashed into
a large drift. When they rescued him they saw that he had worn

through two pairs of thick, navy trousers 'and something more'.[1] Spink found it amusing – or said he did. They sailed for home on 30 August.

Of the two expeditions there can be no doubt which was the most successful. Buchan had discovered how appalling conditions could be in the Arctic, but apart from that had achieved little. He had not even reached the furthest recorded north of 80° 48'. Ross, on the other hand, had mapped the whole of Baffin Bay, had discovered the most northerly tribe of Eskimos and had, with his 'Deep Sea Clamm', brought up a *Caput medusae* from the depth of 1,000 fathoms – a record for a living specimen which would stand for many years. Disastrously, though, he had failed to find the North-West Passage and Barrow would never forgive him for it.

As soon as Ross's expedition returned to Britain, the story of Lancaster Sound began to leak out. Writing from the Shetlands, Parry informed his family, 'That we have not sailed through the North-West Passage, our return in so short a period is, of course, a sufficient indication; *but I know it is in existence, and not very hard to find.* This opinion of mine, which is not lightly formed, must, on no account, be uttered out of our family; and I am sure it will not, when I assure you that every future prospect of mine depends on it being kept a secret.'[2]

The very day after Ross handed in his papers, Parry was summoned to an interview with Lord Melville, First Lord of the Admiralty. 'He conversed with me upon our expedition, and, what was more interesting to me, upon what remained to be done.' Parry wrote on 18 November, 'You must know that, on our late voyage, we entered a magnificent strait, from thirty to thirty-six miles wide, upon the west coast of Baffin's Bay, and – *came out again*, nobody knows why! You know I was not sanguine, formerly, as to the existence of a north-west passage, or as to the practicability of it, if it did exist. But our voyage to this Lancaster Sound . . . has left quite a different impression, for it has not only given us a reason to believe that it is a broad passage into some sea to the westward . . . but, what is more important still, that it is, at certain seasons, practicable; for when we were there, there was not a bit of ice to be seen. This truth has been fully communicated to Lord Melville by Mr. Barrow who had, with his usual discernment, immediately discovered it without any information from me on the subject. Lord Melville conversed with me pretty freely on the probability of a passage there.'[3]

The result of this discussion was that a second Arctic expedition was proposed in December. John Ross wrote to Croker on 29 December offering his services. They were declined. Its command was given in January to Parry.

From the above letters it is clear that some kind of conspiracy was afoot. Before they even returned to Britain, Parry was looking to his 'future prospects'. And the speed with which Barrow learned of Lancaster Sound was breathtaking. Who could have told him? It is unlikely to have been any of the junior officers, for whom it would have been professional suicide to contradict their captain – and none of them, save perhaps Parry, had the standing to approach Barrow for a man-to-man chat on what had really happened. Sabine could have been the one, being an army officer with nothing to lose from naval improprieties. More probably, however, it was a member of Parry's influential family, or perhaps his friend Sir Joseph Banks. Either way, it was a neatly planned *coup* to oust Ross and put Parry in his place.

Ross was later to write of Barrow that 'immediately after my first Voyage of Discovery, circumstances occurred which caused a personal altercation and a rupture of our former friendly relations'.[4] One can imagine only too well the confrontation between these two stubborn men. Never one to burn one boat when two would do, Ross had also fallen foul of Croker. On Ross's return, Croker had invited him to dinner on 16 November. Ross, however, had just learned from his wife that their only child had died, and felt obliged to decline the invitation.

'Damn the child,' Croker replied. 'You'll get more children, come and dine with me.'[5]

Ross's forthright response left the First Secretary 'very much displeased'.

Officially, Ross could not be reprimanded for his failure to find the North-West Passage. No court of inquiry would accept the charge that he had failed to find a seaway which might not exist. Unofficially, though, he was an open target from all sides. No sooner was his journal published in the New Year than the assault began.

Barrow surged into action with a venomous – and anonymous – attack which took up fifty pages in the January edition of the *Quarterly Review*. The existence of a North-West Passage, he wrote, 'so far from being in the smallest degree shaken by any thing that Captain Ross has done, is considerably strengthened by what he has failed to do'. He slammed Ross's 'indifference and want of perseverance'. He condemned his 'habitual inaccuracy and looseness of description'. To give the Eskimos a name like 'Arctic Highlanders' was ridiculous, and to state that they were impressed by mirrors was excessive; did not the ice which surrounded them act as a natural mirror? The crimson snow was 'outrageously (not to say ridiculously) exaggerated'. Even the icebergs were played up. 'Icebergs display no colour at night,' fumed Barrow, who had been to Iceland once and had never experienced the midnight sun. As for Ross's failure to explore Jones, Smith and Lancaster Sounds, he must have been either 'impenetrably dull or intentionally perverse'. It was Barrow's opinion that Ross 'knows no more, in fact, than he might have known by staying at home'. And what really piqued him was that Ross had returned unscathed from his unsatisfactory experience. This was not what exploration was about, as Barrow made abundantly clear. 'A voyage of discovery implies danger; but a mere voyage like this, round the shores of Baffin's Bay, in the summer months, may be considered as a voyage of pleasure.'[6] In short, the man who had doubted the existence of Baffin Bay was calling the man who had mapped it an incompetent, self-serving coward.

After Barrow came Sabine, who published a pamphlet accusing Ross of stealing material from a paper he had written on the Eskimos, failing to credit him for a number of observations, belittling his efforts, sneering at his qualifications as a naturalist – which he had never claimed to be – and making a dog's dinner of his magnetical work. 'I have only to add,' he wrote, 'concerning the magnetic observations that they are incomplete, imperfect, and printed incorrectly; that those on the pendulum are useless in their present state, as every person who understands the subject will perceive.'[7] Not only that, but Sabine accused John Ross of passing off the magnetic observations as those of James Ross, and had a signed affidavit from James Ross to that effect. Finally, he added that he had never heard of Lancaster Sound being blocked until he read Ross's journal, and gave his considered opinion that 'land seen for a short time by a single individual, at a very considerable distance, on a very unfavourable day'[8] was inconclusive proof of the North-West Passage's non-existence.

Then came, most damagingly of all, Parry's private journal, which was quoted by Barrow in the *Quarterly Review*. Here, for all to see, was a version of events which differed widely from Ross's own. 'The more we advanced [into Lancaster Sound],' wrote Parry, 'the more sanguine our hopes were that we had at last found what has been for ages sought in vain. Everything, indeed, tended to confirm this our belief: at noon we tried for sounding with two hundred and thirty-five fathoms of line, without finding bottom; and in the evening, when the sun was getting low, the weather being remarkably clear, we could see the land on both sides of the inlet for a very great distance, but not any bottom of it. But, alas! the sanguine hopes and high expectations excited by this promising appearance of thing were but of a short duration, for, about three o'clock in the afternoon, the *Isabella* tacked, very much to our surprise indeed, as we could not see anything like land at the bottom of the inlet, nor was the weather well calculated at the time for seeing any object at a great distance, it being somewhat hazy.'[9]

Backing this up was an anonymous letter from one of the *Alexander*'s officers – possibly Fisher, Parry's assistant surgeon – which appeared in *Blackwood's Magazine* in December 1818. The appearance of Lancaster Sound 'inspired hope and joy into every countenance', he wrote, 'and every officer and man, on the instant as it were, made up his mind that this must be the north-west passage'. He described events in much the same vein as Parry and concluded that there were no 'grounds for stating, as I perceive has been positively stated in the newspapers, and apparently on demi-official authority that there is no passage from Baffin's Bay into the Pacific. I am perfectly certain that no officer employed on the expedition ventured to hazard such an assertion, because no one is competent to make up his mind to such a decision.'[10]

Ross flailed to extricate himself from the web. He had already suspected Sabine might be trouble and had gone so far as to mention him specifically in his journal: 'My opinions [about Lancaster Sound] were mentioned to Captain Sabine, who repeated, on every occasion, that there was no indication of a passage.'[11] He published a counter-pamphlet which repudiated, more-or-less successfully, most of Sabine's accusations. Further, he collected a number of letters all of which stated that despite their sanguine hopes ('sanguine' was obviously à la mode) the junior officers on both ships had agreed that Lancaster Sound was blocked, had *seen* that it was blocked, had suggested he try further south and if they had suggested otherwise had only done so on 'the impulse of passion'[12] – those last being the words of James Ross.

But his cabal, comprising William Thom, the *Isabella*'s purser, Benjamin Lewis, the ice-master, Lt. William Robertson, Ross's second-in-command, and, occasionally, James Ross, was no match for the one ranged against him.

His opponents had played their cards well. Although everybody knew who had written the piece in the *Quarterly Review*, there was no proof that it had been Barrow. The officer of the *Alexander* was likewise officially anonymous. The one person to give his name publicly to the attack was Sabine, but he was an army man and could say what he liked without jeopardizing his career. Had Ross been buried at sea he could not have been stitched up more thoroughly.

A hearing was held at the Admiralty between 29 March and 30 April 1819, to discuss Sabine's accusations. This was Ross's last chance. He had no direct way of clearing his name, as no naval officer had officially challenged his findings. Nevertheless, he bulldozed his way through the proceedings, using his nephew, James Ross, as a scapegoat. On the penultimate day, a tired clerk recorded Ross's fury in the transcript.

He stated that Mr. James Ross was his greatest Enemy ever
since he knew Capt. Sabine & that Mr. Bushnan was liable to
the same charge.

That a most serious conspiracy existed during the voyage &
still existed against him Capt. Ross.

That Mr. James Ross he would not say refused but hesitated
to make the affidavit [confirming Ross's innocence] tho' there
was nothing in it but what he could and ought to swear.

That on his hesitation he Capt. Ross told him that he would
take him to Bow Street or before the Lord Mayor.

That he gave him the affidavit to read & told him that he
might take it away with him & alter it as he pleased, but that if
he should not swear it, he Capt. Ross would take him before a
magistrate.

That before Mr. James Ross came before the Board
yesterday he (Capt. Ross) believes that he had an interview
with Lieut. Parry.

That he (Capt. Ross) mentions this to show that Mr. James
Ross tho' his nephew is not his friend.

By the next day John Ross had twisted a lot of arms, James Ross
had signed the affidavit, and all was well.

Captain John Ross [continued the clerk, with obvious relief]
being admitted desires to state that he wishes to recall the
observations he made against his Nephew.

He had thought there was a combination between Lieut.
Parry, Captain Sabine and his Nephew against him, but he saw
his Nephew's Brother yesterday Evening who has satisfied him
on this point. He also begs leave to retract the charge relative
to the combination during the voyage as it was probably no
more than the difference which arose from a Land Officer
being embarked with Sea Officers & produced no Injury to the
Service.[13]

The whole business ended inconclusively, with John Ross being cleared but the charge hanging in the public eye. Ross begged Lord Melville for a full court martial, but the First Lord replied evasively that if they had thought Ross guilty of any misconduct they would never have made him Captain – his promotion had arrived on 7 December 1818 – and that, between the lines, was the end of it.

Ross was never again employed actively by the Royal Navy. He retreated to his home above the sea at Stranraer, where he spent his time shooting grouse, watching the ships come and go, fretting about his half-pay and pondering the progress of Parry, who would dominate Arctic exploration for the next ten years.

5

FURTHEST WEST

Barrow would detest Ross for the rest of his life. In 1846 he published a history of Arctic exploration in which he ripped Ross to pieces in the most minute and petty fashion. Every action was castigated, even his claiming the land around Lancaster Sound for Britain, 'with the usual silly ceremony,' sneered Barrow, 'the more silly when the object is worthless, as in the present case – a barren, uninhabited country, covered in ice and snow, the only subjects of His Majesty, in this portion of his newly-acquired dominion, consisting of half-starved bears, deer, foxes, white hares, and such other creatures as are commonly met with in these regions of the globe.'[1]

For all his sneering, however, Barrow was desperately keen that Britain stake its claim to the Arctic and to the North-West Passage. Other countries were already interested in it, particularly Russia and the United States for whom a short-cut between the Pacific and the Atlantic would have been of major importance. Indeed, a Russian expedition was already being planned under Bellingshausen. True, when he sailed in 1820, Bellingshausen perversely sought a short-cut via Antarctica, but Barrow did not know that, and even if he had it would not have made him sleep easier.

Speed was of the essence if the Passage was to be discovered by Britain. The embers of Ross's disgrace were still glowing when Barrow despatched his next two missions. One, under John Franklin, was sent overland to find the sea into which Canada's northern river systems flowed – if this was not the Passage itself, then it would at least be another means of reaching it. The other, under Parry, was to probe from the north and hopefully meet up with Franklin before continuing west.

When Parry sailed on 11 May 1819, his instructions were simple. There was to be no messing around in Baffin Bay, instead he was to head straight for Lancaster Sound and sail through the North-West Passage. If Lancaster Sound was blocked he was to try for an entrance in Smith or Jones Sound. He was not to bother with mapping coastlines, or making scientific observations – although John Ross's Deep Sea Clamm was included in his inventory – but was to reach Russia as quickly as possible, hand in his papers to the Governor of Kamchatka and return home via Owhyhee (Hawaii), maybe even stopping off in China as well. In any event, he was to do, as Barrow petulantly expressed it, that which 'Ross, from misapprehension, indifference or incapacity, had failed to do'.[2]

Parry was given two ships, the 375-ton *Hecla* and the 180-ton *Griper*. With him he took the pick of the officers and men who had served on the previous expeditions. Almost all of them volunteered, and almost all of them were accepted, including Sabine, James Ross, Alexander Fisher, Henry Hoppner, Frederick Beechey and William Hooper. The only notable exceptions were those who had sided with Ross in the Lancaster Sound furore. The *Griper*, however, was given to a newcomer, Lt. Matthew Liddon.

William Parry was a planner. During the first voyage he had decided that the Passage could never be conquered in a single season (just as Scoresby had said). A season, or maybe two seasons, would have to be spent in the ice, and Parry equipped his ships accordingly. The two enemies he envisaged were scurvy and boredom. To prevent the former, which tended to strike after about six months at sea, Parry packed as much Vitamin C as possible in the form of pickles, herbs,

sauerkraut and lemon juice. This last item – often referred to wrongly
as lime juice – was a relatively recent innovation, having first been
introduced in 1795, and normally dispensed in pastilles. Parry insisted
it be extracted from fresh fruit (in this he was far ahead of his time).
Additionally, 'as a matter of experiment a small quantity of vinegar, in
a highly concentrated state, recommended and prepared by Doctor
Bollman'[3] was taken aboard. Vinegar, like lemon juice, was valued as
an anti-scorbutic, and in the cold that they were about to encounter,
Dr Bollman's concentrate would prove its worth.

Another innovation Parry laid great store by was canned food. He
personally spent an hour at the Rotherhithe premises of Messrs
Donkin & Gamble tasting the range of soups available. (Curiously,
nobody had thought of inventing a can opener. The huge quantity of
cans which Parry eventually ordered had to be cracked open with an
axe and mallet.)

To keep his men healthy in mind as well as body he planned,
among other things, a series of musical entertainments. He played the
violin himself, and practised three or four hours a day – to no great
effect, by his own admission. A barrel organ was also taken aboard. It
was a fresh and optimistic expedition. Apart from Parry, twenty-eight
years old, and Sabine, thirty, every officer was under the age of
twenty-three. They were young and they intended to succeed.

As with Ross's expedition, Parry's voyage was the object of intense
interest. The public flocked to Deptford, where the ships were being
strengthened for Arctic service, the engineers working late into the
night under huge oil flares. Lords and ladies came, as did courteous
but critical naval officers and a host of London's middle-class for
whom a trip to Deptford was worth as much, but without the expense,
as an appearance on Rotten Row. By the time the ships were ready
there was barely room to move for the crush of tourists. On 13 April
Parry wrote that 'From 12 till 4 o'clock, the parties came on board by
crowds . . . I had invited Sabine's friends . . . and was in hopes of
having them quietly to ourselves . . . but when they came to my cabin
it was so pre-occupied with other ladies and gentlemen, that no
entrance could be gained until some of the others took their leave . . .

I had scarcely a moment to attend to them, being constantly called on deck by *dozens* of cards that were handed down to me.'[4]

In Parry's albeit prejudiced eyes, no other expedition had attracted 'a more hearty feeling of national interest'.[5] He made the most of it, taking parties up Greenwich Hill to the Observatory, rowing them along the Thames to the strains of the 'Canadian Boat-Song', before finally inviting them aboard the *Hecla* for dinner at 5.30 p.m. When his guests climbed aboard their carriages at 9 p.m., they did so with distended stomachs, some tipsiness, and a feeling that they had been part of a great national enterprise.

In the meantime, as Parry directed his guests hither and thither, he had become increasingly enamoured of a Miss Browne, Sabine's niece, who visited far more often than a sense of national interest warranted. She began to feature regularly in his diary and by the end of April he was confident enough to indulge in a display of Pooterish daring. 'I amused my party yesterday very much,' he wrote, 'by putting my life-preserver on Miss Browne, and making her blow it up, or inflate it, herself!'[6]

In every venture Barrow sent forth there was an element of incompetence. Something, somewhere, was always lacking. The ships might be bad or the supplies inadequate or the clothing wrong or the instructions ill-considered or any other thing. That this was so was not Barrow's fault; he had little money to play with and his ambitions always outstripped available resources. Nevertheless, something was always wrong. In Parry's case that something was the *Griper*. When Parry looked at the *Hecla* he saw 'a charming ship'.[7] When he looked at the *Griper* he could hardly contain his contempt: one of 'these paltry Gunbrigs . . . utterly unfit for this service!'[8] So slow was the *Griper* that it seemed it would never reach Davis Strait, let alone the North-West Passage. Eventually he had to tow the *Griper* behind the *Hecla*, and actually made better time than if they had sailed separately.

In Baffin Bay, Parry made his first important decision of the voyage. He could either go north round the central pack and brave the nutcracker hazards of Melville Bay, or he could forge through the central pack. The former was known and unsafe. The latter was unknown and unsafe. He plumped for the latter. In June 1819 he sailed into the central pack and immediately became beset among the bergs. By the time he had extricated himself, a week later, he had drifted thirteen miles to the south and was still on the Greenland side of the pack. For his next attempt he sailed along Greenland's coast, following Ross's old course, until he reached the latitude of Lancaster Sound. At night, when the fog came down, they fired muskets to keep in contact. Once, in the gloom, they sighted a whaler which was recognized by its green lower masts as the *Brunswick* from Hull. Beating a broom against the deck the men of the *Brunswick* drummed a message across the ice. Nineteen blows: nineteen whales. They had a full hold and were going home.

It was comforting to know they had company in these waters. But the *Brunswick* was going one way, they were going another. At about 73° north Parry turned the *Hecla* west and butted his way through the central pack, the reinforced bows of his ship clearing a way for Liddon's slower, feebler *Griper*. The pack here was an estimated eighty miles wide, but it was weaker than it had been to the south, having been broken up by the weather. For three weeks Parry warped and towed his ships through the channels. Sometimes he also 'tracked', which was a cross between towing and warping, where his men heaved on a hawser until the ship sprang free of the ice. It was tiring and dangerous work. One day they hauled for eleven hours to make four miles. On another they sawed for seven hours to free the *Hecla* from the ice only to find her frozen in again at nightfall. Sometimes the anchor could break free from the ice, its pent-up pressure sending the warpers flying across deck.

Parry watched over his men like a mother hen. He saw them out of wet clothes after a day's hauling, and tempted them into dry ones with drams of rum. His efforts paid off. On 28 July, the two ships broke through into clear water, and a few days afterwards they sighted the flag, still flying, that Ross had planted with such 'silly ceremony' by the mouth of Lancaster Sound. Here, on the very doorstep of the North-West Passage, they were forced to wait for a favourable wind. It came on 2 August and, having arranged to rendezvous with the *Griper* at the 85th meridian, Parry raised sail and entered the sound. 'It is more easy to imagine than describe the oppressive anxiety which was visible in every countenance,' recorded Parry, 'while, as the breeze increased to a fresh gale, we ran quickly to the Westward.'[9] This was the moment of make or break. If Ross's range of mountains did exist, then the North-West Passage was probably unattainable. And worse still, despite having kept himself legally clean over the Ross affair, Parry would be hurled into the darkest lockers of naval pariahdom for his failure. He had already seen what Barrow could do.

Parry was not alone in his worries. 'I never remember to have spent a day of so much fearful anxiety,'[10] wrote his co-conspirator, William Hooper. Little wonder that he and the other officers crowded the rigging for hours on end. The same fate awaited all of them. On 4 August their worst hopes were realized. Land was spotted dead ahead. Every face was filled with 'vexation and anxiety'[11] until the land proved to be a mere island. The Sound was clear. Croker's Mountains did not exist. Ross had been wrong.

Triumphant cheers arose from the crew of the *Griper* as they finally caught up with the *Hecla* and beheld the wide, empty expanse of Lancaster Sound stretching to the west. Few could 'avoid feeling a secret satisfaction that their opinions have turned out to be true',[12] wrote Alexander Fisher in his chatty diary, which he had begun with a brief description of the beauties of England in the spring. Hooper, meanwhile, was delighted. Not for him such secret relief. Gone were the anxious and woe-laden faces, replaced now by self-righteous justification. 'There was something particularly animating in the joy which lighted every countenance,' he thrilled. 'We had arrived in a sea which had never before been navigated, we were gazing on land that European eyes had never before beheld . . . and before us was the prospect of realizing all our wishes, and of exalting the honour of our country.'[13]

There was no denying the excitement of the occasion. Before them lay the clear waters of Lancaster Sound, at least eighty miles wide. To the north were the fissured precipices of Devon Island, separating

Lancaster Sound from Jones Sound, which rose 500 feet from the stony beaches at their base. To the south was a flat plateau riven by broad channels, each of them as clear and navigable as Lancaster Sound. Parry named them as he sailed westwards: Navy Board Inlet, Admiralty Inlet and Prince Regent Inlet. Each represented a possible route to the Pacific should Lancaster Sound prove a dead end, but none was more tempting than Prince Regent Inlet, a magnificent forty-mile-wide thoroughfare.

By the time they reached Prince Regent Inlet, Lancaster Sound had begun to narrow, giving Parry an excuse to call it Barrow Strait. Conditions worsened, and at 89° west their way was blocked by ice. But nothing could dishearten Parry on this extraordinary trip. Pausing only to marvel at his first sight of narwhals, and the appearance of a school of white whales – between eighteen and twenty feet long, and passing beneath the ships with 'a shrill, ringing sound, not unlike musical glasses when badly played'[14] which ceased as soon as they came above water – he turned back to Prince Regent Inlet and tacked into its promising depths. He travelled 120 miles before turning back at 71° 53' 30". In that brief distance, however, he was able to name numerous headlands, capes and inlets – the land to his west became North Somerset, later renamed as Somerset Island – and discovered from his instruments that the North Magnetic Pole was very close. But there was something about Prince Regent Inlet which did not appeal. As opposed to the dramatic cliffs of Barrow Strait, with their striated layers of snow and rock interspersed at regular intervals by natural buttresses of stone, the land past which he sailed was often bland and flat. Beechey, Hoppner and Sabine explored a section of the east coast and found it 'more barren and dreary than any on which they had yet landed in the arctic regions; there being scarcely any appearance of vegetation, except here and there a small tuft of stunted grass, and one or two species of saxifrage and poppy, although the ground was so swampy in many places that they could scarcely walk about'.[15]

One can forgive Parry for not wanting to investigate further. What was this grubby inlet when set against the clean-cut passage and clear waters of Barrow Strait? But before he left, he wrote an assessment of his situation that would have important repercussions in the future: 'I saw no reason to doubt the practicality of ships penetrating much farther south . . . if the determining the geography of this part of the arctic regions be considered worth the time which must necessarily be occupied in effecting it.'[16] Back he went to Barrow Strait where, by a miracle, the ice was beginning to clear. On 19 August, after battling his way through wind, rain, sleet and snow, he was able to continue his journey west.

This time it was the north shore which drew his attention. As Somerset Island passed monotonously to the south, Parry found first a 'noble channel',[17] clear of land or ice and thirty miles wide, which he called Wellington Channel – could this be another route to the Pacific? – followed by a lump of coastline which he named Cornwallis Island. The topography was different this far west. Instead of the limestone plateaux and cliffs which they had encountered earlier the islands were low, sandy hills with, here and there, smooth, brown stretches of land coated in the most 'luxuriant moss'.[18] This moss was the northernmost grazing of America's caribou reindeer, which had not migrated this far north yet, but would do so in due course. The Arctic was coming to life before them, and were it not for the constant presence of ice most would have judged themselves near the point of exit. Parry named his discoveries the North Georgia Islands.

By this time, the North Magnetic Pole had so muddied their compasses that Parry ordered the binnacles on which they were mounted to be dismantled as so much 'useless lumber'.[19] He retained only one, to track the course of magnetic change. Meanwhile, the ships steered themselves, using their last true position as a point of reference: the *Hecla* kept the *Griper* in line with its stern, and the *Griper* kept the *Hecla* in line with its bow.

In this manner they entered a wide sea which Parry named Viscount Melville Sound, and approached a steep-sided island which Parry also named Melville. It was here, halfway along the southern shore of Melville Island, off a point which Parry later named Cape Bounty, that they crossed the 110th meridian on 4 September, thereby winning Parliament's first prize of £5,000. Parry took the opportunity, after Sunday prayers, to break the news to his crew with a schoolmasterish warning that they had done very well but must do a lot better yet if they expected to achieve their goal. 'The enthusiasm excited by this short . . . speech was truly astonishing,' wrote Fisher, not to be cowed by his superior's caution, 'for the ardour that it inspired might be seen in every countenance.'[20]

The following day they dropped anchor for the first time since leaving England. In celebration the ships raised every scrap of bunting available. It excited Parry to a display of understated emotion: 'It created in us no ordinary feelings of pleasure to see the British flag waving for the first time, in these regions, which had previously been considered beyond the limits of the habitable part of the world.'[21] The mood was one of quiet jubilation. Even though the thermometer was falling, the nights were drawing in – it was now dark from 11 p.m. to 1 a.m., with an hour's dusk either side – and the ice was thickening, nobody seemed to care. There was coal to be found on Melville Island and unlimited amounts of game to be shot. As one seaman said, 'The Duke of Wellington never lived half so well. We had grouse for breakfast, grouse for dinner, and grouse for supper, to be sure.'[22] True, there were one or two cases of frostbite, and a hunting party was lost for three days on Melville Island. But what were such irritations compared to the magnitude of the expedition's achievements?

On 17 September Parry reached his furthest point west, 112° 51', near a headland called Cape Providence. (It was here that the hunting party was rescued.) By now, winter was beginning to nip. They experienced their first really cold night, when the thermometer dropped to 10 °F, and the sea took on a flat, glossy appearance heralding a new season's growth of ice. 'During the first formation,' Parry explained, 'it is the consistency of honey, which makes it, according to the technical phrase, *tough*; i.e. difficult for the ships to get through without a fresh gale.'[23] Luckily there were gales aplenty, and Parry sped eastward on their strength, flanked by bergs which slopped untidily from the north, towering above his ships and threatening at times to crush them.

On 22 September, Parry made for a cove on Melville Island that he had previously marked as a promising spot for overwintering. Bay ice had already formed – thick, solid plates rather than the honey mush – and every officer and man was called out to work the ice saws. They toiled beneath the wooden triangles from which the saws were suspended, hauling and dropping, until the ice was carved into rectangles of between ten and twenty feet. These were then sliced diagonally so that they could be pulled to clear water. With paternal pride Parry noted that the men 'who are always fond of doing things in their own way'[24] had eased their task by raising canvas on the freed chunks and sailing them out of the channel. 'Our crews are composed of no common men,' he wrote. 'They do everything cheerfully and well.'[25] Three days after they had started, working in temperatures that reached 9 °F at the most and which froze at sundown the channel they had just cut, the men had completed a channel two and a third miles long and wide enough for the ships to warp their way to a safe anchorage.

At 3.15 on 26 September the *Hecla* and *Griper* reached their winter quarters with three loud and hearty cheers from both ships' companies. And cheer they might. In the two months since they had entered Lancaster Sound they had mapped more than 1,000 miles of coastline, had won a parliamentary prize – that same prize which Scoresby had doubted worth the trouble – had proved the existence of a seaway which, if not yet the North-West Passage, was certainly a passage of some kind, and had done so without a single death, without even a major injury. They were, in short, as they snugged into what Parry called Winter Harbour, very sanguine. 'Our prospects, indeed, were truly exhilarating,' he wrote. 'The ships had suffered no injury; we had plenty of provisions; crew in high health and spirits; a sea, if not open, at least navigable; and a zealous and unanimous determination in both officers and men to accomplish, by all possible means, the grand object on which we had the happiness to be employed.'[26]

Parry, the self-effacing self-promoter, laid his achievements at the door of another. In the candlelit gloom of his cabin he summarized their progress in his journal. 'We had actually entered the Polar Sea,' he wrote. 'I [therefore] ventured to distinguish the magnificent opening through which our passage had been effected . . . by the name of Barrow's Strait . . . both as a private testimony of my esteem for that gentleman, and as a public acknowledgement due to him for his zeal and exertions in the promotion of Northern Discovery.'[27]

6

WINTER AT
MELVILLE ISLAND

Parry had been extraordinarily lucky. He had managed to cross the central pack of Baffin Bay, thereby gaining several more weeks of clear sailing than if he taken the northern, coastal route. And on emerging at Lancaster Sound he had hit one of those rare seasons of Arctic clemency when the region was relatively ice-free. Such conditions would not recur for more than a decade and even then it would be impossible to travel as far west as Melville Island. But Parry was not to know this. On crossing the 110th meridian he had impressed upon his men 'the necessity of the most strenuous exertions . . . assuring them that if we could penetrate a few degrees farther to the westward, before the ships were laid up for winter, I had little doubt of our accomplishing the object of our enterprise before the close of the next season'.[1] Indeed, they had been strenuous, had penetrated the vital few degrees, and were looking forward eagerly to the next season.

From Parry's journal it appears that he studied the map only with regard to his quest: where he had come from, where he was headed, what new channels might open the following season. Had he looked at it in any other light he surely must have quailed. The *Hecla* and

Griper were in the furthest, darkest, coldest domain known to humankind. As the crow flew east, they were 1,200 miles from the nearest permanent settlement on Greenland. The nearest white men were the fur trappers of Canada, 700 miles to the south. To the west it was another 1,200 miles to the shores of Russian Alaska and more miles still to the sparsely inhabited lands of mainland Russia itself. They rested on an island to which not even Eskimos bothered to come, but to which was now given the name of an infinitely distant English viscount.

Parry did not dwell on his isolation. Far more important were his duties which, as he wrote, were of 'a singular nature, such as had, for the first time, devolved on any officer in His Majesty's Navy, and might indeed be considered of rare occurrence in the whole history of navigation'.[2] His first duty was to prepare the *Hecla* for the coming winter. He dismantled the upper masts and rigging, and used the lower yards to support a pitched roof of planks and canvas covering the entire deck. The galley chimney was extended to funnel smoke to the outside, and a complicated array of pipes was laid from the galley stove to channel warm air (it left the pipes at 87 °F) wherever it was needed. A second stove was placed in the main hatchway as back-up central heating and also to keep the air circulating. Snow was packed around the outside of the ship to insulate it from wind-chill. His aim was to provide quarters that were as warm and dry as possible. He also needed them to be spacious, given that the men would be confined aboard ship when winter reached its worst. To this end he ordered every inessential item to be moved out: boats, sails and tackle were piled on shore, and covered with snow; a portable observatory was erected 700 yards away for Sabine's scientific equipment; and a small house was built on Melville Island from wood which had been ear-marked for the construction of extra boats, to store their chronometers, compasses, dipping needles and other essential, but temporarily redundant, navigational items. It was double-skinned, insulated with moss, heated by a single stove and manned around the clock by two marines. Similar preparations, meanwhile, were carried out by Liddon on the *Griper*.

The mechanics of overwintering had been thought out long before. The canvas with which they roofed their ships, for example, was the very same material which had come home, unused, on the *Alexander* and *Isabella*. (It had rotted in places and had to be repaired with patches dipped in hot tar.) The regime of overwintering, however, was of Parry's own invention and relied on one golden rule: everybody must be kept busy at all times. Parry's routine started at 5.45 a.m. when all hands turned out to spend the next two and a quarter hours scouring the deck with stones and warm sand. This was followed by breakfast and at 9 a.m. by a general muster in which the officers inspected the men for health, warmth and tidiness. Once passed they were allowed to walk around the deck while the captain inspected the lower decks. If all was clear they were given another, captain's, inspection, then sent ashore for a further exercise until lunch at noon. If the weather was bad they were herded at a trot round the deck, keeping step to a tune on the barrel organ. While the men were eating the officers took their own shoreside constitutional, before dining at 2 p.m. By this time the men had finished their meal and were set to knotting rope or, if conditions were fine, they were allowed out to shoot game. At 5.30 they were given half an hour to prepare for their third inspection of the day. After this they had their dinner and were allowed to sing and dance until lights-out at 9 p.m. The officers, whose amusements were of a 'more rational kind'[3] – reading, writing, chess, perhaps a tune on the fiddle – stayed up until 10.30. Throughout the night watches were kept with the same regularity as if they had been afloat. On Sundays the routine was altered to accommodate divine service complete with sermon. Once a week the surgeons checked the crew's shins and gums to ensure they were free from scurvy and at the same time the lower deck's bedding was fumigated with a mixture of powder and vinegar called 'devils'.

It was the nearest Parry could devise to normal shipboard life. Naturally, there were some differences. Condensation was a major problem, for example, and despite hanging a screen around the galley to trap the steam from the pots and pans, the roof nevertheless dripped a constant, disheartening patter on the heads of those below.

The dampness spread to the timbers themselves, which had to be regularly scraped free of ice, rubbed down with cloths and then dried with the aid of the galley's hot-air pipes. Fire was an ever-present menace which, as the days darkened, and lamps were lit throughout the ship, required a half-hourly patrol by quartermasters and the twice-daily digging of a fire-hole in the ice to provide a ready source of water.

Rations were different to those to which the men were accustomed, being adjusted to account for future shortages and the possible outbreak of scurvy. The bread allowance was reduced to two-thirds (it was baked on board), and 'a pound of Donkin's preserved meat, together with one pint of vegetable or concentrated soup, per man, was substituted for one pound of salt-beef weekly . . . and a small quantity of sour kraut and pickles, with as much vinegar as could be used, was issued at regular intervals'.[4] Game shot by the hunting parties was always served instead of, rather than in addition to, the standard meat ration. Beer, being valued as an anti-scorbutic – mistakenly – took the place of the normal allowance of spirits, until it was discovered that the brewery caused an unsustainable amount of condensation, and a daily dose of lemon juice was administered to every man under the watchful eye of an officer.

Parry ran a tight ship, leaving little to the discretion of his men, whom he considered 'children in all those points in which their own health and comfort are concerned'.[5] But he also ran a fair ship. When it came to food, 'in no one instance, either in quantity or quality, was the slightest preference given to the officers'.[6] In little more than a week he had carved out a 'snug and comfortable'[7] community in the ice. The two vessels sat on their tees of snow, lights twinkling, organ music wafting forth merrily and the smoke from their chimneys rising against a backdrop of the aurora borealis.

The scene was deceptively secure. Although winter was not yet upon them it was knocking at the door. The day they settled in their harbour the temperature fell for the first time below zero Fahrenheit. The next day their canal, so laboriously sawed, was frozen solid. On 1 October they spotted a polar bear which was completely white, rather than its customary dirtyish yellow – a sure sign in all Arctic land mammals that winter is nigh. On 16 October the sun began to sink. Arctic foxes huddled around the ships for warmth and after them came wolves, whose baying filled the night. By the end of the month the entire sea was iced over, and snow began to fall, not in flakes but in tiny spicules of ice that descended invisibly, innocuously, and were blown across the landscape to form ankle-deep drifts.

The thermometer dropped, but in the few remaining hours of sunlight it was still possible to walk on Melville Island, and it was still possible to hunt game. There were grouse and ptarmigan aplenty and also a few caribou, though these were harder to hunt thanks to the absence of cover and the difficulty of aiming and firing a musket wearing thick gloves, 'at least,' wrote Parry, 'so for the credit of our sportsmen, we were willing to allow'.[8] (For rationing purposes all game was declared common property, the marksman being allowed the head and the heart.)

Parry was entranced by the tricks the Arctic could play. In the utter stillness, sound was magnified a thousandfold: conversations could be heard clearly from more than a mile. Distance was a baffling matter of guesswork: large outcrops of rock which seemed at least half a mile away across the snow became, after a minute's walk, a small stone which they passed from hand to hand in wonder. During the regular storms which blew from the north, their vision was obscured by snow-drift which prevented them seeing more than 300 yards in any direction; yet, directly above them, the stars shone clear and bright.

Less entrancing was the bitter cold which descended at night, and when the snow-drift storms blew. When the wind was up Parry reckoned 'that no human being could have remained alive after an hour's exposure to it'.[9] He ordered lines to be strung between the ships and signposts to be erected on every high point within a radius of two miles to guide wanderers back to base. Now, if men went hunting they did so at their own risk and with strict instructions to be home before sundown. Those who failed to find their way back – and there were several, despite the signposts – suffered accordingly.

The effects of severe cold on the human frame fascinated the captain of the *Hecla*. When search parties brought back John Pearson, one of the *Griper*'s marines who had lingered too long in search of caribou, Parry noted that his hands were frozen as if he was still carrying his musket (three fingers came off). A few days later, when a couple of other stragglers made their way in after dark, Parry observed that they 'spoke thick and indistinctly, and it was impossible to draw from them a rational answer to any of our questions'.[10] Not until they had thawed out and regained their senses could he persuade himself that they had not been drinking. He put this down in his journal as a warning to future Arctic commanders. 'I cannot help thinking . . . that many a man may have been punished for intoxication, who was only suffering from the benumbing effect of frost.'[11] To prevent any further casualties he ordered that 'the expense of all rockets and other signals used in such cases to guide them back, should in future be charged against the wages of the offending party'.[12] It had the desired effect, but soon became unnecessary with the departure on 16 October of the last covey of ptarmigan and the last few caribou.

On 18 October the cold intensified. At noon their thermometers registered –9 °F in the sun, sinking to –16° in the shade. But in the absence of wind 'not the slightest inconvenience was suffered'.[13] In fact, the weather was remarkably mild. On the 26th sufficient light came through the windows of Parry's large, south-facing cabin to permit reading and writing from 9.30 a.m. till 2.30 p.m. And the air was clear enough for magnificent sunrises and sunsets, which turned the horizon a rich, bluish-purple merging into a bright arc of deep red.

Eleven days later, however, the noon temperature was –24 °F and smoke no longer rose vertically but skimmed sideways along the ships' housings. Exposed metal burned like fire to the touch, removing skin at anything more than a fleeting contact. Gloves became an essential item of outdoor clothing and the eye-pieces of sextants and telescopes were covered with soft leather lest the officers' faces be destroyed. It was noted with wonder that these same instruments, when brought in after a prolonged period outside, gave off wreaths of smoke-like condensation which turned, after a few minutes, into miniature snowclouds extending two or three inches from the chilled metal.

On 4 November they saw the sun for the last time, although a few agile bodies could still catch a glimpse of it from the masthead, James Ross being the last to do so on 11 November. It would not rise again until 8 February – a period of ninety-six days. From this point their only light came from the night sky, or from their candles – rationed to an inch a day – over which they hunched in their frigid quarters. Most of them had already witnessed the midnight sun of the Arctic summer, but none had ever experienced its winter counterpart, the midday moon. Despite the energetic routine he had set in motion, this was the dark time Parry feared most. He wrote: 'I dreaded the want of employment as one of the worst evils that was likely to befall us.'[14] But he was equal to the task. On 5 November, their first full day without sun, the curtain rose on the Royal Arctic Theatre.

The theatre was a masterstroke. It appealed to the men's sense of the ridiculous, it gave them something to do – apart from the actual performance it took at least a day to erect the stage and another to dismantle it – and they could watch the officers make fools of themselves. The first performance, a work by Garrick called *Miss in Her Teens*, was cheered loudly. It was widely agreed that Parry sustained the role of Fribble to perfection. Parry played down his triumph bashfully, 'considering that an example of cheerfulness . . . was not the least part of my duty, under the peculiar circumstances in which we were placed'.[15] Such was its success that the theatre became a fortnightly event.

Rosy-cheeked, fresh-faced midshipmen took the parts of young girls to the delight of their sallow audience. Young James Ross was a major starlet, playing Corinna in *The Citizen* on 8 December, Mrs. Bruin in *The Mayor of Garrett* on the 23rd, and a little later, when the available library was exhausted and the officers had to concoct new dramas, he played Poll in a musical entertainment called *The North-West Passage; or, the Voyage Finished*. On 6 January he was finally allowed a male role as Colonel Tivy in *Bon Ton; or, High Life Above Stairs*. Ross's relief to be back in trousers must have been enormous, and not just because of salvaged male pride. The theatre was on the upper deck, and despite a stove and a few handfuls of heated shot, it was no laughing matter to act a gauzy sea-nymph or shepherdess when the temperature on stage was several degrees below zero, as was discovered by one man who volunteered for a part in Parry's later production of *Heir-at-Law* and endured the last act with two of his fingers frost-bitten. Nevertheless, 'The good effect of these performances is more and more perceived by us,' wrote Parry. 'And we shall certainly go on with them, till we can have a nobler employment.'[16] But secretly he confided to his journal his despair at 'the dull and tedious monotony which, day after day, presented itself'.[17] They were alone. Even the wolves and foxes had left them by now. Their only company was Arctic mice, which they never saw, but whose tracks riddled the snow.

Lest the theatre pall – and for the midshipmen it probably did – Parry had another trump card up his sleeve: the *North Georgia Gazette and Winter Chronicle*. This weekly newspaper, edited by Sabine, was not the nobler employment Parry had in mind – which was, naturally, the completion of their voyage. In fact it was downright appalling, crammed as it was with dreadful puns and overblown items like the report which covered legal proceedings against Non-Contributors in the Court of Common-Sense. But it provided yet another vital diversion, right down to the letters box which was pinned to the *Hecla*'s mast and to which, to ensure anonymity, only Sabine had the key.

In this manner, they saw in the shortest day of the winter, 22 December. Once again, despite a forbidding thermometer, it was still possible to walk outside for a good two hours. On Christmas Day they enjoyed a fair meal with a small increase in food and drink, the officers being served a side of beef which had been preserved by the cold since May. Two days later, feeling 'that some additional exercise was necessary after the Festival of Christmas',[18] Parry took every able-bodied man on a six-mile walk. On 30 December the temperature dropped to 75 °F below freezing. Normally it would have stayed there. But the next day it rose some 50°, warmer than it had been for eight weeks. This was without doubt a very mild winter.

January came and went without incident, save for a few distant meteors. On the 11th Parry recorded the coldest temperature yet: 49 °F below zero. 'In going from the cabins to the open air,' he wrote, 'we were constantly in the habit . . . of undergoing a change of from 80° to 100°, and in several instances of 120°, of temperature, in less than one minute.'[19] And yet, it did them no harm. 'Not a single inflammatory complaint,' wrote Parry, 'beyond a slight cold, which was cured by common care in a day or two, occurred during this particular period.'[20]

On 3 February, the sun was sighted from the masthead, fifty-one feet above sea level. Five days later its rays reached the ships. This should have been a good sign. But in fact February was the hardest month yet. The temperature fell and fell, reaching an absolute minimum of –55 °F. The entire expedition began to congeal. Two chronometers stopped. Lemon juice and vinegar froze and burst their bottles. When hatches were opened a cold fog flowed in, covering the bedding with clots of ice and forcing the crew into hammocks. Their supply of coal, which had seemed so exorbitant on loading, began to run out. The main cabin became scarcely habitable, and officers huddled over their chess sets wearing greatcoats.

In the light of his candle stub, Parry drew up evacuation procedures: 'Plan of a Journey from the North coast of America towards Fort Chepewyan, should such a measure be found necessary as a last resource.'[21] Beneath his cool exterior he was worried that they might have to abandon ship.

The first case of scurvy manifested itself in Mr Scallon, the *Hecla*'s gunnery officer. 'Mr. Scallon,' wrote Parry, 'is past the middle-age of life, and has perhaps eat a good deal of salt-beef in his time.'[22] Parry was right to blame salt-beef which, in the absence of fresh food, was a diet for disaster. But he did not know that he had contributed directly to Scallon's illness. According to the doctrine of the times, scurvy could be held at bay not only by lemon juice but by beer and constant exercise, which was precisely what Parry had provided. Unfortunately, as would be found out a century later, alcohol and exercise serve only to progress the disease.

Parry – who really was an extraordinary man – responded to Scallon's condition with ingenuity. Ordering his officers to keep the presence of scurvy secret lest the mere mention of it demoralize the crew, he started a small hothouse of Vitamin C. On the warm pipes which ran from the galley he placed several seed trays of mustard and cress. These little plants flourished and six days later he was able to harvest a pale but nutritious crop. Scallon ate it with avidity and within nine days was boasting that he could 'run a race'.[23] 'I shall be most thankful, should it prove that we can cure, or even check this disease by our own resources,' Parry wrote, 'for I cannot help feeling that, under Providence, our making the North-West Passage depends upon it.'[24]

On 24 February they experienced their worst disaster to date: the house ashore, in which was stored their most valuable navigation equipment, the chronometers and compasses, caught fire. Fortunately the crew were on deck for their morning exercise when the first smoke was spotted and they ran to extinguish it. For three-quarters of an hour they battled with the flames, tearing off the roof and knocking down walls in order to shovel snow onto the blaze.

When they finally had it beaten, and had piled snow over the blackened ruins to prevent a further outbreak, they had saved all the precious instruments. But they had done so at a fearful cost. Almost every firefighter had been frostbitten on the nose and cheeks – the telltale white marks appeared after only five minutes in the open, Parry noted – and despite the standard treatment of rubbing snow on the affected parts some sixteen men remained on the sick list, four or five of them for several weeks. The worst case was Sabine's manservant, who had been in the house at the time and had actually started the fire by drying his handkerchief on the stove. On seeing the flames, he had snatched up the dipping needle and taken it to safety outside. In his haste, however, he had forgotten to put on his gloves. Half an hour later, when he was brought before the surgeon, his hands had the appearance of translucent marble and were so cold that the bowl of water into which they were plunged froze over. His act of heroism cost him seven fingers.

In March more men came down with scurvy, and Parry stepped up his mustard-and-cress plantation. In this month, however, they saw the first signs of a thaw. On 1 March, to great excitement, walkers reported a patch of snow that was glazed and slippery, as if it had melted and then frozen over. On the 6th the thermometer rose above zero for the first time since 17 December of the previous year. And on 7 March, the ice began to melt over the dark areas of the ships' black-and-yellow paintwork. Tentatively, Parry washed a silk handkerchief and hung it outside. To his delight it dried. It was the first item of laundry in six months to dry without the aid of artificial heat.

The thaw was a mixed blessing. Ever since the onset of winter they had been kept dry, if cold, by the immediate freezing of any atmospheric moisture inside the ships. Now, however, everything began to stream with water and on the lower deck the released condensation of the men's breath threatened a serious flood. On 8 March Parry ordered the area to be dried out, and over 800 gallons of ice and water were brought up.

In April the snow fell more heavily than it had during the whole winter and the temperature dropped once again. Sabine, who had taken to spending the night in his observatory to conduct pendulum experiments, frequently had to be dug out in the morning. But the sun shone intermittently, once for seventeen hours, despite readings of –31 °F, and on 8 April Parry was able to record a fascinating phenomenon whereby the sun was surrounded by two haloes in which refraction gave birth to three mini-suns. He was the first to see this sight in such a tight configuration and in 1920, by which date it had been witnessed only six times, it was named Parry's Arc.

On 30 April the temperature was higher than it had been since 9 September of the previous year, imparting such a summery feeling that Parry had to forcibly restrain his crew from throwing off their clothes. Optimism ran high, particularly on 6 May when Parry ordered the ships to be cut free and made ready for sailing. The ice, which had been only seven inches thick when they had sawed into their winter positions, now measured as many feet, and it was eleven days before the task was completed. When the *Hecla* was cleared on 17 May it sprang eighteen inches into the air, a measure of the fuel and food they had consumed during the winter.

'Our little colony now presented the most busy and bustling scene that can be imagined,'[25] Parry wrote cheerfully. There was plenty to do: stone ballast, which had been piled on the shore the previous month, needed breaking and weighing; the boats and sails needed to be dug out of their winter storage; every seam on both ships had opened in the frost and needed to be caulked with at least three lengths of oakum; and amidst the commotion, hunting parties came and went, bringing back the game which had at last begun to reappear on the island. So bright was the sun that several men developed snow-blindness. But even this could not extinguish their high spirits; they wandered cheerfully below deck wearing black crepe eyeshades or dark glasses until they were fit to resume duties.

At 8.30 p.m. on 24 May it began to rain. Everybody hurried on deck to witness this good augur. Undoubtedly the ice would melt soon. But the ice did not melt, and by the end of the month Parry was getting worried. As he admitted secretly, his sole purpose in having the ships made ready was to give the men a sense of hope. There was no sign yet of the ice melting to a degree which would allow them to sail out. Unless it relented they might have to remain there for another year. Unobtrusively, he ordered everyone onto two-thirds rations.

As was his habit in moments of stress, Parry larded his otherwise concise journal with long sentences as if by weight of word he could force back the troubles pressing upon him. The ice, he recorded on 30 April, was still very thick. 'When to this circumstance was added the consideration, that scarcely the slightest symptoms of thawing had yet appeared, and that in three weeks from this period the sun would again decline to the southward, it must be confessed that the most sanguine and enthusiastic among us had some reason to be staggered in the expectations they had formed of the complete accomplishment of our enterprise.'[26]

Parry took advantage of his entrapment to make a partial survey of Melville Island. Taking eleven men and a cart of provisions to last three weeks, he set out for the interior on 1 June. The cart carried a relatively light load of 800 pounds, which was made up by a 'conjuror or cooking apparatus' with a minimum of wood to keep it alight, two 'horsemen's tents', rudimentary affairs each consisting of two uprights – boarding pikes – and a cross pole on which was hung a blanket, plus daily rations of one pound of ship's biscuit, two-thirds of a pound of Donkin's preserved meat, one ounce of salep powder (the ground tubers of orchids, a presumed anti-scorbutic), one ounce of sugar and half a pint of spirits per man. In knapsacks, meanwhile, they carried twenty-four pounds of spare clothing and bedding per person.

Travelling by night, such as it now was, in order to have hard ground to haul over, and sleeping by day, when the soil was warm and their clothes could dry in the sun, they made their way over the desolate expanse of Melville Island. It was dreary beyond belief, comprising icy plains interspersed with swamps and deep ravines, through which they steered by sightings as if they were at sea. Here and there the land rose into hills, but they were paltry, fetid things, covered with sand and limestone rocks which, on being cracked open, emitted a stench of decay.

The land was not entirely lifeless: there were ptarmigan to shoot; one day they were followed by a frolicsome reindeer which they did not have the heart to kill; and here and there wild sorrel poked up its red, sixpence-sized flowers. But generally, it exuded an aura of the grave. Separated from the relative security of the ships, they received the strong impression that no man ever had, nor ever would, live long in this landscape.

On 5 June, snugged into a suitably funereal ravine, they toasted the King's birthday, a day in arrears, unaware that 'our venerable monarch had many months before paid the debt of nature'.[27] Then they mustered themselves and continued north. Six days later they reached a steep cliff from which they saw a wide expanse of frozen water. It was here that the wagon fell to pieces, as they tried to lower it down almost perpendicular slopes. Philosophically they left the red-painted wheels where they were, to be found by future travellers, and used the rest as firewood to cook a fine roast of ptarmigan. 'It is not, perhaps, easy for those who have never experienced it,' wrote Parry, 'to imagine how great a luxury any thing warm in this way becomes, after living entirely upon cold provisions for some time in this rigid climate. This change was occasionally the more pleasant to us from the circumstance of the preserved meats . . . being generally at this time hard frozen, when taken out of the canisters.'[28]

Parry very much wanted to be back on board the *Hecla*. First, however, he had to prove that they had reached the sea rather than an inland lake. He ordered a hole to be hacked in the ice. It was a hard, if not impossible, job given that the only tools available were knives and the boarding pikes that supported their tents. But they persevered and after scraping and chipping their way through fourteen feet of ice, they finally reached salt water.

Having mapped as much as they could of what Parry named Hecla and Griper Bay, they trekked south to find sea on the south coast. By luck they had chosen to reconnoitre the area where the ocean pinches Melville Island at the waist, and they reached its southern side within a few days. Parry paused only to name the bay after Liddon, and headed for home. On 15 June, at 7 p.m., they reached the haven of their ships.

While he had been away, Parry had hoped that the ice would have melted, if not across the bay, then at least around the ships. But he was disappointed. All was as it had been. And by the end of the month, when there was no material change, he began to fear they had sawed themselves into a trap. Out to sea they could hear a terrible grinding, audible from a distance of several miles, as the main pack disintegrated and sent its bergs south and west. Winter Harbour, however, offered only a watery dissolution. Holes appeared, and puddles formed, bringing to the surface three dead fish and a few putrid shrimp which had been caught in the winter freeze. The ice was melting, as was clear from a pile of straw which they had thrown out in May and which, thanks to its insulating properties, now stood two feet proud of the surface. But it wasn't melting fast enough. There were less than ten weeks left of the navigable season.

In mid-July Parry became worried and waxed fulsomely. The men were in excellent health, he wrote, but, 'Gratifying as this fact could not but be to me, it was impossible to contemplate without pain the probability, now too evident, that the shortness of the approaching season of operations would not admit of that degree of success in the persecution of the main object of our enterprise, which might otherwise have been reasonably anticipated in setting out from our present advanced state with two ships in such perfect condition, and with crews so zealous in the cause in which we were engaged.'[29] He spurred his men to gather food. Sorrel was now plentiful and the men were sent to 'graze' it, bringing back handfuls of the anti-scorbutic growth to which, fortunately, they had taken a fancy. Meanwhile the hunting parties continued to load the ship with a month's supply of fresh meat. All the same, 'It is not a very pleasing truth,' wrote Parry on 5 July, 'that we have now been in this harbour, frozen up, during a part of every month in the year except one.'[30] They had entered Winter Harbour in September of the previous year. Only August separated them from their anniversary.

By this time the bay was clear of ice save for a barrier which remained firm across the entrance. On the last day of July this barrier floated bodily out into the sea and the two ships hurried after it. Behind them they left the body of their only casualty on the whole trip, a man named Scott, who had died of a lung complaint and who had been buried ashore, his headstone facing optimistically west, and a 'remarkable block of sandstone'[31] in Winter Harbour, resembling the roof of a house, on which they had carved the ships' names.

For most men, the experience of a winter on Melville Island, however well managed – and Parry had managed it superlatively – would have been enough to send them running home. Parry, however, was not most men. Once again they retraced their path of the previous year along the coast of Melville Island. Despite all evidence to the contrary he sincerely believed that it was possible to complete his mission.

On 7 August, Parry dropped Beechey ashore to see what he could see from the nearest hill. His report was double-edged. There was land to the south-west, possibly the northern shore of the American continent, and possibly the exit to the North-West Passage, but the intervening sea was choked with bergs. Parry went after him to check this out for himself. He named the distant shore Banks Land (now Banks Island), but was determined to give the bergs a try. To his disappointment he sailed no further than he had the year before. On 23 August he gave up the struggle after many 'vexations, disappointments and delays',[32] not to mention dangers. Banks Land was a good 800–900 miles away, he reckoned – erroneously, as it would later transpire – and they had travelled no more than sixty miles in the last fortnight. Previously he had judged the end of the sailing season to be 7 September, maybe at a pinch 14 September. But with new ice already one and a half inches thick around him, he was forced to re-evaluate.

Bearing down on him was the full weight of the never-melting Arctic Sea which would soon clog the channels he had so fortunately sailed through. Naively, however, Parry decided it was not this that blocked his way, but the manner in which it had been approached. 'It now became evident,' he wrote, 'that there was something peculiar about the south-west extremity of Melville Island, which made the icy sea there extremely unfavourable to navigation.'[33] Before he returned home he determined to follow the ice as far south as he could in the hope that he might reach an easier route to the south. 'It was natural that such a hope should be indulged,' he explained, 'because it was evidently desirable, on all accounts, that we should, if possible, get upon that coast rather than remain boxing about among the islands.'[34]

There was no opening to the south, and Parry had to admit defeat. Pursued by the rapidly encroaching ice, which he warned future explorers 'must be as closely and unremittingly watched as an enemy in a state of blockade', he skimmed east through the cliffs of Barrow Strait. It took him a matter of days to reach Baffin Bay, the west coast of which he proceeded to chart anew, considering Ross's previous mapping to be 'wretchedly manufactured'.[35] He reached Peterhead on 31 October 1820, and left his ships to find their way home, while he hurried south to deliver his report.

*

Nothing could have been more dissimilar than Parry's homecoming compared with that of Ross. In Baffin Bay he had taken the precaution of summarizing his achievements in a letter which he gave to a whaling ship. Unknown to him the whaler had returned before his own ships, and when his carriage clattered into Whitehall on the morning of 3 November 1820, he found himself the hero of the day. Barrow was wreathed in smiles; Lord Melville was there to congratulate him in person; and before midday Croker pressed into his hand a message 'to acquaint you that in approbation of your Services, their Lordships have promoted you to the rank of Commander'.[36]

The press trilled him to the sky. John Murray bought the rights to his journal for 1,000 guineas. And in his hometown of Bath he was given not only the keys to the city but 'a massive elegant piece of plate', raised by public subscription. 'The form is that of the celebrated Warwick Vase,' reported the *Bath Chronicle*, 'but divested of the Bacchanalian emblems, and decorated with others more appropriate to the nature of the service intended to be commemorated.'[37] Among the more suitable emblems were dolphins, an optimistic fantasy of his completion of the passage. In very English fashion, the Bath and West of England Society for the Encouragement of Arts &c. voted to award him their gold medal rather than the silver they had originally decided upon.

Barrow pulled out all the stops for Parry. He put his name forward for election to the Royal Society, and wrote enthusiastically of his journal that 'No one, could rise from its perusal without being impressed with the fullest conviction that Commander Parry's merits, as an officer and scientific navigator are not confined to his professional duties; but that the resources of his mind are equal to the most arduous situations, and fertile in expedient under every circumstance, however difficult, dangerous or unexpected.'[38] During the winter of 1820, Parry was the most famous man in the realm. 'Even strangers in the coffee-room introduce themselves, and beg to shake hands with me,' he said.[39]

Officially, Parry was equal to this optimism. In his journal he wrote that, 'Of the existence of such a passage, and that the outlet will be

found at Behring's Strait, it is scarcely possible, on an inspection of the
map . . . any longer to entertain a reasonable doubt.'[40] Further, he
urged 'that no time might be lost in following up the success with
which we had been favoured, should His Majesty's Government consider it expedient to do so'.[41] He did, however, suggest in muted
tones that maybe they ought to try for an entrance further south –
Hudson Bay, for instance – where they had a better chance of reaching the North American coastline, and where 'there certainly does
seem more than an equal chance of finding the desired passage'.[42]

Privately, he was less gung-ho. As he told Barrow, the northern
route through Lancaster Sound was out of the question. 'I *knew* the
difficulties of the *whole* accomplishment of the North-West Passage
too well to make light of them, and am not so sanguine of entire success as those who judge from the actual result of our last voyage. The
success *we* met with is to be attributed, under Providence, to the con-
currence of very many favourable circumstances.' And if Barrow chose
to follow his suggestion of trying further south, whether it be by
Hudson Bay or Cumberland Strait – the fourth and last possibility
from Baffin Bay – 'it must always be kept in view that we have thus *to
begin again*, for who shall pretend to say that either of those inlets will
lead into the Polar Sea and conduct us to the Northern Coast of
America?' In fact, Parry was 'confident another Expedition will end in
disappointment to all concerned and interested in it, *because* so great
has been our last success, that nothing short of the entire accomplishment of the North-West Passage in to the Pacific will satisfy the
Public'.[43]

He said all this and more to Barrow, concluding cunningly 'that I
was still as ready as ever I was, to do my best towards the accomplishment of the object in view, and that I was the more inclined to it,
from a fear of the Russians being beforehand with us'.[44] The Russians
had already begun tinkering at Icy Cape, the most westerly discovered point of Bering's Strait and, as Parry knew, nothing infuriated
Barrow more than the thought of foreigners trespassing on his blanks.

On 25 November 1820, prior to decommissioning, Parry visited
'our dirty old ships' in dock. The men cheered him aboard. 'It is this,'

he wrote pompously, and probably honestly, 'which constitutes my truest satisfaction, not a little enhanced by the happiness of seeing them all safe and well at Deptford among their families and friends.'[45]

Parry had mastered Victorian sentimentality well ahead of his time. Beneath the skin, however, he was blatantly ambitious. He knew there would be another attempt at the North-West Passage and he knew he would command it. 'I hear nothing of any other Expedition,' he wrote home on 24 November, 'from any-body at the Admiralty, though it is talked of every-where else. I shall not wonder if it turns out so, and if so I suppose they will give me the refusal of Command. It is not improbable, however, that they will not like my terms. I *must* have the Commander of the second ship, and my first Lieut. to be officers in whom I place implicit confidence, without which I will not consent either to risk the loss of the little reputation I have gained, or to be cooped up for an indefinite period with people whom I do not like. With respect to the ships, I have no doubt they will do what I should recommend. Say nothing of this to any-body . . .'[46]

It would not have been done, of course, to mention the subject of money. But Parliament's reward still held good and perhaps, as he waited for his orders to come through, Parry pondered a catchy little verse that had appeared in the *North Georgia Gazette*:

> *Fired with fresh ardour, and with bold intent,*
> *Our minds shall, like our prows, be westward bent,*
> *Until Pacific's waves pour forth sweet sounds,*
> *Chiming to us like –* Twenty thousand pounds![47]

7

VICE-CONSULS
OF MURZOUK

In the same year that Parry returned from Melville Island, the people of Zeetun, a coastal town in the Regency of Tripoli, had an unexpected surprise. A bearded, sunburned man, dressed in long desert robes and riding a lame camel, slid down the hills towards them singing 'Rule Britannia' and 'God Save the King' at the top of his lungs. This was Lt. George Lyon RN, the only surviving officer of Barrow's latest brainchild: a trans-Saharan expedition to find the Niger.

Barrow was not a man to be thwarted once he had set his mind on an objective. Despite the failure of Tuckey's expedition he was determined to chart the course of the Niger, and if it could not be done by ship then it would have to be done on foot. There was, in fact, a land expedition already in the field. Shortly after Tuckey had sailed for the Congo, one Major Peddie had struck inland from Sierra Leone with 100 soldiers and a small clutch of civilian scientists. But his progress had been blocked by internal African politics. By the time the expedition returned in 1821 almost everybody had died of disease and no new territory had been discovered. It had been a complete failure, and an expensive one to boot: before leaving Sierra Leone Peddie had already run up bills amounting to some £13,000; the sum would later reach £40,000; and accountants would be mulling over his expenses for another eight years.

Although Peddie's expedition had yet to return, Barrow was aware by 1817 that it had cost a great deal and was likely to be unsuccessful. Thus, for his next attempt, he chose a new route and a new method. Instead of sending a large, costly force he would send an inexpensive two- or three-man group which might be able to weave its way through the country with less difficulty. And instead of sending it through the unhealthy zones of West Africa he would land it at Tripoli from where it would travel across the Sahara and hit the Niger from the north. This approach had the advantage that if the Niger flowed east into the Wangara swamps, and thence into the Congo, or ran cross-country to join the Nile – as Barrow was beginning to think it might – the expedition would intercept its course without having to enter the fever-ridden coastal region.

As so often, Barrow's sense of reality failed him. Crossing the Sahara was a terrible ordeal. True, people did it – an estimated 20,000 slaves per annum were brought north on the ancient caravan routes – but they did it at great personal risk. Oases were few and unreliable, and travellers could go up to eighteen days without water. In 1805 a caravan of 2,000 had perished when a strategic waterhole had dried up. In certain areas the routes were plagued by bandits. All in all, the Sahara claimed about 8,000 lives every year. To complete the journey, top to bottom and back again, five times in a lifetime was considered a feat by Arabs. For Europeans to do it at all was unheard of. Yet in Barrow's eyes it was as simple as catching a coach to Harrogate.

From one Captain Smyth, based at Malta, Barrow had learned that the Pasha of Tripoli was willing to safeguard any British expedition to the Niger. To Smyth's questions the Pasha had replied unequivocally that he would send 'emissaries' to see it to its goal. At the same time, Barrow heard that caravans left Tripoli for Timbuctoo every year. It would be a simple matter, he reckoned, for his group to hitch a ride on one of the caravans and plod its way to Timbuctoo and thence the Niger under the Pasha's protection.

By no stretch of the imagination could the Sahara have been described as Barrow's domain. Exploring such places came under the jurisdiction of Lord Bathurst, Secretary of State for Colonial Affairs. But in Barrow's eyes the Sahara was an honorary sea. Men who travelled there would have to steer by the stars, there being no obvious features on which they could take bearings, and it was well known that military men could not do such a thing. So it was that Barrow, in collusion with Bathurst and the Under-Secretary Henry Goulbourne, set the expedition in motion, directed its course and chose its leader.

The man Barrow picked to discover both the Niger and Timbuctoo was a twenty-nine-year-old civilian named Joseph Ritchie. Little is known of Ritchie save that he had trained as a surgeon, was a keen natural historian, was a close friend of Keats (and had written a few poems himself), was private secretary to Sir Charles Stuart, the British Ambassador in Paris, and was, in 1817, willing to go.

Ritchie was ordered to find a single naval officer plus one other seaman to accompany him. He was given permission to draw on the Treasury to the extent of £2,000, from which he was to fund the entire trip, including scientific equipment, trade goods, necessary bribes, and the salaries of whomever he chose to take with him. Ritchie did his best. In Paris, he located one Captain Marryat, the Victorian thriller writer, whom he considered ideal for the purpose. But Marryat, on second thoughts, refused the job because he would not be guaranteed promotion. Somewhat nervously, Ritchie hired a Parisian gardener by the name of Dupont, who would collect specimens 'if the difficulties presented by the Prejudices of the Inhabitants can be surmounted'. But, he hurriedly assured London, he would not allow the advancement of science to 'compromise the Success of the principal object of the Mission, the determination of the leading geographical features of the Interior of Africa'.[1]

Poor Ritchie was too cowed by his responsibilities to question the imprecise nature of his mission. He did, however, realize that he hadn't enough money to do the job properly. As he told Bathurst, he wished his instructions 'had been more explicit upon the subject of pecuniary affairs'.[2] And as he pointed out to Barrow, if he reached his goal he would need extra funds 'in order to prevent my being reduced to an unpleasant Situation from the necessary difficulty of communicating with Tripoli at a distance of 1200 miles'.[3] He continued: 'The present opportunity seems infinitely more favourable than any of those which have hitherto presented themselves for getting into the interior of Africa & it is but fair that it has as good a chance as preceding ones.'[4]

The money was not immediately forthcoming. Ritchie, who seems from his letters to have been overwhelmed by the mere fact of communicating with such powerful figures, mentioned finance no more. At Marseilles he and Dupont boarded a British ship bound for the port of Valetta, Malta, from which Rear-Admiral Sir Charles Penrose commanded the Mediterranean station. He still had not found the naval men who were to make up his team. But Barrow did him a favour. In an official Admiralty order, he instructed Penrose to furnish Ritchie with whatever two persons were willing to go on the expedition.

Into the breach bounded Lt. Lyon. A moustachioed extrovert aged twenty-two, George Francis Lyon was not, on the face of it, suited to African exploration. He had no fondness for hot places or even warm ones – the Mediterranean 'does not quite agree with me',[5] he once wrote. And his main interests in life were 'balls, riding, dining & making a fool of myself'.[6] But he would do anything to advance his career. At the close of the Napoleonic War he had procured a statement from Lord Melville that he would be promoted as soon as a chance to serve his country availed itself. He clung to this promise like a leech, even though Melville had probably said the same thing to a hundred others. Ritchie's expedition, pitiful as it was, was the opportunity he had been waiting for.

There was one obstacle. In paternal fashion, Sir Charles Penrose – who maybe knew his man – refused to let Lyon go to Africa until he had cleared it with his friends and family in England. Ritchie was disappointed. 'Lieutenant Lyon, of the *Albion*, [is] an excellent Draftsman,' he reported. But alas, 'I cannot hope to have the advantage of his assistance for the present.'[7] Instead Ritchie was given a carpenter called Belford from the Valetta dockyards, 'who is likely to prove a very useful man',[8] and was all the more useful for accepting 100 guineas for the first year out and £120 for the second – 'something less than his regular wages in the Dockyard',[9] Ritchie wrote with pride.

Thus, with a carpenter and the hope of an officer, Ritchie sailed for Tripoli on 30 September 1818 aboard a man-of-war – it would create the right impression, he was assured. Tripoli, a rotting outpost of a rotting Ottoman Empire, ruled by a disinterested Ottoman pasha, Yussuf Karamanli, was not naturally friendly to Britain. However, since Britain's Mediterranean fleet had recently crushed a pirate's nest on the nearby Barbary Coast and could, if it wanted, swat Tripoli like a fly, the Pasha was perfectly willing to receive Ritchie's little group, especially as Ritchie carried a letter of introduction from Sir Charles Penrose warning the Pasha that Britain had no interest in conquering his country, 'while we have possession of Malta and the Ionian Isles, and with their ports and the British Navy to sally from then, what need we more to command in the vicinity should we be at war, though in peace liberal and just persuasion are the only arms we wish to use'.[10]

When Ritchie landed at Tripoli in October 1818 he soon learned how weak his situation was. The idea of a scheduled caravan service to Timbuctoo was laughable. True, caravans did go there occasionally, but the route was long and hazardous, passing through deserts which were ruled by predatory Tuareg tribesmen. The only caravans which left for the interior at even remotely regular intervals were those organized by the Pasha's vassal to the south, the Bey of Fezzan, who gathered an annual levy of slaves from Bornu, an African kingdom some 1,000 miles east of Timbuctoo.

What was more, the Pasha had no intention of fulfilling his offer of support. The promises he had given Captain Smyth became a denial of any help beyond his own borders and those of Fezzan. But if Ritchie wished – and bearing in mind Admiral Penrose's letter – he and his fellow officer, if he turned up, could term themselves Vice-Consuls to Murzouk, the capital of Fezzan.

This behaviour was only to be expected, according to one member of the Foreign Office. On learning that Ritchie was putting his trust in the Pasha, he reminded Barrow and Bathurst that the Pasha had murdered his eldest brother to get the throne and that if Ritchie's 'success depends on the agency of the Pasha of Tripoli he is desperate, as from my knowledge of the man, so far back as 1793, a greater villain never infested the earth'.[11]

Fortunately for Ritchie, the British Consul at Tripoli was Hanmer Warrington. This energetic, capable and opinionated man, who would facilitate most of Barrow's African expeditions, is long forgotten. But during his residency from 1814 to 1846 he did a great deal to extend British influence in the Sahara. He was so close to the Pasha that he virtually became his foreign secretary. By 1825 he was acting Consul for Austria, Hanover, the Netherlands, Portugal, the Kingdom of the Two Sicilies and Tuscany; in addition to this he mediated for the unsatisfactory Consuls of Sweden and Denmark. Under his influence British Vice-Consuls were despatched to the most unlikely of places, and his home became a semi-official asylum for political refugees and runaway slaves.

Warrington's one weakness was the King of Sardinia, whom he could not abide. The King of Sardinia reciprocated and, throughout Warrington's tenure, the two men enjoyed a covert vendetta of insults and petty intrigues. At the time of Ritchie's arrival, Warrington was deeply involved in the case of a Sardinian spy who had attempted to cash a draft for several hundred Spanish dollars – the currency of North Africa – using Warrington's forged signature. In retaliation he was planning a sweep of Malta, whose scurrilous population he considered to be a hotbed of pro-Sardinian agitators.

Magnanimously, Warrington put his quarrel aside. By mid-November Lyon had been given clearance to join the expedition, and he and Ritchie, with Warrington, held an audience with the Pasha, taking great care to have the meeting minuted and signed by all parties lest any promises on the Pasha's behalf went the same way as those made to Smyth. Lyon, in anticipation of his promotion and not wishing to diminish the expedition's importance, announced himself as captain.

The Pasha, for all his bad reputation, was reasonableness itself. He regretted his inability to help them as fully as he had previously wished, but the interior kingdoms were in a state of 'anarchy and confusion';[12] his only friend had been the King of Bornu but he was now dead and 'no mission of His to any part of Soudan would be respected'.[13] Helpfully, he advised Ritchie and Lyon to grow beards, wear native clothing and travel as converts to Islam. And in parting, he told them that the Bey of Fezzan was due shortly in Tripoli to raise funds for a slave-gathering expedition. Their best bet was to join his caravan.

Ritchie floundered. 'It will be evident,' he wrote to the Colonial Office, 'that the position in which I am placed is not the one which I anticipated on leaving Europe . . .'[14] He had envisaged an arduous but organized passage to the Niger. Tagging onto a slave train of uncertain destination was not the same thing. As the days of preparation passed, Ritchie grew more and more silent. He roused himself on occasion, to report snippets of news such as Dupont's hasty return to Paris thanks to 'an unpleasant affair occasioned by the son of the French Consul'.[15] He also managed to record an interview with a sixty-year-old schoolmaster born in Timbuctoo of Tripoline parents who described his home town as a drab place whose houses were built of mud, sometimes two storeys high, around a central palace. The royal troops wore red, the main articles of trade were cotton cloth and gold ornaments, market-days were Tuesday and Thursday, and the surrounding countryside was flat. Half a day's journey to the south was a river, full of boats and so wide that a gun could not carry to the other side. The schoolmaster called this river the Nile, a name that was given to any large river in that part of Africa; according to him, looking at it from the north, 'the Nile comes from your right hand and flows towards the left'.[16] Without a doubt he was describing the Niger. 'It is commonly supposed,' Ritchie wrote, 'to form the Western Branch of the Nile, but this improbable theory is not supported by any evidence.'[17]

While Ritchie mulled over these disheartening revelations, 'Captain' Lyon became increasingly the man on whom the expedition depended. Lyon was irrepressible. He threw himself into his disguise with glee. He learned Arabic, grew a beard and, under the name of Said ben abd Allah, received instruction on Islamic religion. Yussuf el

Ritchie and Ali (Belford) trailed resignedly in his wake. When Mohammed el Mukni, the Bey of Fezzan, came into town it was Lyon who took the lead, meeting this fine-looking man – 'of an insatiable ambition and excessive avarice'[18] – with such fellow feeling that the Bey promised to treat them all as if they were his brothers.

The Bey had been in Tripoli only a few weeks before he brought Ritchie more bad news. He had changed his mind about crossing the Sahara, and could take them only as far as his capital, Murzouk. Ritchie listened listlessly. Could anything else go wrong? By the time the Bey of Fezzan departed on 22 March 1819 Ritchie had given up all hope.

Lyon, on the other hand, was revelling in Arab life. He had explored Tripoli's surrounding hills and countryside, had slept in the same defensive towers as had the Pasha and his forefathers, and had learned how to catch a snake or a scorpion without being harmed. He had impressed himself on his Arab companions to a degree that they considered him a fellow Muslim. Wherever Lyon looked he found something of interest. At their first stop he was drawn inexorably to Lilla Fatima, the gigantic widow of a local ruler, whose calves were as big as a man's thigh. Tattooed across her body, Lyon revealed, were the names of God and all her numerous men-friends. Lyon and Fatima entertained themselves with a naked floorshow until Ritchie wandered in, reminding Fatima so depressingly of her late husband that she pulled up her veil and ordered the dancers home.

As the Bey's caravan travelled south, carrying with it the white men on horses, their goods loaded on twenty-two camels, Lyon recorded everything he encountered. Here he saw Roman ruins, whose inscriptions he dutifully took down; there he saw empty water-holes, dug by preceding caravans, whose depth he estimated at more than 200 feet. On entering the Sahara, on 24 April, he was astonished by the detritus of previous caravans. Dead animals lay everywhere, their remains desiccated by the sun. Sometimes they faced sand-storms of up to twelve hours' duration. Now and then a slave train moaned by; bones, human and otherwise, littered the trail. 'The road,' he wrote, 'was a dreary desert, having but few wells and those of salt water.'[19] He gave precise instructions on how to combat the heat:

water must be drunk in the morning and from the hand; a wet cloth
on the back of the neck would avert sunstroke. Oil yourself down
after a long day, he counselled, and be careful with your horses when
approaching an oasis.

Thirty-nine days after leaving Tripoli they reached Murzouk where
Fatima, who had reached some kind of arrangement with Lyon,
marked the occasion by dismounting without assistance. Admirers
rushed from every quarter to help her to her feet. Murzouk was a town
of 2,500 people, whose windowless homes were enclosed by a fif-
teen-foot-high-wall. In the centre loomed the Bey's palace, a
ninety-foot edifice in which he lived with his guests, courtiers and
harem. The 'Vice-Consuls' were not among the Bey's guests; instead
they were billeted in a windowless, one-roomed house in which a
murder had recently been committed.

Lyon was becoming seriously worried as to their chances of success.
Earlier he had recorded that 'I do not think that the funds allowed to
Mr. Ritchie are adequate to the purposes of safety or enquiry.'[20] Now,
to his horror, he found that Ritchie had spent all but £75 of his £2,000
allowance before even landing in Africa, and most of that was gone.
The goods he had purchased for trade in the interior were worthless
in Murzouk and the only saleable commodities they possessed were
their horses and firearms, to part with either of which would spell an
end to the expedition and also, quite likely, an end to any hope of
returning to Tripoli.

To deepen their gloom further, they were racked by fever. Lyon
and Ritchie spent the months of June, July and August confined to
bed, waited on only by Belford, who had become deaf during the
journey and was himself 'much reduced'. The Bey, who had been so
affable when the white men were healthy and, apparently, wealthy
turned a blind eye to their distress.

Ironically, in this relatively bountiful oasis, they found themselves
in direr circumstances than Parry's men in the furthest wastes of the
Arctic. 'Our situation was daily becoming more deplorable in all
respects,' Lyon wrote at the end of August. 'Our rate of living was
reduced to one *saa*, or quart of corn per diem, with occasionally a few

dates, amongst [all] of us.'[21] Not even a widely believed rumour that Ritchie was married to the King of England's daughter, and Lyon to the King's niece, could help. If anything it only exacerbated the problem as hordes of Murzoukians clamoured at their door demanding money and medicine. Lyon dismissed the money-grubbers but was unable to refuse the sick. However, he 'took good care to give such doses as were not easily forgotten',[22] and soon they were left alone save for an occasional request to treat the Bey's harem, a duty that Lyon felt he could not ignore.

By September 1819 they had recovered sufficiently to purchase a few pounds of camel flesh, the first meat they had tasted in six weeks. Ritchie responded apathetically, lying on his bed against the wall, saying little. Lyon, however, sallied into town, making friends with Murzouk's lowlife and attending illicit parties where he danced and drank bouza, a date brew, until the small hours. In October, Belford made a ceremonial coach for the Bey, which garnered them an invaluable seven dollars. But no sooner had they been paid than Belford and Lyon fell ill, leaving Ritchie to nurse them. And when they recovered, Ritchie once more went down with fever. He finally rallied in mid-November, but only for the briefest period.

On 17 November, Ritchie looked in the mirror and saw that his tongue was black. Jokingly he remarked to Lyon that, if he did not know this to have been caused by the cup of thick coffee he had just drunk, he would have to assume he had bilious fever in which case they might as well say goodbye to him. He died three days later.

On 21 November, one hour after Lyon had finished reciting the first chapter of the Koran over Ritchie's grave, a message came from Tripoli that the British government had granted them an extra £1,000. Lyon was almost beside himself with frustration. If the news had arrived a few months or even weeks earlier it could have averted great suffering and maybe saved Ritchie's life. Infuriatingly, now that the money was available he could not even spend it; so low had their stock fallen that nobody in Murzouk would offer him credit – whatever his royal connections – and if he wanted the cash he would have to go back to Tripoli to collect it.

Lyon's final despair came when he inspected a stack of boxes which Ritchie had directed were not to be opened until they reached the interior. Envisaging a host of tradable goods, he found only the following: one camel-load of corks for pinning insects, two loads of brown paper for wrapping plants, two chests of scientific instruments, eight hundredweight of books and 600 pounds of lead. These and other non-essentials, such as a magic lantern, amounted to eight camel-loads out of the twenty-two they had started with. Moreover, on searching for Ritchie's journal, Lyon discovered that for a long time he had not bothered to keep one. 'Much, very much, valuable information has been lost,'[23] he stormed.

At this point Lyon would have been justified in packing up and heading home. For some time he had been sleeping with his favourite weapon by his side – a sword with a pistol in its hilt – to protect himself from the would-be assassins who pattered across his roof at night. But instead he sold Ritchie's horse plus a quantity of gunpowder and used the proceeds to pay for an exploratory trip to the south with enough left over to cover his passage back to Tripoli. He would not find the Niger but at least he would map a bit more territory for those who would follow.

On 14 December 1819 he set out on a whistle-stop tour of the land immediately south of Murzouk. Following him came the long-suffering Belford, who was now not only deaf but dizzy and frequently fell off his horse. There was little for them to find save a general hatred of the Bey of Fezzan, whose slave trains campaigned through the land once a year. As Lyon wrote to Bathurst, 'their little children are taught to curse him as soon as they can speak'.[24] By 18 January 1820, with his money running out and Belford barely able to stand, Lyon was back in Murzouk. Five days later he celebrated his birthday with a group of locals; to mark the occasion Fatima performed a dance with much dropping of veils. Shortly afterwards, he, Belford and Fatima left on a slave caravan bound for Tripoli.

Crossing the Sahara once again, in conditions of such dryness that his horse's tail switched sparks of static, Lyon's observant eye went to work. The solitude awed and excited him. 'In some parts [of the desert],' he wrote, 'the only living creature seen for many days is a small insect somewhat resembling a spider.'[25] On one occasion he was able to follow the tracks of a single beetle through the sand for a distance of two miles. When he left the campfire at night he was stunned by the clarity of the stars and by the utter silence. All that could be heard was the gentle soughing of the wind – which he later realized was the sound of his own breathing.

Mirages taunted him continually. Lakes abounded, as did forests. Many a time he cantered towards a large tree only to find it was a 'bush which did not throw a shade sufficient even to shelter one of my hands'.[26] His travelling companions found this hilarious, and were forever giving him a nudge and asking him to investigate some illusory landmark. Midway on their journey they stopped at an oasis whose inhabitants made a kind of caviare from tiny mud-worms. Of course, it was nothing like *real* caviare, Lyon reassured his journal readers, but in the circumstances, once one became used to it, it was very tasty indeed.

Back at Fatima's home town, Sockna, fond farewells were said and a celebratory dinner was held indoors. Lyon recorded that flies fell 'by the spoonfuls'[27] into food and drink alike. He reached Zeetun on 18 March, and on the morning of 26 March 1820, fifty days after having left Murzouk, he re-entered Tripoli. It was exactly one year to the day since he had left the town.

On returning to Britain, Lyon had four matters to discuss with the authorities: slavery, the course of the Niger, the measures to be taken by future explorers who travelled through the Sahara and, most important of all, his promotion.

On the matter of slavery he was outspoken. He had been disgusted by the sights he had seen in the Sahara and recommended a pragmatic approach. Unlike Ritchie, who had suggested unrealistically that Britain pay the Arab nations compensation for stopping the slave trade, Lyon advised a programme of trade and education under which the Africans would become so secure that they would no longer need to deal in human beings, and would be able to defend themselves against predators. There would be no obstacle to this, he argued, because 'the whole of the negroe country is open to any peaceable man or woman'.[28] He backed up his reasoning with sound, if depressing, economics: in Tripoli you paid £20 for an African woman; in the impoverished south you could swap a horse for twenty of them.

As for the Niger, it most certainly did not flow into the swamp of Wangara. 'It is quite impossible from the varied accounts given of it,' Lyon wrote of Wangara, 'to form any idea as to its actual situation, or even existence.'[29] In his opinion, Wangara was most likely a generic name for swamps, much as the Nile was a generic term for large rivers. He backed this up with the information that he had heard of many Wangaras, and none of them seemed credible places. One Wangara, for example, was supposed to be inhabited by an invisible tribe which only traded by night. Elsewhere, in another Wangara, there was a circular city whose covered streets were lit twenty-four hours a day by lamps. The city was bisected by a wall, on either side of which pale citizens plotted how to conquer the other half. In the face of such tales it was hard to argue Wangara's existence.

If the Niger went anywhere, it flowed into a lake called Tshad. From what Lyon had been told, this lake (Lake Chad) was a mighty expanse of water that shrank in the dry season to a river which flowed west to east. Nobody knew where the river came from or through which lands it later flowed, but everybody agreed, whatever route it took, that it eventually joined the Nile.

On more solid ground, Lyon asserted that any future expeditions would have to go native if they were to have any chance of success. 'We found that it was absolutely requisite to conform to all the duties of the Mohammedan religion, as well as to assume their dress.' Had they not done so, he continued, 'our lives would have been in constant jeopardy'. 'I am confident,' he concluded, 'that it would never be possible for any man to pass through Africa unless in every respect he qualified himself to appear as a Mohammedan; and should I myself return to that country, I would not be accompanied by any one who would refuse to observe these precautions. It is possible, that as far as Fezzan, a traveller might, by great good chance, escape detection;

but the further south he proceeded, the more bigoted would he find the people, and a cruel death would, in such a case, inevitably terminate his journey.'[30]

Finally, there came the difficult matter of promotion. In vain did Lyon present the argument that he had been serving the nation's interest and so, according to Lord Melville's letter, should be advanced. On every front he was greeted by stony faces. His father, and eventually his mother too, petitioned Lord Bathurst, but to no avail. Only with difficulty could they persuade the government to even pay their son for his troubles, his last salary having been received in 1818.

After much to-ing and fro-ing, Lyon's father let his feelings be known. Having received 'your most disheartening & studiously evasive letter', he wrote tipsily to Lord Bathurst with many capitals, underlinings and the odd Latin quote, 'Do you not think that my son has suffered as much, exerted himself as much, & as much benefited the Country as those many officers who were made Commander for sailing round the Isle of Wight in the Prince Regent's Yacht?'[31]

Lyon senior was an 'independent Gentleman', he informed Bathurst, a position 'which has ever been supported unsullied by my family, [and] I proudly consider myself the equal of any man however high his temporal Rank'.[32]

Bathurst directed him wearily to the Admiralty, where Barrow directed him back to the Colonial Office. And so the war of Lyon's promotion went on.

But Lyon had one card to play. Barrow very much wanted him to go on another expedition to Africa. He told him as much within days of his return – 'not in the most courteous or encouraging manner but with official coldness',[33] wrote Lyon Senior – suggesting that September of 1820 would be a good time to start. Lyon looked him in the eye and announced that 'when he found his *past* services properly appreciated, & fairly rewarded, it would then be time enough to talk of the future'.[34]

Lyon said the same thing to Bathurst's Under-Secretary on 25 August, prompting a frantic note: 'Dear Barrow, What should under these circs. be done as to our African Mission?'[35]

Lyon became even more intransigent when he heard of Parry's promotion following his return from the Arctic. No matter that Parry had done the unheard of and that Lyon had survived a trip to a small, dirty town in Africa. No matter that Parry had 'interest', or patronage, and that Lyon had none. A principle was at stake. He poured out his complaints to Lord Bathurst on 8 November 1820. '*His* report and explanation have been immediately attended to,' Lyon wrote of Parry, '*he* has been admitted to the presence of his highest employers & by them has been received with favour and distinction, *I* on the other hand, am denied to your Lordship's presence, have had no opportunity offered me for examination, & have for the period of three months been referred from your Lordship to the Admiralty & from thence back again to your Lordship, without hope or chance of being eventually attended to by one or the other party.'[36]

Lord Bathurst did not reply. So when Lyon finished his journal – a lively book, illustrated by vibrant prints of his own watercolours – he wrote to tell him so on 13 November, and sent copies of the letter every succeeding day until Bathurst promised to look at it. Simultaneously, Lyon let it be known that he alone held the clue to the Niger. 'High and dazzling offers were made me in a particular quarter to renew my researches into the Interior,' he wrote, 'and I will proudly say that had I accepted them, I *would* & *could* have fulfilled the utmost wishes of my employers, by solving in six months from the time of my leaving Europe, the important questions respecting the Niger.'[37]

Barrow had had enough. Time was pressing and there were scores of men clamouring to be sent to Africa, any of whom who would suit the job. He would have liked to send Lyon back to the Sahara. But as the young man was making such a nuisance of himself and was obviously in need of a lesson, and because Barrow had a sense of humour, he sent him to the Arctic instead.

8

FAILURE AT FOXE BASIN

At the end of 1820 Barrow directed two of His Majesty's ships to be made ready for Arctic service. Parry was commissioned to the *Fury* on 30 December and a fortnight later his old command, the *Hecla*, was given to Lyon. For someone who had insisted that his senior officer be a man in whom he could place implicit confidence, Parry was politely fatalistic about Barrow's choice. Lyon, he wrote, 'is spoken of, by all who know him, as an exceedingly clever fellow, and his drawings are the most beautiful I ever saw'.[1]

Parry may have been thwarted as to his second-in-command. When it came to the ships, however, his demands were followed to the letter. Previously, naval wisdom had dictated that Arctic expeditions take two vessels of different sizes: a large one for clear water and a smaller one for shallow, coastal work. But, as Parry pointed out, the advantages in this were few. The difference in draught amounted to no more than a few feet at most, and should the larger ship sink the smaller could not possibly accommodate two crews and their supplies in anything approaching comfort. Far better, he counselled, to have two identical ships, either of which had space for the other's crews in case of a disaster, whose equipment was interchangeable in

case of breakages, and whose joint provisions could see them through
as many winters as were required. If close exploration was necessary
it could be carried out by small parties in boats.

At 375 tons apiece, *Fury* and *Hecla* were twin sisters. The *Fury*
was strengthened to the same standard as the *Hecla* and both ships
were modified to last a winter in the ice. Their interiors were insulated with cork, even down to the fitting of cork shutters for the
captains' windows, and stoves were stationed amidships to provide
central heating for the whole vessel but particularly for the officers'
cabins which, being higher up and more exposed, were among the
coldest areas. The stoves were designed by a Mr Sylvester, who
claimed that 'the velocity of the warm air current through an aperture
two feet square is about five or six feet per second'.[2] This remarkable
output was produced solely by convection and could be sustained for
twenty-four hours at an expenditure of only five pecks (one and a
quarter bushels) of coal.

During his stay on Melville Island Parry had been concerned by
the amount of fuel needed to provide fresh water. Snow was not like
rain. If you ate it, or rather sucked it, you did little to slake your thirst
and only succeeded in reducing your body temperature. Eating snow
was the Arctic equivalent of drinking sea water. All snow, therefore,
had to be pre-melted for consumption. To get round this problem,
Parry installed water tanks around the stoves' chimneys. These metal
cylinders, open at the top and fitted with taps at the bottom, could
melt enough snow to provide sixty-five gallons of water daily in conditions of 0 °F, more than enough to supply their needs.

Parry took equal care over the provisions. He ordered from Donkin
& Gamble two pounds of tinned meat and one quart of vegetable
soup per man per week. Spirits were taken aboard at 35° above standard proof, to be reduced later, allowing him to squeeze 140 gallons
into the space normally required for 100. The standard issue of ship's
biscuit was halved, and augmented by flour – three hundredweight of
flour occupied the same area as one hundredweight of biscuit. Vinegar
was concentrated. Lemon juice was mixed with rum to prevent it
from freezing, and was stored in casks rather than bottles. Against

the peril of scurvy he packed tinned carrots, plus 'crystallised lemon acid, cranberries, lemon marmalade, tamarinds, pickled walnuts and cabbage, essence of malt and hops, essence of spruce with molasses, dried herbs for tea',[3] and a quantity of mustard and cress seeds.

Altogether he was prepared for three years in the Arctic. He hoped to be out sooner but, just in case he was delayed, he arranged for a supply vessel from the South American station to meet the expedition in Bering Strait in 1824.

The ships having been equipped, Parry cast about for men and officers. As before, he had little difficulty finding takers. Almost all the old hands volunteered for the voyage. Hoppner, Hooper and James Ross were there, as was George Fisher, Buchan's astronomer, who had recently been ordained and took the novel post of astronomer-chaplain – a man of the cloth being 'in every respect desirable',[4] according to Parry. New additions were Edward Bird and Francis Crozier, midshipmen to the *Hecla* and *Fury* respectively.

Parry's orders were much the same as before save for the point of entry which, this time, was to be the uncharted seas north of Hudson Bay. Europeans had been there before: Luke Foxe had discovered the Foxe Basin above Hudson Bay in 1631 and had declared it a dead end. Little more than a century later Christopher Middleton had sought a North-West Passage through the south-west corner of Foxe Basin, only to be turned back by ice at a spot he named Repulse Bay. Like Baffin, however, Foxe and Middleton had fallen into disrepute. Foxe Basin, for all anybody knew, was a positive colander of routes leading westward. But, in one of Barrow's baffling leaps of geography, he decided that out of all these hypothetical routes Repulse Bay might be the one that did not exist. If it did exist, however, it might not be a bay and was therefore worth a try.

Parry was thus to sail for Repulse Bay and if thwarted was to probe the western coastline of Foxe Basin for an alternative opening. Having found the sought-after 'vent' he would, hopefully, find open water leading to America's northern coastline which would, also hopefully, be ice-free. He was then to make for the Pacific as speedily as possible. Should he encounter Franklin's overland party he was to give it every assistance. Otherwise he was forbidden to stop for 'any other object not of imperious importance'.[5] He was not even to map the American coastline.

Parry's orders – like those of every Arctic expedition before and after – included the usual, worn generalities: that he was to record refraction, to take magnetic observations, to make friends with the Eskimos but to beware lest they be enemies, and to keep his crew healthy etc. From the Royal Society, however, he received more exact instructions. Among other things it wanted him to ascertain whether the aurora borealis made a noise, and to see whether sound travelled at the same speed over ice as it did overland. But these were minor details. Hitherto Barrow had emphasized the scientific importance of his Arctic voyages, but Parry's new venture was to barely scrape the surface of scientific observation. Parry did not care, nor did Barrow. As everyone tacitly agreed, by far the most important thing was to find the Passage before someone else did.

By 2 July the ships were off Resolution Island whose tricky currents guarded the door to Hudson Bay. Lyon, who was seeing an Arctic summer for the first time, rhapsodized over its beauty. 'At a quarter past ten the sun set: the sky overhead was of the purest azure, here and there sprinkled with light silvery clouds of the most fantastic forms. At about mid-heaven, in the western sky, a range of purple clouds, edged with vivid gold, formed a delightful contrast with the softened crimson of the setting sun.'[6] In his opinion it was better than the finest Italian sunset. Parry, who knew what lay ahead, noted only the 'prospects of utter barrenness and desolation such as these rugged shores present'.[7]

Lyon soon modified his view. On 21 July they finally passed Resolution Island, having sailed and warped their way through the unpredictable ice which choked the sea. Obviously shaken, Lyon recorded that it had taken them nineteen days to cross sixty miles of water. During this time the *Hecla* lost five six-inch hawsers and its bow anchor had 'broke off at the head of the shank with as much ease as if, instead of weighing twenty-one cwt., it had been of crockery ware'.[8]

They were now in the vast and secretive realm of the Hudson's Bay Company. For almost two centuries this powerful, quasi-autonomous entity – run almost entirely by Highlanders – had exploited the natural resources of northern Canada, ruling the region as a commercial fiefdom in tandem with its sole competitor, the North West Company, which took its men from the Orkneys. Its shadowy hand reached ever outwards, quelling Indian rebellions, building forts, setting up colonies, and despatching trapping parties to extract the furs which sold for fortunes in Europe. Such was its wealth that, in a rumour worthy of modern times, it was suggested that the company had bribed John Ross to turn away from Lancaster Sound in 1818 to deter would-be competitors.

If anybody could have found the North-West Passage in this area it was the Hudson's Bay Company. But for the moment it had no interest in the profitless Arctic tundra. Parry was thus left to his own devices, seeing little of the Company's activities save three ships off Resolution Island which were carrying 160 Dutch colonists to a new life in the north. The men and women danced cheerfully on deck, Lyon observed through his telescope, probably celebrating a wedding.

The Company ignored Parry. But Parry could not ignore the Company. Wherever he landed he found the Eskimos had been tainted by its presence. Along the Savage Islands, which lined the northern coast of Hudson Bay, they were accosted by Eskimos shouting 'Pilletay!' ('Give me!') so loudly that they could 'hardly hear ourselves speak'.[9] Far away were the unspoiled Arctic Highlanders of northern Greenland. 'It was impossible,' Parry wrote sternly, 'for us not to receive a very unfavourable impression of the general behaviour and moral character, of the natives of this part of Hudson's Strait.'[10]

Lyon took a more lenient view. 'It was a favourite joke to run slily behind the seaman, and, shouting loudly in one ear, to give them at the same time a very smart slap on the other,' he recorded good-humouredly. But after he had been saluted in the same manner he found it less amusing. 'The joke,' he wrote frostily, 'consisted in

making the person struck look astonished, which, as may be supposed was always the result.'[11]

The Eskimos stole everything they came across, particularly iron
implements, which only served to exacerbate Parry's poor opinion of
them. Lyon, having re-established himself, was more forgiving: 'A
few instances of dishonesty occurred where iron lay neglected in view;
but it is scarcely to be wondered that such a temptation should prove
irresistible: had small golden bars been thrown in the streets of
London, how would they have fared.'[12]

By 20 August they had left the Savage Islands far behind and were
sailing through Frozen Strait, passing at the end of the day the northern extremity of Roes Welcome Sound under a moon that hung like a
shrivelled orange in the sky.

On the night of 21 August they were battered by a fierce storm
which drove them under cover of darkness out of Frozen Strait and
into Repulse Bay. As everybody could see, when the winds died down
the following morning, it was indeed a bay. Their first opening had
been denied them, but at least they knew where they stood. 'We
were now indisputably on our scene of future action, the coast of
America,'[13] wrote Lyon. Having found the coast, all they needed to do
was follow it and the North-West Passage would fall into their hands.

During the remainder of the season they inched northward. Parry,
magnanimously, gave Lyon permission to explore the first opening to
the west. It was a dead end. Parry took the second opening, another
dead end which he named Lyon Inlet. Then, with winter closing in,
they took refuge on Winter Island off the mouth of Lyon Inlet, pausing only to investigate a slope of the same crimson snow over which
John Ross had been so ruthlessly castigated. It was more diluted in
colour than Ross's version and reminded Lyon of raspberry sorbet.

Compared to Melville Island, Winter Island was a featherbed. The
sun was visible for the whole winter. Open water was never far away,
steaming with frost-smoke that froze and blew like dust onto the
nearby ice. And Sylvester's stoves performed admirably. Within
twelve hours of their being stoked both ships were bone dry. In the
Fury the air left the tubes at 120 °F on the lower deck, falling slightly

to 100 °F in nearby cabins, and emerging in Parry's quarters, forty-six feet away, at an impressive 74 °F. So overbearing was the heat that Parry had to cut their fuel consumption by 20 per cent to four pecks of coal per day.

The winter followed in typical Parry fashion. Both ships were insulated with snow, their decks were roofed with canvas, and the same routine was put in place that had served them so well on Melville Island. The hot pipes were lined with trays of mustard and cress which soon began to sprout and were fed to the men at twice-weekly intervals. By spring they had produced 100 pounds of anti-scorbutic growth. On 9 November 1821 the Royal Arctic Theatre reopened, the officers shaving off their whiskers to act female parts and adorning themselves with a variety of costumes and props which they had bought before leaving England. Lyon was stage manager. Their first performance was Sheridan's *The Rivals* in which Parry played Sir Anthony Absolute.

Other amusements included magic lantern shows, played on a device provided by an anonymous donor, and musical evenings for the officers which took place in Parry's cabin. In addition, evening schools were arranged for those who could not read or write. 'Suffice it to say,' Lyon wrote, 'that every arrangement which could contribute to our general comfort and health was made by Captain Parry.'[14]

Christmas was ushered in with two farces from the Royal Arctic Players and a display of 'phantasmagoria' on the magic lantern. On the *Hecla* 'a well-meaning, but certainly not very sober crew'[15] called Lyon down to the lower deck to drink his health and give him three cheers. On the more respectable *Fury*, Parry beamed with pride as the sailors came up like bashful schoolchildren to present him with examples of their writing. There was not a single man who had not learned how to do his alphabet. 'It is, I confess, with no ordinary feelings of pleasure,' Parry later wrote, 'that I record the fact that on the return of the Expedition to England, there was not an individual belonging to it who could not read his Bible.'[16] Everybody was in high spirits. During the plays the audience rose and cheered whenever England was mentioned. Overwintering had become almost embarrassingly easy.

January was a month for scientific observation. Astronomical readings were taken by the thousand, balloons were sent aloft for upper-air measurements, sea water was analysed, gravitational experiments were conducted, the aurora borealis was listened to diligently – Parry found it hard to confirm anything because his ears froze as soon as they were uncovered; Lyon, who claimed he was better able to withstand the cold because he still retained the heat of the Sahara, announced that after several hours in the open he had heard nothing but his own breathing. The speed of sound was tested by a system of muskets and flags with the peculiar, and as yet unexplained, result that one sound-wave apparently overtook another. On the *Hecla*, in a personal set of observations, Lyon noted that port and white wine displayed different characteristics when frozen.

The only excitement that month was when Parry's cabin caught fire. The flames were soon doused but Parry was distressed to learn that, for all its heat, the soot from his stove froze against the walls of the chimney pipe in a solid crust – like the flesh of a coconut on its shell, Lyon suggested dreamily – and when it grew too thick it fell down upon the coals with disastrous consequences. From this point every section of stovepipe was dismantled regularly and beaten to free it from soot.

On 1 February they met their first Eskimos. The chatty people came aboard with little fuss – they had met 'kabloonas' or white men before and had no fear of their ships – and amazed everyone with their lack of acquisitiveness. They didn't shout 'Pilletay' and 'if we dropped a glove or a handkerchief without knowing it, they would immediately direct our attention to it'.[17] Altogether, Parry and Lyon decided, they were of a better type than the Savage Islanders – even if they did peck through the ships' middens on a daily basis.

Parry, Lyon and four others walked over to their village of igloos and brought a group of Eskimos singing and dancing back to the *Fury* to make their acquaintance. Lyon led the way with choruses of 'Toll De Riddle Loll' to 'loud screams of admiration and a great deal of jumping'.[18] The subsequent evening went so well that for the rest of the winter Eskimos and Europeans kept constant company. The Eskimos came aboard, ate with the officers, slept in their cabins and cultivated useful friends among the seamen. In return the officers walked over the sea-ice – it sprang like shoe leather, Lyon recorded – to experience life as Eskimos lived it.

Parry was mainly interested in a display of igloo building. In less than two hours the Eskimos constructed for his benefit a brand-new igloo, its six-inch-thick walls creating a cavern that looked from within as if it was made of frosted glass, admitting direct light only through a single pane of ice.

Lyon was more adventurous. He tasted a sample of reindeer fat – 'sweet and good'[19] – and discovered that Eskimo women were tat-tooed head to toe. Without a moment's hesitation he drew up his sleeve and demanded a tattoo. Expecting the pierce-and-smear method recorded by Captain Cook in the South Sea Islands and made popular by his own seamen, he was taken aback to find the Eskimos sewed their tattoos using a bone needle and soot-drenched thread. Elaborate patterns were sketched on his arm – 'they all enjoyed a good laugh at the figures, which perhaps conveyed some meaning I could not fathom'[20] – before the operation began. But Lyon would allow them no more than forty stitches, or two inches of tattoo, before he halted the experiment. It stung a little and the colour turned the same light blue as decorated his sailors' arms. Later, a little irrespon-sibly, he took Midshipman Bird to have the full treatment. Unfortunately, Bird's tattooist was a half-blind woman who 'stitched away as if it was an old shoe she was operating on'.[21] Lyon was left with an intricate set of pictures; Bird came out with an armful of meandering, unconnected and indelible patterns.

On a more practical level, the Eskimos gave the white men useful information about the local geography. To the north lay a body of water which was ice-free in summer and whose western coastline led into a navigable strait beyond which lay more open water. Parry asked them for a map and a woman named Iligliuk obliged with a sketch that mir-rored much of what they already knew and showed to the north a reasonably straight coast dotted with islands. On the largest of these, named Igloolik, Iligliuk said she had been born. It all sounded very hopeful. But 'our business was to see not to speculate',[22] Parry warned.

While waiting for the ice to melt, they made exploratory overland trips. Parry tried his hand at dog-sledging but was disappointed. 'After being upset twice and stopping at least ten times,' he completed a journey of two miles in twenty-five minutes. All in all, 'it seemed to me more bodily labour . . . than if we had walked the whole way'.[23] Until they knew what they were doing, he decided, they would stick to man-hauling the sledges.

On 15 March, Lyon took a small group of men to explore the coast, dragging behind them a sledge containing a tent, blankets and food for three days. The weather had been so mild that they expected little trouble. Hardly had they left the ship than the temperature began to fall. Snow sheeted out of the sky, reducing visibility to twenty yards and forcing them to take refuge in the tent before they had travelled six miles. By midnight the temperature was –32 °F. The following morning the tent was half-covered with snow, the sledge was buried so deep that they could not find it and the landscape was altered beyond recognition. With the gale raging unabated, Lyon had no option but to retreat. Carrying a few pounds of bread, a little rum and a small spade they tried to retrace their steps. Within hours they were completely lost, and with only an occasional glimpse of the sun had little chance of finding their position. Soon they were stumbling like drunkards from one landmark to another, every time supposing it to be a feature they had passed on the way out, and every time finding it was not. Some were snow-blind, most of them were frost-bitten and all were in a state of cold-induced stupefaction. The worst case was a marine, Sergeant Spackman, who was unable to walk unaided and whose face had frozen into a ghastly mask, his eyelids stiff plates of ice and his mouth drawn back in a rictus that exposed his teeth and gums. Just as Lyon calculated that they had no more than an hour to live, they stumbled upon a path made by Eskimos. Ten minutes later they were back aboard ship. The swift and unexpected horror of the trip shook Parry as much as it did Lyon. Future exploration would have to wait until the season was more advanced.

Lyon used the days to become better acquainted with the Eskimos. On 18 March he was treated to a display of dancing by a group of

Eskimo women whose 'gestures became indecent and wanton to the highest degree'.[24] Their husbands being away, they had posted children to keep look-out while they entertained the white man. Lyon returned after three hours. 'This was the first instance of any exhibitions which had the slightest indelicate tendency,'[25] he wrote levelly.

For his part, Parry experimented with a new method for drying the ship's laundry. He was pleased to find that wet clothes hung on a black-painted cloth dried in three hours, despite a temperature of 5 °F above zero. However, his attempts at constructing a greenhouse failed. Although the temperature sometimes reached 100 °F under glass, the vegetables were wretched.

By May the Eskimos had departed for their northern hunting grounds, and the igloo camp was empty. As he surveyed the remains, whose once-pristine frosted-glass walls were now blackened with soot, and whose floors were strewn with a slurry of frozen blood and blubber, Lyon wrote that 'of all the miserable places on earth, a snow village recently deserted is the most gloomy'.[26] Even the ice 'windows' had been removed for re-use later on.

It was another month before the ships could push on. Four men died during that period of various ailments. None of them had scurvy, which was a blessing, but the casualty rate was nonetheless uncomfortably high.

By mid-July, after an aggravating voyage during which the *Fury* and *Hecla* were grazed, nudged, heeled over and sprung at by icebergs and floes, they were off Igloolik Island, having found the Eskimo charts to be perfectly accurate. And a few days later they were rowing ashore to the coast of North America. In a sign of divine approbation the sea was now so calm that the spray from their oars ran like mercury in little, silvery globules across the surface, resting there for five or six seconds before the brilliant drops suddenly merged with the water below.

At this point they split into two land parties. One under Parry went north to spy the presumed strait which led to the west. The other under Lyon travelled with a guide from Igloolik to purchase salmon from a nearby Eskimo settlement. Lyon inquired with typical gusto into Eskimo life. Since he 'had fortunately served a kind of apprenticeship to bad and unsavoury food',[27] he had no difficulty eating the Eskimo diet. Raw venison was so good that he was 'confident that were it not from prejudice [it] might be considered a dainty'.[28] He and his companion 'made our breakfast on a choice slice from the spine, and found it so good, the windpipe in particular, that at dinner-time we preferred the same food to our share of the preserved meats'.[29]

Lyon ate everything he was offered – 'had it been carrion, I would not have hurt them by refusing it'.[30] He even partook of a special delicacy, the half-digested contents of the deer's stomach, 'on the principle that no man who wishes to conciliate or inquire into the habits of savages should refuse to fare as they do'.[31] He recorded manfully that it tasted 'as near as I could judge a mixture of sorrel and radish leaves'.[32] He attended wild parties and slept the night off in an Eskimo hut. 'But at midnight I was awakened by a feeling of great warmth, and to my surprise found myself covered by a large deer-skin, under which lay my friend, his two wives and their favourite puppy, all fast asleep and stark naked. Supposing this was all according to rule, I left them to repose in peace and resigned myself to sleep.'[33]

He went hunting with the men and killed a deer, having mastered the art of making a deer-call. He endeared himself to the women, two of whom added to his collection of tattoos. And he made friends with the children, who were 'so very rosy and pretty, that in spite of their dirt, I longed to kiss them'.[34] He taught them how to do cats' cradles and how to play leap-frog but failed to master the trick they offered in return – that of drawing a piece of sinew up a nostril and producing it out of the mouth.

While Lyon was enjoying himself in this manner, Parry was toiling northwards. He returned to the ships on 21 August with the gratifying news that a large but frozen passage lay to the west-north-west through which rushed a strong, eastward-flowing current; beyond it he had seen open water. He named it the Strait of Fury and Hecla and within a few days had the ships hovering off its entrance, ready to drill through any gap that seemed in the slightest promising.

As had happened on the voyage to Melville Bay, Parry's compasses became temporarily so sluggish as to be useless. This delighted Lyon, who wrote with misplaced confidence to a friend that 'we have found the magnetic pole – but this entre nous, until my observations are laid before the Board of Longitude'.[35] Parry was more cautious, surmising only that the North Magnetic Pole must be somewhere in the region between Fury and Hecla Strait and Prince Regent Inlet. However, the interference was so strong that he ordered his men to build a temporary lighthouse on shore, manned day and night, to keep them in their positions. He was not put off by the apparently solid mass of ice which blocked his way. As he had noted so often before, a choked coastline could clear itself in a matter of minutes given a good wind.

There was plenty of wind that September but the ice did not open. Reluctantly, Parry sawed the ships into a harbour on Igloolik and prepared for another winter. 'It required indeed but a single glance at the chart,' Parry wrote on 1 October, 'to perceive, that whatever the last summer's navigation had added to our geographical knowledge of the eastern coast of America, and its adjacent lands, very little had in reality been effected in furtherance of the North-West Passage. Even the actual discovery of the desired outlet into the Polar Sea, had been of no practical benefit in the prosecution of our enterprise; for we had only discovered this channel to find it impassable, and to see the barriers of nature impenetrably closed against us, to the utmost limit of the navigable season.'[36]

This was pessimistic stuff indeed, coming from a man like Parry. Nevertheless, he decided to give the strait one more season. It would be impossible, however, for both ships to make the voyage. By now they were halfway through their supplies and Parry calculated that even if they did find the passage it might take them several years to reach the Pacific. He therefore ordered Lyon to take the *Hecla* home as soon as the ice cleared, leaving the bulk of his food and fuel with the *Fury*.

The winter was little different from any other save that the ships, being in separate harbours a mile apart, were too distant to allow the

theatre to open. Deprived of this amusement, they contented themselves with studying the Eskimos. To Parry the Eskimos were a
mystery. He did not dismiss them out of hand because they looked
different – two men he described as 'perhaps as fine specimens of the
human race as almost any country can produce'.[37] Nor did he deny
them the ability to feel: on asking one man if he would like to come
to England and being refused on the grounds that it would make the
man's father cry, Parry enthused that 'these people may justly lay
equal claim with ourselves to those common feelings of our nature'.[38]

At the same time, he could not bring himself to admit any real
equality between Europeans and Eskimos. So many of their customs
were alien, such as abandoning babies if their mother died and strip-
ping newly bereaved widows of every possession. Their laws of
ownership outraged him: he simply could not understand how they
walked off with anything that took their fancy – he even threatened a
man with flogging for his theft. Their ingratitude was another puzz-
ling trait: why did they not say thank you for the many presents of iron
or wood? And their eating habits were something that simply staggered him. The sight of an Eskimo man lying on his back while his
wife stuffed his mouth with huge lumps of meat, chopping off the
excess with a sharp knife, and pausing only a moment before forcing
more in, until his stomach was like a drum and the man was in a near
stupor, was one that Parry would never forget. Eskimo table habits,
more than anything else, were what horrified Parry and every other
European who visited the Arctic. Even the broad-minded Lyon was
given pause. 'I am confident that starvation tends greatly to promote
merriment and good humour with an Esquimaux,'[39] he wrote.

That winter Parry put an Eskimo to the test. In the space of
twenty-one hours, eight of which were spent in sleep, the man put
away 10 lbs 4 oz of solids, 9 gallons of water, 1¼ pints of soup, 3½
glasses of raw spirits and one tumbler of grog (strong). Parry could not
believe it. Lyon, not to be outdone, put forward another contender. In
nineteen hours Lyon's man consumed 9 lbs 15 oz of walrus, seal,
bread, butter, candles, flour-and-oil, plus 2 quarts of soup and 4 quarts
of water. He lost narrowly. 'It must, however, be remembered,' said

Lyon the gamesman, 'that [Parry's] had two hours more time than my man who would in the same period have beaten him hollow.'[40]

Neither Parry nor Lyon truly understood what they were seeing. To them, any life that did not conform to European standards was inherently wrong. It was interesting, but it was wrong. They noted that the Eskimos survived in their environment, but they did not ask the question: how did they survive? How did they avoid scurvy, for example? The answer was that the Eskimos survived because they ate fresh meat whenever they could get it, however disgusting this may have seemed to Europeans. That, primarily, saved them from scurvy, along with the occasional piece of greenery from a deer's innards. It would be many years before Europeans realized the value of an Eskimo diet.

When the Eskimos began to leave in April, Parry turned his mind back to the quest. He had the *Hecla*'s stores transferred to his own ship, and trenches were dug around both vessels so that they could be caulked for the coming season. The prospects looked good for an early departure. The weather was mild and exquisitely beautiful, the deep purple horizon softening into a delicate rose sky across which floated gold-trimmed clouds. The snow melted, allowing Lyon to record a quite inexplicable sight: a series of long ridges, between four or five inches high, composed entirely of mouse dung. By July the ice was not only melting but positively erupting. In one place the floes convulsed with such power as to throw a block of ice measuring eight feet thick, and forty yards in circumference, more than 500 yards' distance.

Despite the promising conditions, Parry was worried about the expedition's health. For some reason his battery of anti-scorbutics was no longer working. On 30 July he reported that nine of his men were down with scurvy and the rest of the crew were much weaker than they had been a year before. 'We had at length been impressed,' he wrote, 'with the unpleasant conviction that a strong predisposition to disease existed among us, and that no very powerful exciting cause was wanting to make it more seriously apparent.'[41] When Mr Fife, the *Hecla*'s master, died on 6 August Parry began seriously to wonder 'whether the probable evil [of continuing] did not far outweigh the possible good'.[42] His mind was made up when he visited the strait and saw nothing but 'one vast expanse of solid ice'.[43]

The ships left Igloolik on 12 August and battled their way south. For much of the time they were beset amidst drifting floes and by the time they reached clear seas Parry estimated they had sailed only forty miles out of the last 160. They reached Lerwick in the Shetland Islands at noon on 10 October, having been away for twenty-seven months. That night every house in town was lit up in celebration, the church bells rang, and barrels of burning tar smoked in the streets.

As Parry himself acknowledged, the expedition had been 'a matter of extreme disappointment'.[44] True, he and Lyon had made interesting and original studies of Eskimo life, and the men had learned how to read a Bible. But they had made little progress towards finding the North-West Passage. 'Long and laborious . . . and extremely unsatisfactory'[45] was how Lyon described the voyage. It had also been, if rumours were to be believed, somewhat tense. Douglas Clavering, a fellow Arctic hand recently returned from surveying the coast of Greenland with Edward Sabine aboard the *Griper*, wrote of 'quarrels, misbehaviour and insubordination'.[46] From information passed to him by James Ross via Sabine it seemed that besides being a failure the expedition was 'also thought most disgraceful'[47] – so disgraceful that Parry intended taking none of his officers on his next voyage.

What was this disgrace? No hint of discord appears in either Parry's or Lyon's journals. More than forty years later, however, the American explorer C. F. Hall met an ancient Eskimo woman from the Igloolik region. In his diary he recorded her version of events. Parry, she said, had been her lover but had been ousted by Lyon and had become exceedingly jealous. In a further lurid snippet she revealed that Lyon had left two Eskimo sisters pregnant on his departure.

It is impossible to tell whether any of this is true. Parry definitely did take several of his officers on his next trip. And if there was any animosity between himself and Lyon it did not stop him giving him a chest of plate 'fit for the captain of a frigate', which Lyon saw as 'most delightful proof of the approbation of my conduct'.[48] Most likely the 'misbehaviour' and 'disgrace' revolved not around sex – Hall questioned his witness's reliability when he heard that she later accused him of trying to seduce her – but around some mundane matter such as wearing an inappropriate uniform to dinner or, the worst offence of all, daring to venture an opinion as to course, heading, weather or any other trifle with which the captain did not agree.

If not worthy of tabloid attention, the rumours do at least suggest that life on an Arctic expedition was not the pious progression of musical evenings, Sunday schools and theatrical performances that Parry's chronicle would suggest. More of this might have been aired in public had not Parry's achievement – and it was an achievement – been eclipsed by that of the long-forgotten John Franklin.

Franklin's overland expedition through Canada, which had left London in 1819, had returned during Parry's last winter at Igloolik. Their experiences had been the most appalling of any Arctic expedition to date, their story one of starvation, cannibalism and unimaginable hardship. Even to those who were by now used to journals of life in the frozen north, which Barrow's friend John Murray published so seamlessly, Franklin's odyssey was without compare. He was regarded with near-superstitious awe. Parry may have been a capable explorer but Franklin – he was a hero.

Parry, the Arctic superman, had been hoping to augment his fame. But what had he done of note compared with Franklin? As Lyon wrote, 'his quarto will, I fear, appear to great disadvantage by that of the suffering & patient Franklin'.[49]

Franklin was the only name on people's lips, even a year after his return. Society devoured him and ordinary people pointed him out in the street. His journal had become an overnight bestseller and was in such demand that second-hand copies changed hands for ten guineas. He was popularly known as 'the man who ate his boots'. And he had, too.

9

THE MAN WHO ATE
HIS BOOTS

In 1819 the geography of North America was little better known than that of Baffin Bay. It was widely accepted, even by Barrow, that Canada had to stop somewhere. But its northern coastline had only been touched upon in two places. In 1789 Alexander Mackenzie had followed the river since named after him and found open sea at a point about 1,000 miles east of Bering Strait. He had been preceded in 1771 by Samuel Hearne who had done the same with the Coppermine River, meeting the ocean 500 miles east of the Mackenzie. Franklin's job was to fill in the gaps.

Barrow's intention was that Franklin should travel overland with boats and canoes to the Great Slave Lake, follow the Coppermine River from there to its mouth and then take to the sea. He would take a bare minimum of naval personnel, using hired help supplied by the Hudson's Bay Company or its larger competitor, the North West Company. Orkney boatmen would see him through the first part of his journey, after which their place would be taken by Canadian porters, or voyageurs, who would escort him from the Great Slave Lake to the coast. Indian and Eskimo guides would assist him and provide whatever food was necessary should his stores run out. On reaching the coast he was advised to go east, either to rendezvous with Parry or to make his way to Repulse Bay, but if he wanted he could go west to the Mackenzie and if he really felt like it he could even go north into the unknown.

The vagueness of Franklin's instructions was perhaps forgivable. Less so was the spirit of penny-pinching that underpinned them. Instead of being a self-contained venture, the expedition was to rely entirely on outside help. Directors of the two Canadian companies had met Franklin in London and offered him their support. But the official announcement bore no resemblance to reality. Only four years earlier the two fur behemoths had been in a state of open war, mobilizing Indian tribes to attack and imprison each other's agents. Although the situation had calmed down, the area was still riven by rivalry. Cooperation was a flag of convenience which could be lowered at any moment, and neither company was actually keen to expend valuable resources in the frivolous and unprofitable cause of exploration. Essentially, Franklin was being ordered to hitch-hike through a war zone into a wilderness.

There was one baffling aspect to the expedition, which was politely not mentioned at the time. Of all the people available to lead it, why had Barrow chosen Franklin?

Born in 1786, in Spilsby, Lincolnshire, into a family with no history of naval service, John Franklin was a beefy, genial giant who literally could not hurt a fly. He was formal, painfully shy and abnormally sensitive: to order, let alone witness, a flogging made him tremble from head to toe. His religious conviction was profound – but lacking Parry's zeal – to the extent that he refused to sully the sabbath even by writing a letter. He carried with him a twelve-point check-list entitled 'Have I this day walked with God?' As for fame, he wanted none of it. In April 1819 a panorama was shown at Leicester Square of Buchan's expedition. Franklin featured prominently. 'I shall not venture to approach very near,' he told his sister, 'for fear the passers-by should say, "There goes the fellow in the panorama."'[1]

On the face of it this hesitant and rather nice man lacked all the qualities necessary for such an expedition. Buchan would have been the obvious choice, being an experienced leader who had not only commanded the 1818 expedition to the North Pole but had previous experience of land exploration in Canada. However, Buchan seems not to have been approached – or if approached had refused. So the lot fell to Franklin.

Franklin was brave, determined and would obey orders to the letter. He had a good war record, having served at the battle of Trafalgar and the battle of New Orleans. He had also sailed with Flinders on the first-ever circumnavigation of Australia, a feat of which Barrow was eternally admiring. The deciding factor, however, seems to have been Franklin's charm. Everyone who met him agreed that this was his outstanding characteristic – it was impossible not to like him.

It is hard to gauge the extent of Franklin's likeableness from his letters. To family and fellow officers alike he seems to have maintained an aloof stiffness, and yet he managed to catch an exceptional wife: Eleanor Porden, a beautiful, fiercely intelligent but consumptive blue-stocking who had attended Royal Society lectures since the age of nine and at sixteen had written a poem on scientific discovery which was received so well that she had been admitted to the French Institute in Paris. She and Franklin had conducted an awkward romance ever since his return from the North Pole in 1818 and were eventually married in 1823.

It can only have been Franklin's charm that won him the leadership of the 1819 Canadian expedition because he had nothing else to recommend him. Aged thirty-three, he was overweight and suffered from a poor circulation that left his fingers and toes cold even in an English summer. He was unfit and had no experience of land travel. He could not hunt, canoe or trek. Three meals a day were a must; he could not move without tea; and even when he could move he could manage no more than eight miles a day unless he was carried. These last details were recorded with dismay by Governor George Simpson of the Hudson's Bay Company, who had responsibility for the Athabasca district through which Franklin was to travel.

The large doughty man – 'The Happy Voyager', as one biographer describes him – left Gravesend on 23 May accompanied by five Britons. As Franklin's right-hand man Barrow had chosen Dr John Richardson, a solemn, diligent Scot who had been a surgeon in the Royal Marines. He was to be the expedition's naturalist, a post which he accepted readily because, 'if I succeed in making a good collection, I have no doubt of promotion on my return'.[2] He admitted that 'my knowledge of these subjects is very limited',[3] but that seemed to worry no one. As draughtsmen and artists Barrow appointed two midshipmen, the shy, romantic Robert Hood and a conceited bounder named George Back who had served under Franklin in the *Trent*. Two ordinary seamen were chosen to accompany them: John Hepburn and Samuel Wilks, the latter of whom retired sick on reaching Canada.

From the start there was a disorganized note to proceedings. The ship stopped temporarily off the Norfolk coast where Back found a need to engage himself 'upon some business at a house two or three miles from Yarmouth'.[4] Then, while Back was tucking his shirt in, a favourable wind arose and Franklin had to sail off, leaving Back to find his way to their next stop in the Orkneys. Thrashing his way north by coach and finishing with a thirty-mile boat crossing, Back arrived at Stromness nine days later, only a few hours behind Franklin, to find a celebratory dance already underway in the local hall. Unfazed, he threw himself into proceedings with vigour and 'could not be prevailed to withdraw from the agreeable scene until a late hour'.[5]

Here Franklin met his first obstacle: very few Orkney boatmen wanted to join the expedition. The way in which they dithered, dickered and weighed up their chances formed 'a singular contrast with the ready and thoughtless manner in which an English seaman enters upon any enterprise, however hazardous, without inquiring or desiring to know where he is going or what he is going about'.[6] In the end, only four men signed on and even then only until Fort Chipewyan on Lake Athabasca.

By 9 August they had reached Resolution Island and twenty-one days later they were at York Factory, the main port on the south-west corner of Hudson Bay. From here it was 500 miles to Cumberland House, a depot on the Saskatchewan River, and from there another 850 miles to Fort Chipewyan and a further 350 miles to the Great Slave Lake. To complete this immense journey Franklin was supplied by the two companies with a boat that was too small to hold all his supplies – the remainder would be sent on, he was cheerfully informed – and yet too heavy to surmount the various portages they would encounter along the Saskatchewan. Having on one occasion dragged the boat through a quarter of a mile of deep bog, and on another having spent a whole day covering a stretch of 1,300 yards, the men insisted Franklin unload part of his stores or he would never reach Cumberland House. Thus another chunk of cargo was left behind – hopefully, once again, to be forwarded.

The expedition reached Cumberland House in October, the spray from their oars freezing before it hit the water. By the first week of November the river was frozen over and all hope of further travel was postponed until spring. Cumberland House was little more than a log cabin, with reindeer parchment stretched across the windows in place of glass. It housed some thirty Hudson's Bay men, and was served by 120 Cree Indian hunters who brought in produce from an area of 20,000 square miles. Normally the Cree lived their own separate existence but this winter, which was exceptionally bad, they poured into Cumberland House to collect provisions. Franklin was told that conditions were so appalling that some families had started eating each other.

Franklin left on 8 January for Fort Chipewyan, taking Back and Hepburn with him, to arrange voyageurs and supplies for the next leg of their journey. He was quite unprepared for the long march overland through Canada's pine forests. The weather was abominably cold: their thermometers froze, their scientific instruments froze, their tea froze seconds after it had been poured. At night they too froze, in the absence of any tents. They counted it a stroke of fortune if an insulating layer of snow fell on their blankets.

Almost as bad as the cold was the discomfort of travelling in native snowshoes, which for a man like Franklin was even more arduous than walking. As Hood described the journey, 'The sufferer feels his frame crushed by unaccountable pressure; he drags a galling and stubborn weight at his feet, and his track is marked with blood . . . When he arises from sleep, half his body seems dead, till quickened into feeling by the irritation of his sores.'[7] In spite of the discomfort, Franklin remained in stolid good humour. In fact, his companions were awed by his placidity. Once when a mosquito landed on his arm he simply blew it off. Hepburn asked why he didn't give it a good swat. Franklin's eerily saintly reply was that there was enough room in the world for the two of them.

Led by Canadian guides who drove the suffering tenderfoots along at an average eleven miles per day, they reached Fort Chipewyan on 26 March 1820, having covered precisely 857 miles – eleven miles less than the distance from Land's End to John O' Groats. The journey brought 'a great intermixture of agreeable and disagreeable circumstances', Franklin wrote understatedly. 'Could the amount of each be balanced, I suspect the latter would much preponderate.'[8]

At Fort Chipewyan, Franklin was lucky enough to meet someone who could tell him a little of what lay ahead. Peter Dease, a North West Company employee, had spent several winters north of Great Slave Lake and was able to provide a sketchy outline of the topography and the conditions ahead – snow and ice featured prominently in both cases.

But that was where Franklin's luck ended. The voyageurs, whom Barrow had considered so easily hired, showed no interest in the scheme. They did not like the idea of the sea; they feared the possibility of marauding Indians; they were unused to such long and arduous journeys – 160 miles or so was their usual distance; and they did not know the country. As for food, the best Franklin could elicit was the promise that hunters would supply their needs along the way, and that the chief of the Coppermine Indians was willing to help them. Nobody had enough that year. At one post he had been informed that they had only 500 pounds of dried meat for the coming season; five years earlier they had had 30,000 pounds.

Anticipating something of the sort, Franklin had ordered

Richardson and Hood to collect supplies from trading posts as they came up from Cumberland House in the summer. But when Richardson's party finally arrived at Fort Chipewyan on 12 July, it brought disappointing news: the North West Company had given them ten bags of pemmican – a nutritious Indian recipe of pounded, dried meat mixed with fat – which were so mouldy they had to be thrown away; and the Hudson's Bay men had given them nothing at all, having eaten the provisions put aside. All Richardson could show for his exertions was pemmican sufficient to last one day.

Somehow, Franklin managed to scratch up a limited amount of food and a gang of sixteen voyageurs consisting mostly of the men Richardson had brought with him from Cumberland House. Three of the voyageurs' wives also joined the group – with their children – to make moccasins and clothes at the next winter stop. Few of the voyageurs were up to the standard required. But what could Franklin do? Every man worth his salt was needed to fight the two Companies' 'disgraceful and barbarous'[9] internal war. 'The complement required for this arduous enterprise was complied with but the quality caused some little demur,' sympathized a Hudson's Bay employee, Colin Robertson, that summer. 'This [is] a most unfortunate juncture for an undertaking of so much hazard ... men of known fidelity accustomed to the manners and habits of the natives are so necessary in the present contest, that I fear the Captain's portion of good men bears no proportion to those of inferior character. He appears to be an amiable, gentlemanly man, and I regret the painful situation he is placed in, from the strong party spirit that at present exists in this part of the country.'[10]

Franklin left Fort Chipewyan on 18 July and reached his next stop, Fort Providence on the north shore of Great Slave Lake, ten days later. Here, through the agency of a North West interpreter, Mr Wentzel, he made contact with the Indians who would be hunting for him in the months to come. Their leader, a man 'of very grave aspect'[11] named Akaitcho, smoked a pipe, downed a dram then embarked on a long 'harangue'[12] in which he explained that happy as he was to see them he would be even happier if he profited from the meeting. And what exactly was the purpose of their journey? Akaitcho was an intelligent man, 'of great penetration and shrewdness'.[13] He quickly grasped the concept of the North-West Passage and listened contentedly to Franklin's half-truths that its discovery would bring valuable commerce to the region. He inquired about Franklin's expedition and asked some surprisingly acute questions about Parry's pincer movement coming from the north. Then, with an air of innocence, he wondered why, if it was so important to trade, the North-West Passage had not been discovered before. Franklin was stumped.

Having made his point, Akaitcho set out his terms. He would do his best to help them provided he was rewarded with cloth, ammunition, tobacco, weapons, a few tools and the discharge of all debts he and his men had incurred with the North West Company. Most importantly, however, he did not want to enter Eskimo territory. The harmless, happy-go-lucky people whom Parry and Ross had encountered were viewed with fear and hatred by the Indians. Usually each side kept to themselves, but on their traditional border, the climate line between mostly frozen land and mostly unfrozen land, they occasionally fought battles. On Samuel Hearne's journey down the Coppermine River, for example, an Eskimo group had been massacred at a place called Bloody Falls by a party of Indians. It had been such a hideous and traumatic occasion for both peoples that neither was willing to approach the area. The Indians feared retaliation, the Eskimos a recurrence. Further, Akaitcho warned that game would be scarce in the northern regions, particularly in this hard year, and that a constant supply of food could not be guaranteed. That being understood, Akaitcho declared himself satisfied with the deal.

Barrow's plan was springing apart at the seams. Instead of the tight group living off available resources, which had been envisaged, Franklin's party had already amassed nineteen dependent voyageurs. Now it had collected at least an equal number of Indians who would have to feed themselves as well as their charges. Barrow's skeleton approach to land travel was correct but in this instance its application was flawed. Had Franklin been travelling through Africa, say, where food was more-or-less readily available, his core of European explorers would have been fine. Had the party been smaller – two or three fit men – it could have foraged its way across the Arctic with little difficulty. But this expedition fell between two stools: it wasn't an opportunistic darter of the kind that would later criss-cross the Arctic (ironically in search of Franklin himself) nor was it a self-contained bruiser like Parry's, currently stuck at Melville Island.

Franklin's intention was to travel to a suitable spot near the Coppermine, where he would build a home to see them through the winter. The next summer his group would make its way downriver until they reached the sea. At this juncture his guides would be sent back and a reduced party would take to the sea in canoes, mapping the coast to the eastward for as long as their supplies lasted. If they reached Repulse Bay they hoped to obtain sufficient food from local Eskimos to carry them back to York Factory. If, however, they were unable to reach their goal they would retrace their steps or take a short-cut home through the so-called Barren Lands, whichever seemed best.

The plan was haphazard to the point of foolhardiness. But in that respect it differed little from the overall tenor of the undertaking. As George Simpson wrote, with some asperity, 'it appears to me that the mission was projected and entered into without mature consideration and the necessary previous arrangements totally neglected'.[14]

On Sunday, 20 August, a forest fire engulfed a portion of land about 150 miles from Fort Providence, clouding the area with smoke for three days. Akaitcho, who had been expecting a small signal fire to announce Franklin's presence at the chosen winter camp, must have sighed in exasperation. Still, the white men had arrived safely.

This exuberant display of incompetence marked the completion of Franklin's eighteen-day voyage from Fort Providence. In the frigid Canadian winter fire was feared more than the cold. Surrounded as they were by trees, and with all available water frozen over, the voyageurs had long learned to be careful with flame. But this was the third fire Franklin had allowed to get out of hand. One conflagration had already burned down his tent and only Hepburn's quick actions had saved the stock of gunpowder which had been stored within. Another had almost destroyed the entire camp, causing its rapid evacuation. On a fourth occasion, which did not quite qualify as a major incident, Back's fur blanket had caught light while he was sleeping in it.

Tough, tundra-wise people, the voyageurs began to have serious misgivings about their leader. He knew nothing about the land. To compound their doubts, Franklin's food had begun to give out on the third day from Fort Providence. By the tenth his stores were exhausted. Only a few deer carcasses brought in by Akaitcho's men had seen them to their present position.

The voyageurs have often been targeted as the weak point on this fateful expedition – unfairly. They weren't the finest of their kind but they were nevertheless professionals who were at home with their job and had a good understanding of what it entailed. Given enough food, and a fixed goal, they would have been capable of achieving anything. However, they were going into an uncharted region under a man who knew not the first thing about survival and who could not even provide them with enough food. For men whose efficiency was related directly to calorie intake this was an unforgivable sin. They made their discontent clear, forcing Franklin to quell a mutiny with harsh words: 'I therefore felt the duty incumbent upon me to address them in the strongest manner on the danger of insubordination, and to assure them of my determination to inflict the heaviest punishment on any that should persist in their refusal to go on, or in any other way to attempt to retard the Expedition.'[15] The placid Franklin, it seemed, could rouse himself when the occasion demanded it.

The spot Akaitcho had chosen for the winter was perfect, being near a river and surrounded by pine trees mature enough to shelter them from the worst gales. Franklin's fire had compromised the shelter but his men were soon at work felling charred trees to construct an encampment called Fort Enterprise. It comprised a five-room log cabin for the four officers with a rather smaller one for the sixteen voyageurs. Left to their own devices, Akaitcho's forty Indians huddled round as best they could.

Throughout the winter Franklin was beset by problems. Supplies came through only intermittently thanks to the rival Companies' habit of either appropriating them for their own use or, in some cases, simply dumping them because one or other side was not doing its fair share. Ammunition supplies became so low that Franklin was forced to melt down pewter mugs for bullets. But the five rounds he was able to give each hunter were simply wasted – the Indians had no heart for hunting when they could stay in the relative comfort of Fort Enterprise. Finally, Franklin sent Back to stir the authorities into action. He returned after a remarkable 1,200-mile trek in snowshoes 'having succeeded in the procuration of supplies beyond [Franklin's] most sanguine expectations'.[16]

Back was an effective ambassador, giving short shrift to anyone who stood in his way. He browbeat both Companies' representatives at every stop between Fort Enterprise and Cumberland House so successfully that George Simpson complained about his 'impertinent interference in our affairs'.[17] He wrote to one trader that Back had got away with too much. 'That Gentleman seems to think that every thing must give way to his demands,'[18] he stormed.

Back's extraordinary journey benefited the expedition in more ways than one. Shortly before he left, he and Hood had been at log-gerheads over the daughter of one of the Indian hunters, a beautiful sixteen-year-old Indian girl called Greenstockings. Both men fancied themselves as Lotharios: Hood adopted a subtle and effective approach, fathering at least one child during the winter; Back took a more direct, aggressive tack which seems not to have worked. Greenstockings became such a bone of contention that the two mid-shipmen were ready to fight a duel over her, and would have done so had not Hepburn secretly removed the charges from their pistols. There was, Simpson wrote, 'a want of unanimity among them-selves'.[19] Back's prolonged absence can have done nothing but good.

The want of unanimity was not confined to the officers. It engulfed the whole enterprise. The North West clerk at Fort Providence, a man named Weeks, had been spreading rumours about Franklin and his men. They were opportunists, he said, who lived off the

Company's credit and the goodwill of their employees. He refused to honour Franklin's bills and advised the Indians to go no further. The Hudson's Bay Company was also against Franklin, thanks to reports – unsubstantiated – of his having taken sides in the Companies' dispute. Simpson wrote a stern letter to one of his factors, advising him to give Franklin no more supplies, and warning him that Back was probably a spy for the other camp.

At the same time, the voyageurs were getting restless. Spurred by two of their number, the interpreters Pierre St Germain and Jean Baptiste Adam, they complained that the expedition was heading for certain death. This time Franklin's bluster was ineffectual. On being threatened with a trial in England, St Germain laughed. 'It is immaterial to me where I lose my life,' he said, 'for the whole party will perish.'[20] The situation would have become ugly had not Wentzel intervened. He placated the Indians, pointing out that they had entered into the agreement with the full knowledge that Franklin could only pay them by writs which would be honoured at a later stage. He also mediated with the voyageurs until the *status quo* was restored. But a lingering notion of distrust was not dispelled until Akaitcho was satisfied that Franklin had not concealed hidden stores for the use of himself and his men. Thus the winter passed in discontent until 4 June 1821 when Franklin set out for the Coppermine.

Once moving, the expedition's squabbles faded, but were soon replaced by other problems. The Indian guides, who knew the region little better than Franklin himself, proved useless. Crossing a frozen lake they directed him to its west shore, then, suddenly remembering an important feature in the landscape, they sent him to the north-east. The ocean was now distant, now near. 'Our reliance on the information of the guides, which had been for some time shaken, was now quite at an end,'[21] Franklin wrote on 14 July, having climbed a hill to get a view of the promised sea to find 'a plain similar to that we had just left, terminated by another range of trap hills, between whose tops the summits of some distant blue mountains appeared'.[22] Richardson, however, always more willing to trust the natives, walked another three miles that evening and spied the sought-after Arctic

Ocean. To his disappointment but no great surprise, it was covered with ice. He brought his news back to camp as the sun's last rays fell on the surrounding peaks.

They had crossed the line dividing Indian territory from Eskimo and Akaitcho's men were becoming increasingly nervous, especially when they reached Bloody Falls to find an Eskimo encampment still in place. But its occupants had already fled at the Indians' approach, leaving their dogs, tents and food behind. If Franklin needed a reminder that food was scarce, the Eskimo camp provided it. The dried salmon was putrid and covered with maggots. Hung out to dry on wooden frames was their future sustenance: a number of small birds and two mice. Apart from one elderly cripple and his wife, who had been unable to evacuate and who prodded feebly at the intruders with a brass-tipped spear, the Eskimos kept their distance. Occasionally, they could be spotted hovering singly at a safe distance, but despite all attempts to draw them into conversation they could not be tempted nearer.

Even this, however, was too much for the Indians. They left for home on 18 July, according to the agreement Akaitcho had made with Franklin. The following day Wentzel also left, leaving Franklin with fifteen men: the two interpreters, St Germain and Adam, plus thirteen others whose names were Augustus, Junius, Michel Teroahauté, Joseph Benoit, Credit, Registe Vaillant, Jean Baptiste Belanger and Solomon Belanger, Gabriel Beauparlant, Fontano, Ignace Perrault, Joseph Peltier and François Samandré. Of these, St Germain and Adam wanted to go with Wentzel, arguing not unreasonably that their services were no longer needed now the Indians had gone. However, much as Franklin would have liked to rid himself of the trouble-makers, they were the best hunters in the party. He put them under twenty-four-hour watch until Wentzel and the Indians were a safe distance upriver.

To every man who left, Franklin gave strict instructions that depots of food were to be left at various points inland and, in particular, that a large supply of dried meat was to be cached at Fort Enterprise. This last was of vital importance because Franklin feared that should

he fail to reach Repulse Bay – and it was looking increasingly likely
that he would – he would nevertheless have gone sufficiently far to be
cut off from the Coppermine by winter ice. Therefore he would have
to travel overland through the uncharted territory of the Barren Lands
to Fort Enterprise, relying for food on whatever could be shot or
trapped *en route*. As the ground was almost certainly empty at that
time of the year they would be near starving-point by the time they
reached base and thus it was imperative that Fort Enterprise be well
stocked.

Franklin drummed this fact into Wentzel. Then, a few days later,
he set off for the coast in three bark canoes containing fourteen days'
provisions and a group of voyageurs who were terrified of the sea –
they had never seen it – who were equally terrified of the Eskimos
they might meet on land, who had limited hunting skills and who
were appalled at the prospect of hunger. 'It is of no use to speak to a
Canadian voyageur of going upon short allowance,' wrote Richardson.
'They prefer running the risk of going entirely without hereafter, that
they may have a present belly full, and if it is not given to them they
will steal it and in their opinion it is no disgrace to be caught pilfering
provisions.'[23] Several men, he noted, had 'secreted and distributed
among themselves a bag of small shot. They hope thus to be
enabled . . . privately to procure ducks and geese and to avoid the
necessity of sharing them with the officers.'[24] These words, which
appeared in Richardson's journal on Thursday 19 July 1821, were followed with supreme lack of concern by a one-page description of the
starry flounder.

The three canoes reached open sea – Richardson had either miscon-
strued the state of the ice or it had opened since – and scuttled
eastwards. They followed the coastline along every creek and inden-
tation for 555 miles before Franklin called a halt. During this time
storms had arisen which broke fifteen timbers in one canoe, nearly
separated the struts from the bark in another and had the voyageurs
gibbering with terror. Despite frequent landings they had amassed
only a bare sufficiency of food – for which Franklin blamed the baleful

influence of St Germain and Adam: 'we now strongly suspected that their recent want of success in hunting had proceeded from an intentional relaxation in their efforts to kill deer in order that the want of provisions might compel us to put a period to our voyage.'[25]

On 18 August, Franklin walked overland to mark his furthest point east – the aptly named Point Turnagain. Then, on 22 August 1821, the very day, unknown to him, that Parry had sailed into Repulse Bay, he turned back for Fort Enterprise. As he had feared, Franklin had explored himself into a corner. The seas were too rough to reach the Coppermine, and the deer had already begun to move south for the winter. He therefore made for the mouth of what he called Hood's River, a spot they had visited on their outward journey, which seemed to lead in the direction of Fort Enterprise and where they had sighted plenty of game. This would be the short side of a triangle that would lead them back to their winter base with its stores of dried meat.

The voyage to Hood's River took three days, during which Franklin was pleased to see that the voyageurs were at last exerting themselves, driven by the prospect of being once more in their element. On landing he ordered the large, sea-going canoes broken up to build two smaller, portable versions that could be carried overland and launched whenever one of Canada's unpredictable rivers blocked their path.

The voyageurs were overjoyed to be on land again. But they were less happy when Franklin forbade them dinner. The deer had migrated south and those that remained were too shy to be shot. Pemmican was limited. That evening, the first of many, they went without dinner.

The canoes were hard to carry. They blew about in the wind and scraped against sharp rocks which also ripped the men's moccasins to shreds. The going was treacherous, and as Richardson remarked, 'If any one had broken a limb here, his fate would have been melancholy indeed, we could neither have remained with him, nor carried him on with us.'[26] Had they had the opportunity to escape, the voyageurs would have fled *en masse*. But they had nowhere to go.

The expedition's woes started in earnest in September with the premature arrival of winter. Confined to their tent by a howling storm, they ate their last piece of pemmican on 4 September. Three days later, when the weather had lessened, they resumed their march. Before they even started Franklin fainted from a combination of hunger and exposure. That same day the voyageurs dropped one of the canoes, rendering it useless (this was a greater disaster than at first realized as the remaining canoe had been accidentally built too small and was therefore unable to cross a river of any size without being lashed to its larger counterpart). Franklin had strong suspicions that the canoe had been dropped on purpose, but making the best of things, he used the remains as firewood to heat the last of their supplies – a tin of soup.

From now on they had nothing to eat save what could be had from the land. The game had not altogether disappeared. They were able to shoot the occasional deer but it was not enough to satisfy their hunger, and even when they made a kill they were so overburdened that they although they got a good meal at the time they could not carry the excess with them. The voyageurs, whose standard ration was eight pounds of meat a day, and who were carrying some ninety pounds apiece, were hardest hit. One can blame them for their stupidity, but little else, when they secretly threw away the expedition's weighty fishing nets. The loss infuriated Franklin. But by now even he was willing to jettison articles. In a belated purge, he deposited Richardson's natural history specimens, most of the expedition's scientific instruments and the hefty manuals which were required for their operation.

As the winter worsened the game became scarce, then it vanished altogether. They were driven to eating lichen from the rocks, an acrid and barely nutritious growth which induced severe diarrhoea. Many of them could stomach no more than a few mouthfuls. In a sleight of hand worthy of the finest restaurant, they dubbed it *tripes de roche*.

On 14 September, while crossing a river, the canoe overturned. With it went Franklin's journal. Solomon Belanger was stranded in mid-river, up to his waist in freezing water for several minutes until he was rescued. 'He was instantly stripped,' wrote Richardson, 'and being rolled up in blankets, two men undressed themselves and went to bed with him – but it was some hours before he recovered his warmth and sensation.'[27]

The following day they were lucky enough to shoot a deer. But that, apart from another deer on 25 September and a single partridge on 29 October, was to be their only game for another two months. During that period they lived off *tripes de roche*, augmented by a few scraps of deer skin from which the hair had first been singed. Occasionally, if they were lucky, they might find the remains of a wolf kill left over from the previous season. Although lacking any meat, the bones could be made edible by heating them in the fire. Anything that could be eaten was eaten, right down to their spare shoes which, having been either roasted or boiled, were 'greedily devoured'.[28] In fact, their shoes were probably the most palatable item on the menu. The *tripes de roche* caused diarrhoea, and the charred bones were so acrid, even when made into soup, that their mouths became ulcerated. The few sections of putrid spinal marrow which they managed to suck from the backbones of dead deer took the skin off their lips.

The expedition began to break up, both physically and mentally. The line elongated and split as the stronger members forged ahead, and the weaker dropped behind. Back led the way, with some of the fitter voyageurs. But while Richardson was able to keep pace in the centre, Franklin and Hood fell back to the rear. Hood, racked by diarrhoea from the *tripes de roche*, which seemed to affect him more than the others, was fading fast.

The voyageurs, meanwhile, were well nigh uncontrollable. On 23 September Richardson recorded with despair that 'The canoe was broken today and left behind, notwithstanding every remonstrance. The men had become desperate and were perfectly regardless of the commands of the officers.'[29] Only with the greatest difficulty could they be persuaded not to drop everything and make a mad dash for Fort Enterprise. That they did not do so owed less to the officers' commands than the fact that they did not know where Fort Enterprise was.

The men's belief that Franklin knew where he was going was all
that kept them even vaguely obedient. But the truth was that
Franklin did not really know where he was. The countryside was
hilly and unfamiliar. The magnetic deviation for this area was
unknown, making it impossible to adjust their compass readings with
any degree of accuracy. And in weather conditions that ranged from
thick snow, through thick rain, to thick mist, they were unable to
take their bearings from the sun. When they did catch a brief glimpse
of the sun and adjusted their course accordingly, it merely sowed the
suspicion that Franklin was lost.

A mutiny would have been inevitable had they not reached on 26
September a river which, from its size and course, could only have
been the Coppermine. From his calculations Franklin reckoned Fort
Enterprise was only forty miles away. The news cheered everyone, as
did the discovery of a deer carcase whose meat, although putrid, was
cooked and eaten on the spot. When this failed to satisfy, the
intestines were scraped up and thrown into the pot. The chance discovery of a number of cranberry and blueberry bushes added further
to their joy. But even so, wrote Richardson, 'nothing could allay our
inordinate appetites'.[30]

After the euphoria came disappointment. They may well have
been forty miles from Fort Enterprise but in order to reach it they first
had to cross the swiftly flowing Coppermine which was here 120 yards
wide. They could possibly have managed it had they had even one
canoe. But they had none. 'They bitterly execrated their folly and
impatience in breaking the canoe,' Richardson wrote, 'and the
remainder of the day was spent in wandering slowly along the river,
looking in vain for a fordable place and inventing schemes for crossing, no sooner devised than abandoned.'[31]

The voyageurs, in the depths of despondency, all but gave up.
They became 'careless and disobedient, they had ceased to dread
punishment or hope for reward'.[32] At length, however, they rallied
round to construct a raft from the meagre willow trees which grew
along the river's bank. It was a poor vessel, the wood being green and
heavy with sap. At best it could carry only one man. And it was quite

unnavigable, the available trees being neither thick enough to make a paddle nor long enough to make a pole capable of reaching the bottom. However, if it could make just the initial trip, carrying a line to the opposite bank, then the expedition could be ferried across one by one. But the raft never reached the opposite bank. Driven back by adverse winds it went no further than the voyageurs, waist-deep in freezing water, could push it.

Then Richardson stepped forward. If the raft could make no headway maybe a swimmer could. Back was scouting ahead with his hunters. Richardson was the strongest officer left. Tying the line around his waist he launched himself into the river. For a man who was already reduced to skin and bone, and who suffered accordingly from degrees of cold that would normally have been disregarded, to willingly immerse himself in temperatures of less than 38 °F was an act of enormous bravery. Sadly, his courage achieved nothing. Only a short distance from the bank Richardson's arms became so numb that he could not move them. Turning on his back, he kicked on with his legs. He had almost reached the other side when his legs too gave out and he sank to the riverbed. Seeing him go under, the others hauled on the line and drew him back to safety. When they dragged him ashore he was unable to move and could barely speak. Following his muttered instructions they placed him beside a fire and waited for sensation to reappear. Several hours later he was finally strong enough to crawl into a tent. But the whole of his left side was paralysed and although feeling was gradually restored his left arm and leg did not regain their full strength for another five months. To make matters worse he had stepped on a knife just before diving into the river and had cut his foot to the bone.

In any other circumstance Richardson would have been carried as an invalid for the rest of the journey. But hunger allowed neither invalids nor carriers. They were all in the same state. Richardson's body, when stripped of clothes, was a horrible mirror to the others of how far they had sunk. 'I cannot describe,' wrote Franklin, 'what everyone felt at beholding the skeleton which the doctor's debilitated frame exhibited.'[33] The voyageurs were aghast. 'Ah! que nous sommes maigres!'[34] they exclaimed simultaneously.

Ironically, it was St Germain, the voyageurs' discontented ring-leader, who came up with a solution. He volunteered to make a canoe from willow branches and the canvas in which their bedding was wrapped. It took him two days to complete the task, during which time the whole party almost disintegrated. The voyageurs, utterly downcast by Richardson's failure, reconciled themselves to death. They refused to gather *tripes de roche*, declaring they would rather die than waste their last hours harvesting such a revolting crop. Junius wandered off, presumably to find his own way home, and was never seen again.

Of the officers, Richardson was lame, Franklin was prostrate, Hood was so thin that he hardly cast a shadow and even the redoubtable Back could not stand without a stick. It was left to John Hepburn, the hero-seaman of the expedition, to gather a few scraps of lichen for his commanders. Their weakness can be gauged by Franklin's attempt on 3 October to visit St Germain at his canoe-building site. The voyageur was working in a grove of willows three-quarters of a mile distant. Franklin returned after three hours having been unable to reach his objective. They were now so famished that they did not care whether they ate or not. 'The sensation of hunger is no longer felt by us,'[35] Richardson recorded. Yet the memory of food lingered obstinately in their minds – 'we are scarcely able to converse upon any other subject than the pleasures of eating'.[36]

St Germain finished his slight, one-man canoe on 4 October. They 'assembled in anxious expectation'[37] as he set out and cheered as he carried a line to the other side. One by one they hauled themselves across, the canoe sinking lower with each crossing until the last men were in water to their knees. Their heaviest bundle, the spare clothes and bedding, was soaked through when it arrived.

They had crossed the Coppermine and had only forty miles to travel before they reached Fort Enterprise. At their previous rate of about six miles per day, salvation was only a week's march away. As they struggled forwards, however, it became obvious that even a week was too much for some. Far behind everybody else the two weakest voyageurs, Credit and Vaillant, collapsed. When Richardson tracked back to see what had happened, Vaillant was 'unable to rise and scarcely capable of replying to my questions'.[38] He died that day. Credit was never found.

Franklin split his party into two. Back, still hobbling on a stick, was sent ahead with Solomon Belanger, Beauparlant and St Germain to contact Akaitcho's Indians at Fort Enterprise and to bring supplies to the men who lagged behind. But once Back had gone, Richardson put forward another proposal: he himself was lame and Hood was so weak as to be incapable; why not leave the two of them, with Hepburn to act as nursemaid, while Franklin went ahead to intercept Back's supplies? Without the drag of its two weakest members, ran Richardson's reasoning, Franklin's party would have a better chance of survival. 'I was distressed beyond description at the thought of leaving them in such a dangerous situation, and for a long time combated their proposal'; Franklin wrote, 'but they strenuously urged that this step afforded the only chance of safety for the party, and I reluctantly acceded to it.'[39]

Franklin went only four and a half miles before he had a crisis. Two voyageurs – Michel and Jean Baptiste Belanger – declared themselves too weak to continue and asked permission to return to Richardson's camp. The voyageurs were by now in tatters, literally, having thrown aside their tent and cut the canvas into a manageable blanket. Franklin waved them off wearily. A little later another man, Perrault, burst into tears, declared he could go no further, and asked permission to follow Michel and Belanger. Once again Franklin consented. No snow had fallen, the tracks were still clear, and Perrault would have no difficulty finding his way back. A fourth voyageur, Fontano, was sent with him, having become so slow and weak that he was seriously jeopardizing the chances of the others. 'I cannot describe my anguish,' Franklin wrote, 'on the occasion of separating from another companion under circumstances so distressing. There was, however, no alternative. The extreme debility of the party put the carrying him quite out of the question, as he himself admitted.'[40]

Franklin heaved himself and his remaining five voyageurs forward to Fort Enterprise. There was no game to be shot even had Adam, his hunter, found any or been strong enough to lift his gun. The Barren Lands were truly barren. 'There was no tripes de roche,' Franklin regretted, so 'we drank tea and ate some of our shoes for supper.'[41]

They reached Fort Enterprise on 12 October. It was empty. There were no supplies, there was no store of dried meat, there were no Indians. What they found was a note from Back saying that he had been there two days earlier and was going in search of Akaitcho, God willing that he and his three companions should survive so far. Believing that the white men were doomed, Akaitcho had taken his men hunting.

The only food available was *tripes de roche*, and the detritus of last year's stay: bones from the ash heap, and a pile of skins which the Indians had used as bedding. This, Franklin decided optimistically, 'would support us tolerably well for a while'.[42] Two days later, while they were feeding the floorboards into the fire – the one point in Fort Enterprise's favour was its availability of wood – the door burst open to reveal Solomon Belanger, one of Back's voyageurs. Belanger was covered in a thin coating of ice, and could barely speak. He did, however, have the strength to give Franklin a letter. Back had seen no Indians and requested further instructions.

Once again Franklin split his party. Sending Belanger back with the message that Back was to change course for Fort Providence in the hope of intercepting the Indians as they made their way back to winter quarters, he decided to set off upriver himself in the same direction with Augustus and Benoit. Peltier and Samandré, meanwhile, would stay at the fort to look after Adam, whose legs had swollen so much he could not walk.

Two days into the trek, Franklin's snowshoes fell irreparably to pieces, forcing him to return to Fort Enterprise while Augustus and Benoit struggled on. Over the following week snowstorms blew around Fort Enterprise while the four men within sank into a hunger-induced stupor. Adam and Samandré lay in bed, sobbing quietly. Franklin and Peltier, slightly stronger than the others, did their best to collect food and firewood, but they moved like zombies. 'We perceived our strength decline every day,' Franklin wrote, 'and every exertion began to be irksome. When we were once seated the great-est effort was necessary in order to rise, and we frequently had to lift each other from our seats.'[43] But they were cheered by the thought that either Back, or the two voyageurs, would surely have caught up with the Indians by 26 October. It could only be a matter of days before help arrived.

It was now four weeks since any of them had tasted meat.

Michel reached Richardson's camp on 9 October 1821. He was alone. He explained that he and Belanger had split up on the march back and as he had not yet arrived he assumed he must have got lost. Of Perrault and Fontano he said nothing save that the former had given him his rifle and ammunition before he left, with which he had been able to shoot a partridge and a hare.

What doubts they may have had about Michel's story were swept away when he produced the food. To Richardson it was as good as a miracle from the Almighty, 'and we looked upon Michel as the instru-ment he had chosen to preserve all our lives'.[44] They pampered him as much as they were able. When he complained of cold Richardson gave him one of the two shirts he was wearing; Hood offered to share his buffalo hide blanket.

Two days later Michel was once again the Almighty's instrument of salvation. While out hunting he found a wolf that had been killed by a deer. They devoured the strange-tasting meat with unbounded grat-itude. But as the days wore on, with no sign of Belanger, who they now presumed dead, Michel became surly and evasive. He disap-peared for short periods, declining to say where he had been. He brought back no more meat and refused to gather *tripes de roche*. At night he did not sleep in the tent, preferring to lie in the open. By the 16th he was threatening to leave them.

Puzzled by his behaviour, and equally puzzled as to why Franklin had sent no supplies, Richardson and Hood decided that if Michel would hunt for four days, they would let him go forward with Hepburn to see what was happening at Fort Enterprise. At this his attitude became even stranger. He would not hunt. 'It is no use,' he said, 'there are no animals, you had better kill and eat me.'[45] Later he began to rave against Europeans, claiming they had eaten his uncle.

Richardson's account of those days is the only version available. It was written later, following consultation with Franklin, and does not say when the first doubt formed in Richardson's mind. It does, however, reveal what both officers agreed must have happened. On the way from Franklin to Richardson, Michel had killed Belanger. Being surprised by Perrault, who was last seen carrying his gun and heading for the smoke of Michel's campfire, he had killed him too. Fontano had suffered the same fate. During subsequent days Michel had used the three corpses as a private larder, visiting it whenever he felt hungry. The 'wolf' meat he had brought back was almost certainly human flesh. Possibly he planned the same fate for Richardson, Hood and Hepburn.

On 20 October, Richardson was scrabbling together a few handfuls of frozen lichen. Hepburn was chopping willows for a fire. Michel, who refused to do anything, remained at the tent arguing with Hood. A few minutes after noon there was a shot. Richardson and Hepburn hurried back to find Hood dead. A bullet had entered the back of his skull and emerged neatly through his forehead. It had been fired at such close range that his nightcap was still smouldering. Michel greeted them with a gun in his hand.

Michel's explanation ran as follows: there were two guns in camp, a long one and a short one; Hood was cleaning the long one, and had asked Michel to fetch the short one from the tent; while Michel was doing so the long gun went off, whether by accident or by design he did not know. Suicide, accident or murder? Richardson was no detective, but it was obvious what had happened. The long gun was of the outdated type which Britain sold to native soldiers. It was so long that it was near impossible for a man to press its barrel against his head and simultaneously pull the trigger. It was even more difficult for a man to shoot himself in the back of the head with such a weapon. And for a man to do such a thing while holding in one hand a copy of Bickersteth's *Scripture Helps* was beyond the realms of likelihood.

Michel protested his innocence and, having a gun in his hand, was listened to with attention. From that point he was never unarmed and refused to let Hepburn and Richardson be on their own. If either opened their mouths he leaped forwards, waving his gun and demanding to know if they accused him of Hood's murder. The two Britons were at the mercy of a deranged man. Hepburn had a gun, and Richardson a small pistol. Both were too weak to cope with physical violence. Michel, on the other hand, was not only healthy but carried a gun, two pistols, a bayonet and a knife. 'He also,' wrote Richardson, 'for the first time, assumed such a tone of superiority in addressing me, as evinced that he considered us to be completely in his power.'[46] Which they were.

On 21 October Michel tried to lure Richardson into joining him on a hunting expedition. Richardson wisely refused. They set out for Fort Enterprise on 23 October, cajoling the madman in their midst with a semblance of purpose. Michel responded to the routine, but all the time he was reeling inwardly between guilt, self-justification and despair. Despair won. That day, for the first time, he announced his intention to gather *tripes de roche*. He told the other two to go ahead and he would catch them up later.

Alone at last, Richardson and Hepburn conferred. They agreed that Michel had definitely murdered Hood and had probably murdered Belanger too. Hepburn offered to shoot Michel but Richardson decided the duty was his. 'Had my own life alone been threatened,' he wrote, 'I would not have purchased it by such a measure; but I considered myself as intrusted also with the protection of Hepburn's, a man, who, by his humane attentions and devotedness, had so endeared himself to me, that I felt more anxiety for his safety than for my own.'[47] When Michel caught up with them, Richardson took his pistol and shot him in the head. 'His principles,' intoned Richardson, 'unsupported by a belief in the divine truths of Christianity, were unable to withstand the pressure of severe distress.'[48] Then they set out for Fort Enterprise.

'It is impossible to describe our sensations,' Richardson wrote, 'when, on attaining the eminence that overlooks [Fort Enterprise] we beheld the smoke issuing from one of the chimneys.'[49] During their journey he and Hepburn had lived off nothing but *tripes de roche* and Hood's hide blanket. Richardson was now so weak that he fell down twenty times covering a distance of only 100 yards. However, the prospect of salvation gave them strength and on the evening of 29 October they flung open the door of Fort Enterprise.

'No words can convey an idea of the filth and wretchedness that met our eyes,'[50] Richardson wrote. The floor had been pulled up, the partitions had been demolished and the skin off the windows was gone. Of the four men present – Franklin, Samandré, Adam and Peltier – only Peltier seemed able to move. He had risen, expecting them to be an Indian relief party. Now he sank back in despair. Accustomed as Hepburn and Richardson were to the sight of each other's emaciated frames, 'the ghastly countenances, dilated eye-balls, and sepulchral voices of Captain Franklin and those with him were more than we could at first bear'.[51]

Richardson and Hepburn had been expecting Franklin to help them. Now they found themselves having to help him. Despite their weakness they were both far stronger than any man in the building and from that day they undertook the chores of chopping wood and carrying it home. They also went hunting, but were too enfeebled to hold the gun steady on the rare occasions when they encountered game. Franklin, meanwhile, dragged in deer skins from the pile which had been discarded the previous winter. The pile was thirty yards away. Franklin managed to bring back three skins in a day. There were about twenty-six skins in all, thin, rotten things, riddled with warble-fly grubs. The explorers devoured them avidly, right down to the warble grubs which they squeezed out of the hide with their fingernails. They tasted 'as fine as gooseberries'.[52]

Contrarily, while Peltier had previously been one of the healthiest in the group, he now collapsed, and Adam showed signs of renewed life. Richardson diagnosed Adam's swollen limbs as the result of protein-deficiency oedema and incised his abdomen, scrotum and legs, whereby 'a large quantity of water flowing out he obtained some ease'.[53] But there was nothing he could do for Peltier or Samandré. They both died on the night of 1 November.

Richardson and Hepburn now began to flag. On 3 November
Richardson noted that Hepburn's limbs were beginning to swell – 'his
strength as well as mine is declining rapidly'.[54] That day they ate the
last of the bones.

On 5 November Adam began to wander, leaping to his feet and seiz-
ing his gun with the promise of a good day's hunting and food for all,
before subsiding into a dejection so deep that he could not even be
persuaded to eat. The others were little better off. They tried not to
talk about their situation, chatting instead about 'common and light
subjects'.[55] But as Franklin wrote, 'our minds exhibited symptoms of
weakness, evinced by a kind of unreasonable pettishness with each
other. Each of us thought the other weaker in intellect than himself,
and more in need of advice and assistance. So trifling a circumstance as
a change of place, recommended by one as being more warm and comfortable, and refused by the other, from a dread of motion, frequently
called forth fretful expressions, which were no sooner uttered than
atoned for, to be repeated, perhaps, in the course of a few minutes.'[56]

They were all so thin that it hurt even to sleep. Their bones ached
against the floorboards but they put up with it because the pain of
turning to a more comfortable position was even greater. To this was
added initially the pain of constant hunger. But once the pangs had
eased – after three or four days – they usually enjoyed a few hours in
which they dreamed of limitless food.

On 7 November Richardson and Hepburn were in the storehouse,
trying to separate logs from the frozen pile stored there the previous
winter, when they heard a shot. Three of Akaitcho's Indians were
outside. They had been contacted by Back two days previously and
on hearing his tale, and on taking in his shrivelled appearance – he too
was pathetically reduced, and had lost one man from his party – they
had immediately set out with emergency rations comprising fat, some
dried venison and a few deer tongues.

Sending the youngest of them back for further supplies, the
remaining two Indians swiftly took control. They cleared Fort
Enterprise of its corpses, swept out the wet, blackened filth of charred
bones and singed hair that covered the floor, and built up a crackling

fire. The ease with which they did all this stunned Richardson. 'We could scarcely,' he wrote, 'by any effort of reasoning, efface from our minds the idea that they possessed a supernatural degree of strength.'[57]

Then came the feeding. Despite Richardson's injunction to 'be moderate!', they all suffered severely from overeating. Richardson, who should have known better, devoured the food as extravagantly as the others. For days afterwards – weeks, in Richardson's case – they suffered from distention and indigestion. The passing of a stool caused immense pain. Only Adam, who had to be spoon-fed, escaped the effects of sudden indulgence.

The Indians treated the survivors 'with the same tenderness they would have bestowed on their own infants'.[58] They persuaded them to wash and to shave their beards which had not been touched since they left the coast and which had grown to a 'hideous length'.[59] On learning that the Europeans had eaten too much meat they strung lines across the river and came back with four large trout. In every respect they could not have been more solicitous.

But hardly had salvation arrived than it departed. On 13 November the Indians vanished, leaving behind them a handful of pemmican per man. For a while Franklin feared his men would have to revert to their old diet, save that instead of deer skins they now had fish skins. It transpired, however, that the Indians, fearing their messenger had not reached base, had left on a twenty-four-hour march to fetch more supplies from Akaitcho's camp. The Indians reappeared on the morning of 15 November, having walked through a stormy and snow-filled night with two of their wives and Benoit, one of the voyageurs who had accompanied Back. Once again the survivors were faced with an abundance of food, but this time they measured their pace. On 16 November, a sunny Thursday, they left Fort Enterprise for good.

They reached Fort Providence on 11 December, where they were at last reunited with Back. Then began the recriminations. Why had no food been left at Fort Enterprise? In his defence Akaitcho stated that three of his best hunters had drowned and that he had been unable to obtain ammunition from Fort Providence. But he was quite open about the reason for the lack of provisions: he had believed that Franklin's journey was insanity and that none of his expedition would be seen again.

Wentzel the interpreter was equally to blame, having been repeatedly instructed to make sure sufficient food was left behind. But he drew attention away from his failings with an open attack on Franklin and Richardson. The whole party had acted 'imprudently, injudiciously and showed in one particular instance an unpardonable want of restraint'.[60] Richardson was a murderer who should be brought to trial, he said.

Wentzel was right, in a way. There was nothing to prove that Richardson's story was true. For all anyone knew he and Hepburn might have killed all four voyageurs and Hood, and eaten them. 'To tell the truth, Wentzel,' Back had written, 'things have taken place, which *must* not be known.'[61] In classic conspiracy fashion, Wentzel also stated that when he had joined the mission Franklin and his officers had been all over him. When the business was finished he *must* come to London for reunion, they had said, nothing could make them happier. But when the business *was* finished, the same men had advised him to stay in the Arctic for a few more years. It would be in his best interests, they had told him. There should have been some sort of investigation. Had Franklin lost a ship instead of an officer he would be facing a court martial. But Hood was not a ship, and the only witnesses to those fateful days were sticking to their story. In the end both parties dropped their accusations and the matter was swept aside.

The easiest target was of course Akaitcho. But Franklin could not bring himself to attack him. The Indian chief had shown them great kindness and sympathy during their rescue. Moreover, thanks to the usual administrative disputes, he had not yet been paid for any of his troubles. Akaitcho shrugged this off. 'The world goes badly,' he told Franklin. 'All are poor; you are poor, the traders appear to be poor, I and my party are poor likewise; and since the goods have not come in, we cannot have them. I do not regret having supplied you with provisions, for a Copper Indian can never permit white men to suffer from want of food on his lands without flying to their aid.'[62]

Franklin reached York Factory on 14 July 1822, where Governor George Simpson took a quiet delight in their failure. 'They do not feel themselves at liberty to enter into the particulars of their disastrous enterprize,' he wrote on the 16th, 'and I fear they have not fully achieved the object of their mission.'[63] This was putting it mildly. Franklin had travelled 5,500 miles across land and water, had lost eleven of his twenty-strong party, and had returned with the news that he had mapped a minuscule portion of a coastline that everyone already knew existed. Almost every stage of the journey had been mismanaged, and by his decision to press eastwards at any cost, further than his supplies could last, Franklin was directly responsible for the deaths of his men.

But when the story broke, nobody considered Franklin's failings. To do so would have called in question the wisdom of those who sent him. Only Douglas Clavering voiced the worries of his fellow explorers: 'Was the undertaking worth the suffering his party endured?'[64] he wrote to a friend. The answer was no. But what did the public care? Franklin was a hero. He was the man who had eaten his boots.

10

LYON'S DEPARTURE

On his return from Foxe Basin in October 1823, Parry had been greeted at Lerwick by a mixed bag of letters. One informed him that his father had died the previous year. Another, from Barrow, told him with a hint of reprimand that a rescue mission was on the point of being sent out to find him – and that he had been promoted to captain in November 1821. A third was from Franklin, offering his congratulations and giving a brief account of his own tribulations in the Arctic. 'I need not be ashamed to say that I cried over it like a child,'[1] Parry wrote.

Parry was no longer the man of the moment. True, on his arrival in London he was asked by Lord Melville to accept the post of hydrographer. But this well-paid job could not compare with the glory of discovering the North-West Passage and Parry feared that if he accepted the offer it might blight his chances of active service. Melville assured him there was no conflict – but naturally he could not draw both salaries simultaneously.

Parry asked Barrow's opinion. Barrow, in turn, spoke to important figures and advised him that he could still sail to the north and be hydrographer at the same time. After all, what did the post entail?

Nothing but the occasional supervision. 'Do not think of quitting this situation,' said Barrow, 'for, altho' it is true that you are to receive no salary for it, as soon as your ship is commissioned, still it is your *sheet-anchor*; keep hold of the Admiralty while you can – you do not know to what it may hereafter lead.'[2]

Parry accepted the job. 'I now stand on very high ground indeed,'[3] he wrote to his brother. Shortly afterwards, however, he became ill and was confined to his bed in a London hotel with a delirious fever. Tongues began to wag – Parry was not as forgotten as he suspected – although what they wagged about is unknown. Did it have anything to do with the 'disgrace' of his recent voyage? Lyon rushed to his leader's support. 'Reports of the cause of his illness have risen to an enormous & shameful bulk,' he wrote. 'Disappointment in a matrimonial engagement is the true cause.'[4]

It was true. The man who had spent most of the past five years in the Arctic without even catching a cold had been brought low by affairs of the heart. Sabine's niece, the Miss Browne whose life jacket Parry had so daringly inflated all those years ago and with whom, in Parry's eyes at least, he had reached an 'understanding', had been inconstant. Inconstancy could mean a wide range of things in those days. Merely being seen with other men was prima facie grounds for inconstancy. But Miss Browne had gone a step further; she had not only been inconstant but had become engaged to another.

This was a terrible shock for a man of Parry's romantic sensibilities. But worse was to come. Miss Browne's mother – perhaps hoping to drive the Arctic hero back to her daughter, perhaps angling for some breach-of-promise compensation, perhaps having caught a whiff of the unspoken Foxe Basin scandal or perhaps just trying to stir things up – let it be known that Parry had dishonourably broken the engagement. His father had just died, his career had been overshadowed, his love had left him for another man, and now he was being calumniated. No wonder Parry had a slight turn. And his health was not improved by a well-meant ditty which was doing the rounds of London's salons:

Parry, why this dejected air?
Why are your looks so much cast down?
None but the Brave deserve the Fair,
Any one may have the Browne![5]

'I have always been susceptible to attachments of this kind,' he
wrote to his brother Charles. 'I have always felt a desire to be *attached*
somewhere – I have never been easy without it, and with less disposition, I will venture to say, than 99 in 100 of my own profession, to
vicious propensities, either in this or other ways, I have always contrived to fancy myself in love with some virtuous woman. There is
some romance in this, but I have it still in full force within me, and
never, till I am married, shall I, I believe, cease to entertain it.'[6]

Parry recovered eventually, driven in part by the machinations of
Miss Browne's mother. 'I confess a feeling of wounded pride arose
within me,' he wrote, 'which did a great deal to shake off in a short
time the more bitter and less remediable feelings by which I had at
first been agitated.'[7] He found it difficult to face Sabine, the uncle, for
a long while afterwards. They could not help meeting, both of them
being members of the Royal Society, but they went through the
niceties all the same. 'We avoided mentioning *the* subject, and he
behaved well about it,'[8] said Parry.

However, Parry had only a little time to dwell on his loss. On 17
January 1824 he was commissioned to the *Fury* which, with its sister
ship the *Hecla*, was to sail for the Arctic that spring.

Parry had been coy about the North-West Passage following his
recent failure. The Foxe Basin expedition had 'at least served the
useful purpose of shewing where the passage is *not* to be effected',[9] he
wrote in his journal. But he stated that 'There is no *known* opening
which seems to present itself so favourably for this purpose as Prince
Regent's Inlet.'[10] So Barrow sent him there.

Parry's was just one of four expeditions which Barrow sent out
that year. Lyon – 'mad with joy'[11] – was given command of the
Griper, in which he was to sail to Repulse Bay, then trek overland to
Point Turnagain. Franklin was ordered to prepare himself for another

overland assault with Richardson on the Canadian coast, this time travelling down the Mackenzie River rather than the Coppermine. And Captain Frederick Beechey in HMS *Blossom* was instructed to sail around Cape Horn and attack the passage from the west via the Bering Strait. Lyon and Parry were to find Franklin's open water, and Franklin was to find Beechey's. The scale of it all, fuelled by the excitement of Franklin's grisly débâcle, caught the popular imagination. In 1824 anybody connected even remotely with the Arctic was now a hero – even if they had not eaten their boots.

On 24 March 1824 the main participants in all four ventures met at a dinner party hosted by Franklin and his wife of eight months, Eleanor. Among the guests was a young woman by the name of Jane Griffin who penned an interesting series of portraits. 'Captain Parry was in the room when we arrived – he is a tall, large, fine-looking man, of commanding appearance, but possessing nothing of the fine gentleman – his manner and appearance rather excite the idea of a slight degree of roughness and bluntness – his figure is rather slouching, his face full & round, his hair dark & rather curling. – Captn. Lyon was the next object of interest – he is a young man of about 30, of good height & gentlemanly-looking – he has large, soft, grey eyes, heavy eyelids & good teeth & is altogether very pleasing. Mr. Barrow of the Admiralty sat at the top of the table – he is said to be humorous & obstinate & exhibited both propensities. Captn. Beechey was another of the heroes of the same class – he is a prim looking little man & was very silent.'[12] Richardson she described as 'a middle sized man & appears about Captn. Franklin's age. He was not well-dressed – & looks like a Scotchman as he is – he has broad & high cheek bones, a widish mouth, grey eyes & brown hair – upon the whole rather plain, but the countenance thoughtful, mild & pleasing.'[13]

It was a lively occasion in which they discussed everything from opera – 'Captn. Franklin told me he had never been & did not think he could sit it out. Captn. Lyon has never been but once & does not mean to go again'[14] – to craniology. 'The Lyon' showed the ladies his tattoos under the table, and Barrow, for no good reason, had a go at old

Isaac D'Israeli – the future prime minister's father – which left him
'evidently much hurt & vexed'.[15]

The only person not to enjoy himself was Parry. 'He occasionally
bursts into hearty laughs & seems to enjoy a joke,' wrote Jane Griffin,
but for the most part he seemed 'far from lighthearted & exhibits
traces of heartfelt & recent suffering'.[16] This was possibly a hangover
from the Browne affair. Yet there was something deeper. By contrast
with Lyon, he did not appear to relish his forthcoming voyage. 'Captn.
Parry seems to be going [north] again rather against his inclination –
he complained to Fanny [Jane Griffin's sister] that he had seen nothing of any other parts of the world . . . Fanny remarked . . . what a state
of excitement he and his ship must be in when they first arrived in a
situation where they could get news of their country and particularly
of their friends. Captn. P. replied with deep emotion, "Ah, indeed!
Nobody knows."'[17]

For once in the history of Barrow's expeditions one gets an inkling
of what his officers must have felt. To the public they were presented
as diligent, devout and, above all, dedicated men who pursued their
goals with loyal and thrusting ardour. This was true only to an extent.
The thrill of exploration did move them – as did the prospect of promotion, higher salaries and fame. But for many the price was not
worth paying. Many officers and seamen chose to return to the Arctic
year after year. But an equal number chose not to. For this last group
the hardship, and possible death, which they might face were not
half so enticing as a quiet life without promotion on one of Britain's
many naval stations around the globe.

Parry was edging towards the quitters' side. He was no longer as
young as he had been; his joints were stiffening with rheumatism and
he wanted to find his 'virtuous woman'. He dreaded the years of
imprisonment in the ice which another voyage might entail, and as he
said to Fanny Griffin, he wanted to see more of the world.
Nevertheless he was, at this point, still locked into his career. He
would go wherever Barrow sent him. But that did not mean he
wanted to.

*

The usual brouhaha surrounded the *Hecla* and the *Fury* as they were readied in Deptford. Six thousand people signed Parry's visitors' book, among them several members of the royal family and a young lady called Isabella, daughter of Lord Stanley of Alderley, whom Parry invited into his cabin for wine and cakes. In a reserved manner – no life jackets here – he fell for her.

Public confidence was high, and when Parry held a ball to mark his departure, the press reported it luminously. All the Arctic heroes were there, as well as all the present officers, including Lt. Henry Hoppner as second-in-command, Lt. Foster as astrologer-chaplain, Lts. James Ross and, new to the Arctic, Horatio Austin, plus Midshipmen Edward Bird, Francis Crozier and the purser William Hooper who had sailed with Parry on every single one of his voyages. Disappointingly for Parry, most of the attention centred on John Franklin. 'I suppose the newspapers have told you how the ladies pulled him to pieces at Captain Parry's ball,' wrote Franklin's wife, Eleanor. 'He was in such request that I wonder they left a bit of him for me. I do not quite know what to say of his flirting in such a manner with half the Belles of London . . .'[18]

Sadly the confidence was misplaced: this was to be Parry's most calamitous mission to date. Indeed, it has been said that if Parry's third voyage had been his first he would never have made a second. They departed on 19 May 1824 but from the moment Parry arrived in the Arctic things began to go wrong. He reached Baffin Bay only to find the central pack was twice as wide as normal. By the time he had battled through it to reach Lancaster Sound on 10 September he was a month behind schedule and almost at the end of the navigable season. Three days later, when both ships were caught in the ice just twenty-one miles from Prince Regent Inlet, he consulted with Lt. Hoppner of the *Fury* whether they should turn for home. Both men agreed that such a course would be disgraceful. Far better to carry on, overwinter, and see what the next year brought. Meanwhile, westerly gales opened the sea and drove both ships back until they were nearly spewed out of Lancaster Sound. Then the wind turned and the ships were blown back again. They reached Prince Regent Inlet, sailed down it for about fifty miles and readied themselves for winter in a bay on the east coast that Parry called Port Bowen.

As usual Parry had something up his sleeve: not a theatre but a festival – 'masquerades without licentiousness', he wrote, 'carnivals without excess!'[19] On 1 November, in as actorly manner as he could contrive, Parry wrapped himself in a huge cloak, walked over the ice to the *Fury*, and revealed himself as an old beggar whose face and wooden leg was familiar to anyone who knew the streets of Chatham. 'Give a copper to poor Joe,' wailed Parry, scraping wildly on his fiddle, 'who's lost his timbers in defence of his King and country.'[20] He almost brought the house down.

Others came in his wake. Henry Hoppner dressed himself up as a fashionable lady, Midshipman Crozier arrived as a black footman. Throughout the winter a host of unlikely characters flounced across the decks performing quadrilles, waltzes and various other dances. There were Highlanders, Turkish odalisques, chimney sweeps, rag-and-bone men, country bumpkins, city bricklayers, oriental princesses and fashionable Parisian fops. Deep in the intestines of the Arctic, Parry's officers whirled and capered as if they were at a Venetian ball.

Parry, though, was more distant than usual. All the winter offered him was 'inanimate stillness' and 'motionless torpor'.[21] His rheumatism was biting, and James Ross, his midshipman, was often asked to take observations. 'Dear Ross,' ran one of Parry's orders, 'You will much oblige me by taking the Needles, as well as the Vibrations, during your hours on the hill to-day . . . I have so much pain in my loins, when in motion, that I shall not be able to fetch the hill to-day. Yours very truly, W. E. Parry.'[22]

The winter finally ended on 20 July 1825, when the ships sprang free of the ice. Prince Regent Inlet was theirs for the taking. However, ten days after leaving Port Bowen, during which they had made only sixty miles or so down the west coast of Prince Regent Inlet, both ships were in trouble. They were driven landwards and although the *Hecla* extricated herself, the *Fury* was nipped by a massive berg which threw the ship against the shore ice. Hoppner listened helplessly as the *Fury* broke beneath him. First came the trembling; then the violent cracks as the beams gave way; the rudder went with a report like gunfire; water gurgled in through leaking seams. When the berg finally relented, Hoppner's men were working the pumps around the clock. It was clear that the *Fury* would have to be grounded for emergency repairs.

The *Fury*'s stores were unloaded on a beach at the northern cape of Cresswell Bay and the crew were transferred to the *Hecla*. For a fortnight the men and officers from both ships fought to get the *Fury* into a position where she could be repaired, but gales, blizzards and icebergs thwarted their every effort. On 21 August, with some of the men so exhausted that they could scarcely comprehend Parry's orders, work was brought to a halt by the severest gale to date. They were forced to flee southwards in the *Hecla* and when they returned four days later they found the *Fury* lying on its side in a foot of water on the same beach where they had deposited its stores. There was nothing that could be done.

Parry had no choice but to return home. This dismal chronicle of events did nothing to help his reputation or his self-image. 'The only real cause for wonder is our long exemption from such a catastrophe,'[23] he wrote phlegmatically in his journal. Others took a more critical view. According to the *Gentleman's Quarterly*, 'the last two expeditions undertaken by Captain Parry have been particularly unfortunate. Literally nothing has been accomplished.'[24] Even Barrow, writing in the *Quarterly Review*, was forced to admit that Parry's latest effort 'has added little or nothing to our stock of geographical knowledge'. The state of the North-West Passage was 'precisely where it was at the conclusion of his first voyage'.[25]

To further compound Parry's humiliation he had to attend the obligatory court martial which followed the loss of any ship. 'By a curious necessity,' he wrote to his sister Gertrude, 'there not being Captains enough to form a Court without me, I sat as a member, although it was, in fact, myself on whom the responsibility of the abandonment of the *Fury* rested.' All were of course acquitted and the court 'passed a high and flattering encomium on the exertions of all engaged in the Expedition'.[26] Nevertheless, Parry's failure was exhibited to more than 100 naval officers who had come to watch the proceedings.

If Parry's voyage to Prince Regent Inlet had been a miserable failure, it was nothing compared with Lyon's expedition to Repulse Bay. On 9 November 1824, while Parry was wintering in Port Bowen, Lyon had staggered back to England only five months after he set out, having endured the most hellish sea voyage yet experienced by any of Barrow's men.

The *Griper* – 'that coffin',[27] Lyon called it in disgust – had never been popular with any of its commanders and its faults were fully demonstrated on this mission. It pitched appallingly, with a draught that was a foot lower in the bow than the stern, and was so sluggish even with full sail that its accompanying transport, the *Snap*, struggled to keep it in sight without losing all headway and eventually had to tow it across the Atlantic. When they reached the entrance to Hudson Bay in August 1824, the *Griper* took on board the *Snap*'s supplies and immediately proved too small to contain them comfortably. 'We found our narrow decks completely crowded by them,' complained Lyon. 'The gangways, forecastle, and abaft the mizzenmast, were filled with casks, hawsers, whale-lines, and stream-cables, while on our straightened lower deck we were obliged to place casks and other stores, in every part but that allotted to the ship's company's mess tables; and even my cabin had a quantity of things stowed away in it. The launch was filled high above her gunwales with various articles, and our chains and waist were lumbered with spars, spare plank, sledges, wheels, &c.'[28] All the gear and provisions to last thirty months were squeezed into a ship which, as Lyon plaintively pointed out, had carried no more than a year's supply on Parry's voyage.

Adding to the chaos were two Shetland ponies, which Lyon had purchased as an experimental mode of transport for the overland leg of his expedition. They were pleasant companions, walking about the decks 'as familiarly as large dogs',[29] but in a ship so small they became a serious inconvenience, and the vast quantity of hay required

to sustain them for such a long period strained the *Griper*'s capacity
still further.

Never before had a single ship been sent out for such a potentially
long voyage. Perhaps Barrow, lulled by the apparent ease in which
Parry had overwintered, had decided a back-up was superfluous. But
in the light of Parry's own opinions on the necessity of having two
ships, the Admiralty was obviously pinching pennies. Lyon felt the
lack – so sorely that not even the beauties of the Arctic sky, which had
previously driven him to rhapsodies, could compensate. 'Lovely as
the surrounding dazzling view may have been,' he wrote, 'I could
not but yield to a sensation of loneliness which I had never before
experienced on the last voyage; and I felt most forcibly the want of an
accompanying ship, if not to help us, at least to break the deathlike
stillness of the scene. The agreeable visits from ship to ship, which so
pleasingly break in on the monotony of a Polar voyage were now
denied us.'[30]

For a man on his first solo command, Lyon was understandably nervous. But he was not going to admit defeat. 'We had already in our
passage across the Atlantic arranged our little plans of improvement
and amusement, and I looked forward with pleasure to the approach
of winter.'[31] It would be nice to have seen Lyon's 'plans of amusement' in action for if anyone knew the meaning of entertainment it
was him. Unfortunately they were never put into operation.

Normally the northern reaches of Hudson Bay were ice-free in
August, but the season of 1824 was unaccountably thick. The sea was
crowded with ice 'and in many places closely packed as far as the eye
could reach'.[32] Lyon turned disadvantage to good purpose by using a
large floe as a rest stop. He had washing lines erected on the ice
which were soon strung with drying clothes. The men played leap-
frog, the officers wandered about taking potshots at passing loons,
and the ship's ponies, geese, ducks and hens were let loose to wander
at will. Meanwhile the *Griper* waited with loose sails, ready to evacuate 'our floating farm-yard'[33] at a moment's notice.

As he pressed on, Lyon noted that the sea was not only icier but
foggier than usual. Like previous voyagers he noted the peculiar

qualities of Arctic fog. They could often see no further than 100 yards
yet overhead shone a sky of 'most provoking brilliancy'.[34] Icicles grew
so fast on the rigging that it was possible to measure their increase
with the naked eye. When the fog lifted, as rapidly as it descended,
the entire ship glistened as if it were made of glass.

Lyon might have wafted his way poetically to Repulse Bay had he
not made a strange decision for which he gives no explanation in his
journal and which would baffle later commentators. Instead of sailing
to the north of Southampton Island, through Frozen Strait, as he had
done with Parry, he decided to go south and approach Repulse Bay via
the stretch of water known by the idiosyncratic and misleading name,
Roes Welcome Sound. Lyon was trying too hard. He wanted not only
to reach Repulse Bay but to map all the approaches to it. He had
already tested the approach to Hudson Bay by attacking it from the
south, rather than through the tricky currents off Resolution Island to
the north, a process which had left him much shaken and in full agreement that the traditional route was best. His detour to the south of
Southampton Island had exactly the same effect. Expecting a
panorama of sheer-sided cliffs, as had been charted by previous navigators, he found a treacherous labyrinth of shoals extending a full
mile into the sea that tested the *Griper* to its balky limits.

Here and there he was able to make a landing, where he encountered Eskimos and bartered with them for supplies of fresh salmon.
They were different from the tribes he had previously met, in that
they scooted across the water on inflated hides, or in large, skin-hulled
boats powered by translucent sails made from walrus intestines. But in
other respects they displayed no novelty of behaviour that Lyon could
add to his already respectable catalogue of Eskimo life. There was
one thing, however, that Lyon would remember forever. On wandering through an Eskimo cemetery, he came across the grave of a
particularly small individual. Driven by previous reports of a race of
pygmies who lived in the region, he removed the stones covering the
corpse. Instead of the expected pygmy he found the body of a little
child, preserved in a pristine state by the cold. On its neck lay the nest
of a snow-bunting – the Arctic equivalent of a robin – which had

wormed through the chinks to find a home for its young. For once
Lyon was at a loss. 'I could not, on this occasion, view its little nest,
placed on the breast of infancy, without wishing that I possessed the
power of poetically expressing the feelings it excited.'[35] The image
was so strong that even Barrow was later moved by it and, to make up
for Lyon's lack of poetic flair, he commissioned a ghastly poem by
'Georgiana' whose three, mercifully brief, verses utterly missed the
pathos of the occasion.

By 1 September Lyon was in the 'Welcome' and was in serious
trouble, 'the ship pitching bows under and a tremendous sea running',[36] while the winds drove them towards a shore which had a tidal
drop of fifteen feet – considerably less than the *Griper*'s draught. He
flung out his anchors, one of which was lost immediately. Fearing the
total destruction of the ship, which would be inevitable when the
tide fell, he had all boats readied for evacuation, though it was obvious
to all that only one boat, the longboat, had the slightest chance of surviving such seas. The men drew lots calmly, accepting their fate
without murmur, even though the *Griper*'s two smaller boats would
have been swamped the second they were launched. 'The surf was
running to an awful height,' Lyon wrote, 'and it appeared evident
that no human powers could save us.'[37] By 3 p.m. the tide had
dropped and only six feet of water separated the ship from the seabed.
They threw out every inessential item they could lay their hands on
in order to reduce their draught. But to no avail. Every wave that
came in lifted the ship and crashed it against the bottom, simultaneously swamping it with water.

Lyon ordered his men to put on 'their best and warmest clothing, to
enable them to support life as long as possible'.[38] The officers meanwhile grabbed some of the precious instruments, 'although it was
acknowledged by all that not the slightest hope remained'.[39] Then
Lyon called the whole crew aft and asked them to pray, while simultaneously bidding them farewell. 'I thanked every one for their
excellent conduct, and cautioned them, as we should, in all probability, soon appear before our Maker, to enter His presence as men
resigned to their fate.'[40] They sat down in small groups on the deck,

drenched by torrential waves, awaiting their imminent deaths, and dozed off. Those who could not sleep began to chat.

At 6 p.m. a heavier swell than usual caused the rudder to rise in its housing and break the after lockers. Miraculously, no major leak followed and even more miraculously, it was the last big swell. They were saved.

In the small hours of 2 September, when the weather had cleared and the *Griper* was riding steady, Lyon saw the shore on which he and his crew would have had to land. 'Not a single green patch was seen on the flat shingle beach, and our sense of deliverance was doubly felt from the conviction that if any of us should have lived to reach the shore, the most wretched death by starvation would have been inevitable.'[41] He named the spot 'Bay of God's Mercy'. Then, 'the ship being now somewhat to rights',[42] he called everyone up for a quick prayer of thanks, and pressed on.

Two days later, with a pang of guilt, he remembered the Shetland ponies. At the first signs of foul weather they had been strapped in slings near the bow. Since then they had swung forgotten throughout the turmoil, pelted with snow, ice and water, and were amazingly still alive – though whether they were still sane was another matter. However, there was no longer anything for them to eat, the hay having long since been jettisoned, and Lyon regretfully ordered them to be killed. They were probably then eaten, though this was passed over in Lyon's journal.

Lyon's compasses were useless by this time, and he spent an interesting if unnecessary few hours swivelling the *Griper* round to see where the Magnetic Pole might be – north-west by north from their present position, he judged, though after his last disappointment with Parry he was unwilling to admit the existence of a Magnetic Pole.

On 12 September more foul weather threatened and Lyon dropped all anchors again, halfway up the western coast of Southampton Island. The tide was running at two knots on the surface and at a greater velocity below. Bearing down on them were two or three streams of solid ice which a normal ship would have been able to ride out but which the *Griper*, its bowsprit plunging underwater with every wave, could well have done without. Luckily they met the lighter edge of the floes and lost merely 'the bobstays and larboard iron bumpkin'.[43] But they were so heavily laden that every wave crashed over them in icy sheets. 'That night was piercingly cold,' Lyon wrote, 'and the sea continued to wash fore and aft the decks while constant snow fell. As the lower deck was afloat, our people and all their hammocks thoroughly soaked, no rest could be obtained.'[44]

A hurricane blew up. The ship pitched so sharply that it was impossible to stand upright below decks. Those who ventured above were whipped by sharp snow flakes and showered with water whose warmth they welcomed until it almost immediately turned their clothes to ice. Lyon strove desperately and in vain to control his ship. But with every floe that burst upon him he dreaded that his cables would part. Worse still was the prospect that his bowsprit would be caught and once that went it would bring down the masts. 'We were all so exhausted, and the ship was so coated with ice,' he wrote, 'that nothing could have been done to save them.'[45] Throughout the night the wind increased. The watch lashed themselves to the mast and huddled there, encased in ice. When Lyon went up to check on them he could barely reach the mast, so heavy were the waves which pounded over the deck. He had never seen such a dark, fierce night. Over the heads of the watch, rocking in the tumult, a small lantern swung to and fro.

On the 13th the gale still blew with 'terrific violence'[46] and water sloshed aboard faster than the sluices could discharge it. At 6 a.m. the sea rose to unprecedented heights and snapped every single cable. They were now anchorless and driving fast before the wind for Southampton Island. The ship was broadside to and heeled over so far that the crew could not keep their footing on the sheet ice which covered the deck. For the second time in less than a week all hands came on top and prayed.

Once again the prayer worked. The wind changed direction and the *Griper*, its lee gunwales in the water, was able to move offshore. But the Arctic wasn't finished with them yet. 'At eight,' Lyon wrote, 'the fore trysail gaff went in the slings, but we were unable to lower it, on account of the amazing force of the wind, and every rope being encrusted with a thick coating of ice.'[47] A wave rose and stove the larboard waist boat against the side of the ship. Then at 11 a.m. another one swept it away.

Their compasses were useless, they had no anchors, the gale was blowing them south to they knew not where, the ship was so poor as to be unworkable 'even in *moderate* weather',[48] and its overburdened draught so great that they could not enter any nearby anchorage. They were without any bearings, they had lost one of their boats, and several of the crew were incapacitated by rheumatism. Their water was in such short supply that they were rationed to one pint per man per day. The foremast was 'much wrung', the bowsprit was 'injured' and the main mast was splitting. The sky was still black and their only means of navigation was by constant sounding, the men hauling and dropping the lead weight until their hands numbed.

In these conditions, Lyon had no choice but to turn back. Bouncing from shore to shoal, awash with water and taking in more with every wave that swept over it, the *Griper* somehow wallowed out of Hudson Bay and on 2 October 1824 began its 1,000-mile trip back to England. 'For the first time since the 28th August,' Lyon wrote, 'a period of five weeks, I enjoyed a night of uninterrupted repose.'[49]

On the way home, shrouded by constant fog, they met stray elements of the whaling fleet making their way home from Lancaster Sound. Lyon tried to identify them but they drove balefully past on all quarters. On the few occasions when contact was made, the whalers begged for food, which Lyon duly despatched, catching the tubs that they floated down to him on lines and filling them with bread. Once, on 19 October, a whaling captain named Valentine, commanding the *Achilles* of Dundee, came aboard and recounted his tale of woe. Whales were scarce that year, and most ships had stayed out so long that they had exhausted their supplies of food. He himself had caught two whales and considered himself a lot luckier than most. 'Mr. Valentine informed me that he had been exposed, for nearly a month past, to a continuance of the worst weather he had seen in thirty-four years' experience, in these seas, and that the past season had been the most severe he had ever known.'[50] Lyon, with water pouring onto his head from the battered and leaking deck, was in full sympathy.

On 9 November Lyon was in the Channel, lurching his way past the Start and Berry Head, the Portland Lights, and the Needles. On the 10th, he was nearly home. 'In our distressed state, without anchors, I determined on running into Portsmouth Harbour, as the tide would serve until two P.M., and the wind was so fresh, that had we lost the flood, we could not have remained under sail all night in safety at Spithead. Accordingly, after having shewn our number, and signalized that we had lost all our anchors and cables, we ran into the harbour in a heavy squall.'[51] They moored against a three-decker battleship and three men were immediately transferred to hospital. 'Thus,' Lyon wrote tightly, 'ends the journal of our unsuccessful expedition.'[52]

Few of Lyon's men ever went to the Arctic again – only one of them, incidentally, had ever been before – and neither did Lyon. Like John Ross before him, he had aroused that strange and unpredictable fury which Barrow reserved for those who had failed, through no fault of their own, to achieve the goal he had set them. There was no official reprimand, but Lyon was considered to have taken undue risks by going to the south of Southampton Island, and for a naval captain to lose all his anchors was beyond the pale.

Twenty years on, when he wrote his *Arctic Voyages*, Barrow seemed to have forgotten Lyon's failure and spoke nostalgically and kindly of the expedition. He even included a small line drawing of a gift Lyon had given him – a figurine carved out of walrus ivory of a dog gnawing a bone. Absentmindedly, he wondered why on earth the expedition had been equipped with only one ship, and such a poor one at that. The reason, which obviously slipped his memory, was that he himself had ordered it so.

Parry was outraged at the treatment Lyon received and told his brother Charles so in a long letter containing 'much secret and treasonable matter',[53] ordering him to destroy it as soon as it had been read. Fortunately, his brother kept it in his records. 'I cannot express the indignation,' wrote Parry, 'with which I view this too common attempt on the part of the Admiralty, to let the blame for failure lie on any shoulders but their own. This is certainly the case now, with respect to the Griper, a vessel of such lubberly, shameful construction as to baffle the ingenuity of the most ingenious seaman in England to do anything with her. I know nothing of the absolute merits of the case, on the occasion in which Lyon lost his anchors, and was in consequence obliged to return – but this I know, that a good vessel would not have incurred the same risk or the same necessity, and it *is the Admiralty* with whom the principal, original and most glaring fault lies.'[54]

And so one of Barrow's most interesting, entertaining and likeable explorers left the scene.

Franklin had not even left England when Lyon returned from Repulse Bay. Remembering the horrors of his previous overland mission, he had taken the time to organize his present expedition down the Mackenzie River with ruthless efficiency. This time everything was to be arranged in advance. Never again would he put himself in the hands of Canadian voyageurs or the squabbling fur companies – although the latter had by now reconciled their differences and with an eye on Russian encroachment from Alaska were embarrassingly voluble in their protestations of support. George Simpson, who had been so against them before, now gushed that there was not a man in the Hudson's Bay Company, himself included, 'who would not be happy to form a member of the Expedition and share your danger'.[55]

Franklin took Simpson up on his offer to the degree that he accepted the services of Peter Dease, the man who had previously advised him at Fort Chipewyan, to facilitate the laying in of stores preparatory to the expedition's arrival. But in every other respect he intended the expedition to be as self-contained as possible.

The pre-planning occupied most of 1824 and, until Parry's departure for Prince Regent Inlet, Franklin was in daily contact with him, plotting their respective routes and discussing what provisions and equipment were necessary. Parry, who had hitherto been slightly wary of the man who had stolen his glory and whom he had not met since 1819, fell under Franklin's charm. 'The steadiness with which

Franklin pursues his objective is very admirable,' he wrote. 'I esteem his character more and more, as I become better acquainted with it.'[56]

Vast quantities of stores were sent out to Dease throughout 1824: macaroni, sugar, coffee, chocolate, two years' supply of tea, etc., all wrapped in three layers of waterproof canvas – the first time Mr Macintosh's excellent invention had been used in the Arctic. Franklin placed an order for pemmican so large that the entire region could not meet it until the following spring. In no hurry, Franklin decided he could wait.

As well as food, Franklin equipped himself with specially built boats whose design was his own but whose construction was supervised by his erstwhile commander Captain Buchan. They were light enough to be carried but strong enough to handle the rapids. The largest was twenty-six feet long and could hold nine men and three tons of equipment yet could be carried by only six people. Lest he face a recurrence of his earlier disaster with river crossings Franklin also took a novel, collapsible canvas boat called the *Walnut Shell*, which was light, portable and, as Lyon stated, 'can be packed like a large umbrella'.[57]

He also made sure his expedition was manned almost entirely by Britons. As before he would have to depend on Indian hunters to replenish his supplies, but the active members were men entirely of his own choosing. Richardson was his right-hand man and for draughtsmen he chose Lt. John Bushnan, a reliable young officer who had sailed as midshipman on most of Parry's Arctic voyages, plus a Midshipman E. N. Kendall, who had sailed with Lyon. There was a naturalist named Drummond and a squad of British seamen who could be relied upon to obey orders in any eventuality.

Bushnan died before the expedition set out and was replaced by Back. This was not altogether as Franklin would have wished, some unknown difference having arisen between himself and Back. 'You know I could have no desire for his company,' he wrote to Richardson, 'but I do not see how I can decline it, if the Admiralty press the matter, without . . . publicly making an exposure of his incapacity in many respects.'[58] The Admiralty did press the matter and Back, who

had become one of Barrow's favourites, arrived post-haste from a promotion station in the West Indies to take his place in the party. Other
than this the organization was left entirely to Franklin, with the result
that the expedition was one of the most successful to date.

The one shadow across Franklin's exemplary preparations was his
wife's health. In 1824 Eleanor Franklin had been diagnosed as fatally
consumptive and by the time of her husband's departure on 16
February 1825 it was clear she was dying. Oddly, it was a relief to both
of them. The marriage had been a mistake from the start. Eleanor was
a London intellectual of great charm, inquisitiveness and lively talent.
Franklin was a provincial naval captain of great charm, pre-set values
and stolidity. She disliked his religion and his oxlike temperament,
but had been swayed by his fame. She recognized the mismatch,
writing before their wedding that 'The question is not, my dear Sir,
whether you and I can mutually esteem each other as friends, but
whether we are calculated to live together in the closest domestic
union. On this point I feel . . . a distrust even more of myself than of
you.'[59] But they had gone ahead, had produced a child – called
Eleanor after her mother but looking like Franklin 'through the wrong
end of a telescope',[60] according to one of his fellow officers – and had
settled down to a life of conjugal incompatibility peppered by sad
squabbles about Sabbath observance and the like. There was no hint
of infidelity, but gossips noticed that Eleanor was still in touch with
one of her earlier suitors, and that Franklin was often seen in the
company of Miss Jane Griffin, even inviting her to take the *Walnut
Shell* for a trial paddle at Woolwich.

By the New Year of 1825 Franklin was torn between Barrow and his
wife. Barrow won. The decision immediately prompted a flurry of
'idle & contradictory gossip'[61] concerning the state of his marriage.
But Eleanor supported his decision. 'It would be better for me that
you were gone,'[62] she agreed wearily. It escaped neither of them that
Franklin himself was embarking on a voyage from which, despite his
forearming, he might not survive. 'He was obliged to settle all his
affairs,' wrote Jane Griffin, 'as if his wife would certainly not recover
and as if he himself would not return.'[63]

1. John Barrow, the up-and-coming Second Secretary

2. *John Ross and Parry meet the 'Artic Highlanders'. As depicted by their Eskimo interpreter Sacksheuse, 1818*

3. *The first overwintering.* Hecla *and* Griper *at Melville Island, 1819–20*

4. Cutting a channel through the ice. Hecla *and* Fury
at Winter Island, 1821

5. The view from Lyon's ship at Igloolik, 1822–23

6. Franklin's canoes bound for Point Turnagain, 1821

7. An Eskimo watching a seal hole, sketched by Lyon, 1823

8. *The western outlet of Fury and Hecla strait, 1823*

9. John Ross

10. William Edward Parry

11. John Franklin

12. Jane Griffin, later Lady Franklin

13. George Back

14. John Richardson

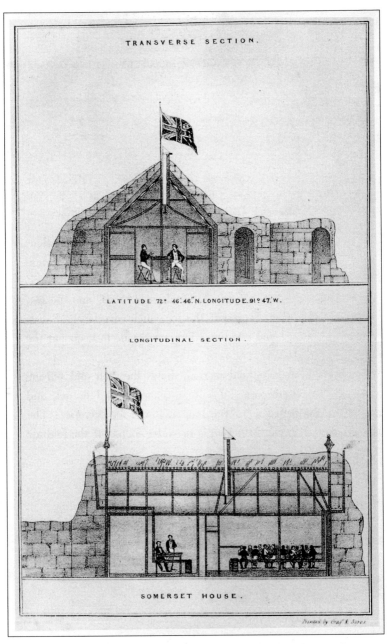

TRANSVERSE SECTION.

LATITUDE 72° 46'.46".N.LONGITUDE.91°.47'.W.

LONGITUDINAL SECTION.

SOMERSET HOUSE.

*15. Somerset House, home to John Ross and his crew during their fourth
winter in Prince Regent Inlet, 1833*

In this atmosphere of mutual despair they sat through a night together reading the funeral service and toasting their doom with the verse from Corinthians: 'O death where is thy sting? O grave where is thy victory?' Then Eleanor gave him a silk Union Jack, which she had embroidered especially for his expedition. Others had by now joined the death-bed, and in an agony of self-justification Franklin wrote that Eleanor 'expressed before the whole party her decided wish that I should not delay in going on the expedition, that it has ever been her desire, and that she is not of the opinion that the circumstance of my going has hastened the crisis of her complaint'.[64]

Her last rites having been read, Eleanor began to improve. 'Even now,' Franklin wrote, 'there are hopes for her recovery, faint as they may be and as I shall consider them.'[65] He wrote to her regularly for the first few weeks of his voyage, only learning on 22 April, when he landed in North America, that she had died six days after his departure. As the news came he was in the middle of a letter to her. 'Your flag is yet snug in the box,' he was writing, 'and will not be displayed till we get to a more northern region. Mr. Back and the men have arrived . . .' The letter stopped abruptly. '7 P.M. The distressing intelligence of my dear wife's death has just reached me.'[66] For all that their marriage had not been perfect, Franklin was stricken. He had had no wish for it to end this way.

Personal tragedy aside, Franklin's expedition was so well organized as to allow little scope for failure. He swanned triumphantly through Cumberland House and Fort Resolution and reached the Mackenzie delta on 16 August having encountered no difficulties whatsoever. Here he hoisted Eleanor's silk flag and the entire company gave three cheers and celebrated the occasion with some spirits which had been saved for the purpose. The sight of the flag caused Franklin a brief surge of grief, but not so much as to draw his attention from the fact that his celebratory brandy had been mixed with sea water and was undrinkable.

The trip to the delta had been only for reconnaissance purposes, and having seen the sea free of ice, Franklin retired to a pre-built

encampment on Great Bear Lake – source of one of the Mackenzie's
tributaries, just to the north of Great Slave Lake – which had been
named Fort Franklin in his honour. It was amply stocked with everything from food to a small library. They passed the winter in total
comfort, the men playing shinty and blind-man's buff, while Franklin
lounged back reading Dante and Milton. 'I wish you could pop in and
partake of our fare,' he wrote to his friend Roderick Murchison. 'You
would be sure of a hearty welcome, and you should have your choice
of either moose or reindeer meat or trout, weighing from forty to fifty
pounds; but you must bring wine and bread if you wish either for
more than one day.'[67]

In late June 1826 the whole company set off down the Mackenzie,
leaving Dease as caretaker at Fort Franklin. On reaching the delta
they split into two groups. Franklin was to follow the coast westwards
with Back as his second-in-command and fourteen men among whom
was Augustus, the Eskimo voyageur-come-interpreter who had been
so bizarrely unaffected by Franklin's previous voyage that he had
offered his services again. Richardson, meanwhile, was to take Kendall
and ten men to chart the seas in between the Mackenzie and the
Coppermine. Both parties were effortlessly successful.

Richardson reached the Coppermine on 7 August, abandoned his
boats and walked back to Fort Franklin, arriving in safety on 1
September. Franklin achieved his furthest point west – coincidentally
on the same day Richardson achieved his furthest east – at a place
called Foggy Island, where worsening conditions and lack of food
finally forced him to retreat. This was the point 'beyond which perseverance would be rashness'.[68] He arrived back at the fort just three
weeks after Richardson.

Together, they had all but conquered the Canadian coast.
Richardson had travelled nearly 3,000 miles, of which slightly more
than 1,000 had never been seen before by Europeans. Franklin had
covered more than 2,000 miles and had mapped 610 miles of new
coastline. During their journeys they had suffered only one incident
and a threat. The incident came when Franklin's boat was nearly
overturned by avaricious Eskimos, and was saved only by Back's

ordering a musket volley to be fired into the air. And the threat came
when Franklin heard that a group of Indians were planning an
ambush because they feared the white men were endangering their
trade with the Russians. Franklin duly changed course on the advice
of two Eskimos and left the Indians to wait in hiding for as long as
they liked.

They spent the rest of the winter in the comfort of Fort Franklin,
where Back entertained them with a display of puppet theatre – his
cardboard figures maybe lacked the oomph of Parry's winter fests, but
were popular enough to merit a run of three nights.

Franklin and Richardson returned to Britain on 1 September 1827.
Back and the others arrived shortly after. It had been a glorious success, for which they were rewarded by promotions and ennoblements.
Back was promoted to commander – such was Barrow's enthusiasm for
his new protégé that the news reached Fort Franklin while Back was
still fiddling with his cardboard cut-outs – and both Franklin and
Richardson received knighthoods.

Their success was heightened by Beechey's voyage in the *Blossom*.
Beechey had sailed round Cape Horn, at the bottom of South
America, and had pressed through Bering Strait as commanded. He
had passed Icy Cape, the furthest discovered point east, and with a
small boat had winkled through the ice until he was only 160 miles
from Foggy Island. Had either Franklin or Beechey realized how
close to each other they were they would certainly have pressed on
and achieved one of Barrow's greatest desires – the emergence on the
west of a group that had started from the east.

The Beechey–Franklin venture was Barrow's most successful to
date. It had also thrown up an item of interest that Barrow could not
resist. In 1789, Captain Bligh had lost his ship, the *Bounty*, in the
South Pacific in one of the best-publicized mutinies in the history of
the Royal Navy. Bligh had been set adrift in a boat to find his way
home – which he did – while the mutineers departed for a life of
untouchable bliss on as remote a place as they could find. They
chose Pitcairn Island, and it was on Pitcairn Island that Beechey
stopped by chance for water while making his way around South

America. His discovery of the mutineers and their descendants set
Barrow thinking.

In 1827, when Beechey and Franklin came home, political circumstances had thrown the Admiralty into a state of flux. Money was
even shorter than it had been before. Barrow therefore dropped his
plans for the Arctic and devoted the next four years to writing the first
history of Captain Bligh and the mutiny on the *Bounty*, a work which
was hugely popular when it came out in 1831 and was still in print 130
years later.

This did not mean he had given up on the Arctic. Far from it. But
for the moment he was obliged to bide his time.

11

SQUABBLES IN
THE SAHARA

Barrow's great surge of activity in the first half of the 1820s was not confined to the Arctic. The Niger still puzzled and frustrated him and, as he wrote to Banks as early as 1817, conditions were ripe for its discovery: 'we shall not be able perhaps to find another Lord Bathurst at home, or another Pasha at Tripoli so favourable for the undertaking'.[1] Bathurst and the Pasha were still in place in 1821, the year after Lyon's return from Murzouk, and conditions were even more favourable than before. While Lyon was plaguing the Admiralty and Colonial Office over his promotion – to grant which would have cost but a few hundred pounds – the Pasha sent an offer that he would guarantee the safety of a party to Bornu and back for the sum of £5,000. The offer was snapped up.

The men chosen by Barrow for this second attempt through the Sahara were Dr Walter Oudney, a serious-minded naval surgeon from Edinburgh, and another Scot, the brawny, adventurous Lt. Hugh Clapperton, who stood over six feet tall, boasted a red beard, had a great capacity for port and had risen to his present position from a humble start as cabin boy. He was 'not exactly cut out for a drawing room',[2] and had maybe fathered some illegitimate children, but he was Oudney's friend and, as the doctor told Barrow, he was 'a gentle-man of excellent disposition, strong constitution and most temperate habits, who is exceedingly desirous of accompanying the expedition. He wishes no salary, his sole object being the love of knowledge.'[3] Overwhelmed by this offer, Barrow granted Clapperton the sum of £150 – later reduced to £100 – should he do all that was required of him. (He could hardly have done otherwise; compared to the cost of Parry's current mission that of Oudney and Clapperton was a bar-gain.) Barrow also gave permission for them to take a third naval man, a carpenter from the base at Malta by the name of William Hillman. There was a fourth member too, who was not of Barrow's choosing but who had been appointed independently by the Colonial Office: a capable but arrogant army officer called Major Dixon Denham, a ladies' man of the Back mould, who had presented a plan for the dis-covery of the Niger in consultation with Lyon.

Unfortunately, it was a bad mix. The two Scots assumed that they were the core of the expedition, and it was understood, if not explicitly stated, that Oudney was its leader. Denham, on the other hand, saw himself as the commanding officer. When the three men met for the first time in Barrow's office in August 1821, the matter of command was not discussed and so they went their way in a cloud of confusion that would eventually swell to a thunderstorm of animosity.

Their instructions were equally penumbral. Beneath a cloak of respectable intentions – to investigate the region's natural history, to open the area to British commerce and to inquire into the nature of sub-Saharan life – they were to search diligently for any large river 'principally with a view of tracing the course of the Niger and ascer-taining its *embouchure*'.[4] But, as usual, there was doubt about where this *embouchure* might be. Clapperton was of the opinion that the Nile flowed into the Gulf of Benin. Denham thought it went east into Egypt. Perversely, therefore, Denham was ordered to look for the Niger to the south while Oudney and Clapperton were told to find Lake Chad, which Lyon had mentioned as a possible outlet, and ascertain whether the Niger joined the Nile.

And there was one other matter, ridiculous now but of prime importance then: what clothes should the members of the expedition wear? Lyon had previously stressed the importance of going native. But this was considered demeaning. How could the Africans be impressed with the importance of the mission – and, incidentally, the importance of trading with Britain – if its members wore Arab costumes? There was national pride to think of too. Should the world's leading power shuffle ignominiously into Bornu clothed in robes and turbans? No, of course it should not. It was decided, therefore, that the expedition should wear, wherever possible, their full dress uniforms displaying all the shiny buttons, epaulettes and medals of British might. The decision was reached partly through genuine worries that Britain might be misrepresented, but mostly at the urgings of Consul Hamner Warrington, who was currently in need of a bit of pomp to remind the Pasha of Tripoli that he, Warrington, was a very important person and thereby to reaffirm his position as the Pasha's indispensable international factor.

Oudney and Clapperton left England in September 1821, with their uniforms, to be followed a month later by Denham and his. The two Scots arrived in Tripoli that October in a final squirt of Admiralty meanness. Instead of being given a naval ship they were obliged to hire a 'small Sicilian boat at Malta'[5] to take them over. 'We not only felt our ardour dampened but our feelings hurt,'[6] Oudney complained. He was even more disgruntled when Denham swept into Tripoli a month later on a naval schooner. But they recovered their sense of importance on meeting one of Barrow's Arctic heroes – Lt. Beechey, the same 'prim' man who would later be sent in the *Blossom* to join up with Franklin's second expedition across Canada.

Barrow had despatched Beechey on a boring mission under Captain Smyth to survey the coast of North Africa between Tripoli and Alexandria. Ostensibly the survey was solely for the purpose of obtaining a good set of charts. Underlying it, though, was Barrow's desire to ensure the Niger did not take a drastic northwards slant and emerge at some point in the Mediterranean before it reached the Nile. In the event, Beechey's survey was limited to a few hundred miles and failed to set Barrow's mind at rest on the Niger, but he did have three useful, and very un-prim, points to make about the present expedition.

His first was that Tripoli was a hellhole – 'I do not think I have ever left any place in my life with so much satisfaction as I do this,' he wrote to Barrow. 'I have certainly never experienced such cheating and roguery from any set of men I have hitherto met with as I have from the people of Tripoli.'[7] His main gripe was the local rate of exchange between English pounds and Spanish dollars, and he advised Barrow never in the future to send out an expedition without buying dollars in advance.

His second point concerned the matter of clothes. 'The travelling in European dress is the only part of the plan I would not venture to recommend, as it will at any rate expose them to much unnecessary annoyance, even supposing it should not endanger their personal safety. The Consul, however, seems very anxious for the experiment and the Pasha affects to be of the same opinion – whether he really be so or not, I will not venture to decide; but those of the natives here, whose opinion I would much rather take, are very decidedly against it.'[8]

Finally, he ventured his opinion on the characters of Oudney and Clapperton. 'Let me . . . congratulate you upon the choice of the two travellers to Bornu,' he wrote. 'They are both decent fellows and entirely well calculated to travel together. The impetuosity and enterprise of Clapperton is well restrained by the caution and prudence of the Doctor, who is certainly a man of a good deal of information and well acquainted with several of the sciences – they are both very zealous in the pursuit of this object and there really appears to be every prospect of their success.'[9] Beechey, the draughtsman son of one of the age's most popular portraitists – William Beechey – even felt a moment of envy. If the Niger led to the Nile, the explorers might stumble across undiscovered remains of ancient Egypt. 'If I had not so interesting a service upon my hands,' he told Barrow with a touch of irony, 'I think I should have been half-tempted to volunteer with Clapperton.'[10]

But it was too late for Beechey's advice to be of any influence. The team left Tripoli in March, clad in their finery and having been thoroughly fleeced. They had the impression that they were very much in the second rank of explorers, most of the available goods having been purchased by Messrs Beechey and Smyth who had gone so far as to snap up Ritchie's telescope, which had somehow found its way onto the market.

At Sockna, however, they were greeted with cries of 'Inglesi! Inglesi!', and their hearts swelled. Perhaps they were not so second-rank after all? 'We were the first English travellers in Africa who had resisted the persuasion that a disguise was necessary, and who had determined to travel in our real character as Britons and Christians, and to wear on all occasions our English dress,'[11] wrote Denham. The inhabitants were awed by the foreigners' waistcoat buttons, by their watches and by their trouser pockets, into which they thrust their hands in amazement. 'This to us was highly satisfactory,'[12] Denham recorded. He saw it as a complete vindication of their strategy. 'I am perfectly satisfied that our reception would have been less friendly had we assumed a character that could at best have been ill-supported. In trying to make ourselves appear as Mussulmans, we should have been set down as real impostors.'[13]

They reached Murzouk in one piece but shaken by desert conditions. Denham, who had never experienced a sandstorm, was driven to prolixity: 'The winds scorch as they pass,' he wrote, 'and bring with them billows of sand, rolling along in masses frightfully suffocating, which sometimes swallow up whole caravans and armies, burying them in their pathless depths.'[14]

The Bey of Murzouk, not to be overawed by their uniforms, billeted them in the same haunted house in which Lyon and Ritchie had previously stayed. It caused Oudney a moment of worry – 'I hope we shall not split on the same rock that poor Ritchie did.'[15] But Oudney and his men were safe from all monetary concerns. They had thirty-seven camel-loads of trade goods and could draw bills on Warrington's credit to a limitless extent. They were in as strong a position as they could possibly be.

At Murzouk, however, internal rivalries began to show. Barrow's instructions had done nothing to clear up the issue of command and if anything had muddied the matter further by telling Oudney in one place that Denham was not under his orders and in another assuring him that the whole expedition was under his command. As for Clapperton (whom the orders referred to as Shakleton) he was left in a leaderless limbo. Naturally, he looked to Oudney as his superior. Denham, however, considered Clapperton as his subordinate. 'In the choice of my companions, I do not think H.M. Government have shewn their usual sagacity,' Denham wrote to his brother. 'As one of them is under my orders and . . . Dr. Oudney and myself independent of each other, no small jealousy exists on their part, and to push me off the stage altogether would be exactly what they wish. My Lieutenant's conduct has been such . . . that had I reported it, he must have been broke or at least sent home, so vulgar, conceited and quarrelsome a person I scarcely ever met with.' As for Oudney: 'this son of War, or rather of Bluster, completely rules; therefore any proposition coming from me is generally negatived by a majority'.[16] They were, anyway, he decided, 'ill calculated to undertaking a long and tedious journey'.[17] Oudney had stayed in a cold wind after heavy exertion and had come down with a bad cough that proved to be tubercular. Clapperton was already feverish, so was Hillman. Denham alone was healthy.

Denham was ill-suited to any kind of compromise. He was also ill-suited to the frustrations inherent in travelling through the Sahara. When the Bey of Murzouk casually told him that there would be no expedition south until the following spring because the Pasha had not sent the necessary escort, Denham stormed back to Tripoli on 20 May 1822, exchanged hot words with Warrington, and left on the next boat for England via Marseilles to arrange the lieutenant-colonelcy he had been promised for his participation. Shockingly, he told neither Oudney or Clapperton of his plans, merely that he was going to get letters of recommendation for their journey from the Pasha.

The two Scots waited optimistically for his return. 'I hope that in five months after this you will her from us . . . on the banks of the

Niger,'[18] Clapperton wrote to Barrow on 4 June. They were still waiting in September when a courier informed them that Denham had
left for England. 'You may judge of our surprise,' Clapperton wrote to
Barrow. 'However, his absence will be no loss to the mission and a
saving to his country for Major Denham could not read his sextant,
knew not a star in the heavens and could not take the altitude of the
sun.'[19] Oudney was more vigorous in his condemnation: 'I have never
borne so much from any man as from him . . . Had I known the man,
I would have refused my appointment, and allowed some other to
reap the honour attached to it. But it is now too late and what I have
undertaken I hope to accomplish with credit to my Country and
myself.'[20]

   To prove his point he led Clapperton and Hillman on a short mission to the oasis town of Ghat, a few days' journey west of Murzouk.
Along the way they encountered Lyon's lakes of caviare worms.
Oudney sniffed them but forbore to have a taste, being repelled by
their 'strong slimy smell'.[21] Otherwise they discovered nothing of
interest save that elderly Arab gentlemen dyed their beards with
henna. Denham later recorded gleefully that Clapperton, who was
very proud of his bushy, reddish beard, was taken for a feeble old man.
They returned, coughing and sweating, to Murzouk, where they collapsed into their haunted house and did not rise for more than two
weeks. Whatever else they may have seen is lost, thanks to Denham
and Barrow, who jointly declared in the published journal that the
voyage home was 'wholly uninteresting, and is therefore omitted'.[22]

   Oudney and Clapperton were still prostrate in November when
Denham unexpectedly rode into town. He brought good tidings: he
had persuaded the Pasha to send an escort and the expedition could
now proceed. But nobody was there to hear the news. Disappointed
that he had not been met in the style he deserved, he peered into
Oudney's house. 'Nothing could be more disheartening than their
appearance,'[23] he recorded in disgust as he saw his fellow explorers
lying on their beds. The story which he then spun was that through
his efforts the Pasha had been prompted into action. In fact, the
prompting had come entirely from Warrington and when the news

reached him in Marseilles Denham had hurried back to Africa to present the change of heart as his own *fait accompli*. Crossly, Bathurst instructed him to act in future 'with more circumspection'.[24]

Oudney was fed up. 'Really,' he complained to Barrow on 4 November 1822, 'I have been much harassed since I left England – our prospects at times gloomy, at times smiling, alternating so that a sensible impression was made on our spirits.'[25] His one comfort came from not having to wear Arab clothes. 'I have not experienced any opposition on account of being a Christian and a Briton. There is not that hatred for the Christian name, not those prejudices which one might suppose. It is much easier for us to support our own character than one that must not but be hard even after several years of experience. I am sparing of paper,' he concluded. 'It is scarce here and we have a long journey ahead of us.'[26]

They left Murzouk shortly after Denham's reappearance, heading south along the slave trail to the interior. They were all ill, except for Denham, and were in no fit state to travel, but they could not turn down the opportunity after so many months of inaction. 'The road is perfectly safe and our personal safety is ensured by an escort of 60 or 70 Arabs,' Oudney wrote. 'For my part I would have dispensed with them as I dread they may be a thorn in our sides, but let us hope for the best.'[27]

Oudney's complaint was almost unheard of in the history of African exploration: he was being offered too much help. The Pasha was far more honest than anyone had given him credit for. Having undertaken to see Oudney's party to its goal and back, he was terrified lest any harm befall it and had accordingly instructed his cavalrymen – who numbered 210, as opposed to Oudney's estimate of sixty or seventy – not to let the Europeans venture into perilous zones. It had been he who had temporarily blocked the expedition earlier in the year, and although his hand had been forced by Warrington, he had no intention of letting Oudney stray beyond the parameters of the agreement with London. The white men would go south, they would come back alive, and the Pasha would get his £5,000. 'I was consequently not left a free agent,' Oudney explained to Barrow, 'but secretly opposed in any undertaking that had the slightest danger so as to try to deter me from it.'[28] Nonetheless, 'I am sanguine of success & think we shall be able to throw some light on a subject you have taken so much interest in.'[29]

The road from Murzouk to Lake Chad was 700 miles long and strewn so thickly with the remains of the some 8,500 slaves who died annually on the journey north that Oudney's party moved with an audible crunching sound. Denham, who had been dozing on his horse, 'was suddenly awakened by a crashing under his feet, which startled me excessively. I found that my steed had . . . stepped upon the perfect skeletons of two human beings, cracking their brittle bones under his feet, and by one trip of his foot separating a skull from the trunk, which rolled like a ball before him. This event gave me a sensation which it took some time to remove.'[30]

For days on end they trampled through the brittle remains. In places – wells which had obviously failed in past seasons – the skeletons lay in drifts 100 deep. Sometimes the bones were scattered in all directions – 'here a leg, there an arm, fixed with their ligaments at considerable distances from the trunk. What could have done this?' Oudney asked in wonder. 'Man forced by hunger, or the camels?'[31] Sometimes, more movingly, they retained the postures of life. 'Those of two women, whose perfect and regular teeth bespoke them young, were particularly shocking,' Denham wrote. 'Their arms still remained clasped around each other as they had expired, although the flesh had long since perished by being exposed to the burning rays of the sun, and the blackened bones only left: the nails of the fingers, and some of the sinews of the hand, also remained; and part of the tongue of one of them still appeared in the teeth.'[32]

By and by Denham became accustomed to the horrors: 'One of the skeletons we passed today had a very fresh appearance; the beard was still hanging to the skin of the face and the features were still discernible.'[33] A merchant suddenly recognized the man as a slave he had abandoned four months ago, whereupon one of the Arab escorts told him to hurry up and get him to market before anyone else claimed him. They all, Denham included, laughed heartily. Denham loved it. Not only were the Arabs 'a great and most necessary protection', but they 'enlivened us greatly on our dreary desert way by their infinite wit and sagacity'.[34] Oudney and Clapperton did not share his enthusiasm.

Soon the going became so arduous that the Europeans wondered if they too might not take their place amongst the skeletons. They wandered through shifting dunes where their footsteps were obliterated within an hour, and where the camel drivers hung onto the animals' tails as they slipped down the treacherous slopes. They plodded through canyons of sand sixty feet high, charting their course from the outcrops of sandstone which littered the unmappable desert. For days on end they never saw water, and when they did it was only revealed by hours of digging. Oudney was now so feeble that he could not walk more than 100 yards without resting. Hillman was worse still. He could not walk at all; he could not even get on and off his mule without help and was so shocked by the trail of bones that, according to Denham, who chose to cast him as the expedition's fool, he needed 'all the help and encouragement I could administer to him'.[35] The very camels were collapsing. One died of exhaustion on New Year's Day 1823 to be followed shortly by four others.

And yet, despite their troubles, they managed to keep up their bickering. Goaded by Denham's constant orders to take latitude readings for his journal, Clapperton set his feelings down on paper. 'You take upon yourself a great deal to issue orders which could not be more imperative were they from the Horse Guards or the Admiralty,' he wrote to Denham. 'You must not introduce Martial System into what is civil and scientific; neither must you expect from me what it is your duty to execute.'[36]

Denham responded that Clapperton was well-nigh ungovernable. He 'has thrown off all restraint', he wrote to Bathurst, complaining of the 'extreme intemperance, irregularity and insubordination with which his conduct has been marked'.[37] Denham also attacked Clapperton for mistreating his servants, knocking them down and threatening to shoot them. Further, he accused him of having sexual relations with one of them. Casual sex with the 'natives' was nothing exceptional on any expedition, whether in Africa or the Arctic. Denham himself had been smitten by the charms of African women – he was forever annotating their measurements and availability – and wrote that were it not for his high morals he would have enjoyed the 'luxury of possessing half a dozen of these . . . beauties'.[38] (He had in fact acquired at least one of the beauties under the pretext of marrying her to one of his servants.) But in Clapperton's case it was different. According to camp gossip, the servant with whom he was supposed to be sleeping was a man. 'The continued extreme impropriety of your conduct is no less discreditable to the mission and the country than to your self as an officer,'[39] Denham thundered.

Oudney was instructed to investigate the rumour but did so indignantly. 'He is not the man to disgrace himself so,' he wrote to Warrington. 'The whole has so much improbability that the most disinterested would pronounce it a Vile, Malicious report.'[40] In the end Oudney could find no evidence to support the accusation. Lord Bathurst decreed that it was unfounded. And Denham quickly asserted that he had never believed it in the first place. But the rumour, true or not, was out, to Clapperton's 'great mental uneasiness'[41] and to the further dissolution of the expedition's precarious unity.

On 4 February 1823, sixty-eight days after leaving Murzouk, they reached the great expanse of Lake Chad, 'glowing with the golden rays of the sun'.[42] Their relief was so enormous that for a moment they forgot their quarrels. The sight gave Denham a 'sensation so gratifying and inspiring that it would be difficult for language to convey an idea of its force and pleasure'.[43] The lake teemed with pelicans, flamingos, and every kind of bird, so tame that they did not move when he walked through them. Along the shore roamed herds of buffalo, antelope and elephant, wild boar, rogue cattle and flocks of guinea fowl. Monkeys chattered from the trees and edible snakes, eighteen feet long, hung pendulously across their way. Fish could be plucked out of the water by hand. From prosperous villages peeped 'good-looking, laughing negresses, all but naked'.[44] Food was ridiculously cheap. As they travelled around the lake, heading for Kuka, the region's capital, they wondered at the man who ruled this Arcadia. He was probably a simple chap, they decided, who would receive them 'under a tree, surrounded by just a few naked slaves'.[45]

On 17 February Denham was riding ahead of the others when he found his way blocked 'by a body of several thousand cavalry, drawn up in a line and extending right and left as far as I could see'. They moved in with 'an appearance of tact and management in their movements which astonished me'.[46] As they drew closer Denham saw that some were clad head to knee in chain mail, while others wore metal helmets. Their horses also wore armour of iron, brass and silver. This disciplined and well-armed formation, moving without noise or confusion, could have been plucked straight from a history of the Crusades. It belonged to Sheikh Mohammed El Kanemi, the ruler of Bornu.

Oudney and his party were flabbergasted. Here, in the middle of the desert, where they had expected a rabble of ignorant natives, was a nation of sophistication and power. They were escorted to Kuka through lines of spearsmen, and taken to the Sheikh's home, where soldiers with crossed spears guarded the steps to El Kanemi's inner sanctum. One by one the Europeans were admitted. Even Denham felt nervous.

El Kanemi sat in a small dark room, dressed in a blue robe with a headdress wrapped casually around his shoulders. Two black guards stood beside him, pistols at the ready. Muskets hung on the walls. What did the Christians want? he asked. 'To see the country merely, and to give an account of its inhabitants, produce and appearance,' Denham reassured him, 'as our sultan was desirous of knowing every part of the globe.'[47] Hesitantly, he proffered a letter of introduction from the Pasha of Tripoli.

To their unbounded relief the 'Sheikh of Spears' – as Denham called him – gave a big smile. They were welcome! Huts would be built for them to live in. His men would look after them. And when they had recovered from their travels he would show them whatever they wanted to see. Gratefully, they 'crept into the shade of our earthy dwellings, not a little fatigued with our entré and presentation'.[48]

They were woken a short while later by the sound of a camel-load of fish being dumped outside their front door. A second delivery was thrown at them that evening.

For two months they stayed at Kuka, pottering about and enjoying the hospitality of the Sheikh who treated them with paternal generosity. They reciprocated with gifts that included two small pieces of field artillery and let off a few Congreve rockets (true, military projectiles rather than fun squibs) whose impressive passage, 100 feet above the city, astounded the townsfolk and impressed the Sheikh mightily. The Sheikh was equally impressed by Hillman's carpentry and commanded him to prove his skill by building a couple of storage chests.

Once again, though, they were molly-coddled more than they wished. The leader of their escort refused to let them explore for fear they might come to harm. When news broke that Kanemi was commandeering their escort for a slave raid to the south Denham stormed that they would have to tie him up in chains if they wanted to stop him going. He raged that he 'dare not lose such an opportunity of seeing the country'.[49] This outburst, coupled with El Kanemi's sudden recall that the Pasha was holding one of his wives and three of his children hostage in Murzouk against his good behaviour, had the desired effect.

Oudney and Clapperton declined to accompany him – more precisely, he didn't tell them he was going – and so Denham left Kuka as the sole European in an army that swelled as it marched through the countryside to more than 3,000. It was not a happy experience. Conditions were 'almost insupportable'.[50] The temperature reached 113 °F in the shade and flies swarmed round him so thickly that 'my hands and eyes were so swelled that I could scarcely hold a pen, or see to use one'.[51] His travelling companions were unfriendly. On the first evening the Muslim commanders let out a 'general groan'[52] on learning that they had been eating with a Christian, and thereafter treated him with suspicion and contempt. When he ventured out to survey the land he was watched so closely and with such mistrust by his escort that he dared not even 'sketch the shape of a single hill'.[53] His vaunted uniform counted for nothing. At one stop he was informed that the people had heard of Christians 'as the worst people in the world, and probably, until they saw me, scarcely believed them to be human'.[54]

Even when he tried to follow Arab customs he was rejected as an impostor. On approaching the town of Mora, for example, he accompanied his group in the traditional greeting of riding as furiously as possible at the main gate and then skidding to a halt as close as they dared. 'This is a perilous sort of salutation,' he wrote, 'but nothing must stop you; and it is seldom made except at the expense of one or more lives.'[55] On this occasion they rode over an innocent bystander, killing him in an instant and breaking a horse's leg.

The local sultan, a small man with a dyed sky-blue beard, was duly impressed by the display and greeted Denham courteously, but on hearing that he was a Christian refused to have anything more to do with him. Everywhere Denham went it was the same. At one stop he had his food bowl snatched away from him, to be replaced with a separate one, lest believers be contaminated by contact with the infidel. Denham did not mention it in his journal, but going European was clearly not a help.

Shortly after the uncomfortable interlude at Mora, the raiding party reached its target, the district of Mandara. The Africans whom the Bornu men had selected to be driven in helpless droves back to Tripoli proved uncomfortably defiant. El Kanemi's troops were greeted with six-foot-high pallisades, showers of poisoned arrows and massive boulders that were rolled onto their heads from the surrounding hills. They fled, pursued by their would-be victims. One man fell to the ground with five arrows protruding from his head. Denham himself received a graze to the cheek, and rode off with two arrows sticking through his headdress.

In the rout Denham became separated from the main body and his horse was shot from beneath him. He would have been killed instantly had not the pursuing tribesmen stripped him and started arguing over his clothes. As he wrote, 'My hopes of life were too faint to deserve the name.'[56] But while his captors were squabbling over their catch he slipped beneath a horse's belly and fled into the forest. Naked, he sped through the trees, scrambling over thorny thickets, plunging through rivers, dodging leopards and venomous serpents, until he finally made his way back to the Bornu army, most of whom were by now succumbing to their poisoned wounds, blood streaming from their noses and mouths.

Even then he was not safe. 'What is there extraordinary in a Christian's death?'[57] demanded one of the leaders, when told of Denham's weakened condition. He would have been left to die had he not been supported by a man whom El Kanemi had sent, unbeknownst to Denham, to bring him home safely. The group that made its way back to Kuka was a sorry one indeed. The only reward Denham received for this interesting but unproductive insight into African slavery was another reprimand for having countenanced such 'disgraceful proceedings'.[58]

Undeterred, Denham left on a second slave raid in late May, accompanied this time by Oudney, Clapperton and El Kanemi himself. (Hillman was left behind to build gun carriages for the Sheikh.) The proposed quarry was a rebellious group of Bornu subjects who lived to the west of Lake Chad. But when they reached their destination, to be greeted by peace offerings and the ritual submission of hundreds of rebels, El Kanemi graciously forgave them and turned back for home. The fact that a further 12,000 rebel bowmen remained unrepentant and were currently dipping their arrows in poison may have had something to do with it too.

This raid did, however, yield one piece of geographical information. Along the way they crossed the River Yeou (Yobe) which flowed eastwards into Lake Chad. 'As I expected,' Denham wrote, 'every one of the Arabs said this was the [Niger].'[59] The Yeou was a miserable little thing, but it was their best hope yet. The optimistic Oudney considered it the 'only probable' connection with the Niger, but even he had to admit that 'it is too small' – qualified by a plaintive 'almost'.

The discovery of the Yeou prompted the only sortie from Lake Chad in which all four Europeans came together as a team. They set off up the Yeou to ascertain whether or not it joined the Niger, but before reaching its source they were driven back to Kuka by illness and bad weather. The rains had set in, and all four Europeans became violently ill. Clapperton was delirious from fever; Oudney was spluttering with a tubercular cough; Hillman almost died; and even Denham was forced to his bed.

From that point they marched alone. At the end of 1823 Oudney and Clapperton went west, resuming their journey up the Yeou, while Denham set off on 23 January 1824 to explore Lake Chad's southern and eastern shores. With him he took a twenty-three-year-old ensign from the 80th Regiment by the name of Ernest Toole, who had volunteered in Malta to join the expedition. Toole was 'a robust, healthy-looking young man with a double-barrelled gun slung at his back. When he presented himself at the door of my hut, his very countenance was an irresistible letter of introduction,'[61] Denham wrote.

Toole arrived in Kuka on 23 December 1823, having made the journey south in a very respectable three months. Little else is known of him save that he played the flute, that he was 'in every sense a most amiable and promising young officer',[62] and that he died of fever within two months of his arrival. His replacement, another youngster called Mr Tyrwhitt who arrived in May, suffered the same fate but lasted a few months longer.

Of the two missions, Denham's was the most promising and the least successful. Had he been able to complete it he would have solved the question of whether or not Lake Chad was connected to the Nile. (It was, and is, not.) But with his fellow explorers dying around him, and with hostile tribes blocking the way, he got no further than Tangalia, on Lake Chad's south-eastern extremity. There, in late June, his escort refused to go any further. 'The excursion you wished to make was always dangerous,' the leader told him, 'it is now impracticable.'[63]

Denham's one contribution to the Niger question was to cross the River Shari, a 650-yard-wide body of water that flowed into Lake Chad from the south. (It had been sighted previously by Oudney and

Clapperton on a minor sortie from Kuka; but Denham passed it off as his own discovery.) Unlike the Yeou, the Shari was the right size to be the Niger but it came from the wrong direction (quite why the direction was considered wrong is a bit mystifying; Barrow's tangled view of African geography could easily have accommodated a northward-flowing Niger). Had Denham followed it to its source he would have reached a watershed on the other side of which could be found the source of the Benue, a river which actually *did* join with the Niger. But Denham did not trace the Shari upwards – for which one cannot blame him; the region was then in a state of war – and thus the matter was no further advanced than when he had set out.

It would be wrong to denigrate Denham's efforts. He recorded a host of new information concerning the peoples of the region – among which was the revelation that Africans practised vaccination 'by inserting into the flesh the sharp point of a dagger charged with the disease';[64] Europeans had only discovered this trick in 1798. But his interests seem to have been concerned mainly with the comparative beauties of different tribeswomen; he purchased a very nice fourteen-year-old Bagirmi girl for the price of a red cap and a muslin turban.

The voyage of Oudney and Clapperton, conversely, held the least promise but accomplished the most. It was the least promising because they had no fixed landmark, such as Lake Chad, around which to work, and because they did not know where their objectives – Timbuctoo and/or the Niger – were. Yet it was the most successful because, in spite of these difficulties, it came within a few hundred miles of its goals.

There was another factor that militated against the success of Oudney's mission and that was the health of its members. Clapperton had malaria and Oudney was still suffering from tuberculosis. Even El Kanemi wondered whether the doctor was fit enough for the task. Oudney shrugged off the Sheikh's concern. 'Why,' Oudney assured him, 'if I stay here I shall die, and probably sooner, as travelling always improves my health.'[65] Reluctantly the Sheikh acceded to his wishes and sent them off in a 100-strong caravan with a small escort to protect them against marauders.

Their immediate destination was the town of Kano on the upper reaches of the Yeou, just over 300 miles from Lake Chad. From there they intended to strike west to the town of Sokoto, capital of the Hausa nation. Kanemi kindly furnished them with a letter of introduction to its ruler, Sultan Bello. That Bello also ruled Mandara, which Kanemi had recently tried to plunder, seemed no object to friendly relations.

Halfway to Kano, while making for the evocatively named town of Murmur, Oudney died. The combination of hot days and freezing nights did nothing to alleviate his condition, and despite his hopes that travel would 'recruit' him a little, it soon became apparent that it would not. On 28 December he admitted: 'I feel it is all over with me.'[66] Instructing Clapperton to give his notes and journal to Barrow he resigned himself to death. He grew steadily weaker and deteriorated to the point where he was unable to dress himself unaided. He died on the morning of 12 January 1824 while being helped onto his camel.

Clapperton was distraught: 'To me, his friend and fellow traveller, labouring also under disease, and now left alone amid a strange people, and proceeding through a country which has hitherto never been trod by European foot, the loss was severe and afflicting in the extreme.'[67] He buried his companion as best he could, building a small wall around the grave and slaughtering a couple of bullocks as a bribe to prevent the locals interfering with the body. Then he carried on for Kano. Alas, no sooner had he departed than Oudney's remains were dug up and burned.

Hitherto, Clapperton had played a subordinate role. Now that he was on his own, he proved a capable and observant explorer. He traced enough of the Yeou to be satisfied that it was not the Niger then, reaching Kano on 20 January, he primed himself to enter what he had been assured was the major trading town in the district. 'Arrayed in what was left of my naval uniform,'[68] he strode through the gates with as much dignity as his crumpled blue frock coat, grubby white breeches and silk stockings would allow. Nobody took the slightest bit of notice. Clapperton was bewildered. 'Not an individual turned his head,' he wrote. '[They] allowed me to pass by without notice or remark.'[69]

Kano was a bizarre place. Centred on an unhealthy swamp into which every main drain flowed, it was not so much a town as an enclosed suburb. Three-quarters of the area within the fifteen-mile circumference of its walls was given over to ill-kempt fields and gardens. The main body of houses was congregated around the swamp – the marketplace was actually *in* it – and to the north lay two hills, 200 feet high, near which huddled separate villages for the blind and the lame. Kano's inhabitants – 40,000 of them, Clapperton reckoned, half of them slaves – plodded incuriously about their business. It was a trading town, used to odd sights and unfamiliar visitors. A person would have had to wear something a lot stranger than a British naval uniform to turn heads there.

Clapperton stayed in Kano for a month or so while he recovered from an attack of malaria. In between bouts of fever, which was aggravated by the abominable stench from the swamp, he examined the marketplace and found that in spite of its fetidness it was a sophisticated emporium. Among the haunches of goat, sheep and camel meat, its stalls carried French writing paper, Egyptian cotton and Maltese swords. He even purchased a green umbrella made in England – 'an article he little expected to meet with, yet by no means uncommon'.[70] When a packet arrived from Denham containing letters, newspapers, a quantity of Peruvian bark – quinine – and three bottles of port, Clapperton began to feel almost normal. He read the papers, infused the quinine, drank the port and, thus restored, staggered upriver on the next leg of his journey.

He did not leave without asking a 'buxom young girl of fifteen'[71] if she would like to accompany him. Like Denham, he learned that being European was not always an advantage. The girl wept, and 'frankly avowed she did not know how to dispose of my white legs'.[72] He did not press the matter.

The going was easy. Ever since leaving Kuka the country had become increasingly fertile and as Clapperton went on he met grassy swards dotted with trees that stunned him with their resemblance to

English parkland. Heartened by this verdure, he entered Sokoto on 16 March and presented himself before Sultan Bello. An imposing man of forty-four, who possessed an uncommon knowledge of the world, Bello seemed not at all surprised by Clapperton's arrival, and if he was awed by his motley uniform he politely did not mention it. He accepted Clapperton's presents gratefully, and when Clapperton pointed out that the prize gift, a sextant, could help the Sultan direct his prayers more accurately to Mecca, he responded with admirable restraint.

Here, in the darkest depths of Africa, was a civilization Britain had never heard of, yet which seemed perfectly *au fait* with Britain's own activities. Sultan Bello nodded knowingly when informed of the latest instances of gun-boat diplomacy and asked some perspicacious questions about British imperialism in India. He was even acquainted with Britain's press, which he called 'the news of the world', and asked Clapperton to read extracts from the issues he had brought with him. Only in religious matters did he seem a little behind the times, inquiring whether Clapperton was a Nestorian or a Socinian.

It was all quite a shock to Clapperton, particularly when Bello airily revealed details concerning Timbuctoo, the Niger and Mungo Park's fate. Yes, he knew of Timbuctoo. It was a town about 600 miles distant. But he could not advise Clapperton to go there. The journey would lead him through hostile tribes and dangerous territory. As for the Niger and Park, he knew of a river, the Quorra, on which a white man had been killed and all his possessions seized by the local potentate, the Sultan of Yauri. This river was much nearer than Timbuctoo but he could not countenance its exploration for the same reasons. When Clapperton said he was nevertheless thinking of pressing on, Bello replied with veiled menace, 'Think of it with prudence.'[73]

Bello drew a map in the sand to show where the river went. As later transcribed by one of his scribes, it flowed south from Bussa, Park's furthest recorded point, then turned dramatically east. Bello claimed that it entered the sea at a spot called Fundah, but the inscription on the map announced in no uncertain terms that it reached Egypt. There were two possible reasons for the discrepancy. When Bello

spoke of the Niger, or Quorra, he may have been meaning its tributary, the Benue, which did indeed enter the Niger at a place called
Fundah. The river on the map, therefore, may not have been
intended to be read as the Niger at all. A second possibility – the more
likely – is that Bello wanted to keep Britain out of his domain.
Delighted as he professed himself to be with Clapperton and all
things British, he can have had no desire for his nation to be absorbed
by the British Empire. (He had already asked some pointed questions
about Denham's participation in the Mandara slave raid.) By sending
the Niger off to the east he was trying to divert British interest elsewhere.

Clapperton made no comment on this, but he did hear a revealing
superstition: 'It is commonly believed among them that strangers
would come and take their country from them, if they knew the
course of the Quorra.'[74] As ultimately transpired, the superstition was
perfectly correct. Prevented from ascertaining the truth, Clapperton
could bring home only a conundrum – plus two pairs of Denham's
trousers, 'much the worse for wear',[75] and his journal, which had made
their way from Mandara to Sokoto. Racked by malaria, he retraced his
steps to Kano, and thence to Murmur – where he recovered sufficiently to give the local chief a sound thrashing for having desecrated
Oudney's grave – and finally collapsed into his bed in Kuka on 8 July.

Denham, in the interim, had occupied himself collecting specimens of natural history and Hillman, delighted not to have been
dragged off on another expedition, had spent his time constructing a
camel litter for El Kanemi's most important wife. It had been eight
months since either of them had seen Clapperton and when news
reached them of his safe return, Denham rushed over to investigate.
'I went immediately to the hut where he was lodged,' Denham wrote,
'but so satisfied was I that the sunburnt, sickly person that lay
extended on the floor, rolled in a dark-blue shirt, was not my companion, that I was about to leave the place when he convinced me of
my error by calling me by name.'[76]

When Clapperton recovered, he and Denham agreed in a rare
moment of unanimity that it was time to go home, whereupon they

began to argue over the precise route. Denham had a harebrained plan to strike east for Egypt, but in the end they went back the way they had come – waiting until Hillman had finished his latest commission, a chair for the Sheikh – and squabbled their way into Tripoli, onto a ship, through twenty-five days' quarantine in Italy, over the Alps, and finally back to London.

When Denham and Clapperton reported to Whitehall on 1 June 1825 they caused a sensation almost as great as that which Parry had stirred up on his return from Melville Island. 'We scarcely know,' said the *Edinburgh Review*, 'since the time of Marco Polo . . . any instance in which so much new ground has been gone over by a single mission. Regions have been surveyed, the very existence of which was before unknown and others, of which only a faint rumour had reached across the immense deserts by which they were enclosed.'[77]

Barrow took a dimmer view. He praised the expedition's achievements, but lamented the lack of solid information concerning the Niger. 'The information obtained by Clapperton,' he wrote in the *Quarterly*, 'has entangled the question more than before.'[78]

Clapperton had not entangled the question at all. If anything he had made it clearer, but not in the manner which Barrow would have liked. Barrow supported the Niger–Nile theory; Clapperton was a Benin man. Following the discovery of the River Yeou, Barrow had written that 'it unquestionably is' the Niger.[79] When Clapperton's expedition proved that the Yeou could not be the Niger, Barrow was displeased. But he still clung on. His opinion in 1823 had been, 'I think now there is no question that the Niger falls into the Nile.'[80] When Clapperton informed him that it didn't, he saw no reason to change his mind. There was that map from Sultan Bello. Besides, how could one trust a man who was not a gentleman? Barrow disliked people who had risen through the ranks. To him, an education 'in the cockpit of a man-of-war, among young gentlemen'[81] was indispensable. It 'is to the navy what a public school is to those who move in civil society',[82] he explained in his biography of Bligh.

When Clapperton's journal came out in 1826, published as part of a compendium authored by himself, Denham and the late Oudney, Barrow appointed himself editor of Clapperton's section. According to the preface it was Clapperton's own from beginning to end. 'I have carefully abstained from altering a sentiment, or even an expression, and rarely had occasion to add, omit, or change, a single word,'[83] Barrow told the public. He told John Murray otherwise, stressing that he had only made the account respectable by 'dishing and trimming him as much as I dare'.[84] Precisely what he dished and trimmed is unknown. Maybe he gave the text no more than a competent edit. But given his stated opinion that Clapperton's observations were 'not much to be depended on',[85] one gets the impression that Barrow suppressed a few contrary opinions.

Denham had dented the Niger–Nile connection slightly by drawing a map, garnered from local information, which showed Lake Chad as having no eastern outlet. Oudney, too, had put forward the theory that Lake Chad led nowhere, judging correctly that it disposed of its water by evaporation. But Denham's journal also described eddies and whirlpools in the centre of Lake Chad which drove the water into underground chasms, through which it passed until halted by a spur of granite, at which point it resurfaced and continued its journey east. This was much more like it and just what Barrow wanted to hear.

Neither Denham nor Clapperton saw the finished publication. Denham, promoted to lieutenant-colonel – and, to judge by the records, snubbed by the authorities – was sent off to Sierra Leone, 'the white man's grave', where he shortly added his own body to the thousands that were buried there already. Clapperton, now a captain, was despatched by Barrow to complete the job he had left unfinished: to map the estimated 300 miles between Sokoto and the Niger, all that separated his last discoveries from those of Park. He departed within three months of coming home, choosing an approach through the perilous zones of the tropical coast. It was not what Barrow had in mind, but it would do, if only to dispel the canard that the Niger flowed into the Gulf of Benin.

All that remained was to dispose of the animals which the expedition had brought back to England, some as presents for King George

IV from rulers they had met, and others collected by themselves. The menagerie included one horse, one sheep, one ichneumon or mongoose, four ostriches, one monkey, three parrots, a shark, and three slugs. The parrots found a home, and some interest was shown in the monkey. The fate of the others is a mystery. A concerned note lingers in the records from the man charged with their well-being. To an inquirer he writes that 'the sheep is so much attached to the horse that their separation might perhaps be fatal to the sheep'. He warns also that 'the animal called "Sharke" is naturally savage & peculiarly dangerous'.[86] There is no mention of the slugs.

12

THE MADMAN OF TIMBUCTOO

Even before Denham and Clapperton returned, Barrow was angling for another bite at Africa. In 1823 he had pushed a plan to cross the Sahara not via Murzouk but via Ghadames, a major oasis on the alternative caravan route to the west. The expedition's destination was Timbuctoo and its leader was Lyon – 'If the government will give him £1,000 he will ask for nothing more.'[1] The government would not give him £1,000 and so Lyon was sent to the Arctic again. But Barrow was persistent. 'I am very much for encouraging this spirit of adventure,' he told Bathurst, 'and I am sure the public feeling is for it.'[2] Bathurst thought differently, and jotted down a brief minute: 'Mr. Barrow is very impertinent.'[3]

Impertinent or not, Barrow got his way, thus solving forever the question of Timbuctoo and sealing the fate of a neglected army officer called Gordon Laing. Laing was an ambitious, impatient, fanatical and very brave young friend of Sabine's who was obsessed with Africa. He had served with the Royal African Colonial Corps in Sierra Leone, where he had caused a degree of resentment as editor of the local newspaper by filling its pages with 'the most fulsome panegyrics upon himself in prose and rhyme'.[4] He was considered 'unwise, unofficerlike and unmanly',[5] and his commanding officer wrote that 'his military exploits were worse than his poetry'[6] – which is saying a great deal. Nevertheless, during his time there he had come to some inescapable conclusions regarding the Niger. On one foray inland he had come across the source of the Niger, and on measuring its altitude had found that it was lower than the highest known point of the Nile. 'The question of the Niger uniting with the Nile must therefore be forever at rest, the elevation of its source not being sufficient to carry it half that distance,'[7] he wrote. He pressed for the recall of the Denham–Oudney–Clapperton mission. 'It is now very clear that nothing in the way of discovery can be effected from that quarter, and that the attempt is only attended with expense, disappointment and perhaps the loss of valuable lives.'[8]

This did not endear Laing to Barrow. Still less did his assertion that the Niger flowed into the Gulf of Benin. But time was pressing. The French were showing an unpardonable interest in the area and had had the effrontery to offer a prize of 10,000 francs for the first person to bring back information about Timbuctoo. Even the Italian archaeologist Belzoni, fresh from trampling through Egypt's catacombs, had his eyes on the fabled city.* Barrow wanted a Briton to get there first. When Laing offered to go, not being 'influenced by the most distant view to emolument of any kind . . . I shall be perfectly happy to undertake the journey without any salary',[9] and with a proposed outlay of £640 10s for set-up costs plus an annual expenditure of £173 7s 6d, he was not only accepted, but was promoted from captain to major.

Laing remained unrepentant about the Niger. 'The information of Sultan Bello now, in my opinion, sets the matter entirely at rest,' he

* The great Belzoni – Egyptologist, engineer and showman – was a fascinating man who wrote vivid descriptions of being suffocated by clouds of mummy dust. He did have a go at Timbuctoo. He was landed at Benin by a Royal Navy vessel and bade it farewell in inimitable style: 'God bless you, my fine fellows, and send you a happy sight of your country and friends!' He died on 3 December 1823 of dysentery, having covered only ten miles.

wrote, 'or as nearly so as can be until the river is absolutely navigated to its *embouchure*, but I rather apprehend that it will not satisfy Mr. Barrow, who is determined that the Yeou or the Schad *shall* be the Niger.'[10]

It did not satisfy Mr Barrow. When Laing's journal was published describing his time in Sierra Leone and his opinions regarding the Niger, Barrow penned a disdainful review. 'I fully expected that he would object to my having seen the source of the Niger,' Laing wrote crossly to a friend in the Foreign Office. 'It would completely interfere with that theory upon which he has completely staked his reputation, and which is just on the point of being overturned.'[11]

On hearing that Barrow was sending Clapperton out again, Laing vented his competitive spleen: 'Clapperton may as well have stayed at home, if the termination of the Niger is his object – It is destined for me, and [nobody] can interfere with me – Timbuctoo shall be visited, and the Niger explored within a very few months.'[12] In yet more strident tone he declared that, 'If I do not visit [Timbuctoo] the world will forever remain in ignorance of the place, as I make no vainglorious assertion when I say that it will never be visited by Christian man after me.'[13] Off he went to Malta, his stop-off *en route* to Africa, utterly obsessed with the mission. 'I am so wrapt up in the success of this enterprise,' he wrote, 'that I think of nothing else all day and dream of nothing else all night.'[14]

Laing arrived in Tripoli in May 1825, where the crews of two British ships swarmed the rigging and gave him three cheers. 'There are moments in a man's life,' he sighed, 'which he would not exchange for living years.'[15] Then he made his way to the British consulate primed with all the urgency of his mission and promptly fell in love with, and proposed to, Warrington's daughter.

Warrington was horrified. Expediting explorers to the interior was one thing, but becoming familially entangled with them was another. Laing was not the best choice of son-in-law. Not only was he slightly mad but he was also sick. Even before he arrived in Tripoli he had spent a month bedridden in Malta. 'I much fear the delicate state of his health will not carry him through his arduous task,'[16] Warrington wrote home. When it came to Laing's cut-price budget, the Consul could only shake his head. The Pasha's manner was 'cool and hesitating' towards Laing, and as Warrington divined from his glances and the rubbing together of his finger and thumb, he was unwilling to let him proceed without a substantial 'pecuniary douceur'.[17]

Laing was equal to the Pasha. On being informed 'in the most unequivocal language, that the door was shut to me unless I opened it with money',[18] he ordered £2,000 to be issued immediately with the promise of a slightly larger sum to be paid by instalments as he neared his goal. In a single stroke he increased the cost of his mission sixfold. It did not worry him. 'I have, I assure your Lordship, done everything for the best,'[19] he wrote blithely to Bathurst.

Warrington supported the extra expenditure. But he was less than happy about the romance. While he wished his daughter every happiness, he did not wish her to marry a lunatic who would in all likelihood never come back alive. As he told Bathurst, 'every argument and every feeling of disapprobation was resorted to by me to prevent even an engagement under the existing circumstances, the disadvantages so evidently appearing to attach to my daughter'.[20] More galling still, as senior representative of the Church of England in Tripoli, he would be expected to perform the marriage service. Furtively, he inquired whether such a marriage was legally binding.

Laing cared not a farthing. With the calm certainty of the fanatic he sent off for 'a handsome little cabinet of mineralogical specimens, such a one as will suit a lady of taste and refinement',[21] which he could not afford, and commissioned a similarly extravagant miniature portrait of his wife-to-be.

Warrington, the great facilitator, was at a loss. 'After a voluminous correspondence,' he wrote to Bathurst, 'I found my wishes, exertions, entreaties and displeasures quite futile and of no avail.'[22] He married the couple on 14 July but made it a condition, signed by all parties, that the marriage was not to be consummated until Laing had reached his target and returned direct to Tripoli.

This did not upset Laing. If anything, he bore it like a badge of honour. He had already set himself an apparently impossible task.

Now he had the impetus of frustrated desire; he was a latterday medieval knight, striving to impress his unobtainable love – whose name was Emma – with acts of heroism and suffering. 'I shall do more than has ever been done before,' he wrote, 'and shall show myself to be what I have ever considered myself, a man of enterprise and genius.'[23]

This strange, frenzied man, who had descended so abruptly on Warrington's life, hurried into the desert amid a cloud of delusions. Down through the Sahara he plodded, with a few servants, in a caravan largely composed of his own camels. He kept a journal – or said he did – but sent few of its contents back to Tripoli. All that survives is a brief ode to himself written in February 1825 and a few pages describing the countryside written the same August. Instead he charted his course with letters that revealed little of his journey and much about his mental state. He castigated the people he met for their greed; he dwelt darkly on the character of Clapperton, whom he saw as his arch rival in the quest for Timbuctoo – 'I am not over anxious to meet [him],' he sniffed, 'particularly after what my friend Sabine has said of him';[24] he ranted about the rewards he should receive and the sacrifices he had made; he disparaged the efforts of previous explorers such as Lyon – 'Master George never troubled himself much with observations';[25] and although he never wrote to her directly, he included in each letter to Warrington an effusion to 'my dear, dear Emma'.

Now and then his despatches included the occasional sketch or map. Sometimes they included horrendous bills – 2,500 dollars in one instance, for a guide. Laing apologized for the cost. But what was money compared to the glory of reaching Timbuctoo? 'I am sanguine in my hopes of accomplishing a visit to the far-famed capital of Central Africa,' he told Warrington in August 1825, '[and to] the spot where the adventurous Park lost his life, and the problematic termination of the Niger, within the space of six months.'[26] As he explained, 'You shall find that I shall do everything in the Mission which you and the rest of my friends expect from me.'[27]

When Warrington forwarded some advice from Clapperton, Laing rose in fury. 'I care little for any information that Clapperton could communicate,' he wrote. 'I smile at the idea of his reaching Timbuctoo before me. How can he expect it? Has he not already had the power? Has he not already thrown away the chance? . . . He amuses me by saying *you must not eat or drink before a Turk* – if so, how is it that I hear how the Turks speak constantly of the quantities of wine *Abdullah* (his country name) used to drink – four bottles of port wine before dinner whenever he could get it – I am not surprised Mr. C. should not wish to drink before them.' Clapperton's advice was 'worth nothing'.[28]

One of the matters Clapperton had raised was the question of clothes. While Denham had relished the opportunity to display his buttons, braid and jackets, Clapperton seems – in retrospect, at least – to have sided with Lyon in advocating native costumes and customs. Laing had adopted local dress from the start – except on Sundays – and took the suggestion as an affront. '"I must wear a plain Turkish dress", just as "I must be kind and patient with the natives",' came Laing's retort. '"Tis not my nature to be otherwise. "I must not take observations secretly." The sun does not shine in sly corners. "I must not speak disrespectfully of the women." I wonder how he found this out – I might have been a century in Africa and never have made such a discovery. "I must not meddle with the females of the country." Prodigious! "I must have presents to give away." We need not ghosts to rise from their graves to tell us this.'[29]

Laing sent huffy letters to the Colonial Office informing Lord Bathurst of his opinions. To his mind, Clapperton's 'only object seems to be to forestall me in discovery'.[30] At the same time, he pestered Warrington for Emma's miniature. Without it he feared he might go mad and that, as he told Warrington unnecessarily, would not be good: 'The state of my mind may prove much more prejudicial to the state of my health than the climate of Africa.'[31] Again, he was plagued by the spectre of Clapperton. 'Clapperton may as well have stayed at home if the termination of the Niger is his object. It is destined for me. It is due me, and [no] Clapperton can interfere with me,' he wrote to Warrington. 'Only take care of my dearest Emma, and

Timbuctoo shall be visited and the Niger explored within a very few months.'[32] 'I, as I always thought I should, shall be the man,'[33] he wrote. He would perform his journey 'like a Trojan'.[34]

But was Warrington taking care of Emma? When the miniature finally caught up with him, Laing was aghast. Could he have made a mistake in choosing the Spanish Consul-General as artist? Or did his beloved really look like that? Those sunken eyes, those pale cheeks, those colourless lips, that melancholy expression . . . she must be ill and dying. Laing immediately prepared to return to Tripoli. 'What is Timbuctoo? What the Niger? What the world to me without my Emma?' he raved to Warrington. 'Should anything befall my Emma, which God forbid, I no more wish to see the face of man; my course will be run – a few short days of misery and I should follow her to heaven . . . Bear with my weakness, my brain is troubled – I must lay down my pen awhile – oh that picture.'[35]

Warrington was seriously worried – both for the expedition and for his son-in-law's sanity. 'For Heavens sake do not let your powerful feelings operate on you so,'[36] he replied with asperity, assuring Laing that Emma was perfectly well and that he was on no account to turn back. Tentatively, he inquired if Laing would like a doctor to be sent out. Laing had the bit between his teeth. 'It is the mind that will see Laing through,' he retorted. 'Should *it* fail me, what doctor could strengthen it? Really, this world is made up of such commonplace matter that it is painful for a purpose of mind to exist in it. I have not yet decided whether I shall proceed or return to Tripoli.'[37]

Warrington was getting angry. 'I can hardly keep my temper or patience,' he wrote. 'So help me God she is alive and well.'[38]

Laing's mind was finally made up not by Warrington's assurances but by a letter from Denham – 'who writes in a handsome, gentlemanlike style'[39] – describing Clapperton's departure for the west coast. 'I feel assured he will never go beyond Benin! – mark my words. He . . . will arrive at the worst season of the year,' Laing told Warrington. 'I cannot help expressing a hope that he may be prudent enough to return if he finds the bad effects of the climate lay hold of his constitution, which they undoubtedly will.'[40]

Competitiveness, combined with a sudden, paranoid belief that the world was watching and waiting for him to fail, drove Laing forward: 'I had a long argument with myself last night, and I felt too keenly the triumph which my enemies (for I have my share of those miscreants who are jealous of the little reputation I have so hardly earned) would have over me . . . Government may find fault with me if they please; let us go on with our labour with diminished enthusiasm, and if we can not command, let us at least deserve commendation.'[41] Confidence restored, he asked for a warship to patrol the Gulf of Benin ready to pick him up because he had no wish to be kept hanging around once he had traced the Niger to its mouth. He punctured the bluster, however, with a plaintive inquiry as to the pre-nuptial agreement. Would he still be allowed to consummate his marriage, he asked, if he returned to Tripoli by a more circuitous route than planned?

Although sickly, Laing prided himself on his strength. He mentioned fleetingly that he had gone without food for a week *en route* to Ghadames and that the thermometer sometimes reached 120 °F in the shade, during which time he had sustained 'privations and exposure to a degree of heat which I am inclined to believe few European constitutions could stand'.[42] With this in mind, he set out over a desert 'as flat as a bowling green'[43] for Timbuctoo.

The route he had chosen had always been dangerous. Caravans travelling from Ghadames faced the prospect of raids from marauding Tuareg tribesmen who controlled the western desert from Morocco to sub-Saharan Africa. Normally, travellers paid them protection money for a safe passage; Laing either omitted to pay or paid too little. His small caravan was easier meat than most. At 5 a.m. on a January morning in 1826, while the group was three-quarters of the way to Timbuctoo, the Tuaregs struck in a flurry of slashing swords and blazing muskets, killing everybody who did not flee and leaving Laing for dead after they had taken all his possessions.

When the caravan reassembled and picked up the pieces, it departed immediately for its next stop, the oasis of Sidi el Muktar, abandoning Laing where he lay. Luckily, however, it also abandoned a wounded camel driver and a few redundant camels. The two men followed in its wake, Laing strapped onto the back of one camel while the injured driver led the way on another. Laing covered 400 miles in this fashion, suffering pains which can only be described by the following account which eventually reached Warrington in Tripoli. 'To begin from the top: I have five sabre cuts on the crown of the head and three on the left temple, all fractures from which much bone has come away; one on my left cheek which fractured the jaw bone and has divided the ear, forming a very unsightly wound; one over the right temple and a dreadful gash on the back of the neck, which slightly grazed the windpipe; a musket ball in the hip, which made its way through my back, slightly grazing the backbone; five sabre cuts on my right arm and hand, three of the fingers broken, the hand cut three-fourths across, and the wrist bones cut through; three cuts on the left arm, the bone of which has been broken but is again uniting; one slight wound on the right leg and two with one dreadful gash on the left, to say nothing of a cut across the fingers of my left hand, now healed up.'[44]

Almost as an afterthought he added that on arrival in Sidi el Muktar he had caught the plague – 'a dreadful malady somewhat similar to yellow fever in its symptoms'[45] – and had spent nine days 'so ill with fever that it was presumed, expected and hoped that I should die'.[46] While he was sick most of his possessions, including his gun, had been stolen and sent to be sold in the Timbuctoo market. 'I am nevertheless doing well,' he concluded, writing with only the thumb and middle finger of his left hand, 'and hope yet to return to England with much important geographical information.'[47]

Warrington wrote to Clapperton asking him 'for God's sake' to find out what was going on. Meanwhile, Laing entered Timbuctoo on 13 August 1826, a withered but blazing ghost, having travelled 2,650 miles across unmapped, inhospitable desert to reach his goal. He was the first white man ever to see this fabled city. It was a sordid, mud-brick town with nothing to recommend it whatsoever. Laing searched in vain for the universities, red-uniformed armies, palaces and gold of which he had heard. They did not exist. Indeed, Timbuctoo barely

had a government of its own. Nominally it fell within the jurisdiction
of Jenne, which was an outpost of Sultan Bello's empire. Order of
some sort existed within the four-mile circumference of the city walls,
but the surrounding region was controlled entirely by Tuareg bandits.
Timbuctoo was not a glittering capital; it was a frontier town – poor,
dangerous and lawless.

Rather oddly, therefore, Laing told Warrington that the place 'has
completely met my expectations'.[48] It is uncertain what he meant by
this – he was so unbalanced that any expectation could have formed
in his mind – but a possible explanation is that he was trying to drum
up a bit of pre-publication interest in his journal. To date, he had
conjured an air of mystery over proceedings, his letters containing
little of substance and much froth. Perhaps he was biding his time
until he could reveal to the world the full grandeur of his struggle.

Laing stayed in Timbuctoo for five and a half weeks, and wrote just
one letter during his stay, dated the day before his departure. It was a
short missive that contained little solid information but made tantalizing reference to the 'abundant'[49] records he had found. It is hard to
decipher truth from fantasy, but there were probably no records. More
likely it was just another attempt to keep people wondering at the
contents of his journal.

If reports are to be believed, Laing became more deranged in
Timbuctoo than ever before. He strutted through the streets in full
European dress, announcing himself as the King of England's representative, drawing money on the Pasha's account and sneering at any
who tried to help him. He rented a small, mud house from which he
cantered out at night on horseback, accompanied only by his personal demons, to investigate the city's outskirts and its port on the
Niger.

He had previously envisaged a stay in Timbuctoo of about six
months but it soon became clear that he did not have that time. Sultan
Bello wanted him out. Fearing further penetration of the region by a
nation whose 'abuses and corruptions' around the globe he had heard
about and whose emissaries might destabilize his already precarious
fringe territories – Clapperton was at the moment in Sokoto and was

proving most troublesome – Bello sent a message to the ruler of
Jenne, instructing him to order the Sultan of Timbuctoo not to admit
a European to the town. All at once, through no fault of its own and
for the first time in its history, Timbuctoo had achieved a measure of
importance.

Laing was not sure what to do. The Sultan 'trembles for my safety
and strongly urges my immediate departure',[50] he told Warrington.
Clearly, he had to leave town. But where was he to go? Barrow had
suggested he travel east from Timbuctoo 'and make for Bornou as a
point d'appui'.[51] But this might entail meeting Clapperton, and was
therefore untenable. Earlier he had written to Sabine that he intended
to explore the whole region to the south of Timbuctoo before following the Niger to its termination. Now he decided to go south-west to
Sierra Leone. Then, for some unfathomable reason, he changed his
mind and headed north. 'My father used often to accuse me of want
of common sense,' he once confided to his sister. '''Tis true, I never
possessed any, nor ever shall.'[52]

Laing's plan may have been to make for Morocco. Alternatively he
might have decided that a detour north was necessary on the way to
Sierra Leone to avoid troubles in the immediate vicinity of
Timbuctoo. In either case, he never reached his destination. He left
Timbuctoo on a northward-bound caravan on 22 September 1826 and
was killed by Tuaregs three days later. If the account of an eyewitness
is to be believed, Laing died a particularly awful death, throttled by
two men hauling on either end of a turban that had been wrapped
around his neck. He was then decapitated and left for the vultures.
The only survivor was a black servant, who had been badly wounded
and had feigned death. He found his way back to Timbuctoo and
from there brought the news to Tripoli in August 1828.

Overnight, Laing became another Mungo Park. Where was his
body? Where was his journal? What had he discovered? The answer to
the first question, and in part to the last, was revealed by René
Caillée – a Frenchman. Caillée was a very brave man who rode and
walked to Timbuctoo without any consular or governmental support
in 1828. Enduring relentless hardship – at one point, suffering from

scurvy, the roof of his mouth exfoliated and little bits of hard palate crumbled onto his tongue – he reached his goal disguised as a Muslim. He confirmed the few solid facts Laing had reported of Timbuctoo, visited the house in which he had lived, and discovered that his body was buried under a tree to the north of the town. Of Laing's possessions he found only a sextant, which he did not dare buy lest he spoil his cover by showing undue interest in the infidel. He discovered no papers or journal.

Unlike Laing, Caillée lived to tell his tale, and returned to publish the story of his epic voyage in 1830. For many people he became the man who had discovered Timbuctoo, and the French took a very public delight in the fact that 'that which England has not been able to accomplish with the aid of a whole group of travellers and at an expense of more than twenty millions [of francs], a Frenchman has done with his scanty personal resources alone and without putting his country to any expense'.[53] Predictably, rumours began to circulate in London that the whole business was a hoax: Caillée had never been to Timbuctoo and his journal had been drawn up from Laing's papers which had somehow found their way into the hands of the French Consul in Tripoli. Writing in the *Quarterly Review* Barrow lost no time in damning Caillée's book as a complete fabrication: his descriptions of Timbuctoo were 'so obvious an imposture' and his other observations were quite 'unworthy of notice'.[54] 'The ostentatious display which the French attach to the most trifling thing is strongly manifested,' Barrow noted. As to their unseemly crowing, it was merely a manifestation of 'a constantly-recurring consciousness of the intellectual and physical superiority of our countrymen over theirs'.[55]

The rumours were nonsense from start to finish – at least, inasmuch as they concerned Caillée. But when it came to Laing's papers they contained a kernel of truth. As soon as the news came in of Laing's death, Warrington had despatched an Arab private investigator to find the whereabouts of the missing journal. The man returned in 1829 with the news that Laing had been warned of the dangers of his route and had therefore left his journal in Timbuctoo. If he reached his first stop safely the papers were to be sent after him. If anything happened to him, however, they were to be carried back to Tripoli by the same messenger to whom he had entrusted his last letter to Warrington. From his inquiries, the investigator learned that the messenger had carried two parcels as far as Ghadames and had handed them over to agents representing the Pasha's Prime Minister, Hassuna D'Ghies. D'Ghies had then passed them to the French Consul, Baron Rousseau, in return for a 40 per cent reduction in various debts he had run up in France. It was stated by several witnesses that Rousseau, an amateur Africanist, wanted the material for a book he was currently writing on Timbuctoo.

Warrington had previously warned Laing to 'be cautious . . . to whom you communicate, as every Consul here is a sort of spy ready to suck the sweets & to transmit the honey of your industry to his or their Govt'.[56] Now his fears were confirmed. He immediately filed his protests at the theft, and threatened that unless something was done he would call in British gunships to reduce Tripoli to rubble. Greatly alarmed, the Pasha leaned on a number of 'witnesses' and came up with the news that D'Ghies and Rousseau had not only stolen the journal but had been responsible for Laing's death.

The accusations were given further weight when Rousseau promptly fled to the United States and D'Ghies took refuge in the American Consulate from where he was later smuggled to Spain. Both men declared their innocence, a statement that was believed by a French commission set up to investigate what threatened to become an international incident, but disbelieved by a British officer sent out to Tripoli for the same purpose. The matter rumbled on for a few years and finally, in the absence of any conclusive evidence, it was dropped.

Possibly the two men were guilty. Equally likely, the whole affair had been conjured up by Warrington to discredit the French in Tripoli – he had already taken to intercepting his rival's mail. But a third interpretation, which was not considered at the time, was that the journal did not exist. Laing had never possessed the methodical instincts of an Oudney, say, or even a Denham. What place had detailed records in the fantastical world he inhabited? The journal may have been merely a product of Laing's imagination.

If anyone wanted to get to the bottom of Laing's expedition they would have been better advised to ignore the journal and study the progress of Clapperton. For it was his arrival at Sokoto that had largely engendered Laing's predicament.

13

THE ROAD FROM BADAGRY

The hot-tempered, red-bearded, pipe-smoking Clapperton had left Chatham docks in a naval sloop on 27 August 1825 bound for the port of Badagry, a few miles to the west of Lagos in present-day Nigeria. From there he hoped to make his way overland to Sokoto, crossing *en route* the Niger, ascertaining precisely what had happened to Park, and then finding both Timbuctoo and with a bit of luck the Niger's termination. With him he took Captain Pearce of the Royal Navy, whom Barrow described as an 'active and accomplished officer, and a most excellent draughtsman',[1] Dr Morrison, a naval surgeon with a smattering of natural history, about whom Barrow had no opinion, and Dr Dickson, a hot-headed trainee lawyer who had served as a surgeon in the West Indies and whom Barrow did not like, referring to him as 'this person'.[2] Clapperton also hired a Cornish manservant called Richard Lemon Lander, who had spent his childhood in the West Indies.

They departed under a cloud of disapproval for having spent too much. The Colonial Office pointed out sternly that Clapperton had wildly exceeded his budget and drew Barrow's attention to the individually inscribed watches with which each man had been issued.

Barrow was furious and insisted the price of the watches be deducted from the officers' pay. As for the quantity of instruments which Clapperton had purchased, he ordered most of them to be sent back. 'I told Clapperton over and over again that we do not want the longitude of places to the last second nor within a handful of seconds,' he said, drawing a line through a list of 'utterly superfluous' barometers and telescopes. Anyone would think they were going 'to watch the Satellites of Jupiter', he expostulated. 'I have travelled 2,000 miles in Africa with a pocket compass that cost me 5/- and these gentry must have them at £3 a piece.'[3] He advised Hay at the Colonial Office to rake Clapperton over the coals. Give him 'one of those strong doses which all at the Admiralty know so well how to administer and which after all are sometimes called for to keep men in order when armed with a little "brief authority"',[4] he counselled.

Thus chastened, Clapperton's party reached the Gulf of Benin on 26 November. Dickson landed at Dahomey and struck off on his own to meet up with the others at Jenna, a town in Yoruba territory, a few weeks' travel inland from Badagry – 'for what reason it does not appear',[5] Barrow wrote acidly in the introduction to Clapperton's journal, although the very evident reason was to explore more territory.

Dickson was nervous about his solo trip. He had a feeling that he would never see his companions again. Clapperton consoled him with gruff but sensible advice. 'Study the character of the natives well,' he said, 'respect their institutions and be kind to them on all occasions.'[6] Above all, Dickson was to 'set a guard' on his temper lest it lead him into trouble.

'We meet at Jenna, then,' Dickson said, in an anxious, doubtful voice.

'We meet at Jenna,' Clapperton replied. 'May God bless and protect you.'

With that, Dickson 'tore himself from the deck' and they never saw him again.[7]

Dickson's departure left a gloom which intensified as they made their way to Badagry. Gusts of hot, tropical air carried to them the feverish exhalations of the coast on which they were to land. They had all heard of the deadly effects the climate had on a man and they became increasingly loath to leave the security of their ship. They reached Badagry on 29 November, where African canoes splashed out to meet them. Their baggage was taken ashore and they bade an emotional farewell to the officers before themselves taking to the canoes. To cheer their departure Richard Lander produced a little bugle and blew 'Over the Hills and Far Away', to which the sailors responded with hearty cheers. Then they were on their own.

Badagry was not such a bad place after all. The air was healthy, they were able to hire horses and asses to carry their goods and the local chief, Adele, let them go their way after only a minimum of face-saving obstruction.

By the time they set off for the interior, their spirits had risen considerably and their company had swelled to include a local British merchant called Houtson with his servant George Dawson, a multi-lingual West Indian interpreter called Columbus – he signed himself A. A. Simpkins – who had accompanied Clapperton and Denham on their previous mission plus an African interpreter by the name of Pasko who had previously been employed on an ill-fated expedition under Belzoni. They travelled at first on foot, but Clapperton had unwisely taken delivery of a new pair of boots before leaving England. The boots did not fit. His feet blistered and bleeding, he put on a pair of slippers and took first to a horse and then to a ham-mock. He did not walk again for the rest of his journey.

By 14 December they were all sick with a fever that would stay with them forever. But Clapperton mustered the strength to write a glowing tribute to the country and its people: 'I cannot omit bearing testimony to the singular and perhaps unprecedented fact, that we have already travelled sixty miles in eight days, with a numerous and heavy baggage, and about ten different relays of carriers, without losing so much as the value of a shilling public or private; a circum-stance evincing not only somewhat more than common honesty in the inhabitants, but a degree of subordination and regular government which could not have been supposed to exist amongst a people hith-erto considered barbarians.'[8] They came to Jenna and left it, not having seen nor heard anything of Dickson.

Their health was now worsening. The first to die was George
Dawson. Morrison, a 'walking spectre',[9] went on 27 January and
Pearce followed the same day while conducting a long and delirious
conversation with his distant mother. Houtson fled to the healthier climate of the coast where he too died after a brief illness. Columbus,
who had earlier told the others that he was the only man among them
who would survive, was next. Dickson, though they would not know
this for several months, had been killed in a quarrel long before he
even approached Jenna. He had failed to guard his temper, offering to
throttle a man for disobedience, and the man had reciprocated.

In a matter of weeks Clapperton's party had shrunk from nine to
three – himself, Lander and Pasko. When the news reached Barrow,
along with Clapperton's report, a few boxes of specimens and the
dead officers' effects, the Second Secretary was coldly furious. 'There
never was anything so stupid as to send home such rubbish as
Clapperton has done,' he wrote to Hay at the Colonial Office. 'What
you have forwarded me consists of nothing but blank papers, blank
journals, and, with one exception, blank memorandum books.'[10]
Noticeably, he showed not a shred of regret for the deaths. What concerned him was the absence of news concerning the Niger. It was very
unsatisfactory – you didn't get Parry running up huge bills, losing
most of his men and then sending home incomplete reports.

Unaware of Barrow's displeasure, Clapperton swayed in his ham-
mock through Yoruba country. Once again, he was filled with
enthusiasm for the people. He wrote that 'the Yorribas appear to be a
mild and kind people, kind to their wives and children and to one
another and that the government, although absolute, is conducted
with the greatest mildness'.[11] Lander was equally impressed. The
local carvings, he wrote, 'rival, in point of delicacy, any of a similar
kind I have seen in Europe'.[12]

Many of the people Clapperton encountered had never seen a white
man before – which explains in part their friendliness – and though
one chief 'kept his hand wrapped up in the sleeve of his [robe], for fear
the touch of a white kaffir should kill him',[13] they greeted Clapperton's
party with genuine warmth and cheerful acquisitiveness. Guns and

ammunition were in demand by the chiefs, as were rolls of silk, gaudy uniforms, and the cheap swords specially made in London for the African market. Lesser people were happy with beads, imitation gold chains and needles. English porcelain was valued by all. Clapperton had already witnessed the appeal of solid enamelware: in Kano he had been served his meals in a handbasin. But he was patriotically pleased when asked to toast a chief with beer from a Toby jug, and, on an earlier occasion, to drink water from a chamberpot – though Houtson, who was with him at the time, was dismayed to recognize it as an old one of his own, which he had sold at market only a year before.

Clapperton handed out gifts generously, perhaps too generously. At Katunga, the Yoruban capital, for example, they were kept waiting for seven weeks while the Sultan dickered for more presents. This happened with increasing frequency as they travelled north and Clapperton soon developed a brusque line in ultimatums. The reason typically given for any delay was that the route ahead was blocked by warfare and that the local sultan wished to ensure his guests' security. The danger was not entirely exaggerated. The Yoruba were a relatively peaceful people, as yet untouched by the hard-bitten trading ethos of the coastal nations and too far south to be ravaged by the likes of Sheik El Kanemi and Sultan Bello. However, the Yoruba's northern neighbours were a different matter. Some had formed alliances with Bello, others with El Kanemi, and those who were not currently at war expected to be so soon.

Clapperton explained repeatedly that their wars were not his concern, that he was a messenger of the King of England, the dispenser of great wealth, and that if they knew which side their bread was buttered they would let him through to Sokoto. Those who were unsettled by his apparent alliance with Bello were informed peremptorily that he carried gifts and letters for Bello and El Kanemi alike. Luckily for Clapperton, the concept of neutrality was well understood, as was the need to keep the King of England happy, and so he was passed gently from ruler to ruler, his only difficulty being the need to juggle gifts according to the superiority of the chiefs he met along the way.

Everyone in this area of Africa had a friend. So the Sultan of Katunga sent Clapperton to his friend the Sultan of Kaiami, who sent him to his friend the Sultan of Wawa, who forwarded him to his friend the King of Bussa, who decided that the newly appointed Sultan of Nyffee ought to be his friend and directed Clapperton to him, and he in turn sent word via Bulla Bulla and Zeg Zeg to Kano that a white man had arrived with gifts and letters for his very good friend and revered ally Sultan Bello who might, therefore, postpone his plans to ransack the region.

Clapperton went where he was sent, each stop scoring its impression in his journal. At Kaiami the sultan toured the city accompanied by a bodyguard of six naked girls who flitted alongside him carrying three spears in each hand and wearing nothing but a white cloth around their heads. When the sultan entered Clapperton's tent the escort followed him, wrapping a blue cloth about their waists to save the white man's embarrassment. When the Sultan left, they threw aside the cloths and flew after their master, springing like shadows alongside his curvetting horse, the white tails of their bandeaux fluttering in the wind.

At Wawa they encountered the mighty widow Zuma, the richest person in town, who conserved her position by renting out her 1,000 slaves as prostitutes. She was a vast thirty-something – or maybe a twenty-something, accounts differ – who was the daughter of an Arab trader and desperately wanted to marry a white man. Clapperton encouraged Lander's suit with glee, pointing out his servant's charms while lying back, arms folded on his chest, with thick volumes of smoke rolling from his pipe, looking 'as happy and as much at home as if he had been seated by his friends in northern Scotland'.[14] Lander was 'a novice in the art of courtship'[15] and diverted her attentions to Clapperton, who became rather alarmed, put down his pipe and demanded an escort out of town at once. Zuma vowed to follow him to his death.

At Bussa, on the Niger, where Clapperton hoped to find a clue to Park's fate, the widow Zuma caught up with him and he was forced to take her home on the instructions of the Sultan of Wawa. She returned in grand style, entering Wawa preceded by a drummer, a body of armed men, and wearing a stupendous headdress of ostrich feathers on a white turban, set off by a gold silk cloak, red silk pantaloons, red leather boots and riding a horse decked out in scarlet with brass emblems and little pieces of red, yellow and green leather on which were written various charms. The Sultan of Wawa wrung his hands in apology. What could he do? he asked. The widow Zuma was a very powerful person who had enough money and men to displace him. It was very important that she be where he could keep an eye on her. 'I was now let into their politics with a vengeance,'[16] Clapperton wrote. He divested himself of Zuma with as much tact as he could muster and returned to Bussa to pursue the destiny of Park.

As he had made his way inland Clapperton had been deluged by rumours of Park's death which, trickling through generations and across tribal boundaries, had retained a remarkable consistency. They stated that a strange vessel had approached Bussa, comprising two strapped-together canoes with an awning – 'a house' – sitting at its stern in which two white men dwelt. On reaching Bussa's rock-strewn stretch of the Quorra, the vessel had become stuck. At this point there were men lining either bank. Some said the white men fired first, others that they were pelted with arrows from the bank. The outcome in either case was that two white men leaped overboard arm in arm and were never seen again. They left behind them in the canoe a number of treasures – a cloak, a double-barrelled gun, books with writing in them – and a quantity of dried meat. The treasures were taken and the meat was eaten. And in the best tradition of all legends, whoever partook of the meat died a slow and lingering death. The canoe, meanwhile, reappeared on the rocks every Sunday to remind the world of what had happened.

The unravelling of this tale, as far as Clapperton could make out, was that Park had arrived when Bussa was in the middle of a war with the Hausas, under Sultan Bello's father. The people of Bussa had taken his canoe for a Hausa vanguard and had waited until it was stuck on the rocks before opening fire. Park and his companion had either been hit by arrows or had drowned in an attempt to escape them. As if by divine vengeance, the area had then been struck by an epidemic which left thousands dead. The two occurrences became entangled, Park's dried meat being diagnosed as the causative agent, and gave rise to a common saying, 'prevalent amongst all ranks and conditions: Do not hurt the white men; for if you do you will perish like the people of Boussa.'*[17]

When Clapperton returned to Bussa he was shown the scene of the murder. His guides led him willingly but cautiously 'and as if by stealth'[19] to the banks of the Niger. Clapperton looked on it with feeling. On 19 March he had written a blurred and almost illegible entry in his notebook: 'I am so near crossing that I am like a gamester desperate I would stake all.'[20] Now the mighty river was before him, sluicing powerfully over rapids on either side of a central island.

Before he could cross the Niger, however, he had to make further inquiries about Park's belongings – particularly his journal. The Sultan of Bussa quivered when questioned on the matter and developed a stammer. He knew nothing about the journals, he said, nor the other objects which may or may not have been found in the canoe. But if they did exist they were almost certainly in the hands of the Sultan of Yauri who lived upstream from Bussa.

The Sultan of Yauri shortly sent notice that he did, indeed, have a few Park memorabilia, including two books, and that Clapperton could have them for the exorbitant sum of 170 mitgalls of gold. Clapperton countered with the offer of a gun, to which the Sultan cheerily agreed but only on condition that Clapperton collect the goods himself. Alas, Clapperton did not have the time. He needed to be in the healthier climates of either Sokoto or Bornu before the rains came. He told the Sultan to keep the books for now, and crossed the Niger on 10 April in a precarious canoe that was only two feet wide

---

* Laing had heard similar stories in Timbuctoo of Park's warlike activities. Indeed, he had been mistaken for Park by a man who said he had been wounded by one of Park's gunshots. Laing's response was typically self-centred – 'How imprudent, how unthinking, I may even say, how selfish was it in Park to attempt making discovery in this land at the expense of the blood of its inhabitants.'[18]

and ten times as long. Then he struck out for Sokoto through a land-scape where massive ant hills towered above him like 'so many Gothic cathedrals in miniature'.[21] He reached his destination on 19 October.

He could hardly have arrived at a worse time. While Sultan Bello's forces were rampaging to the south and west, Sheikh El Kanemi of Bornu had seized the opportunity to declare war on the Hausa. His army was expected any week, and some of the more easterly towns had drawn up evacuation procedures. Sokoto itself was in a state of emergency, and paranoia was in the air. The sudden appearance of a white man bearing, as he admitted, letters and gifts for El Kanemi, sent rumours flying. One day Clapperton was a spy, the next he was a smuggler. Was he supplying El Kanemi with guns? Undoubtedly, and he was probably scouting the area for a possible invasion, too. 'The common conversation of the town now, is that the English intend to take Hausa,'[22] Clapperton recorded wearily.

The source of the gossip was Sultan Bello, whose nerves were in a highly strung state. He revealed his fears in an open lie, when he told Clapperton that on his last visit to Sokoto El Kanemi had advised that he be killed, 'as, if the English should meet with too great encouragement, they would . . . seize on the country and dispossess him, as they had done with regard to India'.[23] Clapperton responded hotly, pointing out that he had hauled an enormous quantity of gifts halfway across Africa precisely to prove Britain's goodwill. 'At no time am I possessed of a sweet and passive temper,' he admitted, 'and when the ague is coming on me it is a little worse.'[24]

Clapperton in a rage must have been an impressive sight. Clad in a robe and turban, his broad leather belt studded with pistols and knives, and with his beard down to his waist, he looked by this stage 'more like a mountain robber . . . than a British naval officer'.[25] Bello, nevertheless, ignored Clapperton's temper. He confiscated the gifts and letters for El Kanemi, despite a torrent of oaths, and for good measure shortly afterwards took Clapperton's spare guns and ammu-nition. Bello also sent word to Timbuctoo that Laing was to be refused entry – though Clapperton had no idea of this. He would decide in due course whether the white men would be allowed to proceed, Bello announced.

Seething, Clapperton threw his energy into hunting, leaving early in the morning and returning only at dusk to the house in which he and Lander had been quartered – an 'immense bee hive',[26] thirty yards in circumference, windowless and with a door so small they had to crouch to get through it. Here, in temperatures that were a good 10 °F higher than outside, Lander played tunes on his bugle, while Clapperton smoked sullen cigars, pacing about in a striped dressing gown that he had adopted to go with his slippers. Clapperton was desperate with frustration. 'If the road to Bornu be denied me,' he told Lander, 'I really can't tell what we shall do, or how we shall get home. It is certain that if we pursue a different route, my business will be incomplete, and of all things, this lies nearest my heart, the trip down the Niger.'[27]

On 12 March Clapperton received good news. Sultan Bello, flush from a recent victory over Sheikh El Kanemi, summoned him to an audience. The white man could leave, he announced. But when Clapperton asked in which direction he could leave Bello was suddenly swamped by congratulatory courtiers. Clapperton must make another appointment, Bello called over the throng. This frustrating development was the last event Clapperton recorded in his journal. That evening he fell ill with dysentery. 'I believe I shall never recover,'[28] he told Lander. His prognostication was correct. For almost a month he drifted in and out of delirium, in his lucid spells giving Lander precise instructions on what to do once he was dead. He was to sell what he could and abandon everything else except the journals and papers which he was to hand personally to the Colonial Secretary. On his way home, which would probably be across the Sahara, he was to write up his experiences as best he could, so that the record would be complete. 'Remark what towns and villages you come to,' Clapperton advised paternally, 'pay attention to whatever the chiefs may say to you, and put it on paper.'[29]

On 9 April Clapperton tried a native remedy of boiled bark, which seemed to do no good. 'I feel myself dying,'[30] he muttered despondently. That night in his sleep he distinctly heard the tolling of a funeral bell. Yet by the next day he was feeling much better and on the 11th was convinced he would pull through. On 12 April he was able to force down solid food for the first time since falling ill. On the 13th he sat up in bed, not having been able to move a limb for weeks. Then, spasmodically, he began to shudder. Lander, seeing his 'pale and altered features',[31] rushed to his side. Clapperton tried to speak: 'some indistinct expressions quivered on his lips; he strove, but ineffectually, to give them utterance, and expired without a struggle or a sigh'.[32]

Lander washed the body, prepared it for burial and, when Sultan Bello finally gave permission for Clapperton to be buried in a village called Jungavie, slightly to the south of Sokoto, Lander organized the grave-diggers and read the funeral service. Then he was on his own. 'I could not help being deeply affected with my lonesome and dangerous situation,' he wrote, 'a hundred and fifteen days journey from the nearest sea-coast, surrounded by a selfish and cruel race of strangers, my only friend and protector mouldering in his grave, and myself suffering dreadfully from fever.'[33]

Lander's position was outwardly hopeless. He was a servant, a cross between a batman and a travelling housekeeper, not an explorer. He carried no authority, could sign no bills, could draw no money, could command no men, was in a strange land and had no skills with a compass or sextant. Yet he somehow had to extricate himself and his master's journals from Africa.

He took control with complete and astonishing assurance. He parlayed Sultan Bello into letting him leave town, demanded payment for the goods that had been seized – and, remarkably, received part of the sum – then, in defiance of Clapperton's instructions, he set off south instead of north. He was not only going to get home, he was going to follow the Niger to its termination. As he explained airily, he had developed 'an earnest desire, which I could not repress'[34] to ride a canoe down the great river.

His desire was unattainable. As he retraced his steps southward, following the path he and Clapperton had previously taken, he learned that the middle stretches of the Niger were in such a state of war that he would be mad to go there. Disappointed, he continued his journey across country. He scraped up a bit of money by selling Clapperton's clothes, bartered his way here and there with some of the trade goods – by now reduced to cloth and needles, all the more glittering gifts having been disposed of – sold *in extremis* his sword and pistol, gratefully received the hospitality of chiefs he had met before, was fed to the gills by widow Zuma, and finally, having rejected an offer to marry Zuma and take over Wawa, and having regretfully declined another chief who offered him four of his daughters if he would stay behind to act as his prime minister, he reached the safety of Badagry on 21 November, with nothing to his name but Clapperton's trunk of papers, a few bolts of damask and twenty-four pairs of silk stockings.

Hitherto, Lander's experience of slavery had been limited to the relatively benign domestic version which prevailed in the African-ruled interior. In theory it was as brutal and degrading as any form of enslavement. In practice, however, it usually comprised a degree of servitude very similar to the system which existed in England but with greater social leeway: slaves were often treated as part of the family; they shared meals with their masters; and they were frequently granted their liberty. African slavery was no less reprehensible but far more humane than that practised in the West. As Clapperton wrote, the African slave's greatest fear was being taken abroad: 'They are much afraid of being sold to the sea-coast, as it is the universal belief that all these who are sold to the whites are eaten; retorting back on us the accusation of cannibalism, of which perhaps they have the greatest right to blame us.'[35] This was not to say that the process of collecting and transporting slaves for the Western market did not occur. But it was conducted almost invisibly and with some discretion. When a slave train passed it did so quietly, camping a good way from town behind a screen of trees.

Lander had gone along with it, acquiring two female slaves, Aboudah and Jowdie, whom he considered more dependable than hired servants and whom he intended to free once they reached the coast. Aboudah had been given to him as a wife and Jowdie he had purchased for a quantity of needles. Now in Badagry, he encountered the system head-on. The place was teeming; its five 'factories' were crammed with more than 1,000 slaves and a fleet of Portuguese slavers stood at anchor ready to take delivery. When Lander arrived, 400 unfortunates, shackled together by the neck and separated by only nine inches of chain, were being herded into a tiny ship of little more than eighty tons.

Lander was appalled. He had become very fond of Africans, if in a patronizing fashion. He wrote of his 'high admiration of the amiable conduct of African females',[36] likening them wistfully to the West Indian nurses of his childhood. 'In sickness and in health; in prosperity and adversity – their kindness and affection were ever the same. They have danced and sung with me in health, grieved with me in sorrow, and shed tears at the recital of my misfortunes.'[37]

Rather than blame Europeans for the sights he saw, he put it all down to the Badagrians who now became 'without comparison the most rude and barbarous . . . of any of the people in the whole of Africa'.[38] He heard horrible stories of the way they treated their slaves. The elderly and infirm were weighted and dropped into deep water. Others were condemned to human sacrifice, being slaughtered in front of the king who would then eat the victim's heart before consigning the body to be hung on a fetish tree. Lander stumbled across the tree by accident and was almost sick. He described 'the huge branches of the fetish tree, groaning beneath their burden of human flesh and bones, and sluggishly waving in consequence of the hasty retreat of birds of prey; . . . the intolerable odour of the corrupt corpses; the heaps of human heads, many of them apparently staring at me from hollows which had once sparkled with living eyes'.[39] Next to the tree stood the King of Badagry's fetish hut, a court of ordeal, in which the King gave final judgement by means of a poisoned drink. If the offender lived he was innocent, if he died he was guilty. Very few lived, as Lander learned when he peeked inside the hut and saw that it was lined with skulls. He fled in horror.

Putting the Badagrians to one side, he appealed to the Portuguese ships for help. He was thrust away. Not only was he a servant, but a

British servant at that. Who could tell what treachery he planned? A
Brazilian captain kept him well provisioned for a while but his ulterior
motive was to buy Pasko and the two African slaves. When Lander
refused his offer of 100 Spanish dollars apiece, the Brazilian withdrew his largesse.

Lander was stuck. And as if that was not enough, the slavers spread
word that he was a spy. The rumour caught fire. It reached the King's
ears and within a matter of hours Richard Lander was hauled off for
judgement. With great dignity, Adele, King of Badagry, decreed that
he undergo trial by ordeal. Lander could not believe it. He had plodded inland with Clapperton, had plodded back again, had suffered
from malaria and amoebic dysentery, had brought his master's journal
to the nearest known coastline, and now he was being asked to drink
poison. It was appalling, he raged, 'when almost within hearing of my
countrymen, that my life should be destroyed; that my skull should be
preserved as a trophy by heartless savages, and my body devoured . . .
by birds of prey'.[40] Having no other option he put on his best clothes
and went to Adele's court, 'the gloomy sanctuary of skulls'.[41] He was
handed a bowl of colourless liquid. 'If you come to do bad it will kill
you,' Lander was comforted by an attendant, 'but if not, it cannot hurt
you.'[42]

Lander would have liked to run, but outside the hut a crowd
500–600 strong had gathered to watch the white man's death. They
were armed and angry and the fetish tree was waiting. Left with no
choice, Lander swallowed the draught. It was made of sasswood bark,
a definite poison, and tasted 'bitter and disagreeable'.[43] The onlook-
ers surged forward in anticipation of an instant death. It did not come.
Lander strode through the crowd and made his way back to his hut,
feeling slightly dizzy. When nobody was looking he took an emetic
and discharged his stomach's contents. He learned later that the
poison was almost always fatal and that he was the only man to survive
the trial for many years.

Lander's miraculous survival changed everything at Badagry. He
became the man of the moment. He was supplied with all that he
could need, and was treated like royalty up to the moment he was

able to board a British ship. He freed Aboudah and Jowdie and set off home with Pasko.

Shipboard life did not suit Lander. From being an explorer, he became a hired hand whose job was to wash the eyes of the turtles that the captain was carrying home in his bath tub. 'But could I,' Lander wrote, 'who had recently shaken hands with majesty, and lodged in the palaces of kings; who had been waited on by the Queen of Boussa, and walked delighted with the proud princesses of Nyffee; could I who might have become the master of a thousand slaves, and the lord of the high minded and lovely Zuma . . . forget all my dignity, and all my laurels and descend to the menial and grovelling occupation of washing the filthy eyes of turtles?'[44] No, of course he could not. The turtles all died as a result and Lander stepped onto Portsmouth quay on 30 April 1828 where, with his beard and sun-burned, tousled appearance, he was greeted by the Jewish community as a pilgrim from Palestine.

He cajoled the authorities into sending Pasko home, if he so wished (which he did), and made his way to London where, on con-tacting Clapperton's agents and relatives, he handed over to Barrow every item of the expedition's stores that remained, which included a trunkful of papers as well as the watches of Clapperton and Captain Pearce.

Barrow would later be scathing about Lander's achievements, but for the moment he was astounded by the servant's solo journey. He was even more astounded when Richard Lander produced a journal that fitted seamlessly alongside Clapperton's. He was 'a very intelli-gent young man',[45] Barrow told the world.

On the subject of Clapperton, however, Barrow displayed a breath-taking depth of animosity. Having edited the expedition's journal, he wrote that Clapperton was 'evidently a man of no education; he nowhere disturbs the narrative by any reflections of his own, but con-tents himself with noticing objects as they appear before him, and conversations just as they were held; setting down both in his Journal without order, or any kind of arrangement . . . There is no theory, no speculation, scarcely an opinion advanced.'[46] Had Clapperton survived to complete his journal, he would probably have furnished the theories and speculations Barrow required. And had he done so Barrow would probably have castigated him for not sticking to the facts. It was impossible to please the man. 'It may be necessary to observe,' Barrow wrote crossly, 'that it is written throughout in the most loose and careless manner; all orthography and grammar equally disregarded.'[47] As for Clapperton's handwriting, he continued schoolmarmishly, it was almost illegible. 'Much, therefore, has been left out, in sending it to the press, but nothing whatever is omitted that could be considered of the least importance.'[48] Of course, Barrow had said almost exactly the same of Clapperton's previous journal which he had edited with a vengeance.

Having ground Clapperton to dust, Barrow added a perfunctory few words of praise lest it seem he was speaking ill of the dead: 'Clapperton was, in fact, a kind-hearted and benevolent man, of a cheerful disposition, not easily put out of temper, and patient under disappointment.'[49] He even summoned a grudging epitaph for Clapperton's expeditions. 'It may now be said of him, what will probably never be said of any other person, that he has traversed the whole of that country, from the Mediterranean to the Bight of Benin.'[50] Then he spoiled it all by adding, 'but he has not contributed much to general science'.[51]

This lay at the heart of Barrow's grievances. The contribution to general science for which he had hoped was the news that the Niger flowed into Lake Chad. Clapperton's discoveries, however, had suggested the awful likelihood that it flowed into the Atlantic. 'The reports continue to be contradictory,' Barrow wrote, 'and the question is still open to conjecture.'[52] He admitted that the Niger's likely termination was the Bight of Benin. 'But there is still a considerable distance, and a deep range of granite mountains intervening, between the point to which with any certainty it has been traced and the sea-coast.'[53] In a flourish of pique, Barrow concluded that if the river Clapperton had encountered did, indeed, flow into the Gulf of Benin then it was probably not the Niger. Herodotus, Ptolemy, Pliny, and all the other ancients who had written of the Niger could not possibly have travelled that far south. Clapperton therefore must have discovered the wrong river.

'The name of Quorra, or Cowarra,' Barrow wrote, 'ought now, therefore, to be adopted on our charts of Africa.'[54]

But whether it was the Quorra or the Niger, there still remained the matter of Park's journals. Their recovery was 'an enterprise of much interest . . . not only due to the reputation of the lamented traveller, but to the nation to which he belonged'.[55] Barrow was keeping his options open.

Barrow's attack on Clapperton passed Richard Lander by. Having delivered Clapperton's journal and his own to Whitehall, Lander had been rewarded with a job as weighing porter at the Truro Customs House. It paid £65 per year if all went well, but as the salary was pegged to performance, and as few ships entered Truro, Lander could rely only on a basic £25 retainer. He therefore decided to write his own version of the expedition, in collaboration with his brother John, hoping that he might be able to fluster up some extra money. When the manuscript was complete he sent it off to John Murray who passed it to Barrow for his comments.

Barrow was still in a bad mood. 'It appears to me that Mr. Lander's wanderings in Africa, which I have attentively read, scarcely justify the expense of a publication,'[56] he replied. He castigated Lander's brief description of his earlier life as 'utterly unimportant and uninteresting to any reader'. He condemned him for 'deficiences of style' and accused him of 'the sins of egotism'. The scientific notes were 'deplorably meagre'. As for the business with widow Zuma, 'notwithstanding that Mr. Lander himself appears as that it is amusing in the extreme, [it] is written in very bad taste'.[57]

Maybe Lander's description of the fetish rite at Badagry might make a pamphlet, Barrow advised. But even then it would require 'a great deal of toning before it could be prudently submitted to the public eye'.[58] All in all, he concluded, Lander's 'book' (the inverted commas are Barrow's) was quite unworthy of publication.

The manuscript was wrapped up and posted back to Truro. It says much for Lander's spirit that he did not give up after such a crushing rejection. Instead, he sought and found an alternative publisher,

Colburn and Bentley of New Burlington Street, who eventually produced his two-volume narrative in 1830. What he was paid is
unknown – it was probably very little. But the satisfaction of being
published was the most important thing to Lander. He would have
liked to have received a large sum of money, but in its absence he was
very happy with the prospect of public recognition.

14

PARRY TO THE POLE

Three important things happened in April 1827. It was the month in which Clapperton reached Bussa and ascertained the fate of Mungo Park; and in which, some 1,800 miles to the north, Warrington learned of Laing's death and set in motion the investigation that would cause such a furore among the diplomats of Tripoli. At the same time, roughly the same distance again to the north, Captain William Edward Parry embarked on Barrow's most ambitious venture to date: the overland conquest of the North Pole.

The idea of reaching the North Pole across the ice was not a new one. It had been suggested by a number of people, among them John Franklin after his 1818 voyage. Indeed, as early as 1816, William Scoresby had laid out very definite guidelines for anyone attempting such a venture. They should travel Eskimo-style in light sledges drawn by dogs and should set out before spring when the ice was still firm but the temperatures not unbearably cold.

At the time, Barrow had sneered at Scoresby. In the *Quarterly Review* he had derided 'the idle and thoughtless project of travelling over the ice of the sea to the North Pole'.[1] What use would sledges be in the 'Open Polar Sea'? Without boats how could that glorious lump of basalt, basking in its lukewarm bath, be attained? Then, in 1826, he performed a volte-face. He was inspired in part by a sentence from the journal of Lt. Constantine Phipps who, in 1773, had found his way north blocked by 'one continued plain of smooth unbroken ice, bounded only by the horizon'.[2] This was compounded by a recent report from Scoresby which stated that, at certain times, one could drive a coach-and-four across the ice. Perhaps it was possible after all to reach the Pole across the ice – partially at least. But it would have to be done properly and not in the skimpy manner Scoresby advocated.

Barrow dug out Franklin's proposal and passed it to Parry with the recommendation that he send it in as his own. Why Franklin himself was not given the task remains unclear. True, he was in Canada at the time. But the expedition could have waited. Possibly it was deemed incorrect for him to resubmit a proposal which had already been rejected. More likely, though, was that Barrow wanted Parry to have the glory. He was his golden boy. And if the plan was to be accepted – there was no certainty that it would; the Admiralty was on a tight budget and had already spent large sums on Arctic exploration to no great effect – it was as well that its proposer be Britain's most popular and successful Arctic officer.

Barrow was right to have doubts about the plan's acceptability. Parry submitted it to Lord Melville in spring 1826 and for two months heard nothing. It was not until July that Melville, not at all happy as he later confessed, bowed to the pressure of Barrow and the Royal Society and gave his consent.

In April 1827, Parry and a select crew were to sail aboard the *Hecla* to Spitsbergen. Along the way they would pick up a team of reindeer to haul them in boats across the ice. (Scoresby had advocated dogs, preferably from the region in which the expedition was travelling, but he conceded that reindeer might do instead, given that they could travel five or six days without food and were quite happy in cold con-ditions – given, too, that no British officer knew how to handle dog teams.) Once at Spitsbergen the crew would split into two parties. The first would remain with the ship while the second would embark on their overland boats, supported by provision-laden sledges, for the

Pole. In the grand, uncomplicated scheme of things Parry would scoot across the ice, steering his boat-and-reindeer team with the merest shake of the reins, reach the 'Open Polar Sea', and then sail triumphantly for the world's final horizon. It was to be the simplest thing: 'Few enterprises are so easily practicable,'[3] Parry wrote.

Scoresby, when he heard what was going on, was appalled. He stated outright that the expedition would fail, not least because it was departing too late in the season. But Scoresby's opinions, though always correct, counted for nothing. He was not a naval man.

Parry picked his officers with care. Those to remain aboard the *Hecla* at Spitsbergen included Lt. Francis Crozier who had been on all his previous expeditions, Lt. Henry Foster who had served with distinction on his last, and a young, untried Scottish surgeon called Robert McCormick. The Pole boats, meanwhile, were to be commanded by Parry himself and James Ross.

At the same time he oversaw the construction of his polar transports. Each boat was twenty feet long, could hold a crew of fourteen, and weighed 1,450 pounds. They were equipped with sturdy iron runners and massive, detachable wheels for overland travel. In a half-hearted afterthought, lest they prove too heavy for the reindeer, they were provided with bamboo masts. In these amphibious monsters, which at night were covered with awnings to provide shelter for his men, Parry had every expectation of reaching the Pole.

It was a busy time for Parry. Shrugging off the gloom of Miss Browne's inconstancies, in October 1826 he married Isabella Stanley, a pious, whimsical woman of almost-grand ancestry whose parents looked down on her humble sea-captain husband. They doted on each other. She came to Deptford the following February to see the *Hecla* being fitted out and spent a week in Parry's cabin. A fierce winter descended and the Thames froze over. And as she lay in her berth, comforted by the blazing stove with its hearth rug laid on the planks before it and listening to the ice grate against the sides of the ship, she formed a romantic vision of polar life. She relished the way the sailors pampered her and was much taken by the dynamism of James Ross who would occasionally burst in, his features contorted

with excitement. On departing, through an ice channel cut as if she
was in the Arctic, she was so delighted that she gave her husband a
companion to see him through the troubles ahead – Fido, 'your pink
and white doggie'.[4] What Parry thought of this gift is uncertain. More
to his taste was a silk flag, sewn by Isabella, which he was to hoist at
the North Pole. Not wishing to seem ungallant with mementoes,
however, he gave her one of his teeth that had recently fallen out.

The *Hecla* sailed on 4 April 1827 and headed for the Norwegian
port of Hammerfest where they took a crash course in skiing and
picked up eight reindeer, that proved to be 'excellent sailors'[5], plus a
supply of moss for fodder. By 14 May they were off the coast of
Spitsbergen searching for a suitable anchorage. To their dismay the
ice was thick around Spitsbergen that year and sheltered harbours
few. However, they used this to their advantage on Sunday 27 May by
giving the boats a trial run on a suitably flat floe. The boats were lowered, the reindeer were harnessed and the wheels were attached. The
stores were packed aboard. The signal was given. Nothing happened.
Axle-deep in snow, the wheels refused to budge. Even when the crew
gave a helping hand the result was the same. The boats did not move
an inch.

The concept of Santa Claus had yet to reach Britain from Germany.
But even so, the image of reindeer-drawn boats manned by an extraordinary collection of elves dressed in racoon-skin caps, hooded
jackets and blue trousers with white, knee-high canvas gaiters, strain-
ing uselessly for the North Pole, made an impression on Robert
McCormick. 'Never, perhaps before, was witnessed so novel and
exciting a scene as the motley group of officers and men, together
with the boats on the wheels, the sledges, and the reindeer presented
on the ice alongside the *Hecla* this morning.' It was all 'picturesque in
the extreme'.[6]

Despondently, Parry ordered the reindeer back on board. Unless,
by some miracle, he and his men could sail their way to the Pole, they
would have to drag the boats themselves. The enterprise was not
looking so easily practicable after all. Continuing north he deposited
caches of supplies at the tiny Walden and Little Table Islands before

finally returning to Spitsbergen and discovering an anchorage in Treurenberg Bay on 20 June. Parry wasted no time. Pausing only to name the spot Hecla Cove – possession of Spitsbergen was then disputed by Britain and others, so every little bit helped – Parry set off the following day in his boats, taking with him Ross, Midshipmen Edward Bird and Charles Beverly, plus five sailors per boat. (Crozier, Foster, Fido and the rest were left to guard ship.) He took seventy-one days' provisions which, when added to the weight of the boats, meant that each man would be hauling 260 pounds. Three days later they reached the ice.

Conditions were far from what Parry had hoped for. Instead of the flat highway to the Pole which Phipps had described, the expedition was faced with an archipelago of floes – as flat as 'a stone mason's yard'[7] according to his men – interspersed with narrow stretches of open water. Sometimes the channels were navigable. More often they were from five to twenty yards across, just wide enough to give them the labour of launching and hauling up the boats, without the advantage of making any progress by water.

Everything was alien. Here the ice formed tall pressure ridges up to forty feet high. There it rose in smooth cones 'much resembling in shape the aromatic pastiles sold by chemists'.[8] Sometimes it lay in rotten sheets, dotted with holes and terrifying to cross. Seemingly solid, level plains consisted on closer inspection of a few inches of sludgy snow floating on water two feet deep. On one occasion they walked through a field of crimson snow of the kind Ross had discovered in 1818. The crimson had been covered by a fresh fall of white, with the result that they left behind them a trail of glowing pink footprints.

The weather was unaccountable. Generally the temperature was little above freezing point. But on some nights it rose to 66°, forcing them to throw off a layer or two of fur blanket. Sometimes the sun was so fierce that tar oozed out of the boats' seams. And to everybody's astonishment it rained – once for thirty hours without cease. The rain added an extra dimension to the journey. It formed glittering, blue lakes of icy water. When they evaporated they left deceptive fields of 'greenish velvet' which actually comprised vertical needles of razor-sharp ice – 'pen-knives', the sailors learned to call them from bloody experience.[9]

Then, in a further twist, there was time. This far north, where the sun shone for twenty-four hours, it was hard to distinguish between night and day. Although all the officers carried specially built twenty-four-hour chronometers, and they kept a regular routine of travelling only by night when the ice was firmer and the glare less, Parry admitted that 'there were several of the men who declared, and I believe truly, that they never knew night from day during the whole excursion'.[10]

And so they stumbled their way through this surreal world, now baking, now freezing, unsure whether they should be asleep or awake, their feet slashed by 'pen-knives', numbed by immersion in the lakes, drenched by rain and coughing from the tobacco which Parry encouraged them to smoke at night to dry their clothes and raise the temperature of their sleeping quarters – by '10° or 15°' he boasted. (He himself never smoked and covered himself with cologne whenever the men lit up.)

Parry did his best to keep an orderly routine. 'When we rose in the evening, we commenced our day by prayers, after which we took off our fur sleeping-dresses, and put on those for travelling, the former being made of camblet, lined with racoon-skin, and the latter of strong blue box cloth. We made a point of always putting on the same stockings and boots for travelling in, whether they had dried during the day or not; and I believe it was only in five or six instances, at the most, that they were not either still wet or hard-frozen.'[11] Then they breakfasted off cocoa and biscuits, travelled for five hours, halted for a one-hour lunch break, then travelled for another six. The boats were hauled onto a floe and lashed together, everybody changed into dry clothes, and then came supper – 'a time, and the only one, of real enjoyment to us'[12] – when they would eat, smoke, swap yarns and finally sleep, having posted a guard to turn the drying clothes and keep a look-out for polar bears. Seven hours later they were woken by a bugle for a new day's haul.

The going was hard. Ross and Parry floundered ahead through the snow trying to pick a clear way ahead. They became so exhausted that when stuck in a drift they simply sat down and waited for their strength to return. Behind them, hauling the boats, the men 'were often under the necessity of crawling on all fours to make any progress at all'.[13] Once, when dragging their boats through a lake – 'we preferred transporting the boats across them, notwithstanding the severe cold of the snow-water, the bottom being harder for the "runners" to slide upon'[14] – they made only 100 yards in two hours. Generally they averaged seven miles a day, which was far short of the thirteen miles Parry had anticipated. The ice was treacherous. James Ross nearly had his spine crushed when a boat slipped and pinned him against an outcrop. Given, too, that their rations were woefully inadequate – at 10 oz biscuit, 9 oz pemmican, 1 oz cocoa powder and a gill of rum per day this was 10 oz less than Scott allowed his men on his 1910 dash for the South Pole – it became clear that they were not going to reach their destination.

But it was only on 20 July that Parry confirmed that their quest was doomed. On that day he recorded a phenomenon that he could scarcely believe. During the previous three days they had travelled, by his calculation, a good twelve miles. Yet, according to his readings, they were only five miles further north. To his horror, he realized that the ice over which they trudged northwards was drifting steadily to the south. With a northerly wind he reckoned they were moving backwards at a rate of four miles per day. As if in confirmation that their quest was doomed, the floe on which they were resting chose that moment to break, tipping several men into the water.

Parry increased the pace only to find that by setting out earlier they ran the risk of snow-blindness. On 23 July they saw a magnificent rainbow of five complete arches. A few hours later Parry could see nothing and had to ask Ross to lead the way. After that they settled back into their usual routine.

On 26 July, when Parry judged that they had made only one real mile's progress in the last five days and had actually lost three miles in the last four, he called a halt. They were at 82° 45'. It was the furthest north any man had ever penetrated – a record which would stand until 1875 – but they were still 500 miles from the North Pole. By now everyone was suffering from snow-blindness and chilblains were rife. It was futile to continue. Parry announced a twenty-four-hour rest before they turned for home. He hoisted the British flag, ordered a slightly better supper than usual and drank a toast to the King, to which James Ross responded with: 'Mrs. Parry!'[15] Parry burst into tears and continued to weep, while describing the occasion in a letter to his wife which he wrote that night and 'posted' the next day into his luggage.

The journey south – 172 miles, of which 100 were open sea – proved uneventful. Ross shot, and the men ate, a polar bear which made them all very ill – although most of a polar bear is edible the liver, which was most prized on that occasion, is poisonous. Then on 11 August they left the ice. Ten days later they were aboard the *Hecla*, and on 28 August they stood out of Spitsbergen and sailed for Britain. They reached the Orkneys on 23 September, at which point Parry accepted a lift from a revenue cutter and left his ship to find its own way home.

Before they left the ice, however, Parry paid tribute to Ross. 'To the islet which lies off Little Table Island, and which is interesting as being the northernmost known land upon the globe, I have applied the name of Lieutenant Ross in the chart; for I believe no individual can have exerted himself more strenuously to rob it of that distinction.'[16]

Parry took a deserved fortnight's leave, deputing the tidying up to Ross. Here, at last, the reindeer came into their own, being despatched as haunches of venison to as many influential people as Parry could think of.

Later that year Ross and Parry wrote up their journal – having sent their slight Botanical Appendix to be catalogued by the eminent naturalist Professor William Hooker – which was published in 1828. The *Hecla*, still braced for the Pole, was subsequently sent south, last to be heard of in equatorial West Africa. And that was that. As for Parry, he never went to the Arctic again. He had spent the last eight years in the ice and was not going to spend another away from home and hearth.

The 'beau ideal's' Arctic epitaph was written by the poet Thomas Hood in 'Ode to Captain Parry':

> *Parry my man! has thy brave leg*
> *Yet struck its foot against the peg*
> *On which the world is spun?*
> *Or hast thou found No Thoroughfare*
> *Writ by the hand of Nature there*
> *Where man has never run!*
>
> *O come and tell us what the Pole is –*
> *Whether it singular or sole is, –*
> *Or straight or crooked bent, –*
> *If very thick, or very thin, –*
> *Made of wood – and if akin*
> *To those there be in Kent.*[17]

15

ROSS RESURGENT

When Parry and Ross returned from not finding the North Pole Barrow was in a slight state of shock. During their absence the Admiralty's fusty proceedings had suffered an upset. In 1827, the short-lived Prime Minister Canning had resurrected the post of Lord High Admiral, last held in the reign of James II. The man he had appointed was the brother of King George IV, the Duke of Clarence, who had become heir to the throne on the death of his elder brother, the Duke of York.

William Duke of Clarence – William IV as he was crowned in 1830 – was not a typical Admiralty Lord. For a start he had been a professional naval officer and knew what he was talking about. Secondly he did not really care what he was talking about so long as there was enough wine to hand. And thirdly, he said and did what he liked because he knew that one day he would be king. According to the diarist Greville, he distinguished himself 'by making ridiculous speeches, by a morbid official activity, and a general wildness which was thought to indicate incipient insanity'.[1] It was all true and he was a good laugh to boot.

The Duke burst through the Admiralty like a dose of salts. He liked to entertain – 'for you know, my delight is in hospitality',[2] he confided to his master of household – and insisted Barrow give him a tour of Admiralty House so that he could gauge its potential. As the obedient Second Secretary opened door after door, the Duke became ever more excited. It was almost as splendid as anything his brother the King had to offer.

The Duke enjoyed himself thoroughly. He usurped everybody's powers, issued elaborate decrees about uniforms, sold his horses and his silver in order to entertain more lavishly, and turned the navy on its head by ordering officers to go easy on the cat-o'-nine-tails. Indeed, he told the reactionary Croker that he did not like him. More, he was going to sack him as soon as he became king.

'It is a totally different thing from what it was when I left England,' cheered Hydrographer Parry in a letter to his wife, having just been ordered by the Duke to take two weeks' extra leave after his polar expedition, 'and as concerns *my* personal comfort and feelings, improved beyond all conception. [My position as Hydrographer] is now, in short, fit for a gentleman and an officer to hold, which was by no means the case, when a certain person whose name begins with a C, was allowed to govern the Admiralty from top to bottom. This is all over now, and, under the Duke's government, every-body minds their own business.'[3]

Alas, Parry spoke too soon. Croker cranked his influential wheel and word reached high authority that the Duke of Clarence was unfit for office. The Duke of Wellington himself was entrusted to inform the King that the 'machine could no longer work'[4] as long as the Duke of Clarence was at its helm. The King, who loathed his brother, responded eagerly with the announcement that 'an extinguisher must be put on the Duke of Clarence's attempts at rendering himself independent of all authority'.[5]

The Duke gave in with grace. But he had one final insult for Croker – whose demise he would eventually oversee, as promised. 'We were told,' recorded Croker, 'that he came to town with the intention of taking a civil leave from us, but his courage or kindness failed him and he did not see any of us, except Barrow, to whom he made a fine speech and gave a magnificent silver ink stand adorned with the Duke's and Barrow's cyphers.'[6]

Barrow had, understandably, found it difficult to concentrate during this unsettling time. But as he regained his sense of equilibrium he took stock of his latest Arctic conquest. Parry's achievement had been great, and Barrow could not deny it. However, he had not discovered the North Pole and had not proved that it was a piece of land set in the Open Polar Sea, which Barrow desperately wanted it to be. Not even by scouring the appendix to Parry's journal could Barrow discover a hint that a solid Pole existed. Had they found flies, for example, this would have been proof that land was in the vicinity. But to his despair, he learned that they had found nothing save one dead specimen on a piece of ice. This sad fly was given a chapter to itself, headed 'INSECT', which, as Barrow fumed, revealed 'no intelligible information, only that it resembles another species called *A. picea*',[7] which usually fed on the silver fir. So where did the firs come from? That's what Barrow wanted to know. The Appendix told him obligingly that Spitsbergen was covered in such firs and that fallen trunks often floated out to sea. Barrow chose to ignore this. In a separate entry, where Parry described the sighting of another 'couple of small flies', Barrow grasped even more wildly. Yes, but were they living or dead? The answer, he commented petulantly, 'is not recorded'.[8]

Flies! What about the flies? One of the most bizarre voyages in history was reduced in importance to a few dark specks on the polar cap.

At this point in Barrow's Arctic career, budgets intervened. It had been hard enough getting Parry's expedition past Lord Melville and in the period of retrenchment and cost-cutting that followed the Duke of Clarence's extravagance, Arctic exploration came low on the list of priorities. But Barrow still wanted to find the North Pole. Above all he still wanted to find the North-West Passage. One can only imagine his horror when his old enemy, John Ross, offered to do the job for him.

John Ross was still smarting from Lancaster Sound. During the
past decade he had peppered the other, younger men with letters in
the hope of producing a publishable correspondence on the subject – no matter that Parry had since sailed through his mythical
mountains. But they had closed ranks. To them he was an eccentric
and possibly dangerous maverick. Their careers would not be helped
by association with 'the blundering Ross',[9] as Parry now called him.
Franklin, ready to see everybody's good side, reserved judgement: 'I
never was one of those who joined in all the condemnation,' he later
wrote to his wife, 'but ascribed his error to his being satisfied with his
own opinion alone.'[10] Otherwise, Ross's only supporter was Scoresby,
but then Scoresby too was an outsider. Ross badly wanted to restore
his reputation.

Over the years he had thrown himself into an eclectic variety of
studies, from phrenology to engineering. Along the way he had written a treatise on steam power and had arrived at the then
unfashionable opinion that steam was the way forward not only for the
navy but for all Arctic explorers. The notion was famously ridiculed by
Lord Melville, who announced that 'the introduction of steam was
calculated to strike a fatal blow to the naval supremacy of the
Empire'.[11]

Melville's attitude was quite reasonable at the time: steam ships
were notoriously unreliable; their engines occupied too much space,
consumed huge amounts of fuel and tended to break down; their
paddles could be disabled by a single enemy shot. Moreover they
were dirty and unwieldy. Steam ships could not sail. The navy, for all
its administrative uselessness, knew how to use a sailing ship better
than the next nation and did not want to lose that advantage. It would
be many years before they reluctantly bowed to progress.

When it came to the Arctic, however, Ross had a point. From experience he knew how difficult it was to navigate in berg-filled seas.
Only a steam ship could take full advantage of the opportunities presented to it. Additionally, steam ships drew a shallower draught and
could go closer to shore where the ice was always loosest. If the ice
solidified, a steam ship could barge through where a sailing ship could

not. Whatever the form of propulsion, Ross also suggested that the ships be small. His recipe for success was a small-crew, low-draught shore-creeper that could insinuate its way to the Pacific rather than by the battering-ram approach favoured by the Admiralty. In all these things he was right. But when he presented his theories to the Admiralty in 1828 they were rejected. How on earth could a small, combustible device succeed where the navy's finest had failed? Anyway there wasn't the money.

Ross had nothing to lose. He canvassed his many friends and found in Felix Booth the perfect sponsor. A wealthy gin magnate with a philanthropic bent, who had once been Sheriff of London, Booth was only too happy to fund Ross's expedition. As he later stated, 'I had known Captain Ross for some time and I undertook it . . . thinking that he was slighted in his former expedition – that there was a cloud hung over him . . . He said he would very much like to go out again and "I think I could do it at a small expense." I said, "Well then, put down and let me see what you call a small expense".'[12] It says much for Booth's nerves that he did not blanch when Ross presented an estimate showing the small expense to be £10,000. However, there was one further stumbling block. If Ross succeeded he would be entitled to the £20,000 prize which was still being offered by Parliament. Booth would therefore be accused of making a profit rather than contributing to science, a slur he was unwilling to countenance.

Ross learned from his failure with Booth. When he approached his next potential backer, a London merchant called Thornton, he emphasized the benefits to be gained. Thornton would not only get Parliament's £20,000 but the money from salvaging the *Fury*'s stores. Alas, Thornton declined. So did everybody else. Ross even tried the Duke of Wellington, but the notoriously straightforward soldier would have none of it.

Ironically, it was Parliament that came to Ross's aid. In 1828 it abolished the Board of Longitude and with it the polar prizes. Ross hurried back to Booth, who was only too pleased to renew his offer – on the careful understanding that £10,000 was 'the utmost sum required'.[13] Now that Booth's account was open to him, Ross used it for all it was worth. Scouring the country for second-hand steamers he settled on the *Victory*, a short-haul packet which had been operating between Liverpool and the Isle of Man. The *Victory* was given a thorough overhaul. Its sides were raised, increasing its tonnage from 85 to 150, and its internal beams were strengthened. Its paddles were replaced with a new set that could be raised out of the water 'in a minute'[14] to avoid obstructions. From the firm of Braithwaite and Erickson Ross ordered a novel steam engine that did not need a conventional funnel but used bellows to provide the necessary draught. Everything was up to the minute, even if it smacked more of the small-ads than was wise.

In addition to the *Victory* Ross also bought an ex-whaler called the *John*, which was to act as supply ship as far as the Arctic and would then recoup some of the expedition's costs by salvaging the *Fury*'s stores and catching what whales were to hand.

Food and fuel were packed to last a thousand days along with twelve thermometers, six chronometers, five sextants, four barometers, two dipping needles, theodolites, telescopes, compasses and a small library of Arctic reference books supplied by a grudgingly impressed Admiralty. By the time Ross was finished he had spent £3,000 of his own money and Booth's small expense had risen to £18,000.

The instant Ross announced the expedition was ready he was transformed from pariah to conquering hero. Applications piled in from eager officers willing to join his crew. From veteran Lieutenant Henry Hoppner, who had sailed in all of Parry's voyages save his last, came a letter stating that 'I am ready to go with you, in any capacity, and will make over all I am worth for the advancement of your object . . . There is no occupation too lowly that I will not undertake.' And bearing in mind Ross's temper, 'I promise you most implicit obedience; and will never offer an opinion unless required. Be assured of my devotion to the great and noble undertaking.'[15] He was turned down. So too was Back, who on hearing of the news in Italy hurried home immediately and on encountering Ross in Parliament Street all but threw himself at his feet, begging to be taken on any terms. Several other officers offered large sums if only Ross would accept them.

Nothing could have eclipsed Barrow more completely and Ross revelled in it. Had he wanted to, he claimed, he could have manned the expedition entirely with naval captains. As it was, he had already chosen his officers. Second-in-command was James Ross who, like his uncle, was unemployed on half-pay following his stab at the North Pole. The third officer was William Thom, who had served as purser on Ross's 1818 voyage. Both had agreed to serve without pay, like Ross himself. Sharing the same main cabin – but with less cachet since they had asked to be paid – were two fellow Scots, George McDiarmid, surgeon, and Thomas Abernethy, gunnery officer.

From his headquarters at 160 New Bond Street Ross fielded an equal deluge of inquiries from people who wanted to be no more than ordinary seamen. Sifting through them he finally achieved a complement that lacked only a cook. To his delight a letter came in from a thirty-eight-year-old man from Gosport, who was experienced in all aspects of cuisine and had served under Nelson on HMS *Victory*. What was more, the applicant had received spiritual approbation, in that 'three nights following, a person appeared to me in a dream, and said "Go with Captain Ross, he will be crowned with *success*." And not having the smallest thought of such things before, and reading of dreams having led to great discoveries, I put some confidence in this, and make bold to offer my services, should a man of my description be wanted.'[16] He was sent a letter of engagement and replied that he would be in London by next Friday. But just before that Ross received another letter.

April 9, 1829.

Sir,

I have just found out that my husband has made an engagement with you to join your expedition, through a dream, *without consulting me*; I must beg to tell you, sir, that he shall not go – I will not let him have his clothes. He must be mad ever to think of leaving a comfortable home, to be frozen

in with ice, or torn to pieces with bears; therefore I am
determined he shall not leave Gosport, so I hope you will not
expect him.

Yours, Sir, &c., and so forth,
Mary L.[17]

What could Ross do? He hired another cook, called Harry Ayre, and
made ready.

Excitement mounted. Even Ross's critics visited *Victory* and were
moved by its purpose. 'The application of steam as a moving-power to
this object of the N.W. Passage offers, in my opinion, a very great
hope of its accomplishment,' wrote Parry, 'and as Ross has attended a
good deal to *both* subjects I really think he has a better chance of succeeding than any of us.' But he cast a warning note on the gadgetry. 'I
think, however, there is, in the whole thing, rather too much that is
new and untried; and this is certainly not the kind of service on which
novelties of that sort first ought to be tried.' Nevertheless, having
spent a day aboard Ross's ship he declared himself 'much gratified . . .
It is a bold, public-spirited undertaking.'[18]

Parry was not the only visitor to swell Ross's pride. John Franklin
and his new wife Jane Griffin came, as did the Lords of the Admiralty
and as many people as could afford the journey. Everybody wanted to
see what Ross was up to. A trip to the *Victory* became a major social
event. Amidst the glitterati the only notable absence was John Barrow.
But this was too much to expect. As John Ross's biographer says, 'If
John Ross had sailed through the North-West Passage in a butter
firkin Barrow would not have recognized it as a feat of any consequence.'[19]

But if Barrow was having nothing to do with Ross, the Admiralty
was willing to lend a hand. It supplied a sixteen-ton tender – which
Ross named *Kreusenstern* after his hero, the famous Russian admiral –
to be towed behind the *Victory*, and also donated two boats which
had last been used on Franklin's expedition. And in one of his surprising fits of generosity Croker gave Ross a passe-partout against his

reaching the Pacific. On top of Croker's letter he received a good-luck letter from the Duke of Clarence, and was given promises from every ambassador in town that he would be treated as a neutral should war break out while he was gone.

Ross was elated. Through sheer force of will he had confounded the enemy and brought them to his way of thinking. His joy was heightened on 23 May, the date set for sailing, when the *Victory* was inspected by Louis Napoleon, the future King of France, and a swarm of curious French nobility. Then at 3 p.m. Felix Booth boarded, with two friends, with the intention of steaming as far as Margate. Beaufort inspected arrangements and at 11 p.m. so did Braithwaite and Erickson, the engine's manufacturers. Nothing could go wrong. Ross would outshine those pretenders who had proved Barrow Bay false. Where Parry and other youngsters had failed he would succeed. They had relied on traditional methods. John Ross, aged fifty-two, was using state-of-the-art technology.

Yet by the time he reached Margate, where Felix Booth hailed a fishing boat to take him ashore, Ross was having second thoughts. Everything was going wrong. 'Our wretched and discreditable machinery',[20] as he now called it, produced a top speed of only three knots. The boilers leaked, necessitating the constant use of a hand pump. Erickson's incomprehensible suggestion that the flow be staunched with mashed dung and potatoes did nothing to help matters, merely adding to the discomfort of the pumpers as they sweated in the 95° hell of the engine room. Pistons and keys started to break and in the absence of spares were replaced by improvised substitutes. These too broke. Off Galloway, just when engineers and engine seemed to have reached some sort of compromise, a stoker fell into the machinery and almost severed his left arm. Ross had to perform an immediate amputation – his first. 'I should have been much more at my ease in cutting away half a dozen masts in a gale than in thus "doctoring" one arm,'[21] he wrote when it was all over.

Shortly afterwards the teeth stripped from one of the bellows' cogwheels. Then the seams of the boilers gave way, sending water cascading into the furnace. What was more, the ship leaked, requiring two pumps to be in operation night and day. The list of calamities continued. On arrival at Stranraer, where they had agreed to rendezvous with the *John*, Ross learned that the whaler's crew, officers and men alike, had mutinied. Nothing Ross could say or do could persuade them to change their minds. They would not even help shift their supplies onto the *Victory*. Given that the *John*'s hold was packed mostly with fuel for the *Victory*'s steam engine, which did not work anyway, the defection was not the disaster it might have been. But it did Ross's publicity no good. The inhabitants of his home town who had been expecting to cheer the expedition on its way were instead drawn to the harbour by yells, oaths and drunken brawling as the mutineers commandeered the *John*'s boats and ferried themselves ashore to the nearest source of alcohol. In the disorderly rout two boats were stove in and one man fell overboard.

Fortunately Ross was able to make space for some of the *John*'s stores by ditching a small boiler and its accompanying equipment for cutting through ice. There was also room for a belted Galloway bullock donated by a local well-wisher.

Ross's diminished fleet departed for Greenland on 13 June with his luck, seemingly, unchanged. The engines broke down so constantly, with hours required for each repair, that they were hardly fired. Instead Ross hoisted the paddles and used sail. However, one day into the Atlantic they were hit by a gale which removed the *Victory*'s foremast, thereby reducing its already limited seaworthiness. The only good news was that the ship had stopped leaking. Every built-up ship leaked to begin with, Ross noted tersely. It had happened to the others.

When they reached Greenland, fate smiled upon them at last. The Danish governor, accompanied by a fleet of Eskimo kayaks, told them that a wrecked whaler, the *Rockwood*, was waiting to be stripped in the nearby anchorage of Holsteinborg. Its mizzen mast was just the right size to replace the *Victory*'s lost foremast. In addition Ross was able to purchase the whaler's stores and equipment. At Holsteinborg Ross also learned that this was one of the warmest summers on record. The oldest Greenlander could not remember a year so mild.

On Sunday 26 July Ross bade farewell to Greenland, receiving a present of six good huskies from the Governor – as much use as a set of fish forks in John Ross's case; but his nephew would put them to good use – then he pushed north and west through Baffin Bay's central pack. The temperature was warm. Icebergs disintegrated about them. On 2 August Ross reached his furthest north, 74° 18′, and the steam engine rose to the occasion by operating for a record twelve hours before collapsing.

On 6 August Ross entered Lancaster Sound, the scene of his earlier disgrace. To mark the occasion he filled four pages of his journal with a lengthy diatribe. Then, honour satisfied, he limped into the North-West Passage on one paddle, towing the *Kreusenstern* behind him, and disappeared from human ken.

16

THE RIDDLE OF
THE NIGER

With Ross's departure a peeved silence emanated from Barrow on the subject of the Arctic. It was his chosen terrain, the object of his brightest dreams. That it should be sullied by Ross – who might, *horribile dictu*, even succeed in finding the North-West Passage – was almost beyond contemplation. Fortunately, Barrow had another enterprise with which to occupy himself. Richard Lander, that 'very intelligent young man'[1] who had survived Clapperton's expedition in search of the Niger, was pressing to complete the task.

Barrow did not have a high opinion of Lander as a serious explorer. There had been all those faults in his journal, as he had pointed out to John Murray. On the other hand, to a snob like Barrow, these faults were only to be expected of a man whose father kept the Fighting Cocks public house in Truro. The poor man obviously knew no better, so why not let him have a second stab at the Niger? 'No one in my opinion,' Barrow informed the Colonial Office, 'would make their way so well and with a bundle of beads and bafts and other trinkets, we could land him somewhere about Bonny and let him find his way.'[2] And if he died, ran the sub-text, it would be no great loss. Lander himself was aware of his status. His submitted plan ended with the comment that should the expedition perish there was at least the consolation 'that the gap we may make in society will be hardly noticed at all'.[3]

Apart from his dispensability there was another aspect of Lander's expedition which appealed enormously to Barrow: it was very, very cheap. Where the Arctic expeditions had run into tens of thousands of pounds, Lander asked only for £100 or so in travelling expenses, plus free passage to his starting point, rudimentary equipment and gifts from official stores (to the value of £96 and £260 respectively) and a pension of £100 for himself and the same amount for his wife while he was away. Lander's brother John was to accompany him free of charge. The shoestring nature of the expedition was out-lined in a pathetically supplicatory letter written by Lander to Barrow on 16 October 1829. (The latter's pencilled comments appear in brackets.)

Sir,
In obedience to your desire I have fully considered the proposition contained in Mr. Hay's letter for my journey into Africa. The assistance to be obtained . . . includes some description of weapons of defence, which . . . will only be a fowling piece, a small pair of pocket pistols and a sword and tent. It will also be requisite to be furnished with pens and paper and some journal books with a pocket compass and thermometer which I hope may be granted without any expense to me. (Agreed this)

I am not aware whether the allowance for presents will be sufficient but I hope, should it be necessary upon my arrival to the coast, that I may be permitted to exceed the same by a few pounds (only £10) and that some allowance may be granted to the natives who accompany me, which although it may not be a great sum (sum must be specified) yet will be more than I can afford from my own pocket.

I further beg to state that it will be proper for me to be supplied with a small portion of medicine which I hope will

also be granted to me free of any expense. (A small medicine
chest to be given)

I should particularly wish if there be no objection to it, that
my brother, John Lander be permitted to accompany me
(agreed to) as my companion on my lonely journey, and in the
event of its being complied with that directions for his passage
in addition to my own may be given (agreed to – but no salary
to be considered) accordingly. This favour, above all, will not, I
trust, be denied me, for in the unknown countries through
which I shall have to pass, an associate, and that associate my
brother, would reconcile me to any danger or difficulty that
may attend my progress.

I have the honour to be, Sir,

Your very humble and faithful servant,

R. Lander.[4]

Lander's instructions were magnificently vague: he was to find the
Niger, follow it to the sea if that was where it went, or if it did not go
there then to follow it to Lake Chad, where it might or might not end
up, and failing that to follow it to wherever it did go, at which point he
could return home by whichever route seemed convenient. The only
point on which his orders were specific was that he send interim
reports whenever practicable, 'furnishing the bearer with a note, setting forth the reward he is to have for his trouble, and requesting any
English person, to whom it is presented, to pay that reward, on the
faith that it will be repaid to him by the British government'.[5] If
Lander was going to die, as was statistically probable, they did not
want to send a further expedition to retrieve his findings. Paying
some Africans a few pence for his bulletins was much more sensible.

The Colonial Office was not being wholly opportunistic. Barrow
had rejected two other proposals as impracticable (they were pursued
independently nevertheless but both leaders died at the outset).
However, at the end of the day, Lander's was a suicide mission.

Lander's plan was to make his way to Bussa, his last point of contact with the Niger, where he would endeavour to find out more about

Mungo Park's fate and if possible recover the journal of his last days, then follow the river downstream to its mouth. He and his brother left Portsmouth on 9 January 1830, bumping their way round the forts and coastal stations which studded the belly of West Africa, at one of which they engaged the services of Pasko, Richard's old guide, as well as Aboudah and Jowdie, his erstwhile wives, before paddling through the surf at Badagry on 22 March to be 'flung with violence on the burning sands'.[16]

Lander was not going to make the mistake of previous expeditions. From harsh experience he knew that waistcoats and thick uniforms made poor travelling gear in Africa. Instead, he and his brother were to wear straw hats, long gowns and baggy breeches in the accepted Muslim style. The Badagrians greeted them with due hilarity. Everyone knew that white men wore impracticable costumes of thick cloth. This new manifestation fooled nobody. Giggling, they led the strangers to Chief Adele.

Adele was not a happy man: times had been hard. He had lost all his best generals, one of whom had endured the indignity of having his left hand chopped off and his right hand nailed to his head. In addition Adele's house had caught fire. In it had been his store of gunpowder which blew up spectacularly. As the townspeople approached to see what was happening they discovered that Adele's house had also contained his large collection of loaded muskets. The detonating weapons caused widespread injuries. Then, as a finale, the fire took hold and razed much of Badagry. What was more, Adele informed Lander in sombre tones, he had been very poorly of late.

The tale of woe having been told, Adele informed the Landers that the interior was in far too hazardous a state for them to continue and that, as they were his friends, he could not possibly allow them to leave Badagry. So began the endless process of bribes and haggling with which Lander's party was to make its way inland. With him Lander had brought a selection of gaudy uniforms, fifty yards of fine cloth, fifty razors, 100 combs and pipes, 110 mirrors, two silver medals and 50,000 needles – 'Whitechapel sharps' – with which he hoped to fund his progress. A selection was presented to Adele who received them with doleful disdain. The only item to catch his fancy was a naval surgeon's coat but even this he returned sorrowfully, telling Lander that it was meant for a boy and that he was slightly insulted by it. Then he came down to business. What he really wanted was 'four regimental coats, such as are worn by the King of England, for himself, and forty less splendid than these, for the use of his captains; two long brass guns to run on swivels; fifty muskets; twenty barrels of gunpowder; four handsome swords and forty cutlasses . . . a halfdozen rockets and a rocket gun with a soldier . . . capable of undertaking the management of it'.[7] There was also the matter of a chest of carpenter's tools and a set of oils and brushes for, as Adele informed Lander, he had mastered all arts from woodwork to painting and lacked only the skill of a tailor.

Lander asked with misplaced sarcasm whether there was anything else the chief wanted. Adele pondered, puffing a long pipe. Yes, he had forgotten to mention four casks of grapeshot and a barrel load of flints plus a large umbrella. He later added to this list a gunboat with 100 English sailors. And some more pipes would not come amiss. This was not a man to be bought off with a few trinkets.

Fortunately, Lander had come prepared for Adele's demands. As well as the usual rubbish he had laid in forty muskets and twenty signal rockets. These he handed over, with the lie that the remainder of Adele's order would be supplied in due course. This did the trick. Adele informed him that the way ahead was now less dangerous than it had been and Lander left the 'abominable place'[8] of Badagry with relief. The news that he was going to miss a mass sacrifice of 300 people put an extra spring into his step.

As the Landers made their way through familiar settlements Richard noted that his reception, while not actively hostile, was not the same as when he had last passed that way. Then, he and Clapperton had been seen as 'messengers of peace',[9] the bringers of good, soothers of discord. But now they were heralded as dangerous interlopers. 'The rapturous exultation,' wrote Lander, 'which glowed in the cheeks of the first Europeans that visited this country on being gazed at, admired, caressed, and almost worshipped as a god – joined to the delightful consciousness of his own immeasurable superiority, will, in the present age at least, never be experienced by any other. Alas! What a misfortune! The eager curiosity of the natives has been glutted by satiety – an European is shamefully considered to be no more than a man!'[10]

The Landers reached the Niger on 17 June 1830 at Bussa, the furthest point downstream that any European – man or god – had penetrated. They were shown a few more relics of Park's expedition which had been salvaged from the river. For an instant, as the local ruler began to unwrap what was obviously a book, their hearts 'beat high with expectation'.[11] Was this the missing journal? Alas, it was no more than Park's book of logarithms containing also a tailor's bill and an invitation to dine with a Mr and Mrs Watson of the Strand. The book was not to be given away, being revered, as the Landers noted, 'as a household god'.[12] (It was purchased twenty-seven years later by a British officer for the price of a small knife.) However, they were made a gift of a fine robe which they later discovered – although the ruler did not admit it – was the one Park had been wearing when he had drowned.

A trip upstream to Yauri revealed nothing save that the local chief was unfriendly and had no knowledge of Park's journal. 'How do you think I could have the books of a person that was lost at Bussa?'[13] he asked coldly, but not unreasonably. But he did sell them a fine shotgun and a cutlass which Park had sent ashore as a gift. At Yauri the Landers had reached the limits of equatorial prosperity. It disturbed them. On their journey to Bussa they had been impressed at the briskness of the local economy. They had seen people spinning cotton and silk, carving wooden bowls, stitching leather for shoes and saddles, hammering brass and iron into stirrups, bits, chains and fetters. The cloth from Bussa was at least as good, if not as plentiful, as that which was coming out of Manchester. In Yauri, however, the inhabitants were poor and ill-fed, the air was 'humid and unwholesome, being impregnated with all matter of noxious effluvia . . . from the large pools of impure water which existed more or less in every quarter of the town'.[14] They tried in vain to buy a canoe for their journey downriver. But Yauri's ruler was not selling. When Lander attempted to convert goods into currency the chief accepted their trinkets but then reneged. All he could offer in return was a female slave, who was accepted reluctantly and given to Pasko.

The Landers were becoming worried. Their money was running out. The 'Whitechapel sharps' needles which were 'warranted superfine and not to be cut in the eye',[15] proved often to have no eye at all. To save face the brothers had to throw most of the remainder away. They still had no canoe. And the peak period for safe navigation of the Niger was upon them. If they did not take advantage of it they might have to wait another year before conditions were right. But the ruler of Yauri would not let them go. His first excuse was that he had to write a letter to King George to explain the fact that he did not have Park's missing journal. It would take him three days. Then came the news that he had suffered a major setback in a war he was waging and needed time to recover. A little while later they received a number of seedy-looking feathers plucked from the ruler's finest ostrich. They were to be given to King George, the chief explained, but as was clear to anybody they were not of the quality one ruler would expect from another. Perhaps the Landers could wait until new feathers were available? He was doing his best to encourage new growth by rubbing twelve pounds of butter into the unfortunate bird's bottom. The Landers would not mind, he added reassuringly, if he deducted the cost of the butter from the amount he owed them. Then he announced that because of continuing hostilities he could not provide an escort to take them overland to Bussa. They would have to stay. Meanwhile they received daily visits from members of government and the chief's family demanding access to their precious medicine chest.

The Landers' frustration was relieved by the arrival of a letter from Bussa wanting to know why they were being detained and ordering their immediate release. On Sunday 1 August, after a dreary interview with the chief in a courtyard full of swallow droppings, during which they acknowledged their debt to have been fulfilled, they were allowed to go. Feeling that some gesture was needed, they finally

acceded to the demand for medicine. They administered a violent
purge to the chief, his sister and the entire royal family. Then they left
while the going was good.

They arrived in Bussa four days later, and took stock of their situation. The river, they decided, was an unpromising thing, 'not more
than a stone's throw across'.[16] Contemplating it from a nearby rock
they could hardly believe that Park had died in this miserable stretch
of water. Still, it was indisputably the Niger and they intended to
follow it to its end which, they believed, was the sea. However, they
had been told on their journey from Yauri that it veered eastward
and ended at Lake Chad. This disconcerting news would have been
welcomed by Barrow, but the Landers greeted it with despair. After
all their travails were they merely to end up in the middle of the
Sahara?

Their one comfort was the realization that they had an unexpected
source of income. Amongst their stores from England had been cans
of powdered 'portable soup' which they had dismissed after one tasting as 'worthless and unpalatable'.[17] The people of Bussa treated the
contents with equal disdain but the cans became valued style acces-
sories. 'We have been highly diverted,' wrote John, 'to see one man in
particular walking at large, and strutting about with "Concentrated
Gravy" stuck on his head in no less than four places.'[18] As they sold
their soup cans they were relieved to hear that the Niger did not end
up in Lake Chad. The mistake had come about through the naming
of a tributary of the Niger, the Tshadda or Benue, which did indeed
snake northwards towards Lake Chad. But the main river, they were
promised, emptied into salt water.

They were also able to add to their collection of Park-abilia by
purchasing an iron-sprung leather cushion which had been retrieved
from the river at the time of his death. At the same time they heard a
tantalizing story concerning Park's journal. A man in the nearby town
of Wawa had hoarded a collection of books and papers which had still
been in his possession when Clapperton passed through. But since he
had not been asked about them he had not volunteered their existence. In the intervening years they had rotted, fallen to pieces and

been thrown away. If the story was true, and if the documents were indeed Park's journal, the Landers had answered one of the most burningly pointless questions of West African exploration – Park's route had already been retraced so his journal could offer no geographical information and only in the most unlikely of circumstances would it shed light on his death. Still, they could congratulate themselves on having amassed enough of Park's possessions to be assured a warm welcome in Britain whatever happened. In that quarter, at least, things were looking up.

But their prospects of travelling down the Niger seemed to be diminishing daily. A suitable canoe simply was not to be found. One was on its way, the King of Bussa informed them, but when it arrived it was ridiculously small and inadequate. Moreover, it cost them a large part of their dwindling resources. John Lander was beside himself. 'There is infinitely more difficulty,' he fumed, 'and greater bustle and discussion in simply purchasing a canoe here, than there would be in Europe in drawing up a treaty of peace, or in determining the boundaries of an Empire.'[19]

Their stay in Bussa lengthened, and their wealth shrank. When they sent their last main article of barter, a donkey, to be sold at a local market and were told that it had been stolen along the way, they determined to leave with or without a canoe. The King replied that such a course would be 'presumptuous and improper',[20] but finally relented on 19 September. From nowhere a second canoe suddenly materialized and the Landers loaded it up. They took their leave with mixed feelings. For all his obstructiveness the King of Bussa had been a good-humoured and helpful host. But there was no doubting their relief at being free of him. 'When our people were all embarked on the Niger, and ourselves, we humbly thanked the Almighty for past deliverances, and fervently prayed that He would always be with us and crown our enterprise with success.'[21]

On the whole, He did not smile upon the expedition. Both canoes leaked and required the constant bailing of three men to keep them afloat. And at every stop they were stalled by orders to stay awhile – and a while longer, and a while longer still. A mighty canoe lurked forever beyond the horizon but never materialized. 'They have played with us as if we were great dolls.' steamed John. 'We have been driven about like shuttlecocks . . . Why this double dealing, this deceit, this chicanery?'[22] It took all their skills in diplomacy – and most of their remaining gifts, including Park's precious robe – to maintain the impetus.

Down the Niger they travelled, recruiting teams of paddlers as they went. They passed Mount Kesa, a great volcanic plug rising sheer from the river. They tried to investigate the Benue as it flowed into the Niger, only to be swept back by the current. They were attacked by a herd of hippopotami. It was exciting, but not unbearably dangerous, and despite recurrent bouts of malaria the Landers were reasonably cheerful. Their financial situation improved in dribs and drabs. At some stops they were greeted as the gods they had once been and were showered with presents. Elsewhere, by some quirk of riverine inflation, their remaining stock of needles were in such demand that they were able to get a magnificent price for them. Set against this was the old business of the canoe which they solved by reluctantly stealing one here, borrowing one there, and purchasing for an enormous price another – leaking – elsewhere.

On 22 October they saw a seagull. The coast was near. At the same time the river traffic picked up. They were delighted to see a small vessel shaped 'like a common butcher's tray'[23] go hissing past, crewed by ten children. Shortly afterwards they discovered the remains of a European gunpowder barrel. A little later they 'saw an English iron bar, and feasted our eyes on the graceful cocoanut tree which we had not seen for so long. We were delighted also with the mellow whistling of grey parrots. Trifling as these circumstances may appear, yet they made our hearts beat with delight, and awakened in us a train of very pleasing association. We indulged in a delusive, yet fanciful reverie, and we fondly hoped – but what good would it be to tell of what we fondly hoped?'[24]

Even at this stage in their travels the Landers were unaware of the effect so-called 'civilization' had had on Africa. They had seen the barracoons at Badagry, they had seen lines of slaves being marched south for export, they had even acquired several slaves themselves – albeit as gifts rather than by purchase. They knew full well the extent of the slave trade. But to them it was like a strange local custom, unpleasant but irrelevant to the task in hand. For all the hardships and idiosyncracies of the early stage of their journey the Landers had been treated well. The Africans upriver had bargained straightfor-wardly: the Landers needed things from them, they wanted things from the Landers; the outcome was generally decided in merchant-like fashion, even though the Landers resented the fact that they came off worst. Downriver, in contrast, lay the most brutal zone of the Niger: that area which had been influenced by Europe and whose inhabitants had learned from the white man the true meaning of rapacity.

The Landers paddled hopefully towards it. At every stop they were warned to go no further, or at least to wait until there was an escort to guide them through the dangers ahead. But the warnings were ignored. John and Richard Lander had had enough of such delaying tactics. Their progress was heartened by signs of prosperity. One vil-lage at which they stopped spread along the bank for a full two miles. Everywhere were indications of European culture. Meanwhile 'the magnificent Niger [seemed] to be slumbering in its own grandeur'.[25] Surely the end was in sight!

It was. But not in the way they expected. On 5 November the Landers were overjoyed to encounter a flotilla of canoes flying a vari-ety of flags. They were rather odd flags. Some bore pictures of decanters and glasses, some of chairs and tables, one had a man's leg printed on it but, gloriously, some boats were showing the Union Jack. Moreover, the men in the canoes were wearing shirts and coats.

Only when the canoes unveiled cannons did the Landers realize they had fallen into the hands of pirates. After a prolonged tussle, in which the Landers lost their clothes, Richard's journal, all Park's pos-sessions and every article of value they possessed including their guns, they were hauled ashore and told that they were now the prop-erty of King Obie, who was currently away but in a few days' time they would be taken downstream to meet him, at which point their fate would be decided. In the meantime they were placed under house arrest.

A few days later they were shoved into a canoe, with other slaves, and made the hazardous trip through the Niger's delta. In this they were lucky. The delta was understood only by its inhabitants and the Landers with their upriver crew would have been at a loss. In all likelihood they would have foundered in one of its many branches had it not been for their providential capture.

Somehow John Lander had managed to retain his notebook. Even during their capture he had scribbled down blow-by-blow descriptions of events. Richard's journal having been lost, it was now up to John to record their journey downstream to where King Obie awaited them. He noted everything of interest: other canoes, the size of houses, the loudness of their captors' voices 'which Stentor might have envied',[26] and the habit of one fellow slave of brushing her teeth rigorously with a twig – an example of dental hygiene quite astonishing to the two Britons. But nothing struck him so forcibly as the news that there was a British brig lying at the mouth of the river – the *Thomas of Liverpool*, ostensibly there to buy palm oil.

By the time they reached their destination and were brought before King Obie, John was sufficiently roused by the prospect of salvation and by a few meals of roast yam to let his descriptive powers run wild. Obie, a youngish man, was a sight to behold. 'His head was graced with a cap shaped like a sugar loaf, and thickly covered with strings of coral and pieces of broken looking glass . . . his neck, or rather his throat, was encircled with several strings of the same kind of bead, which were fastened so tightly, as in some degree to affect his respiration, and to give his throat and cheeks an inflamed appearance . . . He wore a short Spanish surtout of red cloth, which fitted close to his person, being much too small . . . Thirteen or fourteen bracelets (we had the curiosity to count them) decorated each wrist, and to give them full effect, the sleeves of the coat had been cut off . . . The king's trousers [equally tight] . . . reached no further than the middle of his legs, the lower parts . . . being ornamented like the wrists and with precisely the same number of strings of beads;

besides which, a string of little brass bells encircled each leg above the ankles.'[27]

The Landers stared in astonishment at this over-stuffed man in whose hands their destiny rested. With a full sense of occasion Obie 'shook his feet for the bells to tinkle, sat down with the utmost self-complacency, and looked around him'.[28] After a lengthy period during which Obie listened to the Landers' story through an interpreter, he announced his decision. The white men were his property. However, he was willing to release them to an English ship in exchange for goods to the value of twenty slaves.

The Landers were horrified. This was an outrageously high sum by any standards and certainly by those of the traders who frequented the West African coast. The chances of their ransom being met were reduced still further by Obie's insistence that they could not visit the coast themselves. Instead the business was to be conducted by messengers while the white men stayed where they were. Under these conditions the Landers had no realistic chance of being freed.

The next few days were painful. Weakened by fever and possessing not even a Whitechapel sharp with which to buy food, they were at the mercy of their captors. 'We have been reduced to the painful necessity of begging,' wrote John. 'But we might have addressed our petitions to the stones or trees . . . never had we greater need of patience and lowliness of spirits. In most African towns and villages we have been regarded as demi-gods [this was wishful thinking] but here, alas, what a contrast! – we are classed with the most degraded and despicable of mankind, and are become slaves in a land of ignorance and barbarism.'[29] Ironically, the ignorance and barbarism was of his own culture's making.

By extraordinary good luck, a man stepped forward who was willing to factor their ransom. He was King Boy, a ruler from the coastal region of Brass. He announced that he would undertake the payment owing to Obie in return for a promise from the English ship that he would be paid the required twenty slaves' worth as well as an extra fifteen slaves' worth plus a cask of rum for his trouble. The Landers almost fell over themselves to agree and on 12 November bade farewell to King Obie – who was delighted that they had found such a neat solution to their problem and insisted they visit him again should they ever be in the area – before boarding King Boy's canoe. 'Although distant about sixty miles from the mouth of the river, our journey appeared to me already completed and all our troubles and difficulties I considered at an end,' Richard later wrote with relief. 'Already in fond anticipation I was on board the brig, and had found a welcome reception from her commander – had related to him all the hardships and dangers we had undergone, and had been listened to with commiseration – already had I assured myself of his doing all he could to [help us].'[30]

For the first time in their travels they experienced the joys of swift, easy travel. King Boy's canoe was vast, holding sixty people, quantities of food and trade goods and all the weaponry needed for estuarine warfare. A cannon was strapped to the bows and cutlasses hung ready in case hand-to-hand combat was necessary. Apart from King Boy and his wife there was a captain, a mate, a boatswain, a coxswain and even a cook. It seemed a model of naval efficiency, down to the two enormous speaking trumpets which hung ready at the side of the canoe. With only two inches of gunwale showing above the water they sped downriver, forty paddles plunging in perfect unison.

With freedom in sight, the Landers recovered some of the grouches of civilization. The canoe was too noisy. The Landers had already decided that the men of Brass possessed the loudest voices known to mankind but when they discovered that the speaking trumpets were used not for issuing orders but to add vim to the abuse which the crew hurled at each other throughout the day, they were aghast 'but we are constrained to submit to it in silence'.[31] The canoe was also too cramped. When the Landers fell asleep, they were used as a convenient footrest by 'Mr. and Mrs. Boy . . . It would be ridiculous to suppose that one can enjoy the refreshment of sleep . . . when two or more uncovered legs and feet, huge, black, and rough, are traversing one's face and body, stopping up the passages of respiration, and pressing so heavily upon them at times, as to threaten suffocation.'[32] The Landers pinched the feet until they moved away. Then, when they were dropping off, the feet crept back. So it went on until the man nearest a speaking trumpet awoke and started a new day.

These were petty inconveniences, which John recorded ungratefully considering that King Boy had saved them from slavery. However, the experience did bring them together in a degree of friendship which would benefit the Landers when they finally arrived at Brass. The town was named after the Duke of Northumberland's gardener, one of the first people who had been sent to West Africa in the interests of science. He had brought back a number of interesting plants and had left behind him a settlement bearing his name. These homely associations meant nothing to the Landers. They saw 'a wretched, filthy and contemptible place'[33] whose houses seemed on the brink of sinking into the ground, and whose inhabitants, human and animal, wandered through the streets in a state of festering emaciation. Overseeing it all was the bleary eye of King Forday, King Boy's father.

King Forday was an amiable drunk, who was amazed that the Landers had travelled down the Niger as far as they had and immediately plied them with rum and held a ceremony in their honour. But he was not so amiable as to lose sight of commercial considerations. He informed the Landers that Boy's deal was perfectly acceptable, but just in case they decided to jump continent he would retain John and all their party, allowing only Richard to go to the *Thomas*. The two explorers had no choice but to agree.

Richard was paddled down the delta and at 7 a.m. on 17 November saw two European ships lying at anchor. One of them was a Spanish trader. The other was the *Thomas*. The past year's hardships rolled away. He had found the termination of the Niger, and there was an English boat waiting to sail him home. His ransom would be paid and glory would be his. 'The emotions of delight,' he recorded, 'are quite beyond my powers of description.'[34]

His delight didn't last long. Of the eight men who crewed the *Thomas* only four were still alive, and they were bedridden with fever. Only the captain, a man called Lake, was capable of movement and he was half delirious. Hopefully, Lander produced Barrow's orders, which were read to the illiterate Lake by one of his own stricken men. Lander explained that he wanted a bill written for the money owed his captors. Lake exploded. 'If you think you have a — fool to deal with you are mistaken; I'll not give a b—y flint for your bill, I would not give you a — for it.'[35] Richard Lander's hopes were crushed by a torrent of four-letter words. It was worse than anything he had encountered in all his time in Africa. 'Never in my life did I feel such humiliation as at this moment. On our way through the country we had been treated well; we had been in the habit of making presents as had been expected from us; and, above all, we had maintained our character among the natives by keeping our promises. This was no longer in our power, as my means were all expended . . . I had promised the price of our ransom should be paid by the first of our countrymen that we might meet with, on the best of all securities.'[36]

What Richard did not realize was that Lake was at his wits' end. He was not an inherently bad man. He was stuck inside the bar which ran across the Niger's mouth and had only the prospect of the local pilot, a man who was famed throughout the region for guiding European ships to disaster, to lead him to safety. His crew, the few that remained, were unable to function. Lake was even more desperate than Lander. In the end, this desperation worked in Lander's favour. Lake suddenly awoke to the fact that the hostages were healthy men, some of whom had seagoing experience. If he could get them on board he would have the crew he needed.

When King Boy came aboard to collect his ransom he was given short shrift by Lake. Despite Lander's protestations of Boy's decency Lake replied that if the whole contingent were not freed within three days he would sail without them. And as for getting out of the river, he would be damned if he would pay the pilot a cent. He would find his own way out.

The next day the pilot, who had brought the ship in and had not yet been paid, came up to ask for payment, offering at the same time to lead Lake out again. Lake said he would have nothing to do with him. The pilot calmly pointed out that there were seven brass cannons at the mouth of the river and that if he wasn't paid he would blow Lake out of the water. Lake responded that he did not give a —, and ordered the man off his ship. He then sent his mate, a man named Spittle, to sound the depth of the bar. Spittle was duly captured and held to ransom for £50. Lake did not seem to give a — about this either.

Meanwhile, against all odds, King Boy had returned with John Lander and the other hostages. He delivered them aboard to a volley of curses from Lake who assured him he would not get a penny for his efforts. Then, repenting perhaps of his heartless attitude towards Spittle, he promised Boy that if the mate was not returned immediately he would send 1,000 men-of-war to blast the town and anyone connected with it to smithereens. The captain must have been particularly expressive because, a little while later, Spittle was freed.

The Landers were appalled. King Boy, their friend and saviour, had been dismissed with only a scribbled promise of reward. Their honour had been lost. Moreover, they were now in the hands of a man who seemed a near lunatic, whose behaviour was such that Richard 'shrunk from him in terror'[37] and who, far from delivering them to a safe port, announced that he would drop them on an island off the Cameroons; it was the best he could do.

Lake, on the other hand, was pleased with himself. From a point of near collapse he had single-handedly saved two explorers – not that he cared the slightest about their expedition or their twitterings about honour – had remanned his ship at no cost, had seen off the enemy and was about to do what no European had ever done: navigate the Niger's sand bar.

In their passive drift down the Niger the Landers had never thought what might happen when they reached its mouth. Now they knew. And although neither admitted it, they were very lucky to find a captain as determined as Lake. Compared to the brutality of the coast, their voyage so far had been a tourist trip.

On 26 November, Lake approached the bar but found himself driven back by the sea until he was in five fathoms of water and almost touching dry land directly opposite the coastal battery. This

was the most dangerous point in the Landers' journey. What Lake
needed was an offland wind, but it did not come, and he was forced to
maintain his position by anchor. At any moment the guns could
destroy them. The pilot was spotted watching them through a telescope. Armed Africans waited patiently on the beach to collect the
survivors. It was a waiting game which they were happy to play. It
could not be long before the war canoes of Brass arrived to claim their
money and when they did the *Thomas* would be at their mercy. As
night fell, small fires were lit along the coast.

Whether from fear of the unknown power of Lake's single cannon,
or fear of his 1,000 men-of-war, the battery did not fire. Or maybe they
had read the tides and knew they had no need. When dawn broke so
did the *Thomas*'s cable. A second, smaller anchor was lowered but not
before the ship was almost in the breakers. The watching Africans
waved jovially, pointing out places where the crew could land. Spittle
assured Richard that in a few minutes it would be every man for himself. Then, at 8 a.m., Lake had his last bit of luck. A sea breeze arose
and, by lowering boats to tow him, he was able to scrape over the bar
in less than three fathoms.

To the Landers Lake was an abomination. Yet they owed everything to this rude, violent and effective man.

Thanks to a brief encounter with the *Black Joke*, a tender to a
British naval vessel which was patrolling the waters in search of
slavers, the Landers did not have to land at Lake's Cameroon island
but were deposited at Fernando Po, a British-manned island to the
east of the Niger which Richard knew as a haven to which officers like
Dixon Denham repaired for a fever-free furlough.

Fernando Po was not free of fever. Lieutenant Stockwell, the resident commander of marines, had recently lost five servants and five
children to yellow fever, and malaria was rife. But even this could not
quench the Landers' delight at being in relatively civilized surroundings. They bade farewell to Captain Lake, and that was the last they
would see of him. Standing at the port as Lake drew out, they saw a
ship with 'long, raking masts'[38] surge from behind a headland. Shots
were fired and grappling irons were hurled. Darkness fell before they

could gauge the outcome. When morning came, the sea was empty but it was clear what had happened. Neither he nor the *Thomas* were ever heard of again.

By January the Landers were on a ship to Rio de Janeiro. There they found an English ship, the *William Harris*, to take them home. On 9 June 1831 they arrived in Portsmouth. The next day Richard was reporting his findings in London.

So, the Niger had been 'found' and one of the most controversial questions in African exploration had been answered. It was, in the words of the *Edinburgh Review*, 'perhaps the most important discovery of the present age'.[39] The commercial benefit which Banks had envisaged all those years ago was now within Britain's grasp, as Richard Lander was quick to point out, stating that the discovery of the Niger's mouth heralded the possibility of 'a water communication . . . with so extensive a part of Africa that a considerable trade will be opened'.[40]

Yet he and his brother received little approbation from the government and none at all from John Barrow, whose pet theories they had so soundly debunked. Richard got the £100 he had contracted for – paid from a quasi-official slush fund called 'the King's Bounty' – and John got what he had been promised: nothing.

They were better treated in other quarters. King William granted them an audience in which he kept them talking for a full hour. And John Murray paid them 1,000 guineas for their journal which, interestingly, he did not allow Barrow to edit as was usual, but instead gave to an Admiralty hydrographer who was the editor of the *Nautical Review*. Even so, there was a show of disdain for their achievements. As the introduction explains, 'The accomplished surveyor will look in vain along the list of articles, with which the travellers were supplied, for the instrument of his calling; and that man of science, to form his opinion of it, need only be told, that a common compass was all that they possessed to benefit geography, beyond the observation of their senses . . . Too much faith must not therefore be reposed in the various serpentine courses of the river on the map, as it is neither warranted by the resources, nor the ability of the travellers.'[41]

The book did not come out until 1832 by which time John Lander, its primary author, was nearly destitute. Reluctantly, he approached Bathurst for assistance. A position as clerk or messenger in the Colonial Office was what he wanted or, failing that, a sum of money. Neither were forthcoming. Indeed, he was not even sent a reply. 'May I beg your Lordship will please to inform me what the Government intends doing for me?'[42] he pleaded again to Bathurst. He was greeted with silence. It would not be the last time he wrote. But he was wasting his time. His reward was still nothing.

Richard fared slightly better, securing a decent job with Customs, his task being to taste wine shipments to see if they had been adulterated. But he soon abandoned this when a consortium of Liverpool merchants approached him to see if he would lead an expedition of two steam-boats to set up factories along the Niger. No longer would he be a humble servant of the government. He would be at the helm of a magnificent industrial venture.

He managed to get his Customs job assigned to his brother John – charging him a stiff commission of £100 for doing so – and in June 1832 set off for Africa. He penetrated 100 miles into the Benue and travelled up the Niger as far as Rabba, only a few towns down from Bussa. This was a changed Lander from the one who had finessed his way from settlement to settlement. This was a conquering Lander. His ships bristled with guns and at one point he was constrained to 'chastise' the natives by destroying a town. It was a word he used with increasing frequency and bewilderment. On being attacked in a narrow part of the river by '8,000 or 10,000 all armed with muskets and swords, Bonny, Benin and Brass people', he decided that 'if these savages are not chastised immediately it will never be safe to go up in a boat or canoe'.[43]

But he would not be around to do the chastising. During the attack he received a musket ball – a sawn-off piece of copper bolt – in the thigh. It was a high wound, close to the anus, and the bolt could not be removed. When gangrene set in there was nothing that could be done. Lander died at 2 a.m. on 2 February 1834. His ill-starred expedition slunk home a month later, by which time its numbers had dropped from forty-eight to eight.

The Niger conundrum had ended as it had begun, with a white man ambushed in a narrow stretch of river. Only this time there was no mystery and nobody cared.

17

SECOND SINGAPORES

The Royal Geographical Society – or the Geographical Society as it was then known – was founded in 1830. Its first meeting was held at the Raleigh Club in St James's, and on the suggestion of Francis Beaufort was chaired by John Barrow – 'there could not be a more desirable person to preside over the resolutions',[1] cheered William Jerdan, editor of the *Literary Gazette*.

In his autobiography Barrow distances himself from the Society's foundation, claiming the idea was suggested by the auctioneer William Sotheby. It was in fact presaged by the foundation of the Raleigh Club on the instigation of one Sir Arthur de Capell Brooke, an army captain who had travelled widely and wanted a club where he could eat exotic food – Dead Sea bread, Lapland venison, Mexican ham and the like. Barrow was a founding member. The Raleigh Club's practical extension was mooted by a member of the Asiatic Society in a letter to the *Literary Gazette* on 24 May 1828. 'From the egg thus dropt,' wrote Jerdan, 'the Royal Geographical Society was hatched.'[2]

For all his avowed disinterest, Barrow must have been delighted to chair proceedings. The presidency of the Royal Society was socially beyond him, and anyway it did not recognize geography as a science. In the Geographical Society, however, he had a new pressure group for his ambitions. On the same day that the Asiatic Society man's letter appeared in the *Gazette* Barrow suggested two proposals to the members of the Raleigh Club. His first was 'That a society was needed whose sole object should be the promotion and diffusion of that most important and entertaining branch of knowledge – geography; and that a useful Society might therefore be formed, under the name of THE GEOGRAPHICAL SOCIETY OF LONDON.'[3] His second was that the Society should do everything in its power to facilitate the voyages of any explorers who came forward with good ideas as to how that branch might be extended.

It took two years of regular meetings, at Barrow's Admiralty rooms, before the Geographical Society was officially launched on 16 July 1830. Its membership was taken from the Raleigh Club and the African Association; its President was Viscount Goderich (the new Colonial Secretary); and its four Vice-Presidents included Sir John Franklin and Barrow. Almost every other official was from the Admiralty. John Barrow, of course, was the Chairman. In one smooth move Barrow had put himself in a position to control every exploratory venture which left Britain. Whether through the Admiralty, the Royal Society or the Geographical Society, he was in command.

The Chairman did not have a light touch. One member complained that he 'could not submit to the harsh dictatorial language of Barrow'.[4] And at one point the Secretary, one of Barrow's naval mouthpieces, was charged with 'intentionally and systematically duping and misleading the Council, with mis-stating and mystifying their proceedings in the Minute Book, with sacrificing the interests of the Society to particular objects, and in general with misconduct'.[5]

But Barrow did have a number of ideas to put forward. His first speech started off quietly with one of his better suggestions: that the Society produce 'road-books for different countries, gazetteers, geographical and statistical tables and all such matters as are of general utility'[6] – travel guides of the kind that John Murray would later publish to great acclaim. But then Barrow gathered steam. 'It would seem desirable,' he said, 'to collect and distribute information regarding New Holland, or as it is now more generally called, Australia. Hitherto a country as large as Europe has been presented on our maps as a blank. Yet, as this extensive territory will, in all probability, in process of time, support a numerous population, the progeny of Britons, and may be the means of spreading the English language, laws and institutions over a great part of the Eastern Archipelago, it is presumed that every accession to our knowledge of its geographical features will be acceptable to the Society.'[7]

To their credit, the members resisted Barrow's steamrollering. They preferred less partisan ideals such as the creation of a £50 Gold Medal for exploration, the first of which was awarded in 1832 to Richard Lander (Barrow's annoyance can only be imagined) but was received by his brother John, Richard having already sailed to his doom. As for Australia, the members could not countenance it, having heard only a year previously how Barrow's last stab at the continent had come to an ignominious end.

Back in 1824 Barrow had been diverted from his Arctic voyages to address the problem of Australia. He had envisaged a settlement on its north coast which would come to be 'a second Singapore'.[8] He chose Melville Island, near present-day Port Darwin, whose existence had been reported recently in glowing terms by one Captain Bremer. Barrow's advice was forthright. 'We ought not, in sound policy, to hesitate a moment in forming a settlement on the northern part of New Holland . . . when it is considered how anxiously the Dutch are exerting themselves to re-establish their dominion, and with it their pernicious and narrow system of exclusion in the Eastern Archipelago.'[9] By which was meant that Britain should get in there and operate its own system of exclusion.

Melville Island was duly settled by Captain Bremer with fifty-one soldiers and forty-four convicts. 'There never was a more promising spot,' wrote Barrow, 'in a naval, commercial and agricultural point of view . . . I have no doubt that, in a commercial view, it will become another Singapore.'[10] Alas, it never did. Not only did it fail to attract any trade – being on the route to and from nowhere except itself, it is hard to see how it could have done – but it was expensive to maintain, all its supplies having to be transported 2,000 miles from Sydney. The scheme was abandoned in 1829, to the secret relief of the First Secretary. 'I always considered the establishment as very doubtful policy,' wrote Croker, 'and the circumstances stated by General Darling [the Governor of New South Wales] leave no doubt of the complete inutility of these embryo colonists for the purpose for which they were (in my private opinion, inadvertently) undertaken.'[11]

If he had not chosen the right place for a second Singapore, Barrow was at least right to suggest further stock be taken of Australia, which was being treated in an appallingly cavalier fashion. Despite a perverse view that having been circumnavigated by a Briton Australia therefore belonged to Britain, Britain seemed to have no interest in the continent. Only a small portion of the south-east had been colonized, and that mainly by convicts who arrived at the rate of 3,000 per year. The rest of Australia was consigned to the geographical attic. So disinterested was the mother country that it could not even supply an independent religious hierarchy. Until a late date Australia belonged to the diocese of Calcutta. Given these circumstances, there was no reason at all why France or Holland, both of whom had a major presence in the Far East, should not occupy stretches of Australia's as yet largely unexplored coastline. As ever, in Barrow's estimation, the foreigner must be thwarted.

It was this that kept his interest in Australia burning. And there was another reason, too: in the same year that Melville Island was closed down his friend and favourite, Parry, had left England to become Commissioner for the Australian Agricultural Company. This massive but creaky concern had been founded in 1824 with a million-acre grant of land north of Sydney and £1,000,000 of share capital. Its aim was to turn Australia into a vast sheep and cattle ranch – which to an extent it did. But it had yet to pay its investors a dividend and it needed a commissioner to tell it what was going wrong.

It was at times like these that being an explorer paid off. Franklin and Parry had just been knighted, had both been to Oxford to receive

honorary degrees and, although it had been a few years since either
had hit the headlines, to hear verses sung in their praise. One typical
example ran:

> *But fairer England greet the wanderer now,*
> *Unfaded laurels shade her Parry's brow;*
> *And on the proud memorials of her fame*
> *Lives, linked with deathless glory Franklin's name.*[12]

Companies then, as now, wanted to be associated with famous
names. The Australian Agricultural Company offered the com-
missionership first to Franklin and then to Parry. Both refused, on the
grounds that taking the job would mean relinquishing their Admiralty
pay, thus severing a reliable source of income. However, when the
post was offered to Parry again, he reconsidered. The money was
good, at £2,000 per annum plus an annuity of £300 for life, and a visit
to Lord Melville secured the promise that he would continue to
receive half-pay from the Admiralty. Moreover, he was sick of the
Hydrographical Department. Even if Croker had not been obstruct-
ing his every move he would still have been tired of sitting at a desk
sorting maps. It was almost as bad as Arctic service. 'I am losing both
health and money,' he told his brother. 'This will not do.'[13] His wife
agreed: 'He . . . generally comes home quite tired and worried, only fit
to lie on the sofa and be made much of.'[14]

Parry decided to accept and, at the end of May 1829, handed his
position over to Francis Beaufort. The relief on both sides was palpable.
One Captain Owen, an officer who had done outstanding work in surveying the West African coast, sent a note of congratulation to Beaufort:
'I had some complaints against Parry on which I wrote to him . . . but I
think he was always playing another game than Hydrography.'[15]

Parry's game was no more Australian than it had been hydrographical. He served his four-year term dutifully but innocuously, with his
wife Isabella and a growing number of children (one of whom was
conceived on the journey out). His main achievement was to tell his
employers that they were wasting their time.

I unreservedly state it as my opinion,

1st That from £50,000 to £100,000 of the Company's Capital has been unprofitably expended . . .

2nd That all the Profit which the Company can reasonably expect to realize, is a moderate but remunerating Interest upon that portion of their Capital which has been profitably expended, or is now profitably expending.

3rd That for *that* Portion of their Capital I do not, under the present depressed tho' certainly improving circumstances of the Colony, and especially with the present doubt as to sufficient Markets for the produce, venture to anticipate an adequate Return for at least the next two years.[16]

Sure enough, in 1834, two years after Parry wrote that judgement, and ten years after the investors put in their money, the company paid its first dividend. The experience had been enough to turn Parry grey and to reduce Isabella to a weight less than half her husband's sixteen stone. They left joyfully in March 1834 aboard 'the most uneasy sieve I ever sailed in',[17] with a menagerie of one cow, a kangaroo, an opossum, five sugar squirrels, two diamond birds and seven parrots.

Barrow had kept a keen eye on his ageing prodigy's progress, and the country in which he progressed. He was still worried that France or Holland might snatch Australia from Britain. In 1837 he heartily supported a project to colonize Port Essington, a few miles east of Melville Island. It was vital, he wrote, 'that the whole of this great continent should be held under one undivided power, and that Great Britain, which first planted colonies upon its shore, should be that power; and that, to keep it in secure possession, she ought to draw a ring-fence round its whole coast',[18]

So off went Captain Bremer once again, to make a second settlement in north Australia. As before, he wrote glowingly of the region's attractions. And as before the region failed to live up to expectations. Port Essington became a byword for discomfort. T. H. Huxley, Aldous Huxley's grandfather, visited the place and condemned it as 'the most

useless, miserable, ill-managed hole in Her Majesty's dominions'.[19]
He declared that it was worth 'all the abuse that has ever been heaped
upon it. It is fit for neither man nor beast. Day and night there is the
same fearful damp depressing heat, producing unconquerable lan-
guor and rendering the unhappy resident a prey to ennui and cold
brandy and water . . . Port Essington is *worse than a ship*, and it is no
small comfort to know that this is possible.'[20]

An official from the Colonial Office put it in more gentle terms.
'The fact is, that this was a favourite scheme of Sir John Barrow's and
that in the original eagerness to accomplish it, all financial difficulties
were set aside.'[21] Port Essington was closed down in 1849, one year
after Barrow's death.

Barrow was not greatly troubled by the failures. They had seen the
foreigner off at any rate. 'Happily,' he wrote in 1843, 'the French are
quartering themselves on a different part of the globe and may be satisfied with the larger [i.e. smaller] scope which the Pacific will afford
them.'[22]

Fascinating as Australia and the Pacific might have been, they were
never of more than secondary interest to Barrow. Granted, it had been
he who had proposed the exploration of New Holland to the Royal
Geographical Society in 1830. However, his heart had never been in it.
What he would like to have proposed was another stab at the North-
West Passage. In this he had been thwarted both by budgets and the
forestalment of John Ross and his sputtering little steam ship. But as
1830 turned into 1831, with no news of Ross from either the Pacific or
the Atlantic, a faint glimmer of hope formed in Barrow's mind. It
would be wrong to say he wished his old enemy dead. With every
passing season, though, Ross's demise seemed ever more certain.

18

ORDEAL OF
THE *VICTORY*

John Ross was very much alive, however. On 10 August 1829 his ships reached Prince Regent Inlet and turned south, reaching Fury Beach two days later. The spot was almost exactly as James Ross and Parry had left it four years before. Piles of coal still hummocked the shoreline. The two huge heaps of provisions were undisturbed and in as good a condition as when they had been abandoned. Even the sugar, bread and flour were edible. The sails were well stacked, sound and dry. Amazingly, one of the tents was still standing. There was everything Ross could possibly need, from gunpowder and lime juice to wine and anchors. The only thing missing was the *Fury* itself.

Ross packed the *Victory* to overflowing. He took aboard ten tons of coal, the best sails, the *Fury*'s spare mizzen mast, anchors, hawsers and enough food to last almost three years. Finally he blew up the remaining gunpowder, lest it cause an accident among the Eskimos. The crew rowed back to the *Victory* to cries of 'God Save Fury Beach'. Looking back, the stores loomed as bounteously as before. They seemed hardly to have been touched.

Ross weighed anchor on 14 August and continued south, sliding past the sheer sandstone cliffs of Somerset Island which towered 300 feet above him. Cresswell Bay, named but not explored by Parry, looked promising as a possible route west. For a while Ross faced the enormously satisfying prospect of sailing through Parry's bay much as Parry had sailed through his own. But it was not to be. The bay was a bay, nothing more. Disappointed, Ross restored his spirits with a display of magnanimity. 'I would rather find a passage anywhere else,' he told his nephew. 'I am quite sure that those who have suffered as I have from a cruelly misled Public Opinion will never wish to transfer such misery to a fellow creature if their hearts are in the right place.'[1]

On 16 August he passed Parry's furthest south and the cliffs dwindled to a point where Ross could row ashore and claim the land for Britain. Discarding the name Somerset Island, he called his discovery Boothia Felix after his sponsor. Down the coast of Boothia Felix he went, naming bays, mountains and islands after either his or Booth's family. An anchorage was named Elizabeth Harbour, in honour of Booth's wife; a striking mountain was called Christian's Monument in memory of Ross's deceased wife. By the end of September he had travelled 300 miles further south than Parry and was moored off Andrew Ross Island, christened after Ross's son.

It really did look as if, this time, Ross was going to succeed. He had sailed further down Prince Regent Inlet than any man yet and was only 280 miles from the point at which Franklin had discovered open water in 1821. The weather was mild, game was plentiful and his men found the remains of at least twenty Eskimo summer settlements. So long as Boothia Felix proved to be an island rather than a peninsula, they were in with a chance.

Alas, Boothia Felix *was* a peninsula. Though Ross had no way of knowing it, he was fighting his way into a dead end. And, ironically, he had already passed not only a possible way out but a channel which led into the true North-West Passage. Somerset Island was indeed an island, separated from Boothia by the narrow, treacherous Bellot Strait – as it would be later called after the French explorer who discovered it. However, John Ross had either ignored or not noticed the strait in one of those blind moments to which he was prone.

Hypothetically, Bellot Strait could have led Ross to fame. But so, in Ross's mind, could Prince Regent Inlet.

The *Victory* had served Ross well, but its steam engine had not. It occupied, with its fuel, two-thirds of the ship's tonnage; it worked atrociously at best; and it required the constant attention of four men to keep it running. In fact, Ross calculated that the engine moved the ship no faster than if it had been towed by two boats manned by rowers. He decided he would rather have the space and the man-power, and rely on what he knew best: sail. He asked his officers' opinion. They all agreed with him. So Braithwaite's ingenious new mechanism was dumped ashore unceremoniously on Andrew Ross Island. 'I believe there was now not one present who ever again wished to see its minutest fragment,'[2] Ross wrote.

Winter was coming in. As he struggled south Ross met increasingly hard conditions which he described vividly in his journal. 'Ice is stone,' he conjured, 'a floating rock in a stream.'[3] He invited his readers to 'imagine, if they can, these crystals hurled through a narrow strait by a rapid tide; meeting, as mountains might meet, with a noise of thunder, breaking from each other's precipices huge fragments, or rending each other asunder, till, losing their former equilibrium, they fall over headlong, lifting the sea around in breakers, and whirling it into eddies while the flatter fields of ice, formed against these masses . . . by the wind and the stream, rise out of the sea until they fall back on themselves, adding to the indescribable commotion and noise.'[4]

On 6 October he settled into winter quarters, his crew cutting a path through the ice to reach an anchorage that was called Felix Harbour. The staleness of the name reflected Ross's own weariness. Killing a polar bear was the only event which enlivened 'the tedium of the day, the forerunner of many far worse'.[5] Then he turned the *Victory* to the north to face the winter winds and battened down. 'The prison door was shut upon us,'[6] Ross wrote. 'It was indeed a dull prospect. Amid all its brilliancy, this land, the land of ice and snow, has ever been, and ever will be a dull, dreary, heart-sinking, monotonous waste, under the influence of which the very mind is paralyzed,

ceasing to care or think . . . it is but the view of uniformity and silence
and death . . . where nothing moves and nothing changes, but all is for
ever the same, cheerless, cold and still.'[7]

Ross did not welcome the winter but he was prepared for it. He
insulated the deck with two and a half feet of trodden snow on which
was laid a covering of sand. He used the sails from Fury Beach to
make a tented roof over the ship. And in scientific fashion he met the
problem of condensation not with stoves but with holes cut through
the deck over which were placed upside-down iron tanks. On the
principle that hot air rose, Ross reckoned that the condensation would
freeze in the tanks, and could be chipped off later and thrown overboard. The system worked magnificently, according to Ross. Others
were less sure. An observatory was erected on shore, to be manned by
James Ross. And extra provisions were allotted to the men who
manned the log, barometer and thermometer.

Like Parry, Ross aimed for constant activity. Watches, schedules
and ship's duties were maintained as normal. The central event was
lunch, which took place at noon. The crew exercised on the deck in
the afternoon. And further chores kept them occupied until evening
when, from 6 to 9 p.m., Ross oversaw a school covering reading, writing, arithmetic and navigation. Everyone attended these evening
classes, their main challenge being to convert three of their colleagues
to literacy. Sunday school was at 6 p.m.

Unlike Parry, however, Ross did not stoop to such frivolities as
plays, masquerades and newspapers. His was a stern expedition operating under the wartime rules he was acquainted with.

John Ross drew heavily on the experience of his nephew for his
winter regime, but added a novel touch of his own: fresh food. He
opined that 'the large use of oil and fats is the true secret of life in
these frozen countries, and that the natives cannot subsist without it,
becoming diseased and dying under a more meagre diet'.[8] Decades
before his time, Ross had devised the best anti-scorbutic diet yet. No
more running around to stave off scurvy's effects, or drinking quantities of beer; with further far-sightedness, Ross decided alcohol
made men more prone to the disease and banned its use except in

emergencies and for land expeditions. Instead, all that was needed was fresh food. And for most of the year he had fresh food in plenty. His men shot ptarmigan, hunted caribou and netted salmon. There was no shortage. If anything there was an embarrassing surplus. 'What do you think of 6,376 at one haul?' he wrote to Beaufort concerning his salmon-fishing activities. 'I am afraid I must not stick this in my publications – unless I want a worse name than I have.'[9]

Not all the game was so accommodating as the salmon. On one hunting foray James Ross shot a musk-ox at the unsporting range of fifteen yards. It fell, but immediately arose again and charged its persecutor. Ross ducked behind a nearby boulder against which the musk-ox, 'rushing with all its force, struck its head so violently that it fell to the ground with such a crash that the hard ground around us fairly echoed to the sound'.[10] Amazingly, the animal returned to the attack. It was only five yards away when Ross finally brought it down with a second shot. The incident could have come straight from the pages of a big-game hunter's African memoirs, save that it took place in the Arctic, and Ross was armed only with a musket.

Such sorties were short-lived. As the temperature fell the wildlife disappeared. On 26 November the sun also vanished – they caught its last reflection off the ice a week later. On Christmas Day they were treated to a magnificent show of the Northern Lights and ate the remains of the Galloway steer, accompanied by mince pies and cherry brandy salvaged from Fury Beach. New Year saw them well and healthy at a temperature of 16° below zero. The interior of the ship was warm enough, but not as warm as Parry's had been. This fact was noted resentfully by Ross's steward. Ross, however, dismissed all complaints with the argument that less heat meant less condensation. And anyway, the cold meant little to him. As he explained, 'I have myself been noted, by a physiologist of well known reputation, as possessing in a very high degree the power of generating heat.'[11]

Outside, a stark shape against the snow, a raven fluttered around their ship. Was it an omen for good or evil? Ross dismissed his crew's speculations – 'what their prognostics were, I did not take the trouble to inquire; had they been either absurd or important, it is probable that I should have heard enough of them without inquiring'.[12] But the raven meant something to him. When it was shot, on 29 January, he bemoaned its loss. It had done them no harm. They had killed their lucky charm.

On 9 January they made their first contact with Eskimos, a party of thirty-one men and women who had come from a settlement a few miles to the north. Unlike the Eskimos Ross had encountered in 1818, these people seemed not at all surprised to see the white men's ships. Already, Ross decided, Europeans had lost their novelty value. (He and Lander should have exchanged notes.) However, the visitors were delighted with Ross's gift of a piece of hoop iron apiece and complimented him on the oil and salt beef which he served them. The oil was 'really good';[13] but later they admitted that they were being polite with regard to the beef.

Throughout the winter Eskimos and Britons enjoyed a good relationship. Ross's men visited the Eskimo village – primarily to sleep with the Eskimo women – and the Eskimos were entertained on the *Victory*. Dances were held, with each community displaying examples of their ethnic specialities. Ross scored a diplomatic victory by ordering the ship's carpenter in collaboration with the surgeon to make a wooden leg for an Eskimo named Tulluahin, who had lost the original to a polar bear. It was fitted on 15 January 1830 and became a talking point of that part of the Arctic. Everyone wanted one. More than once Ross had to break the news that a boil or minor abrasion didn't qualify for amputation.

In return, the Eskimos helped Ross with his quest. They told him where the salmon were, where the musk-oxen could be found and when the caribou herds would come back (in April). They also gave invaluable advice on the region's geography. When Ross showed them his meagre map they at once began to draw in coast and rivers. In an interview aboard the *Victory*, charmingly painted by James Ross, they assured him that there was no way out to the south and that his only option was to retrace his steps and look for a route to the north. But, in a manner which would have appealed to Beaufort's hydrographical exactitude, Ross insisted he would find that out for himself.

James Ross explained it more fully. The Eskimos 'gave us no encouragement, assuring us that the land was here continuous from north to south within the whole range of their knowledge, and affirming positively that there was no passage where we fancied that one might possibly exist. But we did not think ourselves at all justified in taking this on their showing: they might not be correct.'[14] Of course, had James Ross been told there was a wide, ice-free canal flowing without obstruction to Bering Strait, he would have thought this quite correct.

As ever, the Eskimos were willing to help the strangers in their unlikely venture. They furnished the Rosses with sledges and dog teams and gave them instructions on their use. The sledges were a source of wonder to the Europeans. The standard model comprised two lengths of frozen salmon, wrapped in hides and joined by cross-pieces of bone. (When times were hard it could be thawed and eaten.) Alternatively they could be made out of ice, carved elaborately into a recognizable sledge-shape, or simply scooped from the ground to form a bowl that slid happily over the snow.

Handling the sledges was a matter of some difficulty. James Ross picked it up quickly enough, although his team frequently ran wild, depositing him in the snow and being retrieved only after a chase of several miles when they would be found, exhausted and with the sledge jammed between outcrops of ice. His uncle had less success. On his first attempt the dogs ran in opposite directions so that he went nowhere; on his second they ran in circles, so that 'the sledge appeared as if it were placed on a pivot, and Capt. Ross within it, resembling a huge teetotum twirled round and round'.[15] Not wishing to embarrass himself further, he confined his travels to short-distance exploration, taking one of Franklin's lightweight boats on man-hauled forays into the interior. The longer distances were left to James Ross.

The Eskimos must have been puzzled by their visitors. There they were, huddled in their ships while a whole community was thriving outside. What was the attraction of those ships? They seemed to have plenty of iron, plenty of food, but why were they so frightened of the outside? The Eskimos could only shrug. On 2 April, with the thermometer showing 22 °F, they coaxed James Ross out of the casket. A dog-sledging expedition was arranged, with two Eskimo guides and ten days of food, to explore Boothia Felix. Almost as soon as the party left it was hit by a violent storm. Snow sheeted down and the wind rose to gale force. Eight days later, at 6 p.m., James Ross fought his way back to the *Victory*. He had crossed Boothia Felix and had seen frozen sea to the west.

Later in the month James Ross made a second sledge trip and returned with the news that Boothia Felix was probably a peninsula, as the Eskimos had said. He had not travelled to its end, but he had gone far enough down its ice-clogged shores to be certain that there was no passage to the west. James Ross went out again and again on the Eskimo sledges. His greatest achievement that winter was to cross a frozen body of water that would later be called James Ross Strait – though he assumed at the time that it was solid land – and to survey the northern coastline of a bleak region he named King William Land. At Victory Point, his furthest west, he saw open water. From here it was only 200 miles to Franklin's Point Turnagain. Another tantalizing piece of the puzzle had been filled in.

But James Ross had made a dangerous mistake. Although he had no way of knowing it, King William Land was in fact an island, not part of the mainland as he had assumed. Below it lay open water which curled round to meet James Ross Strait. There was something else, too. Littered along the coast of King William Land were massive blocks of ice, thrown up to half a mile above the high tide mark, whose presence so far inland baffled Ross. Again, he could not know that these came from the vast ice stream which flowed out of the Beaufort Sea to the north, squeezing its way under enormous pressure through the Arctic archipelago to beat remorselessly at the north-west coast of King William Land. It would never be possible to break through this constantly frozen, constantly replenished mass. And this would not be discovered until it was too late.

James Ross returned on 13 June, to find preparations underway for the return journey. On 20 June the temperature rose to 62 °F. Two weeks later the snow had melted and after another fortnight the ice began to break around the ships. The shore observatory was dismantled and the canvas roof packed away. It looked as if they would soon be home.

Not for the first time, and not for the last, in the tremendously frustrating annals of the North-West Passage, William Scoresby was proved right. He had stated that if the Passage existed it would only be attainable at rare intervals. Ross had sailed down the Gulf of Boothia on one of those fortunate years and was now paying the penalty. He had chosen his anchorage at a period of high tides. This year, however, the tides were too low and his ships were unable to navigate a sand bar which lay across the entrance to Felix Harbour. Only by unloading both ships was Ross able to scrape them over the bar, after which came the tedious business of reloading. Just as Ross had met with high tides, so he had met with ice-free conditions. Now, just as the tides were low, so was the sea frozen. He made three miles on the first day then ground to a halt. By the end of September he had moved another 300 yards. The brief Arctic window was closing. It was obvious that the expedition would have to spend another year in the ice.

They cut a channel to a safe harbour and on 2 November began the laborious task of re-roofing the ships, re-erecting the observatory and re-insulating the deck. Ross called his new home Sheriff Harbour, once again after his sponsor. Ross's charts were now liberally bespattered with associations of gin, and as he gazed at them he must have been painfully aware that it was only two hours' walk, at most, to reach his quarters of the previous year.

His one consolation was that none of his men had come down with scurvy. By this time, on Parry's great voyage, the signs of scurvy had already been apparent. But Ross's men were fit and well thanks to his revolutionary diet. It went down badly with his steward who wrote angrily about the lack of red meat: 'It was impossible to decide on what principle Capt. Ross could suppose that his men could sustain the continual fatigue and labor to which they were exposed on such a weak and watery aliment as fish.'[16] Ross was wiser. 'The first salmon of summer,' he recorded, 'were a medicine which all the drugs in the ship could not replace.'[17]

This second winter was worse than the first. There were no Eskimos to be seen, the weather was colder and, despite Ross's best efforts, there was little to do. With the thermometer standing at −43 °F, they amused themselves by firing balls of frozen mercury through a one-inch plank. 'It was little more than a schoolboy's experiment,' Ross wrote, 'but this had, possibly, not been done before.'[18] (It had, by Lyon.) They tried the same experiment with frozen almond oil but the bullets rebounded like little balls of rubber.

To the boredom was added discord, if the steward William Light is to be believed. His reminiscences, published in 1835 and ghosted by a notoriously inaccurate hack called Robert Huish, may have been based on personal animosity – he was the only man out of the whole expedition whom Ross did not later suggest for promotion or future employment. But, accurate or not, they are the only insight other than Ross's own journal into this extraordinary voyage.

Ross, he claimed, was a tough man who drank heavily and spent most of his time in his cabin, emerging only to issue iron-fisted orders. In Light's words, 'the quarterdeck of a British man-of-war is not the one best adapted to teach a man urbanity and civility towards his inferior!' The *Victory*, in Light's mind, was 'a house divided'. Ross was 'trebly steeped in the starch of official dignity, the maintenance of which he considered to consist in abstracting himself as much as possible from familiar intercourse with those beneath and suffering no opportunity to escape him, by which he could shew to them that he was their superior and commander. The men were conscious that they owed him obedience; they were not equally convinced that they owed him their respect and esteem.'[19] On occasion, he said, the men were close to mutiny.

A lot of this was probably true. Ross *was* a tough man, and was covered in scars to prove it. He was also vain, irascible and intransigent. And maybe he did drink heavily. (Though in one of his later works, a treatise on intemperance in the navy, he claimed that he never touched spirits. This is reinforced by figures from his first expedition:

Ross's men accounted for 541 gallons of spirits and 128 gallons of wine; Parry's on the other hand consumed almost twice as much spirits, three times as much wine and, incidentally, smoked 1,629 pounds of tobacco compared to Ross's 264 pounds.) Certainly, he had none of Parry's light touch. There were no plays or entertainments on his voyage, merely rigid routines. Sunday service, such a mainstay to Parry, became under Ross a hurried and incomprehensible gabble. At times his temper erupted. At one point in the spring of 1831 he spent his fury on his nephew, who reciprocated with vim. 'The fire,' wrote Huish dramatically, 'which had been concentrating for some time in their breasts, like the lava in the craters of Vesuvius and Etna, burst forth with an explosion, which terrified the other inmates of the cabin.'[20]

Where Ross was disliked, his nephew James was popular. It was to him that the men went if they had a complaint and it was he, according to Light, who was 'the very life and soul of all the schemes and plans'.[21] This rings more truthfully than Light's other assertions. Although John Ross was not idle, and made several sledge journeys of his own, he was still fifty-five years old. He was tired and lacked the enthusiasm which had spawned the 'Deep Sea Clamm' of 1818. All he wanted to do was find the North-West Passage and restore his reputation. Failing that, his main concern was to lead his ships to safety. Maybe he did spend most of his time locked in his cabin. His game was survival. Exploration was left to James Ross.

As the long Arctic winter softened James Ross went out on further exploratory trips. This year he was not just going out to see what he could see; he was going out to find the North Magnetic Pole. In 1830 he had come within ten miles of it, or so he suspected, but had not had the equipment to confirm this. Now he was fully prepared. On 15 May he left the *Victory* and sledged west to the frozen sea, at which point he turned north. At 8 a.m. on 1 June he reached the point where his dipping needle pointed almost directly downward and his compasses ceased to move. It took another day to make perfectly sure, but by the evening of 2 June, James Ross was convinced he had found the spot. This was the place which 'Nature . . . had chosen as the centre

of one of her great and dark powers'.[22] At 70° 5' 17" north, and 96° 46'
45" west, on a bland, featureless stretch of coast that he named Victory
Point, he raised the Union Jack, 'and took possession of the North
Magnetic Pole and its adjoining territory in the name of Great Britain
and King William the Fourth'.[23]

'I believe I must leave it to others,' he wrote, 'to imagine the ela-
tion of mind with which we found ourselves now at length arrived at
this great object of our ambition: it almost seemed as if we had accomplished every thing that we had come so far to see and to do; as if our
voyage and all its labours were at an end, and that nothing now
remained for us but to return home and be happy for the rest of our
days.'[24]

If only life was that simple. When James Ross returned to the
Victory on 13 June it became apparent that home was yet a long way
off. It was a cold and stormy summer. By the end of July they were
still frozen fast. On 28 August the ice broke sufficiently for them to
sail four miles. Two days later they were fast again. By October they
were chiselling their way into a fresh anchorage to withstand a third
Arctic winter. On 31 October they shot two hares whose white fur
reminded them that winter was upon them. Ross cursed the ice. It
was 'a plague, a vexation, a torment, an evil'.[25]

By now, everyone was heartily sick of the expedition. 'That it has
been a dull month, I need scarcely say,' wrote John Ross. 'If this was
a durance of few events, and those of little variety, even these had no
longer aught to mark a difference among them, nothing to attract
attention or excite thought. The sameness of everything weighed on
the spirits, and the mind itself flagged under the want of excitement;
while even such as there was, proved but a wearisome iteration of
what had often occurred before. On no occasion, even when all was
new, had there been much to interest; far less was there, now that we
had been so long imprisoned to almost one spot.'[26]

Ross had reached the end of his tether. He was not a waiting man.
He did not have the imagination to invent ways of filling the endless
hours. He did not even seem to have considered doing so. Facing this
third winter, he sank into passive dejection: 'We were weary for want

of occupation, for want of variety, for want of means of mental exertion, for want of thought, and (why should I not say it?) for want of society. Today was as yesterday, and as was today, so would be tomorrow.'[27]

Christmas came and went, 'the only fact worth remarking [being] a round of beef that had been in the *Fury*'s stores for eight years, and which, with some veal and some vegetables, was as good as the day on which it was cooked'.[28] Mince pies and cherry brandy were a dream of the past.

New Year was even more dismal, marked as it was by the steady deterioration of the armourer, James Dixon. He died on 10 January 1832 of tuberculosis and was buried two and a half feet deep, which was as much as could be done for him in the frozen soil. On 31 January Ross wrote that, 'Our medical report begins now to be very different from what it had hitherto been. All were much enfeebled and there was a good deal of ailment without any marked diseases.' Most horribly of all, Ross's ancient wounds, long since healed over, began to bleed. 'I knew too well,' he recorded, 'that this was one of the indications of scurvy.'[29] Below decks, too, the sledge dogs died *en masse*. They had been licking the corrosive fluids that seeped from the old steam engine pipes.

This was the extent of their festive cheer as they entered a winter that was as bad as, if not worse than, the previous two. For 136 days the thermometer did not rise above zero. 'I do not believe,' Ross wrote in despair, 'there is another record of such a continuous low temperature.'[30]

During the dark months Ross made some calculations. He had enough supplies to last at least another year. If the ice relented, they could sail home. But if 1832 was as cold as 1831, as it promised to be, they would face a fourth ice-bound winter. His stores might last, if augmented by fresh meat bought from visiting Eskimos. But if the Eskimos did not appear – and there had been none the year before – he and his men faced a lingering death from starvation or scurvy. On the other hand, there was plenty of food at Fury Beach, where there was also the prospect of open seas. If they travelled overland, hauling the ship's boats behind them, they could replenish at Fury Beach and then sail through to Baffin Bay to rendezvous with the August whaling fleet. But that would mean abandoning ship, something which a naval captain could consider only in the last resort. Moreover, Fury Beach was 300 miles away and the boats, when laden, were very heavy. It was the equivalent, per man, of dragging a large dead sheep from London to Carlisle.

Ross came to a decision: he would quit the *Victory*. Loss of pride was a small price to pay for escaping the ice scuttle of Prince Regent Inlet. And whatever the hardship of the journey, it was preferable to stationary death. The prospect of action restored Ross's spirits. His plan was that a boat would be filled with provisions, dragged so far, and then the men would return to fetch another laden boat and drag it a little bit further, and so on, until there was a line of caches which could nourish them to the point where they made a do-or-die break for Fury Beach. All winter the carpenters toiled over the sledges on which the boats were to be loaded and in April the first contingent set off. Throughout the month Ross fired off his torpedoes of food and by the beginning of May he had constructed a supply line which stretched eighteen miles. His men, meanwhile, had travelled 110 miles to and fro. The weather had deteriorated: in temperatures of 30° below zero, they cut their meat with a saw and thawed it in cups of cocoa. By June the line extended thirty miles from the ship and the haulers had trudged an exponentially large number of miles. It was a bagatelle in terms of the distance still to be covered, but the furthest attainable from the *Victory*. Their final tasks were to bury their gunpowder, chronometers and astronomical instruments in a waterproof bundle and to beach the *Kreusenstern* containing sails, masts, rigging and 'everything which could be of use to us in case of our return, or which, if we did not, would prove of use to the natives'.[31]

On 29 May, Ross said farewell to his ship, having wrapped it around with chains in seamanlike fashion, so that if it became waterlogged it might yet be hauled to shore. The loss saddened him immeasurably. 'The colours were therefore hoisted and nailed to the mast,' he wrote, 'we drank a parting glass to our poor ship, and having seen every man out, in the evening, I took my own adieu of the *Victory*, which had deserved a better fate. It was the first vessel that I have ever been obliged to abandon, after having served in thirty-six, during a period of forty-two years. It was like the last parting with an old friend.'[32]

He stopped, alone, to 'take a sketch of this melancholy desert, rendered more melancholy by the solitary, abandoned, helpless home of our past year, fixed in immovable ice, till Time should perform on her his usual work'.[33] Then he hurried back to his party. Two-thirds rations, he announced, to see them through the journey. That night they huddled together in a trench of snow, wrapping their blankets around them. They had not reached their first cache. Fury Beach was a long way off and the temperature was below freezing.

By this time, people at home were wondering what on earth had happened to the Rosses and their expedition. Barrow for one was convinced they must be dead. Others were less sure. Among them was Dr John Richardson, Franklin's erstwhile travelling companion, who offered to lead an overland rescue party. His proposal was turned down. The Admiralty did not feel it could fund the recovery of a civilian trip.

Forward stepped George Ross, brother of John and father of James. George had all the necessary Ross qualities of anger and obstinacy, to which was allied an unfortunate propensity to failure. All his life he had been trying to get rich, through one ploy or another, and had failed to do so. Now, with an emergency beckoning, he swarmed into action. By prodding, lobbying and making a nuisance of himself, he managed to form a committee to look into the possibility of his brother's rescue. For once, George Ross could not lose. His brother had become a *cause célèbre*. A huge muttering filled the press. What were the authorities doing about the expedition? Did they no longer care about the Arctic, or the naval hero who had steamed forth to conquer it? The commotion spread to Italy, where it reached the ears of a vacationing George Back. The man who had all but prostrated himself before Ross three years ago hurried back to England to save him.

The two Georges met. The one wanted adventure, the other wanted a bit of fame and the chance to run a successful venture. George Ross suggested an overland journey to Prince Regent Inlet, shamelessly hijacking Richardson's idea. George Back agreed at once. The new proposal was better received than Richardson's – Back, after all, was an officer – and the government agreed to provide £2,000 of George Ross's estimated £5,000 outlay on condition that Back lead the rescue mission. By January 1833 George Ross had raised the extra £3,000 through public subscription and the following month Back departed. His plan was to set up base at Great Slave Lake, then travel down the hitherto unexplored Great Fish River to the sea and from there to Fury Beach. If he found no sign of Ross after two seasons in the ice, he would abandon the search and survey the coastline between the Great Fish River and Point Turnagain.

Meanwhile, the ever optimistic George Ross was plugging his latest idea, 'which has long occupied my attention, and which, I trust, will be deemed fully as interesting to the scientific world as that which is about to depart; whilst it is to be hoped that it will give humanity a readier and more speedy exercise as regards the much desired relief to be afforded to my Brother Captain Ross, my son, Commander James Ross, and their adventurous little crew. I mean an ARCTIC EXPE-DITION BY SEA.'[34] He had it all worked out. It would comprise two whalers with a total crew of thirty-five, and would be led by George Ross himself. That he had never been to sea in his life did not deter him a jot, nor did the estimated cost of £5,000. He even wrote to Scoresby, enclosing maps of the route he intended to take and asking his advice. Scoresby's reply was straightforward: it was a 'great matter of prudence'[35] that George Ross avoid being caught in the ice.

On 10 June 1832, while George Ross was agitating in London, John Ross and his 'adventurous little crew' were at a pivotal moment in their trek. They were halfway to Fury Beach, had long passed their last cache and were living off the little food they still had. The ice ahead was so rugged that they could not possibly drag their boats any further. A tentative mutiny broke out. The men, led by Thom, wanted to leave the boats and make a dash for Fury Beach. Ross shouted them down. He pointed out that they did not know what lay ahead. If they abandoned the boats and went ahead on foot they could reach Fury Beach. But what then? What if the past winters had swept away the stores? What if the *Fury*'s boats had also gone? They would have nothing to sail in and nothing to eat. Where they stood they had the option of going forward to the *Fury* or going back to the *Victory*; their present supplies could take them either way. There was always the possibility that the ice would open and allow them to escape in the *Victory*'s boats. But if they left the boats now, and ran for Fury Beach only to find it empty, they would be dead of starvation before they made it back to their present position.

John Ross won the day by sheer force of will, explaining himself 'in a manner not easily misunderstood, and by an argument too peremptory to be disputed'.[36] Seamen, he noted in his journal, were more prone to thought than had been the case during his junior service. The men acquiesced reluctantly. On 11 June 1832, Ross sent his nephew ahead with two men to Fury Beach to ascertain that the provisions were still there. James Ross returned two weeks later with good news. The food piles were intact and although three of the *Fury*'s boats had been washed away there remained another three scattered along the coast which were damaged but seaworthy.

Ross's gamble had paid off. Abandoning the two boats they had lugged 150 miles from the *Victory*, he and his men ran for Fury Beach. Relieved of their load they completed the remaining distance in just six days, arriving on 1 July. 'We were once more at home,' Ross wrote in relief, 'such a home as it was.'[37] After the rigours of their march the half-starved men fell on the scattered stores. Ross tried his hardest to prevent them, knowing the effect a sudden surfeit of food could have on empty stomachs, but his efforts were in vain. When he was asleep that night they crept out and ate their fill. They 'suffered smartly for their impudence',[38] Ross noted with ill-concealed satisfaction.

The next day Ross ordered the construction of a temporary dwelling to see them through the few months before the ice melted and they could sail to freedom. It was to measure thirty-one feet long

by sixteen feet wide by seven feet high and would be walled with
canvas from the *Fury*'s sails which still lay piled on the beach. The
framework was erected in the course of a day, and by the following it
was completed. It was divided into two equal sections, one comprising a large room for the ordinary seamen and the other being split into
four separate cabins for the officers. Ross called it Somerset House.
Meanwhile the ship's carpenters were repairing the *Fury*'s boats and
rigging them with sails for the journey ahead.

At last, things were moving. The mood lightened perceptibly.
Against all odds Ross had led them from near death to near salvation.
On 31 July the ice opened. They packed the boats with two months'
provisions, the two Rosses exchanged copies of their journals and
charts – lest anything happen to either of them – and on 1 August with
a strong, northward-flowing tide, they bade farewell to Somerset
House.

The ice which had retreated so accommodatingly was floe ice.
Unlike bergs, which are driven by deep currents, floe ice is a surface
creature. It reacts to winds, to tides, to any fickle change in the
weather. It is unpredictable. The boats had only advanced eight miles
before the tide came in and the ice changed direction. Ross was alert.
He had the boats unloaded and hauled onto the nearest beach. 'It was
not a minute too soon,' he wrote, 'for the ice immediately came down,
and the two floes nearest us were broken to pieces with a violent
crash.'[39]

Ross was in the exact spot where the *Fury* had been wrecked eight
years ago on the same day of the same month. He was quick to
acknowledge the coincidence. But whereas Parry had been able to
transfer the *Fury*'s crew to another ship, Ross did not have the option.
He crept forward painfully. On 6 August he made three miles. On 9
August he made another two. But that was it. They huddled in
makeshift tents, watching for a change. On 28 August it came. The ice
broke. Once again the heavy mahogany boats were launched. It did
them little good. On 2 September they reached the end of the open
water, a place they called Batty Bay. Ross climbed a mountain and saw
Barrow Strait. It was a plain field of ice. Not even the coast was clear.

They waited until 24 September and, with no easing of conditions, Ross decided that their only hope lay in retreating to Somerset House.

They returned with downcast hearts. Even James Ross, the jaunty explorer, was broken-spirited. As John Ross wrote: 'Within the last days of the month Commander Ross seemed to have more than hesitated respecting our escape; and on the twentieth, I must needs say, with whatever regret, I began myself to question whether we should succeed in passing the barrier of ice this season; in which case there could be no resource for us but another winter, another year, I should say, on Fury Beach; if indeed, it should be the fortune of any one to survive after another such year as the three last.'[40]

Their spirits fell further when they discovered that they were iced in on all sides. It would be impossible to sail back to Fury Beach; instead they would have to walk, and they would have to drag their provisions with them. With considerable ingenuity the carpenters produced some sledges from old bread casks. The stores were loaded, and Ross's band set off, limping and struggling, for Somerset House. They reached their destination on the afternoon of Sunday 7 October, where a shrieking storm that lasted the rest of the month assured them that this winter would be the worst yet.

Ross ordered their quarters to be made ready for the coming winter. In the teeth of gales so fierce that they had to work inside tents, his men constructed a four-foot-thick wall of snow blocks around Somerset House and spread a similar layer on its roof. They pointed the joints between the blocks with wet snow and sealed the whole structure by throwing buckets of water over it. In the –15 °F temperatures in which they worked the walls and roof were soon coated with a shell of ice.

Thus insulated, and heated by two portable stoves, their living quarters achieved a near-comfortable temperature of 52 °F. But if the cold could be kept at bay, hunger and scurvy could not. The *Fury*'s stores, which had previously seemed such a cornucopia, now began to look finite. From 1 November Ross ordered all hands on half rations: carrot soup one day, turnip soup the next; dumplings of flour and water at every meal; two servings of canned meat per week.

Otherwise, their only sustenance came from a few Arctic foxes which they managed to trap. No Eskimos came this year with their life-giving supplies. Christmas Day was celebrated with a meal of roast fox.

New Year arrived with further foul weather and with several men showing signs of scurvy. The worst affected was Chimham Thomas, the carpenter, whose condition deteriorated steadily despite treatment with lemon juice. After eight years in its casks, the anti-scorbutic was beginning to lose its potency. Ironically, it was the one item that was not in short supply. The carpenter died on 16 February. He was buried six days later, during a lull in the atrocious weather. The ground was rock-hard and Ross had difficulty completing the funeral service in temperatures of –45 °F. 'His age was forty-eight,' Ross wrote philosophically, 'and at that time of life, a seaman who has served much is an aged man, if he does not chance to be worn out.'[41]

Chimham Thomas's death was a major blow. The boats left at Batty Bay would undoubtedly have suffered during the winter. The crew could handle small repairs but if there was any major damage Thomas was the only man who could have fixed it. Yet another chair had been kicked from under them.

The first months of 1835 were incredibly severe. Snow fell so heavily that Somerset House was covered almost to its chimneys. Occasionally, when the wind died, Ross's men were able to dig themselves free of their prison. They found a landscape so ridged by ice that even foot travel was rendered impossible, let alone the sledge haul that would be necessary if they wished to drag themselves and their provisions back to Batty Bay. There was no game to hunt, even had it been possible to do so.

Scurvy took a stronger grip. By March, three men were disabled and everybody was weakened. The mood was one of frigid apathy. Even Ross's iron constitution began to fail him as his many wounds, received more than twenty years before, opened one by one. 'My own condition,' he wrote, 'was at this time somewhat threatening. I had now, indeed, some reason to suppose that I might not be ultimately able to surmount all the present circumstances.'[42] Concealing the

1. Franklin's boats on his second mission to the Canadian Arctic, 1826

2. Hugh Clapperton

3. Dixon Denham

4. George Lyon

5. Richard Lemon Lander

6. James Clark Ross

7. Christmas Harbour, Kerguelen Island, 1840

8. Approaching Mt. Erebus, 1841

9. The collision of Erebus *and* Terror, *1842*

10. A gale in the Antarctic pack, 1842

11. McClure's Investigator *trapped in the ice*

12. Richard Collinson

13. Robert McClure

14. John Barrow, elder statesman of exploration

blood as best he could, Ross strode through Somerset House, cursing his men into activity. He forced them to construct a raised, wooden floor so that they no longer had to sleep on ice, and browbeat them into exercising, whenever the weather permitted, in a thirty-six-foot-long pen of snow blocks that had been erected when Somerset House was being walled in for winter. It was little enough, but anything was preferable to idleness: 'better was it,' Ross wrote, 'that they should work themselves into utter weariness, that they should so hunger as to think only of their stomachs, fall asleep and dream of nothing but a better dinner, as they awoke to hope and labour for it'.[43]

Privately Ross too fell victim to the lassitude of scurvy. His journal entries became briefer, more repetitive. However, as he later apologized, what was there to record? 'Let him who reads to condemn what is so meagre, have some compassion on the writer who had nothing better than this meagreness, this repetition, this reiteration of the ever-resembling, every day dullness to record, and what was infinitely worse, to endure. I might have seen more, it has been said: it may be; but I saw only ice and snow, cloud and drift and storm. Still I might have seen what I did not; seen as a painter, and felt like a poet; and then, like painter and poet, have written. That also may be, but let painter and poet come hither and try; try how far cold and hunger, misery and depression, aid those faculties which seem always best developed under the comforts of life . . . Our "*faecundi calices*" were cold snow water; and though, according to Persius, it is hunger which makes poets write as it makes parrots speak, I suspect that neither poet nor parrot would have gained much in eloquence under a "fox" diet, and that an insufficient one, in the blessed regions of Boothia Felix.'[44]

Dreariness was the least of Ross's worries. Even on present rations their food could not last beyond 1 October. Laboriously, Ross began to construct his lifeline to salvation. As when he had abandoned the *Victory*, he set up relays of sledges to carry food for three months to the boats he had been forced to leave at Batty Bay. And as before it was a crippling task. There were four loads, each of which had to be dragged in stages. The actual distance to be covered was twenty-four miles.

But by the time they had finished – a process which occupied a month – the haulers had walked 256 miles. At night their sleep was disturbed by starving polar bears, one of which fell through the roof of John Ross's shelter, almost landing on top of him. And when they reached Batty Bay it was covered in thick drifts of snow. Their boats were nowhere to be seen. They foraged about, found them, and dug them clear. Thankfully, no major repairs were needed.

By 29 May, everything was in place and they returned to Somerset House to await the summer. The spring had done them a slight favour: they had been able to kill enough bears, foxes and seals to last them on two-thirds rations until 1 October. But on 1 July they ate the last of the *Fury*'s meat. However rich the current larder, their reserves were gone. Whether the ice cleared or not, another winter in Somerset House was out of the question.

On 8 July Ross led his ragged party to the boats, dragging their sick men behind them. Besides the scurvy-ridden there was one man who was stricken by epilepsy and blind, another who could barely walk, having lost half his foot to frost-bite, and several with snow-blindness. They reached Batty Bay four days later and started the long wait. The weather was now clearing and there was plenty of game to shoot. But the ice had not moved. Were they doomed to yet another summer of fine weather and frozen seas?

At last, at 4 a.m. on 14 August, a single lane of clear water opened to the north. Those who could leaped to their feet and began hacking at the shore ice to free the boats. Shortly afterwards the tide came in and a westerly breeze arose. By 8 a.m. they were afloat and sailing. For the first time in three years they could move. The Arctic had released them. Ross was beside himself: 'it was a change like that of magic to find that solid mass of ocean . . . suddenly converted into water; navigable, and navigable *to us*, who had almost forgotten what it was to float at freedom on the seas. It was at times scarcely to be believed: and he who dozed to wake again, had for a moment to renew the conviction that he was at length a seaman on his own element; that his boat once more rose upon the waves beneath him, and that when the winds blew it obeyed his will and his hand!'[45]

They fled, three tiny ghosts, through the narrow channels which opened before them. They sailed past the massive cliffs of Somerset Island on 16 August. At 3 a.m. the next day they left Prince Regent Inlet. On the 18th they crossed the mouth of Admiralty Inlet, the longest fjord in the world. When the wind did not come they rowed. Given their debilitated state and incipient scurvy it is astonishing how they managed it. Yet they rowed almost without cease: twenty hours on one occasion, twelve on another. Finally, after a full day's hauling, a gale arose and the men collapsed. Ross ordered them ashore. They had reached the east side of Navy Board Inlet. It was 25 August.

At 4 a.m. the following morning they were woken by the look-out. He had seen a sail. They poured out of their tents. Sure enough there was a ship, probably a whaler, which James Ross described to his audience with the aid of his telescope. They let off smoke signals using wet gunpowder. While they waited for the boats to be made ready they discussed the ship eagerly. Where was it heading, what was its rig? Or was it, as some suggested, merely an iceberg?

The boats were launched and the men rowed desperately towards their saviour. It was a calm day. The ship could go nowhere. Surely they were saved.

They weren't. A wind came and the ship slid over the horizon to the south-east, leaving Ross's flotilla bobbing helplessly on the waves. They were still out there when, at 10 a.m., they saw a second sail. By now the wind had dropped. They had no way of signalling, but they could still row. An hour later they were sighted. The ship dropped a boat which drew up alongside them. Were they distressed seamen, the mate asked ingenuously? Ross and his crew, haggard, horribly pallid, unshaven and near death, admitted that they were. They asked what ship had rescued them. The mate responded cheerfully that he was from 'the *Isabella* of Hull, once commanded by Captain Ross'.[16] Ross rose and gave his name. The mate, taken aback, told him that Captain Ross was dead the past two years. Ross assured him, bluntly, that he wasn't.

*

The *Isabella*'s crew gave three cheers as the castaways came aboard. Ross's men hardly had the strength to respond. 'Never was seen a more miserable set of wretches,' Ross wrote. 'Unshaven since I know not when, dirty, dressed in the rags of wild beasts instead of the tatters of civilization, and starved to the very bones, our gaunt and grim looks when contrasted with those of the well-dressed and well-fed men around us, made us all feel, I believe for the first time, what we really were.'[47]

They fell into the arms of civilization with bewilderment. 'All, everything, too, was to be done at once; it was washing, dressing, shaving, eating, all intermingled, it was all the materials of each jumbled together.'[48] And amidst it all were the questions, from both sides: how had they survived – what party was in government – what was the ice like – who was the new Prime Minister – what had they eaten – were railways now commonplace?

That night Ross tried to sleep in the bunk provided. But after so many nights spent on hard ice he was unable to make himself comfortable. Instead he crawled into a chair by the stove where, eventually, he dropped off.

19

'ANY ANIMAL WILL DO FOR A LION'

'As the season is yet young, any animal will do for a lion; and the animal now dressed in the skin is Captain Ross, who is playing the part at the various *soirées* and *conversazioni*, such as they are, which are now giving.'[1]

The thought of Ross at a *conversazione* boggles the mind. It obviously gave pause to the columnist who wrote those words and who could not help introducing a reference to walruses in the next paragraph. But the fact was that Ross had become Britain's – and Europe's – newest hero. He dined with King William IV and was given a knighthood. (He went straight from the palace to the printers in order to insert this important detail in his journal.) The monarchs of Prussia, Sweden, France and Belgium showered him with honours. Learned societies from Russia to Denmark awarded him their gold medals. He received six gold snuff boxes and two presentation swords from admiring governments and was awarded the freedom of London, Hull, Liverpool and Bristol. More than 4,000 letters of congratulation landed on his doorstep. It became briefly fashionable for women to write him poems and love letters. A panorama of his travels was exhibited at the great, ninety-foot rotunda in Leicester Square.

With this trousseau of *billets-doux*, commendations, medals, chains, keys and diamond-studded decorations, it was hardly surprising that Ross was received rapturously by London's salonistes. He lingered long enough in the limelight to catch a new wife: Maria, the sister of his friend Thomas Rymer. It was a typically bad match, the product of misconceptions on both sides. She thought she was marrying an up-and-coming star in London society. He thought he was marrying a homebody who would look after things at Stranraer. In due course the marriage would fall to pieces. But for the moment all went well, if a little stiffly, with the two of them exchanging hesitant love notes in which their Christian names were never once used.

Ross's sudden popularity irked many of his naval contemporaries and was entirely galling to Barrow, whose jealousy was such that in his 1846 *Voyages Within the Arctic Regions* he could hardly bring himself to mention Ross's achievement, let alone give him credit for it. He tried at first to ignore the voyage, referring to it only passingly in a blast on Lancaster Sound. 'Ross himself had the courage – can it be called moral courage? – to revisit, some years afterwards, this horrible spot in a miserable kind of ship, fitted out at the expense of a private individual for some purpose or other.'[2] Later in the book, however, he returned to his bone. Forgetting his disinterest he devoted a whole chapter (headed 'Miscellaneous') to the voyage, his resentment flowing over to the extent that he copied out in full Ross's entry in Dodd's Peerage, sneering heartily at 'the numerous honours and *et ceteras*'.[3]

Ross had everyone against him. In the case of Barrow it was because of Lancaster Sound. In the case of the others it was because of his book, which came out in 1835. It was a handsome affair, with detailed descriptions of the journey, scientific observations on the Arctic by both uncle and nephew, a number of less scientific observations on the world in general by John Ross, and a gripping account of the discovery of the North Magnetic Pole, the whole enlivened by a series of plates from watercolours by both John and James Ross. It was a weighty tome – seven pounds – and it was very profitable.

The first bidder for publication rights was John Murray, who had contacted the head messenger at the Admiralty, a man called Nutland, the instant he heard of the Rosses' rescue. '[Nutland] called upon them the moment of their arrival,' he wrote to his son on 22 October 1833, 'and obtained a promise to give me the publication of their "Journal". We have got to settle terms . . . I have received a very kind letter from Mr. Barrow, who has undertaken to get a confirmation of the promise.'[4]

Murray could not have chosen a worse intermediary. Having been rejected by the Admiralty, having invested his own time and money in organizing the expedition and having extricated himself from the Arctic without a smidgin of help from the authorities, Ross was now being asked to hand his epic narrative to the official Admiralty publisher on the urging of his worst enemy for a payment that, going by Murray's standard payments, was not likely to be more than £1,000. Whatever Ross's earlier promises, Barrow's intervention ensured he would not honour them. Instead he took the gamble of publishing the book himself, an exercise he defended in self-righteous terms to Scoresby: 'My first object . . . was to get the book up so as to be a credit to the nation and all concerned, my 2nd object was to give it to the public *cheaper*, and to show thereby how the booksellers impose on both the authors and the public.'[5]

His true purpose, however, was to make money which, to everybody's irritation, he did. He set up a subscription office in Regent Street, employed a team of door-to-door salesmen, and by April 1835 was able to tell Scoresby that 'I have 7,000 subscribers amounting to no less than £7,000!'[6] He sent Scoresby a copy for him to review, labouring the fact that he had 'endeavoured to set the public to rights, in regard to the credit of renewing the search of the N.Wt. Passage being due to you – which is indeed only justice'.[7] He did, however, omit both the scientific appendix and the meteorological journal, in which Scoresby might have been most interested, enclosing instead 'some comparative notes, respecting Parry's voyage and my own' which he hoped might be useful to the review. 'PS,' he ended with unnecessary unction, 'There are only portraits in those I give to my friends.'[8]

A friend Scoresby may have been. But as an ally he was impotent.
In 1825 his religious yearnings had got the better of him and he had
quit the sea to join the Anglican Church, sacrificing excitement and an
average annual income of £800 for peace and quiet and a stipend of
£40. He still kept abreast of events – he was present at the opening
of the Liverpool–Manchester railway in 1830, and described in me-
ticulous detail the running down of William Huskisson MP by
Stephenson's *Rocket*. He lectured regularly at the British Association,
of which he was a founding member, and pursued relentlessly the perfection of the magnet. Nevertheless he was too far from London and
too distanced from the naval establishment to be of use to Ross. He
was also preoccupied with other matters, namely commemorating his
second son, Frederick, who had died on 30 December 1834. *A
Memorial of an Affectionate and Dutiful Son* came out the same year as
Ross's tome.

If Scoresby could not review the book there were others, less qualified but far better placed, who would. Among them was William
Maginn. 'The Doctor', as Maginn styled himself for no good reason at
all, was a despairing mix of talent and ruin. A brilliant young Irish
journalist who had come to make his fortune in London, he had been
'discovered' by Blackwood, and had subsequently risen to become
the leading light of *Fraser's Magazine*. He was intelligent and witty,
and could write fluently in any style on almost any subject. 'In any
galaxy he was, indeed, a star of the first magnitude and greatest brilliancy,'[9] enthused his friend William Jerdan. But Maginn's character
conspired against his genius ever rising above the ephemeral. He
drank, spent and womanized, was always in debt and often in prison.
His death in 1842 at the early age of forty-nine, as a consumptive,
alcoholic bankrupt, surprised nobody. But in 1834 he still flourished,
glass in one hand, pen in the other, dashing off effortless columns of
what he called 'squib work' for whoever would pay him.

Although Croker disliked and distrusted Maginn, his services, as he
wrote darkly to a friend, could sometimes come in handy. 'There is a
man whom I am far from recommending for respectability, or even
trustworthiness,' he wrote of Maginn, '[but] he is a powerful and has

been a useful partisan writer.'[10] On this occasion he was undoubtedly useful.

Before Ross's book even came out an article appeared in *Fraser's* 'Gallery of Illustrious Literary Characters'. The Gallery was a vehicle for Maginn's wit – illustrated by his fellow Irishman, Daniel Maclise – that preyed upon famous people of the day. Byron, Scott, Wordsworth, Coleridge and their ilk were its normal fare. But in January 1834 it included John Ross. 'We regret to say,' Maginn began, 'that doubt exists, not, indeed, as to the appearance of the work, because that is a necessary appendage to the voyage . . . but as to the value of its contents. If the Captain has seen the magnetic pole, to use the language of a Scotch newspaper, which evidently considered it to be somewhat like a barber's pole stuck up in the way of a finger-post for the loadstone, he has seen nothing else. His discoveries, as far as we can learn, have been precisely nothing . . . and neither geography nor science in any of their branches have profited a whit by the embedding of Captain Ross within the regions of thick-ribbed ice.' On the opposite page was a sketch by Maclise of Ross 'undergoing the sufferings of his voyage' before a blazing fire with a hot toddy in his hand. 'Let nobody fancy for a moment that we are blaming Captain Ross for taking care of himself while out upon his chilly voyage,' Maginn continued. 'Far be from us such a thought. The only thing for which we think he ought to be condemned was for going at all. He had failed once, and that should have been quite satisfactory. We take it for granted he will never think of failing a third time. He should now be satisfied with the full glory that he has proved, if not exactly that there is no north-west passage at all, yet that he decidedly is not the man to find it.'[11]

Maginn's article was probably written to order. But if it was ordered by either Croker or Barrow, Ross had in part brought it on his own head. Never one to shrink from controversy, he had used his own book as a convenient way to reopen the old argument about Lancaster Sound. In the intervening years his mind had worked at the problem and come up with a new, if rather meagre, twist. Parry, he declared, had been guilty of gross misconduct if he had believed the Sound to be open but had not told his commanding officer. Parry, who had been, by Ross's own assertion, eight miles distant at the time and therefore unable to voice his opinion, was understandably irritated. 'That foolish man, Ross, is determined *always* to get himself into a hobble,'[12] he wrote to Franklin, replying to the latter's exhortation that he respond to the accusation. He did, in fact, have a response: when he had offered to explore Smith Sound with boats, Ross had reminded him sharply that *he*, not Parry, was commanding the expedition. But the thought of entering a protracted public dispute was too wearisome: 'pamphlet would be sure to beget pamphlet, and an endless controversy would ensue, of which one half of the world would not understand the real merits, and two thirds of the other half would not care about it'.[13]

When an infuriated Barrow wrote to Parry asking for ammunition for a forthcoming piece in the *Quarterly Review*, Parry wisely let the matter drop. He was in no mood to intervene on either side of the quarrel between these two long-memoried elephants. Besides he had a career to protect and laurels to rest on. There were others, however, with less foresight than Parry. One was Braithwaite, the operation – or, rather, non-operation – of whose engines Ross had described with disparaging candour. *A Supplement to Captain John Ross's Narrative of a Second Voyage in the Victory, in search of a North-West Passage containing . . . a just appreciation of Captain Sir John Ross's character as an officer and a man of Science* came out in 1835, accusing Ross of experimenting with steam for war purposes, of using the machinery improperly, having unreasonable expectations of the bellows which would naturally wear out and of generally mismanaging the whole business. Ross was a man of 'braggart assurance', who had declared the equipment 'just the thing he wanted',[14] and had Braithwaite known what the ship was intended for he could have designed much simpler and more reliable engines. He also pointed out, between the lines and probably truthfully, that Ross had been using the expedition to prove his currently unpopular opinions about steam power.

Ross hurried delightedly into print for the second time that year.

His *Explanation and Answer to Mr. John Braithwaite's Supplement to Captain Sir John Ross's Narrative of a Second Voyage in the Victory, in search of a North-West Passage* was a blow-by-blow rebuttal to which there could be no reply. Itemizing Braithwaite's shortcomings in detail, he calculated that 'taking the whole distance which the machinery actually propelled the ship, the cost was about £100 per mile!'[15] And as to the bellows, 'after we left the ship, the leather was wanted and made use of to make boots and shoes for the men, which indeed was the only good the bellows or the leather ever did us'.[16] Finally, he quoted a statement written in August 1829 by his two engineers – one of whom had come highly recommended from Braithwaite & Co. – which ended, 'We are also of the opinion that the engines and boilers are so defective in power, and so bad in material and workmanship, that it would be a useless expenditure of fuel to persevere any longer in attempting to work them.'[17]

In a letter to *The Times* Ross told the world that, albeit 'it is not my intention to enter into any controversy', his pamphlet would be issued gratis to anyone who was interested in the boilermaker's 'supercilious attempt to exculpate himself'.[18] But he had to warn potential readers that 'it is lamentable to perceive a tradesman, even of the second class, descending to such unbecoming language'.[19] Braithwaite sank from sight.

Then came Light's damning journal, edited by Robert Huish. This tantalizing book was ill-sourced and hastily produced and bore all the hallmarks of a writer pumping the market dry. Possibly Light's statements were true, but under Huish's slapdash editorship they failed to convince, encompassing as they did every petty gripe and wild accusation – Light, for example, claimed that the North Magnetic Pole had never been discovered at all. This was a shame, because Light's was one of the few insights from the lower deck into life on an Arctic expedition. But one must not blame Huish out of hand. This was a man who, until the 1830s, had spent more than a decade trying to make his name as a writer. Since 1820 he had written a few 'Romances', one or two obviously commissioned religious tracts, a cookery book, and a manual on bee-keeping which reached a second

impression. Then, in 1835, he had discovered his true metier as a
popular historian. While ghosting Light's journal he was also working
on Richard Lander's journal of his discovery of the Niger, the memoirs
of William IV, William Cobbett, Daniel O'Connell and Henry Hunt.
On top of these, to keep the money coming, he was to publish the
lurid tale of one James Greenacre who had been executed at the Old
Bailey for the murder of Mrs Hannah Brown, plus a new edition of his
earlier triumph, *The Female's Friend & General Domestic Adviser*, which
had done very well when it first came out in 1826.

Beyond issuing a few posters damning Light as a liar, the captain of
the *Victory* did not even bother to reply.

Ross had also roused the ire of his fellow officers by the blatantly
self-serving way he went about his journal. Barrow condemned him
immediately for his 'lust for lucre'.[20] James Ross placed a public
advertisement warning prospective buyers that he was not being paid
a penny for his appendix, which accompanied the main journal, and
that they were being duped should his uncle's 'emissaries', or salesmen, suggest otherwise. Francis Beaufort, with a touch of sour grapes,
remarked that he had made no money out of his own journals because
'I did not think that materials acquired in the King's service ought to
be sold.'[21]

Beaufort was also aggrieved at another piece of underhand dealing
whereby Ross had asked him to draw up a map of his discoveries to
present to the King. Beaufort had done so, and seen nothing more of
it, there being no other copies made. Between the Hydrographical
Office and the palace, however, Ross had obviously been at work
with his pen. Lady Franklin reported the following snippet of gossip
in which Beaufort had asked her to count the Clarence Islands, west
of Boothia Felix, as depicted on the current map of the Arctic. 'I
counted nine,' she wrote. 'Three I said were lilac, & all the others
white. "Well", says he, "there are but *3* – & when the chart was first
shewn to me, there were only 3 marked down, but Ross having proposed to the King to call them the Clarence islands, 'yes, yes –' sd the
King, 'call them the Clarence islands' – & then Ross thought it would
be as well to make a few more, so that the Clarences & Fitzclarences

might have one apiece".'[22] The King had been the Duke of Clarence and his many illegitimate offspring were called Fitzclarence. It was widely believed that this flattery had gained Ross his knighthood.

Barrow was enraged. In his history of Arctic exploration he expressed his indignation in Mark-Antonian style: 'A few foreign princes may think themselves *flattered* by having their names dotted along the coastline of a thing called a chart; but the King of England's family are not so easily captivated by baits of this kind.'[23] The backbiting was to continue until both men were dead. But for the time being Barrow could only scowl as Parliament voted £5,000 to recompense Ross for his investment and another £18,000 to Felix Booth, who also received a baronetcy. The Admiralty also agreed to pay Ross's crew for the unexpectedly long time they had been away. Barrow, through gritted teeth, had to carry out their wishes. The sum came to £4,580, 12s, 3d. which was to be accounted for, Barrow insisted, by stamped vouchers from every man.

When Barrow's review eventually appeared in the *Quarterly Review* of July 1835 it amounted to little more than a hysterical rant. The narrative was 'ponderous', Barrow wrote, and drawn up in a 'cold and heartless manner'. It was 'silly' and 'trash'. Ross was a 'vain and jealous man', who was 'utterly incompetent to conduct an arduous naval enterprise for discovery to a successful termination'. The expedition itself was an 'ill-prepared, ill-conceived . . . and ill-executed undertaking', the results of which were 'next to nothing'.[24] The only thing Barrow was willing to praise was the conduct of James Ross whose experience and all-round excellence were the only reasons he could detect for the mission having returned. Did John Ross mention this? Far from it, stormed Barrow. In fact, Ross's journal was notable for 'the unwillingness to give praise or make acknowledgement even to him on whom the safety of the expedition mainly depended'.[25]

Barrow had put his finger on something here. A curious antipathy had arisen between John and James Ross which first manifested itself at the Special Parliamentary Committee which met in March and April 1834 to discuss whether Ross should be rewarded for his

achievements and to investigate, through interviews with members of
the expedition and experts such as Beaufort, what those achievements had been.

The two Rosses put on an extraordinary show. John Ross tried to
claim in as obfuscatory a way as possible that he had discovered the
North Magnetic Pole, adding that even if he hadn't discovered it he
should still get the credit for doing so. James Ross, for his part, stated
even more bizarrely that he had commanded the *Victory* and that the
entire expedition owed its existence to him. He quoted Booth as
saying, 'If you decide that you will accompany the expedition, I will
decide that the expedition shall go; but if you hesitate to say whether
you will accompany it, I must also hesitate to decide.'[26] Booth denied
it all. '[John Ross] was the sole commander,' he said in bewilderment,
'with liberty to appoint whom he pleased under him. I only said, "Let
them be men who will be of great service!" I left the command
entirely to him.'[27]

Again and again uncle and nephew contradicted each other. John
Ross claimed to have found the height in sea level to be different
either side of the Boothia peninsula; James Ross said he had never
heard of such a thing. John Ross announced that the expedition had
conclusively proved that there was no North-West Passage; James
Ross said it had made its existence all the more certain. Utterly baffled, and perhaps remembering the equally tempestuous exchanges
that had followed the Rosses' 1818 expedition, the Committee
decided to approve the rewards and leave the two Scots to sort their
differences between themselves.

James Ross predicted the outcome in an angry letter to Franklin on
29 March 1834, thanking him for a note, probably of support, 'which
could not fail to have been of most material service to me had I had an
opportunity of reading it to the Committee'.[28] By then, however, the
proceedings were running down. No more evidence was being taken
and a report was expected within two weeks. 'I have no idea what it
will be beyond giving Capt. Ross the £5,000 and of course nothing to
me,'[29] James wrote, noting angrily that the Committee was manned
entirely by John Ross's friends. The Committee did, in fact, grant him

a second hearing, but it was a brief pro forma interview that changed nothing. James Ross's assessment of its findings was correct. He received nothing – although his uncle eventually gave him the niggardly sum of £250.

The truth was that before the examination both men had ends to pursue. John Ross wanted to bury his past errors under a torrent of praise. James Ross wanted to advance his career. He had, after all, spent fourteen summers and eight winters in the Arctic. He had received a thousand times the kudos of his uncle, yet was still only at the rank of commander. When they approached the table they delivered their agendas in a confused mish-mash of puffery. If anything about the expedition was poorly managed it was the Rosses' behaviour in its aftermath.

They continued to batter away at each other even after the Committee had reached its findings. In the Royal Society's *Philosophical Treatises*, and in a lecture before the Royal Society in 1834, James Ross delivered his own account of the discovery of the North Magnetic Pole a full year before his uncle's journal appeared. In December that year he wrote to John Ross demanding 'an explicit avowal' that the glory 'belongs solely and exclusively to myself'.[30] He was also very keen to see any alterations John Ross might have made to his contribution to the journal, and hinted darkly that he might forbid its publication if it was in any way altered – particularly since he had glimpsed the elusive first-draft map at Beaufort's office and had noticed that 'some of the very few names which I gave to places . . . have been expunged and renamed'.[31]

Ross responded by publishing his nephew's account in one chapter but following it with another which he devoted to a meandering explanation of the fact that although 'my energetic and philosophical officer had placed his foot on the very spot',[32] it was to be made plain that 'if I myself consent to award that palm to him who commanded this successful party . . . it must not be forgotten that in this I surrender those personal claims which are never abandoned by [the leader of an expedition].'[33] It did him no credit and can only have widened the rift. As Franklin wrote, 'Ross will do himself harm by the eagerness he has shown in this matter, and no one is more annoyed than young Ross, of whom the uncle is very jealous.'[34]

Nothing had changed, then. John Ross was still a pariah. He affected not to notice, diverting his energies into adding a study in the shape of the *Victory*'s cabin to his house in Stranraer – which he now called a castle. James Ross by now had declared his intention to have '*no further communication*'[35] with his uncle, and told his father that he intended to publish his own journal. 'I think he must be mad,'[36] John Ross told a friend, honestly baffled. In the end James Ross never went to publication and the two men settled their differences after a fashion.

But it was an uneasy truce. As late as 1846 John Ross was still raging about his nephew. 'Since [the Committee meeting] my enemies received their warmest ally; in private and in public, at every club and in every society – the Royal, the Astronomical, the Geographical – did I hear of efforts to depreciate my talents, my acquirements, and my services; but I have borne all in silence, because I knew the quarter from whence these efforts emanated, and grief subdued my indignation. Now, however, silence has become impossible. To all the calumnies in Sir John Barrow's works, Sir James Clark Ross has affixed his signature.'[37] It would seem that James Ross's only crime was to lend his name to the map in Barrow's vitriolic *Voyages*.

Barrow's map is indeed a fine map. It covers the Canadian Arctic, the top side of Alaska, what was known about Greenland, a little bit of the Siberian coast, a smaller bit of Norway, and the popular whaling island of Spitsbergen. Around Spitsbergen, names protrude like spiders' legs. Above Canada names are fewer and are replaced by lines – bold for discovered coastlines, dotted for supposed – which revolve optimistically around a large blank. Prince Regent Inlet's southern extremity is a mass of dotted lines, from which further dotted lines and further blanks lead to the west. The lines reveal a peculiar mind. They show that Barrow did not trust Ross's affirmation that Prince Regent Inlet – here the 'Gulf of Akkolee of Iligliuk' – had a bottom, and that it had no outlet to the west. Apart from the bulk of

Boothia Felix there is little to show that John Ross had ever been there. Everything is wiped out and, instead of the territories he had named after the Clarences and Fitzclarences, there is a small, semi-circular inscription west of Boothia. It reads 'Innumerable Islands'.

20

THE OVERLANDERS

By some strange twist of reasoning John Ross's failure to find the North-West Passage became absolute proof of its existence. Everyone was convinced that its discovery was at hand. 'I feel more confident than I have ever previously ventured to feel,' Sabine wrote as early as December 1833, 'that the probability of accomplishing a passage is now so great as *fully* to justify the attempt.'[1] Richardson was equally sanguine. 'I have no doubt that a passage will ultimately be found,'[2] he told James Ross the following year. Before they could act, however, they had to see what Back had discovered on his rescue mission overland.

Back had sailed from England on 17 February 1833 accompanied by three seamen and a waspish little surgeon called Dr Richard King whom Back described as 'very amiable and will make a good voyageur'.[3] Four months later the team were at Fort Alexander on Lake Winnipeg, poised to strike north to Great Slave Lake. From there their destination was the Great Fish River, unrecorded on any map but of whose existence Back had been told by an Indian in 1820 and which he hoped would lead them in the direction of Boothia Felix.

The last time he was in the region Back had been castigated for his overbearing attitude by Governor George Simpson. This time he provoked an opposite reaction from Thomas Simpson, the twenty-five-year-old cousin of George, who was a clerk with the Hudson's Bay Company. In Thomas Simpson's opinion Back was 'deficient, I should say in that commanding manner with the people so necessary in this savage country', but otherwise he seemed 'a very easy, affable man'.[4]

Leading a party that now numbered twenty, Back set off for the Great Fish. His method was identical to that used by Franklin on his two previous missions: boats and portage. And although he spent most of his time scouting ahead of his men in a canoe, leaving the day-to-day organization to King – who commented on the fact – he ran a well-organized and successful enterprise, following the river down 'a violent and tempestuous course of five hundred and thirty geographical miles, running through an iron ribbed country without a single tree on the whole line of its banks'.[5]

By this time Back was no longer trying to rescue Ross, news of whose safe arrival home had been despatched to the Arctic in the closing months of 1833. However, as he was already in place he had been instructed to carry on and find what he could. The general feeling – in Canada, at least – was that it might satisfy his sense of self-importance if he was allowed to map the odd undiscovered mile.

The journey was not without its difficulties, which were noted by a Hudson's Bay man called MacTavish who had a low opinion of Back. They 'have been playing the same tune', he wrote, 'they have starved this winter again'.[6] It was not quite true. Back and his men did not starve, but hundreds of Indians who had gathered outside his encampment did. 'You'll hear what a fine story they'll make out of this bungle,' MacTavish wrote in April 1834. 'They will, you may be sure, take none of the blame for themselves . . . they will return next summer, & like all expeditions will do little & speak a great deal.'[7]

Back's affability had obviously worn off. When he reported that the voyageurs received him 'with a would-be politeness' MacTavish waxed angry. What did Back expect in the wilds of Canada: 'the capers and grimaces of a Frenchified Fool?' The voyageurs had treated him

fairly and that was enough. Back's expedition had 'disgruntled the
Gents. in this country by . . . the returns they made them for their
kindness', he told his sister. Back was utterly 'heartless'.[8]

Heartless or not, Back reached the river's mouth in August 1834,
and charted a bay of clear sea water that he named Chantrey Inlet.
There was land to the north – King William Land and Boothia Felix
as it happened – but he did not have food or fuel to go further. King,
eager with anticipation, wanted him to continue. Had Back done so
he would have discovered two vital pieces of information: that Boothia
Felix was indeed a peninsula, as John Ross had said it was, and that
King William Land was an island. But Back turned away, and for the
second time the truth was missed.

Back returned to England on 8 September 1835, where he was
greeted by Barrow's hearty approbation. Back had borne his ordeal
with 'a degree of cheerfulness and good humour peculiar to himself',
Barrow wrote. 'He never shrunk from difficulties, never murmured,
never desponded. Like a true British seaman, the greater the danger
the more firmly he stuck to the bark, determined to hold on, sink or
swim. The praiseworthy object alone which he had in view took full
possession of his mind.'[9]

This was not entirely correct. Back's mind had not been wholly
occupied by his mission. He had commented on every woman he
met, whether it be a 'good strapping dame' or 'an interesting girl of
seventeen'.[10] Nor had he been particularly cheerful. If anything, the
opposite. Thomas Simpson, previously such a fan of Back, changed
his mind: 'Back I believe to be not only a vain but a *bad* man.'[11] When
Back's journal came out in 1836, Simpson described it as 'a painted
bauble, all ornament and conceit, and no substance'.[12]

Back seemed to have a knack for making enemies. First there was
Franklin, then the two Simpsons and MacTavish in Canada. Now, on
his return, he stirred up trouble for George Ross, John Ross's brother –
whom he privately called an 'old fool' – by suggesting he had been
fiddling the expedition's books. Odiously, the first person he told was
George Ross's son, claiming that his father 'had received subscriptions
from the public, which [he] never had accounted for, and had been

guilty of gross malversation in misapplying the funds . . . to [his] own private ends'.[13] The only evidence to support this accusation was that George Ross had resigned as secretary of the expedition following the safe return of John Ross. But in Back's mind this was clear proof of guilt – George Ross had been found out and had jumped before he could be pushed.

All in all, his fellow explorers agreed, Back was a self-promoting schemer. The only man not to notice Back's faults was Barrow. But then Barrow was in a cheerful mood that year, having just received a baronetcy. 'No one can admit more strongly than does his Majesty the claims literary, scientific and official, which are united in the person of his highly esteemed friend Mr. Barrow,'[14] wrote King William happily, when he informed Barrow of his elevation. The honour was certainly deserved but, alas, it was not given on merit alone. It had been proposed by Croker, who still held considerable influence even though he had been turfed out of office in 1830 when the Duke of Clarence succeeded to the throne.

A rift seemed to have opened between the First and Second Secretaries, as Croker hinted in a letter to Prime Minister Robert Peel in which he referred to Barrow as 'my old friend and now connection'.[15] However, in recommending the baronetcy, Croker was thinking not so much of Barrow as of his own descendants. Croker's daughter Nony was married to Barrow's eldest son George, therefore the title would eventually pass to Croker's grandson.

For a man to whom position meant so much, Barrow was hesitant about accepting. Titles did not come free, but required a certain outlay that he was not certain he could afford. Irritatedly, Croker told him he would supply the necessary monies but he must accept the honour on all accounts, if only for his children's sake. Barrow eventually agreed. The baronetcy was 'unexpected and I fear I may add in all sincerity, unmerited', he wrote to Peel. 'It is a distinction to which I never had ambition to aspire, but I accept it, as I ought, with all humility and thankfulness, valuing it the more on the ground on which you have put it, of long and faithful service.'[16]

*

With Back's return the way was now clear for another stab at the North-West Passage and in 1836 Sir John Barrow urged the Royal Geographical Society, of which he was Vice-President, supported by the Royal Society, of which he was a Fellow, to suggest it to the Admiralty, of which he was Secretary. Naturally, the idea was approved.

Opinions were divided as to its exact route. Barrow favoured an approach south of Melville Island, being convinced against all the evidence that there was open water between Parry's furthest point and Alaska. Beaufort, Franklin and Richardson supported him and the latter, in a fit of optimism, hazarded that a route might even be found *north* of Melville Island. Two years previously, Richardson had privately suggested to James Ross that an overland expedition was 'likely to be fully as efficient as a ship one . . . and much more economical'.[17] But such an opinion was best kept quiet given Barrow's enthusiasm that the Passage was to be crossed by ship. Only one man suggested a land expedition, and when Richardson saw what happened to him, he was glad of his reticence.

The man was Dr Richard King, who had returned from the Great Fish River – or the Back River, as it was now called – brimming over with correct and entirely unfashionable views. In his two-volume journal, published independently of Back's, he attacked every value that the Arctic establishment held dear. He criticized the Hudson's Bay Company for their policy towards the natives – 'the most venemous thing I have read for a long time',[18] Thomas Simpson recorded – and sneered at Barrow's ponderous ship expeditions. What was needed, he explained, was a small overland party – led by himself – which could move on foot or by dog team across the country, living off the land and probing the shores of North America until the passage was found. It would be effective and above all cheap. Compared with the £70,000 bill for Parry's fiasco in the *Fury*, and the £5,000 it had cost to mount Back's last expedition, King budgeted a mere £1,000 for a venture such as the one he proposed. 'The question has been asked,' he wrote, 'how I can anticipate success in an undertaking which has baffled a Parry, a Franklin, and a Back?'[19] Scathingly, he admitted that his chances would be very low were he to follow their cumbersome, time-consuming, money-wasting methods.

He formally presented his proposal in April 1836, describing an expedition whose object was to solve the all-important question of whether or not Boothia Felix was a peninsula. It was greeted with derision. Franklin, the man at whose accomplishments King had just scoffed, got his own back when Barrow asked him to review the proposal. 'The plan of Mr. King,' Franklin wrote in his large, jagged handwriting, 'appears to me so meagre in its detail that it will not furnish any satisfactory information.' All King seemed interested in was Boothia Felix, not the grand object of the passage. 'On the whole this plan seems so uncertain,' Franklin concluded, 'that I cannot recommend it.'[20]

Oddly, though, Franklin felt quite able to recommend an outline put forward in the same year by Barrow which envisaged a ship being sent to Repulse Bay, or its southerly neighbour Wager Bay, and landing a shore party whose objective was to explore the southern shores of the Gulf of Boothia. The unstated goal was to ascertain whether Boothia Felix was a peninsula.

Barrow approached it in his usual roundabout way. He presented the idea to Beaufort and asked him to start a correspondence on the matter with the Royal Geographical Society. Beaufort did as he was told, and Barrow replied with an enthusiastic letter of support – puffing at the same time his favourite route south-west from Barrow Strait with two large ships. Richardson, whom Barrow had also primed to write in, agreed that Beaufort was correct in promoting a land attack via Wager or Repulse Bay. So too, later, did Franklin. Everything was going swimmingly until John Ross wrote (uninvited) to say how they had all got it wrong. Any attempt should be made by sea in just the way he had done it, and as for Barrow's alternative, 'no man in his senses would commit such an act of imprudence'.[21] Being the arbiter of the correspondence, Barrow was unable to block Ross's letter which was duly printed in the *Royal Geographical Journal* alongside his own contribution.

It was three against one. Ross was ignored and the expedition went ahead. Everyone expected James Ross to command it. 'You are now quite without a rival for the command,'[22] Sabine enthused. But in the end Barrow's new favourite, George Back, was the chosen one. He left Chatham on 14 June 1836 aboard the *Terror*, destined for Repulse Bay. Apart from the business of discovery, his instructions included the explicit injunction 'that this Arctic expedition may be distinguished from all others, by the promptness of its execution, and by escaping from the gloomy and unprofitable waste of eight months' detention: it is therefore our distinct orders that every effort shall be made to return to England in the fall of this year'.[23] Barrow had stolen King's notion of economy too.

Back was given a choice of two routes to Repulse Bay: the disastrous one chosen by Lyon to the south of Southampton Island or the preferred one via Frozen Strait to the north, 'which was performed with apparent ease' by Parry in 1821. He naturally chose the latter and endured an appalling ten-month voyage during which he was seized by the ice, buffeted by floes which at one point hurled the *Terror* forty feet up a cliff, and attacked by an iceberg which crushed the ship so thoroughly that Back feared it would sink. Having come nowhere near Repulse Bay, he turned for home. Struggling across the Atlantic, water pouring through the smashed timbers, his fears were realized: the *Terror* was going down. He beached his waterlogged vessel on the shores of Ireland, returned to London and never went to the Arctic again. For this he was rewarded with the Royal Geographical Society's Gold Medal, an Admiralty desk job and, in due course, a knighthood.

James Ross, meanwhile, had been sent on a lowly mission to rescue stranded whalers in Davis Strait. It wasn't what he'd been hoping for but he had the satisfaction of knowing he had been chosen in preference to his uncle, who had also applied for the job, and at least it kept his name before the public – though the only man to show an interest was Captain Edward Belcher, a stupid, blustery officer who had sailed with Beechey on the *Blossom* and who was everyone's acquaintance but nobody's friend. 'They appear to believe,' Belcher told James Ross, 'that if all have not escaped they are wrecked and therefore *do not want aid* until the summer. You must look to this and bring up such information as will settle their hash.'[24] Ross went and came back again, the whalers having disentangled themselves without his assistance.

1836 had been a bad year for all concerned. Back had failed. James Ross had been disappointed. Barrow had been thwarted. In the reserves, meanwhile, both John Franklin and John Ross had fallen on hard times.

John Ross's book had not done as well as he had expected. Booth, his good friend, had advanced £5,000 to cover the cost of publication, and had loaned him a further £6,000. In return he had demanded a half-share in the journal and was charging interest on the rest. Once everything had been paid off there was little profit left. 'If any one will give me £500 down and take all the risk,' John Ross told his brother George, 'I shall make them over all I have to benefit & have benefited by the speculation!'[25]

Ross's prospects of future employment were limited. He would never be given a command while Barrow was still alive, and having made so many enemies in the naval establishment he had little chance of work anywhere in Britain. As a friend wrote from Ireland, 'I am afraid you have some Enemy at Head Quarters. Capt. Jas. [James Ross] is an insinuating fellow and from his plausible stories has made many friends here at your expense. I presume he has done the same in England.'[26] Ross lapsed back into the life of a gentleman amateur, toying with this and that, overseeing the extension to his 'castle' at Stranraer, and juggling the demands of a marriage that was already falling apart. However, his friends in Parliament, who had previously helped him over the inquiry into his mission, finally arranged his appointment as British Consul in Stockholm. It was an ideal post, given his fluency in the language and his previous experience in Sweden. He sailed for Scandinavia in 1839 and stayed there until 1846, returning home only on fleeting visits.

Franklin lacked Ross's self-contained nature. He knew nothing of phrenology, steam power or other modish subjects. He had no castle to build, no grouse to shoot. He had nothing, in fact, but the ability to command ships and lead men. It was what he did best and there was no call for it.

Since his last expedition to Canada Franklin had been on duty in the Mediterranean, overseeing Greece's transition from Ottoman colony to independent nation. On his return in 1834 he had lobbied unsuccessfully for command of the expedition that was eventually given to Back. After that he had petitioned the Admiralty, stating that he was ready for any service. But all they could offer, in time-honoured fashion, was the promise that they would bear him in mind. He tried again in 1836, with the same result. He therefore turned to the Colonial Office, with whom he had had dealings during his Canadian treks. 'I have always felt an interest in new colonies,'[27] he wrote transparently. Disinterestedly, they told him the Governorship of Antigua was vacant. Franklin might have been tempted, but his wife Jane was against it. She pointed out that Antigua formed part of the Leeward Islands, which had their own Governor-in-Chief; Franklin would therefore be a subordinate. And whatever its charms, one could not ignore Antigua's size: the place was a good deal smaller than the Isle of Wight. This was not what polar heroes were destined for. She told Franklin to refuse and to point out in his refusal that the position was beneath him. Franklin did as he was told, to the delight of his friends. Beaufort assured him he had made the right decision and praised Lady Jane as 'a woman of most excellent understanding & judgement'.[28] His refusal could only make the Colonial Office respect him the more, Beaufort said.

Beaufort was right. Within a fortnight Franklin was offered a much more prestigious assignment as Governor of Van Diemen's Land (modern Tasmania). And he was offered it in a grovelling manner with the assurance of a £2,500 per annum salary. This was much more to Lady Jane's liking, notwithstanding that Van Diemen's Land was a convict settlement. As with Parry, when he left for Australia Franklin wondered if his acceptance would hamper his naval prospects. But when Beaufort assured him that his worries were 'all my eye',[29] Franklin signed on at once.

Franklin was still a figure to be conjured with despite his recent absence from the polar scene. When the charming man who had eaten his boots announced his new appointment the whole country was pleased. The citizens of Spilsby, his birthplace, passed round the hat for a piece of silver plate. At Horncastle, near Lincoln, where he was currently staying, schools were given a day off, church bells rang incessantly, and Franklin was guest of honour at a public dinner. The only discordant note came from his friend Thomas Arnold, the Rugby educationalist, who knew Franklin maybe better than Franklin knew himself. 'I am not sure,' Arnold counselled, 'how far this appointment may be a subject of congratulation to yourself, as I am sure it is to the settlement.'[30]

Arnold was right to voice his doubts. Franklin's kind, vacillating personality was not suited to a colony of convicts. But Franklin went there all the same, shepherded along by the restless Lady Jane.

With Johns Ross and Franklin out of the way the other unemployed Arctonauts battered at the Admiralty gates.

Dr Richard King was keen, as always, for an overland mission and submitted his application to the Royal Geographical Society in strident tones. He asked the Fellows to consider how most journeys 'have been either unsuccessful, or attended with prodigious loss or risk – how great an expense they unavoidably incur compared with the amount of real advantage to be expected'.[31] King wondered, undiplomatically, whether 'it be right to recommend to the government the equipment of a fresh expedition . . . until one or two points have been settled by the more economical as well as the more promising agency of overland expeditions'.[32]

James Ross put forward a counter-proposal, in language that sounded suspiciously like Barrow's: 'I will not trifle with your time,' he told the Royal Geographical Society, 'by stopping to confute the absurdly erroneous notions that are entertained by some as to the Expense, Danger, Loss of Life & hardships & privations that those who embark in services of this nature are said to be exposed to, nor will I labour to point out the many advantages that have already resulted from these Expeditions & are likely to result from future perseverance.'[33] His expedition was to follow Barrow's preferred route south-west of Melville Island and was to comprise two large ships of 300–400 tons. Large ships were important, Ross explained in a circular argument of the kind John Barrow favoured, because they had to hold sufficient provisions to feed the large crews that were necessary to haul such large ships through the ice.

In the end no expedition was sent, because there was already one in the field. In 1836 the Hudson's Bay Company had despatched Thomas Simpson and Peter Dease to do the Admiralty's job for it. They travelled light, with just a handful of men and a few boats, and in two years achieved more than Barrow had in the past twenty.

Simpson was arrogant, physically strong and insatiably ambitious – rather like his enemy Back, in fact – to which he added a fanaticism reminiscent of Gordon Laing. Had he been left to his own devices he would probably have hurried the expedition straight to an icy grave. Fortunately, Dease acted as a restraining influence. This calm, laid-back man who had advised Franklin on his two overland journeys was the perfect foil to Simpson and although Simpson would later claim all the credit to himself, the expedition was very much a joint effort.

They left Athabasca early in 1837, travelled down the Mackenzie River and set off west along the coast. By 31 July the men were exhausted and ready to go home. Simpson left them where they were and forged ahead on his own. On 4 August he had the indescribable joy of sighting Point Barrow, the furthest point east reached by Beechey. 'I and I *alone* have the well-earned honour of uniting the Arctic to the great Western Ocean,'[34] he wrote. Retracing his steps he picked up Dease and returned inland, bound for the Coppermine. Throughout the summer of 1839 the two men sailed along the coasts Franklin had so laboriously mapped, passed his Point Turnagain and reached Back's Chantrey Inlet.

It was a towering achievement, accomplished with apparently total ease, that came within a hair's breadth of completing the North-West Passage. The Hudson's Bay men were delighted at the way Dease and Simpson had eclipsed the bumbling British navy. 'I suppose friend Back looks blue upon it now,'[35] one man wrote. As before, needless to say, this corner of the Arctic proved troublesome. Simpson believed that Boothia Felix was an island and that King William Land was not. He was wrong on both counts and his mistaken beliefs, which were given authority by his success in every other department, would have disastrous repercussions in the future.

The journey had had the usual tensions. Simpson declared that Dease had been a deadweight. 'It is no vanity to say that everything which requires either planning or execution devolves upon me,' he wrote. Dease was 'the last man in the world for a discoverer'.[36] Dease agreed cheerfully that he had been an indolent supernumerary from start to finish. This was inaccurate but Dease, who was a wise man, looked forward to a long and trouble-free life. He knew the truth would out eventually. More serious was Simpson's attitude to the mixed-blood voyageurs he had taken with him. 'To the extravagant and profligate habits of the half-breed families I have an insuperable aversion,' he wrote. They were 'worthless and depraved', subject to 'uncontrollable passions'.[37] This was an unwise attitude, to say the least, particularly as Simpson intended leading the same men on a new expedition into the Arctic.

Flushed with success he announced a plan to complete his explorations on a two-year voyage that would take him from Chantrey Inlet to the Fury and Hecla Strait. It would cost a mere £500 which would be supplied by himself. 'I feel an irresistible presentiment that I am destined to bear the Honourable Company's flag fairly through and out of the Polar Sea,' he wrote. The glory would be his and no other's: 'Fame I will have but it must be *alone*.'[38]

The Hudson's Bay Company agreed. So did London where, to Simpson's amusement, his journey had become a debating point between the Whig and Tory parties. And so did Dease, who relinquished all rights to accompany Simpson and slipped back into his happy-go-lucky life with careless ease. Barrow, meanwhile, was delighted. Dease and Simpson had 'quashed by their persevering and energetic labours' all John Ross's nonsense about isthmuses and 'the absurdities to which they gave rise'. Their journal 'carries with it the stamp of truth and modesty', he wrote.[39] He persuaded the Royal

Geographical Society to award Simpson its Gold Medal plus a pension of £100.

But Simpson was dead before he heard of either the medal or his plan's acceptance. The precise details of his death are murky. Suicide was the official explanation, but it seems that while travelling across Canada with four mixed-race voyageurs in the summer of 1840 Simpson voiced his opinions a little too freely. He was taken to a quiet spot in the wilderness and was shot.

21

THE BOTTOM OF
THE WORLD

By 1838 James Ross was very disappointed. Of all Barrow's Arctic hands he was now the only one without a job. But there was hope yet. Barrow had turned his eyes in a new direction, revealed by Richardson in a letter to Ross dated 24 August 1838. Richardson had approached the Admiralty and told them that 'your greatest ambition was either the N. or S. Pole – you did not much care which'.[1]

The South Pole? Here was something truly new and exciting.

Antarctica occupied a somewhat nebulous position in the minds and maps of the world's navigators. The ancient Greeks had said it was there. In the 1520s Magellan had drawn an astonishingly accurate map of it without ever seeing it. It had been circumnavigated by Cook in 1773 and by a Russian, Bellingshausen, in 1820. In 1821 an American sealer called John Davis had landed on the Antarctic Peninsula, the northernmost strip of land which reaches out to Tierra del Fuego.

People were sure Antarctica existed, without any proof, but had no idea of its precise nature. The most popular view held that it was a continent of dry land peopled by outlandish beings of (naturally) great wealth – a cross between Atlantis and Timbuctoo, before the latter had been found wanting. One enterprising Frenchman had even taken shiploads of colonists to the south, only to be driven back by gales and ice.

The myths were not entirely wrong. Antarctica *did* contain wealth, if not the 'minerals, diamonds, rubies, precious stones and marble'[2] predicted by one French explorer. Cook had reported teeming multitudes of seals and whales, both of which were in high demand. Since the 1760s, when a Canton merchant had discovered a way of separating a seal's outer hair from its soft underfur, sealskin had been a sought-after fashion accessory. By the 1820s, however, most of the accessible populations had been wiped out. The northern whale, too, had almost disappeared. But balleen, or whalebone, was now more in demand than ever to satisfy the craze for corsets in an increasingly prosperous and style-conscious world. By 1830, the balleen from a single Greenland whale fetched £2,500, which was more than enough to pay for a journey to the Antarctic and back. Accordingly, during the 1820s and 1830s, American and British firms used their profits from the north to probe the unknown treasures of the south.

The sealers were a hardy race. Dropped on an isolated scrap of rock, the gangs spent months and sometimes years killing and butchering their quarry, fending as best they could until they were picked up (which did not always happen). But they were poor explorers, lacking the expertise to make charts and what was more keeping all discoveries secret for fear of competition. One captain admitted openly that when his holds were full he abandoned his men lest they reveal where they had been and thus jeopardize his find. There were, however, exceptions, such as Edmund Fanning of Connecticut and James Weddell of Lanarkshire. The latter, in 1822–4, sailed further south than Cook, and made a record-breaking penetration of the Weddell Sea that would not be bettered for ninety years. And in 1830–2 a captain from the British firm of Enderby Brothers – whose interest in Antarctic exploration was such that it eventually bankrupted them – had sighted a portion of the continent which would be called Enderby Land.

Back in 1773, Cook had been dismissive about Antarctica. The continent probably did not exist, and even if it did, the conditions he had experienced suggested that it would be a cold, hopeless place. For six decades this had been accepted naval dogma. But with new evidence coming in from sealers and whalers, the British Admiralty was forced to reconsider. Antarctica *was* there. Moreover, it had commercial prospects. And these prospects, unless they were careful, might be usurped by Barrow's bug-bear – the foreigner. The push southwards began in earnest in 1838 and, as with the push northwards twenty years previously, it was given a cloak of scientific respectability.

The prompt came from Sabine – now Colonel Sabine – who addressed the British Association for the Advancement of Science at Newcastle in August 1838. To his earnest audience he pointed out the deficiencies in the study of magnetism, particularly in the southern hemisphere. He called for a year of international cooperation in which European nations would set up observatories across the globe, coordinate readings on fixed dates, and compare results. He also suggested that Britain mount an expedition to determine magnetic variations in the region of the South Pole. His suggestions became resolutions which were passed to the Admiralty and which, after the usual greasing of the wheels by Barrow, received official consent. It was just in time too. The foreigner was already at the gates.

In 1837, Captain Jules Sébastien-César Dumont d'Urville had set sail from Toulon on the *Astrolabe*. He was fifty, crippled by gout, and looked as if he would die before the end of the voyage. (Unsettlingly, he heard one of his men suggest as much as he hobbled aboard.) He didn't really want to go to the South Pole at all. His heart had been set on a pseudo-scientific pleasure cruise through the South Seas. Having already acquired the Venus de Milo for France he had no desire for further glory. But King Louis-Philippe had ordered him south, with a reward for each degree passed beyond 67° and 'whatever you choose to ask for'[3] if he reached the Pole. So south he went.

To everybody's surprise, maybe even his own, D'Urville did magnificently. He did not reach the Pole but he did make the first-ever landing on the main continent. It was not very prepossessing. He discovered a barren wasteland which he described very accurately as 'a formidable layer of ice . . . over a base of rock'[4] and which he named Adelie Land after his wife. And, 'following the venerable custom which the English have carefully maintained, we took possession in the name of France'.[5] Then spying a new variety of penguin he named that, too, after his wife. After which he set sail for home. It was now January 1841.

D'Urville had barely reached open seas when he encountered a ship skating in a fast, haphazard fashion across the ocean. It came within hailing distance but careered on its way without making contact. Puzzled, D'Urville pressed on. The ship he had seen was the *Porpoise*, one of a six-vessel American expedition under the command of Lt. Charles Wilkes which had sailed from Virginia in 1838. The expedition had been proposed in Congress as early as 1821, but only now had it become reality. A collection of beautifully named cockleshells – *Peacock*, *Flying Fish*, *Sea Gull* – the fleet was ill-equipped, shoddily manned, and physically rotten. Yet, under Wilkes, it managed to chart a purported 1,500 miles of Antarctic coastline before returning home. However, the value of its findings was undermined by subsequent bickering in which Wilkes, a heavy-handed man, had to endure courts martial, public investigations and private charges brought by his officers. In due course his name was cleared, but by then his thunder had been stolen by another: James Ross.

By the late 1830s James Ross was the most experienced polar officer in the world and, with Parry out to pasture and Back in shell-shocked retirement, he was Barrow's man of the moment. During the last twenty years he had spent seventeen in the Arctic and overwintered for eight. As the discoverer of the North Magnetic Pole he was a pre-eminent magnetist. He was also, it was said, the handsomest officer in the Royal Navy. What more suitable, more popular and more glamorous person could there be to lead a British expedition to the South Pole?

Ross was given two bomb ships: *Terror*, newly repaired after its service with Back in the Arctic; and its twin, *Erebus*. If any vessel was perfect for polar exploration, a bomb ship was the one. Designed as mortar platforms to pound coastal installations, bomb ships were strong, had capacious holds, and had a shallow draught – eleven feet – so that they could creep close to shore. By now accustomed to preparing ships for icework, the Admiralty dockyards set to on *Erebus* and *Terror* with practised efficiency. The ships' decks were doubled in thickness, with waterproof cloth being sandwiched between two layers of planks. Fore and aft their interiors were braced with interlacing oak beams to resist and absorb shock. Their hulls were scraped smooth and double-planked. Their keels were sheathed in extra thick copper. Treble-strength canvas was fitted.

By any standards the enterprise was phenomenally well equipped,* from its ice saws and portable forges to its stocks of provisions – sufficient for three years and including 2,618 pints of vegetable soup, 2,398 pounds of pickled cabbage and 10,782 pounds of carrots to keep scurvy at bay, not to mention a small flock of sheep – to its stores of winter clothing and to Ross's insistence that 'every arrangement [be] made in the interior fitting of the vessels that could in any way contribute to the health and comfort of our people'.[6]

The men, too, were the best that could be found. While Ross was in command of *Erebus*, *Terror* was given to his old friend Lt. Crozier, who had sailed with Ross on all of Parry's voyages and who had been his second-in-command on the abortive rescue mission of 1836. Each ship held a crew of sixty-four. Ross had Edward Bird, from the Franklin–Buchan voyage of 1818, as first lieutenant, Crozier had Archibald McMurdo who had sailed with Back to Repulse Bay. Oddly, given their scientific aims, there was no provision for scientists. Ross deemed them unnecessary. Those that came had to come in the guise of medics. So Robert McCormick, a hot-tempered geologist who had sailed with Darwin, was chosen as 'surgeon' for the *Erebus* while a

* Ross's equipment even included Mr Fox Talbot's new daguerrotyping apparatus. Unfortunately, however, this early camera was either too baffling or too unwieldy and remained in its case throughout the trip.

twenty-one-year-old botanist called Joseph Dalton Hooker was
chosen as 'assistant surgeon'.

J. D. Hooker – later to become Britain's foremost naturalist – was
bitterly disappointed to be playing second fiddle. He had wanted to
be the expedition's official plant finder. He wanted to go ashore and
discover things nobody had ever seen. But as Ross explained, a 'surgeon' 'must be well known in the world beforehand, such a person as
Mr. Darwin'.[7] Hooker was devastated. He was a friend of Darwin, and
had slept with a copy of his unpublished work beneath his pillow.
'What was Mr. Darwin before he went out?' he countered. 'He, I
daresay, knew his subject better than I now do, but what did the
world know of him? The voyage with the *Beagle* was the making of
him.'[8] Hooker feared that McCormick – who had sailed previously on
the *Beagle* but had left the ship at Rio de Janeiro because his fellow
naturalist, Darwin, was being given preferential treatment – might
steal his glory. He had hoped that the *Erebus* might be his stepping
stone to fame. He was to be sadly disabused.

The equipment he was given met few of his requirements. 'Not a
single instrument or book [was] supplied to me as naturalist' with
the exception of twenty-five reams of drying paper for plant specimens, two botanizing vascula, and two of 'Mr. Ward's invaluable
cases'.[9] And when given his instructions by various members of the
Royal Society, he was astonished at the surly treatment he received.
'None of them seemed cordial to me in the least degree,' he wrote to
his father. 'On leaving the room no one even wished me a pleasant or
successful voyage.'[10] Shrugging his shoulders, he resigned himself to
his position. It could have been worse: one of the Admiralty Lords had
asked what on earth botany and geology had to do with the expedition
in the first place.

Neither of the two ships handled well. Nor did they look pretty.
But when they left the Thames in autumn 1839 they represented the
cutting edge of naval ingenuity. No sailing ships before, and none
since, had been so finely prepared for their task. The *Erebus* and
Terror leaped like eager bulldogs into the Atlantic. 'It is not easy to
describe the joy and lightheartedness we all felt,' Ross wrote, 'as we

passed the entrance to the Channel, bounding before a favourable breeze over the blue waves of the ocean, fairly embarked on the enterprise we had all so long desired to commence.'[11]

Ross's expedition started a year later than its competitors, yet such was its purpose, strength and sheer indomitability that it sailed – literally – through their findings.

No enterprise by Barrow's men could be complete without Scoresby and, sure enough, Scoresby raised his head at the first mention of magnets.

In the past years, when not preaching to his congregation in industrial Bradford, Scoresby had been absorbed by the study of magnetism. Much of his time had been spent on the new craze of 'animal magnetism', or hypnosis, for which the Reverend Scoresby had found an uncanny aptitude, particularly where female subjects were concerned. But he had also devoted time to terrestrial magnetism. During his investigations he had devised a new and improved set of compass needles which 'can be magnetized without taking asunder, and if varnished and placed in pairs, would *never* lose their power'.[12] This was unheard of. Never in all the years of the Admiralty had anyone been able to construct a compass which did not suffer some deterioration. And in the new iron ships that were being built by Barrow's much-feared projectors a stable compass needle was essential.

In 1836, following a successful demonstration at Bristol, Scoresby was invited to send his new needle to the Committee for the Improvement of Ships Compasses. Among its members were Sabine and Beaufort. Its chairman was James Ross. He was invited to test a sample of Admiralty needles which were so poor that Scoresby could only believe they had been deliberately chosen for their uselessness. Beaufort assured him otherwise: 'I am afraid that those sent to you were not worse than the average supply from the Dockyards – at least they were not selected for their badness but taken at random.'[13] Two weeks later Scoresby delivered a damning report on the Admiralty needles and included an example of his own, the patent for which he was willing to forgo provided it would be of use to the Admiralty.

For some reason Scoresby's own needles did not work and he feared they had been compromised by contact with another magnet. The Committee pointed out that a similar design – consisting of 'three thin steel plates (clock springs) as nearly as may be of the same length, breadth and thickness as those of Mr. Scoresby's needles and separated by a barrier of brown paper instead of the wood Mr. Scoresby uses'[14] – had been in existence since 1823. To this judgement, signed by James Ross, Scoresby could only reply that he had 'the honour of acknowledging the reply of the Committee on compasses',[15] and that he would try harder. While he did so the Admiralty introduced a new compass that was in every respect Scoresby's design.

James Ross ploughed south. On 31 January he anchored in St Helena where he set up the first observatory, not far from the house to which Barrow had consigned Napoleon back in 1816. Already McCormick had gathered so many specimens that his cabin was overflowing and his fellow officer, Edward Bird – who had no feeling for natural history – was finding space for them in his own quarters. By St Patrick's Day they were at the Cape where they set up a second observatory and departed on 6 April to the cheers of the crewmen clinging to the rigging of HMS *Melville*. On 15 May the expedition was ensconced in the dramatic bowl of Christmas Harbour, Kerguelen Island.

Christmas Harbour was a 'most dreary and disagreeable'[16] place, Ross recorded. A gale blew for forty-five of the sixty-eight days they were at anchor, reaching such strengths that at times they had to lie flat in order not to be blown into the sea, and there were only three days on which it neither snowed or sleeted. Nevertheless they managed to erect an observatory where for two months, at hourly intervals, they recorded a flurry of extreme magnetic activity. There was enough grazing to keep the sheep well-fed, wild ducks were plentiful and penguin soup, the officers agreed, was very like that made from hare. McCormick peeved Bird with yet more specimens, and Hooker applied himself with mad enthusiasm to his task, chiselling specimens out of the frozen soil or, if the frost was too hard, sitting on them until they thawed. Then they were off again, through gales and hurricanes, the waves driving over them in solid sheets, until on 16 August 1840, their sails in ribbons, they arrived at Hobart, Van Diemen's Land, and settled into an anchorage that would later be called Ross Cove.

Their relief was great. The last leg had been hard with five men washed overboard, one of them – the *Erebus*'s boatswain – never to return. At one stage the *Erebus* had lost its sails and been driven help-less with bare masts. But their relief was nothing compared to that of Sir John Franklin, whose domain they were now entering.

Here, at last, Franklin had managed to find people who disliked him. In this stifling society of 24,000 citizens, 17,592 convicts and 97 indigenous Tasmanians, marbled by veins of snobbery, resentment and despair, Franklin was at a loss. He was a sailor, not an adminis-trator, and no matter how hard he worked he could not hide the fact. The unsophisticated upper crust, perched on their antipodean plinth, saw him as weak, inexperienced and threateningly liberal. His wife, Jane Lady Franklin, was viewed with even more distrust. According to the Colonial Secretary, an 'undermining, cool-headed icicle'[17] called Captain John Montagu, she was 'a clever, mischievous intrigu-ing woman'.[18] She was widely seen as the power behind the throne, her husband 'a man in petticoats',[19] which was not entirely untrue. Seasoned officials were horrified at her attempts to investigate the plight of female convicts, to found a new college and to rid the island of its snakes by paying a bounty of one shilling per dead serpent delivered to her door. Their wives, too, found Lady Franklin overly blue-stocking for comfort. When she introduced the concept of edu-cational 'conversaziones' they threw up their hands in horror. 'Why could not Lady Franklin have the military band in,' wrote one, 'and the carpets out, and give dances, instead of such stupid preaching about philosophy and science, and a parcel of stuff that nobody could understand.'[20] Such was their antagonism that even the genial Franklin noticed 'a lack of neighbourly feelings and a deplorable defi-ciency in public spirit'.[21]

In this atmosphere of hostility, Franklin welcomed his old friends with joy. It was clear he had been anticipating their arrival, for all the

materials necessary for building their observatory were in place and
within a day, once Ross had selected the site, 200 convicts were working on the foundations. 'The arrival of Captains Ross & Crozier has
added much to Sir John's happiness,' wrote Lady Jane, 'they all feel
towards one another as friends & brothers, & it is the remark of
people here that Sir John appears to them quite in a new light, so
bustling & frisky & merry [is he] with his new companions.'[22]

Such was Franklin's enthusiasm that the observatory was
completed, and all its instruments installed, within nine days. Even
the convicts took heart and, according to Ross, were most disappointed at not being allowed to work past 10 on a Saturday night,
despite having started at 6 that morning. The observatory had a surreal, Dali-esque air. Previously, the site had been a wild spot,
swarming with wildlife and covered in trees. Now the trees had been
cleared and in their place rose a grove of granite pedestals, fluted and
pilastered in classical style, on which were balanced the precious
magnetic instruments. No man could touch the instruments lest the
recordings be affected and so a few yards from each pedestal was
another pedestal carrying a telescope through which the necessary
readings could be viewed.

Lady Jane thought it was a load of rubbish. She visited the site and
left soon afterwards, being 'about as wise when we came away as
when we went in'.[23] What she wanted to see was the *Erebus*, where
'Captain Ross has a copy of Negelin's portrait of Sir John in his cabin,
& so it is much visited.'[24] Nonetheless she commissioned a portrait of
Ross, Franklin and Crozier standing before the observatory, which
she intended to send to Sabine. 'There you are all 3 with your hats
off,' she later wrote to Ross, '& you with the dear bunch of wattle in
your button hole – I insisted on this.'[25] The wattle was a flirtatious
token from Lady Jane, who had fallen for Ross in a mild way. Ross
obviously reciprocated, writing later that his memories of Tasmania
were 'precious, almost hallowed'. Hobart was '*our own* home of the
Southern Hemisphere',[26] and he wore the wattle whenever possible,
muttering 'Tasmania' as he did so.

Lady Jane admired Ross, but her real favourite of the expedition was Hooker, whom she described as 'a youth of about 20, very boyish looking, of rather an interesting appearance'.[27] Taking him under her wing she directed his researches with amateur enthusiasm and maternal autocracy. She 'would like to show me every kindness', complained Hooker, 'but does not understand how, and I hate dancing attendance at Government House.'[28] However, he adapted as usual to adverse circumstances. Having been abducted for a three-day botanizing trip aboard the Governor's yacht – 'two of them at sea, and the third, a Sunday, it rained furiously'[29] – he incurred Lady Franklin's displeasure by working on the sabbath. 'But I thought it excusable as being my only chance of gathering *Anopterus glandulosus*.'[30] He also shocked her on a picnic by screaming so loudly she thought he had been bitten by a snake. It transpired he had found a new species of orchid.

Ross's arrival was like a Christmas hamper to the inhabitants of Hobart. Despite their fatiguing journey the officers and men offered more news and entertainment than could be found in several years' worth of colonial life. Even the anti-Franklin press was muted, restricting itself to the accusation that Ross was bribing seamen to join his expedition, a charge which was negated embarrassingly by the flood of people begging to be taken aboard. But Hobart held one major disappointment for Ross. It was there that he heard of the activities of D'Urville and Wilkes. He was not pleased. Regardless of the fact that both expeditions had sailed a year before his own they had, in his eyes, committed an unforgivable act of disrespect. 'That the commanders of each of these great national undertakings should have selected the very place for penetrating to the southward, for the exploration of which they were well aware, at the time, that the expedition under my command was expressly preparing, and thereby forestalling our purposes, did certainly surprise me. I should have expected their national pride would have caused them rather to have chosen any other path in the wide field before them, than one thus pointed out, if no higher consideration had power to prevent such an interference.'[31]

Curiously, while he learned of the French expedition second-hand from local newspapers, he was most affronted by a letter left for him by Wilkes, detailing the American achievement and supplying a chart of the coastline he had seen. It was a well-meant letter, intended to help a fellow explorer. To Ross it was salt in the wound. But no amount of 'forestalling' – a favourite word among nineteenth-century explorers – could keep Ross from the South Pole. 'Fortunately, in my instructions much had been left to my judgement in unforeseen circumstances; and impressed with the feeling that England had ever led the way of discovery in the southern as well as the northern regions [this was not quite true] I considered it would have been inconsistent with the pre-eminence she had ever maintained, if we were to follow in the footsteps of any other nation. I therefore resolved to avoid all interference with their discoveries, and selected a much more easterly meridian on which to endeavour to penetrate southward.'[32]

Wilkes had explored Antarctica between the 100th and 160th meridians, but he had been prevented from landing on the continent by the pack ice surrounding it. From sealers' reports, however, Ross learned that on the 180th meridian they had seen a lagoon-like expanse of open water beyond the pack. Ross reckoned that his reinforced ships might have a chance of breaking through the ice and into the clear water beyond. Wilkes's ships had only displaced 100 tons or so; Ross's ice-crackers displaced 370. Bearing this in mind he bade farewell to the Franklins and set sail on 12 November 1840. Carrying some 800 of Hooker's and McCormick's specimens, plus two pots of jam from Lady Franklin, they headed for what McCormick predicted would be 'a region of our globe as fresh and new as at creation's first dawn'.[33]

On New Year's Day 1841 they crossed the Antarctic Circle, an event which they celebrated by intoxicating 'Billy', the ship's goat. Two days later, while Billy was 'paying the usual penance for his debauchery',[34] they reached the ice pack. The so-called consolidated pack was solid at the edge but inside could be seen stretches of open water – narrow leads rather than the lagoon they had been promised, but open water nonetheless. Ross chose his point and rammed the pack. The ice held, but so did the *Erebus*. For the next hour he repeatedly rammed the same spot – an act of extraordinary seaman-ship – until at last it gave way and the two ships broke through to the mass of loose floes which lay beyond. By noon they had wormed their way so far into the pack that clear sea was no longer visible. By mid-night they were seventy miles into the ice. Ross and Crozier wove their way through the ice, followed by hordes of penguins who wad-dled from floe to floe in pursuit of the strangers and pursued by seabirds which McCormick, after long hours of practice, was able to shoot so that they fell on deck. On the morning of 9 January they sailed triumphantly into open sea. They had broached the inner lagoon.

Conditions could not have been more different to those they had expected. McCormick likened the weather to 'the finest May day in England'.[35] At night the sun skimmed along the horizon while the sky turned an intense indigo. The sea was calm, the air hazy, the light brilliant and, as their ships sailed south past silent, monstrous ice-bergs, following compasses whose dip revealed that the South Magnetic Pole was almost upon them, every man was filled with a sense of near-biblical awe. No human being had ever reached this spot; it was the clean white sheet of creation for which McCormick had prayed.

On 11 January they sighted an outline through the haze. It was lost for an hour or two, but eventually re-emerged as a mountain. It became clear that, as McCormick recorded, 'we had discovered a land of so extensive a coastline and attaining such altitude as to justify the appellation of a Great New Southern Continent'.[36] The land was still 100 miles distant, by Ross's calculations. But as he pressed on to the south-west he discovered a lump of rock rising from the sea at 71° 56' south, 171° 7' east. In the full dress regalia of a Victorian sea captain he took possession of it in the name of his monarch. And so, with a ceremony conducted knee-deep in guano, amidst knee-high hordes of yattering penguins – D'Urville would have appreciated the scene – Possession Island became the first territory claimed for Britain in the name of Queen Victoria.

Soon Ross was bestowing names like confetti. The first summit they had seen on the 11th became Mount Sabine. Rounding a headland – Cape Adare – he sighted an enormous chain of mountains, up to 10,000 feet high, which he called Admiralty Range, each peak being honoured with one of their Lordships' names. Another range was immortalized as 'eminent philosophers of the Royal Society and British Association'.[37] A cape bearing a curious, conical hill was called Barrow. Government ministers, the expedition's officers, Ross's fiancée (a cape), his prospective father-in-law (the island to which the cape belonged) and even his fiancée's uncle (another cape on the same island) entered the charts.

By Saturday 23 January they were at 74° 23', further south than any man had been before. Extra grog was served to the popular toast 'sweethearts and wives', and to less familiar ones 'further south still' and 'the discovery of the magnetic pole'. On Tuesday the Magnetic Pole was only 174 miles away. On Wednesday it was seventeen miles nearer and Hooker nearly killed himself landing on Franklin Island, the latest piece of rock to swell Her Majesty's dominion. On Thursday the Magnetic Pole was nearer still. But on that day they saw something which drove the Pole from their minds.

At 10 a.m. McCormick's 'attention was arrested by what appeared to be a fine snowdrift, driving from the summit of a lofty crater-shaped peak . . . As we made a nearer approach, however, this apparent snowdrift resolved itself into a dense column of smoke, intermingled with flashes of red flame.'[38] Here, at the bottom of the world, surrounded by ice and snow, they had found a live volcano. Nothing, truly, could have been more astonishing.

Rising 12,400 feet into the air, the volcano was christened Mount Erebus. Connected to it by a saddle of ice was a dormant cousin of 10,900 feet, which became Mount Terror. Another small island was sighted, but nobody bothered to claim it. They merely gave it the name Beaufort and left it in peace.

The situation of these two ships, their 128 officers and crew, their diminishing flock of sheep and their pet goat Billy, floating in conditions of utter strangeness, thousands of miles from a homeland which

they might never see again, was encapsulated by Hooker in an
eloquent letter to his father:

> The sun never setting, among huge bergs, the water and sky as
> blue, or rather more intensely blue than I have ever seen it in
> the Tropics, and all the coast one mass of beautiful peaks of
> snow, and when the sun gets low they reflect the most
> beautiful tints of gold and yellow and scarlet, and then to see
> the dark cloud of smoke tinged with flame rising from the
> Volcano in one column, one side jet black and the other
> reflecting the colours of the sun, turning off at a right angle by
> some current of wind and extending many miles to leeward; it
> is a sight far exceeding anything I could imagine and which is
> very much heightened by the idea that we have penetrated
> farther than was once thought practicable, and there is a
> certain awe that steals over us all in considering our own total
> insignificance and helplessness.[39]

The totality of their insignificance was underlined when they
sailed east of the volcanoes – which were, though Ross had no way of
telling this, on an island rather than the mainland – and saw yet
another astonishing sight, in its way even more breathtaking than the
first: a perpendicular wall of ice rising three times the height of their
masts and extending to the east for as far as they could see.

For some time now they had been aware of the ice blink, a cold,
white line which illuminated the horizon, caused by the sun's rays
bouncing off a mass of ice to the south. Now they met its source: the
Ross Ice Shelf – Ross himself, being an explorer, called it the Barrier –
the largest ice floe in the world, comprising a 1,000-foot drop of ice of
which only 15–20 per cent showed above water. Ross's blacksmith and
armourer, Isaac Savage, a man of poetic bent, dictated his impres-
sions to a more literate mess-mate, C. J. Sullivan:

> All hands . . . Came on Deck to view this the most rare and
> magnificent Sight that Ever the human Eye witnessd Since

the world was created actually Stood Motionless for Several
Seconds before he Could Speak to the next man to him.

Beholding with Silent Surprize the great and wonderful
works of nature in this position we had an opportunity to
discern the barrier in its Splendid position. Then i wishd i was
an artist or a draughtsman instead of a blacksmith and
Armourer. We Set a Side all thought of Mount Erebus . . . to
bear in mind the more Imaginative thoughts of this rare
Phenomena that was lost to human view

In Gone by Ages[40]

When Captain Ross came on deck he was equally surprised 'to see the
Beautiful Sight. Though being in the north Arctic Regions one half
his life he never seen any ice in the Arctic Seas to be compard to the
Barrier.'[41]

Ross was not only surprised but also very disappointed. The Barrier
was 'perfectly flat at the top and without any fissures or promontories
on its even seaward face. What was beyond it we could not imagine . . . It was, however, an obstruction of such a character as to leave
no doubt upon my mind as to our future proceedings, for we might as
well sail through the cliffs of Dover as penetrate such a mass . . . It
would be impossible to conceive a more solid-looking mass of ice; not
the smallest appearance of any rent or fissure could we discover
throughout its whole extent, and the intensely bright sky beyond it
but too plainly indicated the great distance to which it reached to the
southward.'[42] At 4 p.m. they turned to follow the Barrier. Mount
Erebus, still visible to the west, erupted in spectacular farewell.

Two weeks and 250 miles later the Barrier showed no signs of
diminishing. If anything it seemed taller and more impenetrable than
before. They discovered a point at which it sank to an unusually low
height of fifty feet, which allowed Ross to climb his mast and survey
the interior. All he saw was an 'immense plain of frosted silver'[43]
reaching in all directions. By now the short Antarctic summer was
coming to an end. Young ice was forming between the consolidated
pack and the Barrier. Even with their stores and the quantities of

penguins and seals available, not to mention the whales, who 'had hitherto enjoyed a life of tranquillity beyond the reach of their persecutors', Ross wrote with melancholy foresight, 'but would soon be made to contribute to the wealth of our country',[44] they could not risk overwintering in the Antarctic. Whereas the Arctic had offered a glimmer of hope, here there was none. No land birds, no salmon, no polar bears, no deer – only the strange, oily creatures that lived in these frozen seas. The crews had already chewed their way through tons of cabbage and carrots and no matter how closely penguin soup resembled that of hare, the average seaman was more interested in fresh beef. Moreover, how could Ross be sure that they would escape a winter in the Antarctic? He had spent four years in the ice a decade previously and was lucky to be alive. Was he going to risk another such ordeal in seas which, as far as he knew, might have opened by a freak and which could close behind him forever?

On 9 February Ross reversed his course, hauling northward at the same time. By 15 February he was back at Franklin Island, in time to see Erebus give a contemptuous belch of fire. The sea was freezing fast. It was time to go home.

22

'YOU SEE HOW OUR HANDS SHAKE?'

Their exit through the consolidated pack was not as easy as their entry. The wind fell at noon on 7 March, leaving them at the mercy of a strong swell that drove them towards a long wall of bergs 'so closely packed together that we could distinguish no gaps through which the ships could pass; the waves breaking violently against them, dashed huge masses of pack ice against the precipitous faces of the bergs, now lifting them nearly to their summit, now forcing them again far beneath their waterline, and sometimes rending them into a multitude of brilliant fragments against their projecting points'.[1]

Initially Ross was unperturbed. But as the hours dragged by, with no sign of a wind, he became more anxious. By 8 p.m. they were within half a mile of the bergs. 'The roar of the surf . . . and the crashing of ice, fell upon the ear with fearful distinctness, whilst the frequently averted eyes as immediately returned to contemplate the awful destruction that threatened in one short hour to close the world and all its hopes and joys and sorrows upon us for ever.'[2] All they could do was pray to the Almighty. Luckily, their prayers were answered and, at the last moment, a feeble breeze sprang up and by putting on full sail they were able to escape.

By 8 March they were free of the pack. Under a full moon, with the aurora australis billowing in the sky, they headed for Tasmania. Just to satisfy his curiosity Ross turned westward and spent an enjoyable few days sailing over Wilkes Land. Where Wilkes had marked a chain of mountains Ross found himself in open sea so deep that 600 fathoms of line were unable to touch bottom. The American had clearly been deceived by refraction, as John Ross had been in Lancaster Sound – and, in fact, as James Ross had been in the Antarctic: beyond the Barrier he had marked a range which he called Parry Mountains; they stayed on the map for sixty-three years until it was discovered they were no more than a few islands which had been raised into the sky by mirage – but Ross was not willing to tread lightly when it came to a man who had 'forestalled' him. Nor was Isaac Savage, who was touched by the muse when he learned what was happening.

> Like the lying yankey who made his boast
> he Saw high land & reached no Coast
> when we returned from Seventy Eight
> a hundred miles Each way we beat
> But Low the land the yankeys See
> was Sunk and Gone neath the Sea.[3]

The rest of the journey passed smoothly and, shortly after midnight on 6 April, Ross slipped into the Derwent River. The pilot came aboard at 9 a.m. the following morning and a little after noon they were being greeted by Franklin aboard his governor's barge.

The expedition had been an unqualified success. Ross had discovered new lands, had travelled further south than any man before him and had debunked Wilkes Land while simultaneously stamping his own name firmly on the map. Above all he had found a way through the consolidated pack. And throughout his odyssey he had not lost a single man either to accident or scurvy. It was a tremendous feat of which he was rightly proud and when the ships had been resupplied and refitted he intended to go back for another stab at the Magnetic Pole. But amidst the excitement he had not forgotten the expedition's main purpose: magnetic investigation. In Hobart he reapplied himself to this dreary task.

For Franklin the task was far from dreary. It was a welcome relief from local concerns. While Ross had been away his fortunes had taken a turn for the worse. His wife had travelled tirelessly across the island, compiling information about anything which caught her eye, be it the price of sheep or the habits of the white macaw. The colonial press, meanwhile, had equally tirelessly denigrated her – 'puffed up with the love of fame and the desire of acquiring a name by doing what no one else does'[4] read one comment. Franklin himself was considered even more indecisive and feeble than he had been before and powerful enemies, headed by Montagu, the Colonial Secretary, were gathering against him.

Matters would become worse still in due course. But for the moment Franklin shrugged off his administrative concerns and busied himself helping Ross erect his portable observatories alongside the permanent one he had put up previously – which was now called, thanks to Lady Jane, Rossbank. The sad truth was that Franklin would do anything rather than face his angry subjects. While Ross had been away he had attended the observatory as if it was a place of worship, spending all his free hours there. As Sophie Cracroft, Lady Jane's niece, reported, 'He is so much interested in Terrestrial Magnetism that nothing could give him greater relaxation.'[5]

During their furlough Ross and his officers travelled over the island, collecting new specimens and casting an inquisitive eye on anything they met, from the fossilized wood of Derwent Valley to the convict settlements of Port Arthur.

On 3 May their presence was celebrated at the Royal Victoria Theatre by 'an entirely new nautical Drama entitled the SOUTH POLAR EXPEDITION'.[6] 'In Act 2, will be introduced a splendid view of the VOLCANIC MOUNTAIN, named by the distinguished navigators *Mount Erebus* . . . And in the last scene will be represented a Grand ALLEGORICAL TABLEAU of Science crowning the distinguished Navigators Captains Ross and Crozier at the command of Britannia, and Fame proclaiming their success to the world. To conclude with the romantic Drama (which was received with such unbounded applause) entitled the ROBBER OF THE RHINE.'[7]

Ross returned the compliment a month later, by holding a ball on the *Erebus* and *Terror* which had been lashed together and roofed over with canvas. It was one of the most magnificent events the colony had ever witnessed. Guests – each officer was allowed to invite ten friends – approached on a 300-yard driveway which had been cut through the surrounding woods and entered via a dark, covered bridge of boats swathed in flags and leafy branches at the end of which marines stood at attention to welcome them into the bright lights of the ballroom. The resident 51st Regiment provided music, along with the Hobart Town Quadrille Band, and the party lasted till dawn. Sophia Cracroft wrote, 'the ball on board the *Erebus* and *Terror* on the 1st of June far eclipsed anything else that has taken place in Van Diemen's Land. We danced in the *Erebus*, and the *Terror* was the supper room. 350 persons were present and all sat down to supper together. You would not have fancied yourself in ships for they were so beautifully arranged with flags and flowers. There were 250 looking glasses (which were brought out for the natives of the islands they visit) arranged round the sides of the ship and reflected the lights beautifully. The chandeliers were formed of swords and had a very pretty effect . . . I had the honour of dancing with both Captain Ross and Captain Crozier. I told Captain Crozier that while I was dancing with him the morning of your birthday was dawning. He said he was very sorry that you were not there dancing too!'[8]

For many years after the event was referred to as 'the Glorious First of June'. In the immediate aftermath Franklin's home was besieged by officers bringing 'specimens of granite, albatrosses' eggs and different things from the South . . .' with which they hoped to impress the womenfolk. The most assiduous visitor was Crozier, who had taken a shine to Miss Cracroft. But alas, as he later discovered, she had eyes only for James Ross.

By the end of June the ships were ready for their next stab at Antarctica. They departed on 7 July, their holds stuffed with three years' worth of provisions and another two jars of Lady Jane's jam. Before they entered the ice they had first of all to discharge their magnetic obligations. This entailed a trip to Sydney where Ross, unable to set up his observatories on his preferred station, Macquarie Island, because it was packed with guns and artillery balls, had to make do with the lesser Garden Island.

On 5 August Ross and Crozier sailed again, this time via New Zealand, where they erected more observatories and encountered one J. H. Aucklick, previously an officer in Wilkes's squadron but now commanding the American navy sloop *Yorktown*. Ross took the opportunity to despatch a letter to Wilkes stating that Wilkes Land did not exist and sailed on feeling that a good job had been well done.

Ross's satisfaction was only slightly spoiled when, after a three-day exploration of the interior, he returned to find a French corvette anchored not far from *Erebus*. To his chagrin its commander, Captain Leviche, was able to give him far better maps of the Chatham Islands – Ross's next stop south – than he already possessed. When Ross eventually sailed on 23 November his pride prevented him from stopping at the Chathams.

This time Ross had decided to attack further west, down the 146th meridian. It was a longer journey than the first. On 15 December the expedition met its first icebergs. By Christmas they were embedded in the consolidated pack. They celebrated the day with 'good old English fare, which we had taken care to preserve for the occasion'.[9] And after another six days, on New Year's Eve, they celebrated in the same fashion, but a little differently. The two ships were moored in the middle of the pack either side of a great floe. As McCormick recorded, 'This being the last day of the old year, great preparations have been in progress all day upon the piece of ice forming a fender between the two ships . . . A Quadrangular space has been excavated in the ice for a dance, albeit a somewhat novel kind of ball-room. On this an elevated chair of the same material has been constructed for the accommodation of both captains: adjacent to this crystal ballroom a refreshment-room has also been cut out, with a table carved in the centre for bottles of wine and grog-glasses for the use of the dancers.

The whole of this sculptured ice almost rivals in hardness and white-ness the finest Carrara marble.'[10]

Meanwhile Hooker and Davis, second master on the *Erebus*, carved a Grecian statue to oversee proceedings – a 'figure of a woman which we called our "Venus de Medici" – she was made sitting down and about 8 feet long and as the snow froze very hard she remained per-fect till we left the floe'.[11] The boatswains served drinks, the crew danced, the captains sang, and one wily shot opened the New Year by shooting a white petrel and presenting it to Ross. When they left, Hooker's and Davis's ice statue floated northwards. If only D'Urville had been there to find it.

The going was harder this time. On 18 January they were still in the pack and the ice had closed around them so that they were impris-oned within a small circle of open water from which there was no visible escape. The next day the Antarctic showed what it was capable of. A hurricane blew up and the ships were battered remorselessly by blocks of ice weighing several tons which surged up from the foaming sea. 'Soon after midnight,' Ross wrote, 'our ships were involved in an ocean of rolling fragments of ice, hard as floating rocks of granite, which were dashed against them by the waves with so much violence that their masts quivered as if they would fall at every successive blow; and the destruction of the ships seemed inevitable from the tremendous shocks they received.'[12] Hawsers snapped, sails blew away, the copper sheathing was stripped from the *Erebus*'s hull. There was nothing they could do except pray. 'Each of us could only secure a hold, waiting the issue with resignation to the will of Him who alone could bring us through such extreme danger; watching with breathless anxiety the effect of each collision and the vibrations of the tottering masts, expecting every moment to see them give way.'[13]

This was not the triumphant revisit they had envisaged, hardened by their previous experience of the pack. At 2 p.m. on 20 January, after twenty-eight hours of tempest, the storm peaked. But even then Ross could scarcely believe what was happening. 'Although we had been forced many miles deeper into the pack, we could not perceive that the swell had at all subsided, our ships still rolling and groaning amidst the heavy fragments of crushing bergs, over which the ocean rolled its mountainous waves, throwing huge masses upon one another, and then again burying them deep beneath its foaming waters, dashing and grinding them together with fearful violence.'[14] Both ships lost their rudders. In addition, a fire broke out in the *Terror* which was only quenched by flooding the hold to a depth of two feet.

Then, as suddenly as it had arrived, the hurricane departed. The ships were battered but unbowed and at least the storm had done them a favour: it had broken up the ice, allowing them to take shelter behind a chain of bergs while they made repairs. Once again they gave thanks for their reinforced hulls, without which they would have been reduced to matchsticks. The repairs were completed and on 2 February they broke through the consolidated pack. As Antarctic veterans they were no longer surprised by what they saw. Everything was familiar, even the icebergs – Ross recognized one he had seen on his first trip, a monster that was at least four miles in diameter.

It was colder this time. On 21 February, while the crew were chopping ice off the bows, 'a small fish was found in the mass'.[15] The fish had been thrown up in the spray formed by the *Terror*'s bow. So low was the temperature that it had frozen solid on first contact with the hull. An intrigued Dr Robertson tried to sketch the fish for posterity. But while he was doing so 'it was unfortunately seized upon and devoured by a cat'.[16]

On 22 February they met the Barrier and Ross turned eastward. He sailed marginally further south than before – 78° 11′ at latitude 161° 27′ – but at that point the Barrier veered north and, after a few miles, merged with the consolidated pack. On 24 February Ross gave the order to head north for the Falkland Islands. Even ships like the *Erebus* and *Terror* could not butt their way around Antarctica in the pack. At 7 p.m. after an uneventful passage – give or take the odd gale – they crossed the Antarctic Circle and headed for Cape Horn.

Theoretically it should have been an easy journey. But out of sight was not out of mind as far as the Antarctic was concerned. As if in revenge for being violated it dealt Ross a final blow. On 12 March, in what should have been clear seas, the barometer began to sink, the sea took on a sullen aspect and by the afternoon, as snow fell, it became clear that there were bergs in the vicinity. That night at 1 a.m. a massive, slab-like mountain of ice loomed in front of *Erebus*. Ross reefed sails and turned his ship to avoid it. Unfortunately he turned his ship directly into the path of *Terror* which had either not seen, or been unaware of, the danger and still had her sails on.

The *Terror* ploughed straight into the *Erebus*. 'The concussion when she struck us,' wrote Ross, 'was such as to throw almost every one off his feet; our bowsprit, foretopmast, and other smaller spars, were carried away.'[17] People sleeping below were shaken brutally awake. 'So sudden was the collision,' recorded McCormick, 'that there was scant time for dressing, and an officer might have been seen clinging to the capstan in his nightshirt only.'[18] The two ships, tangled together by their rigging, performed a hideous vertical dance in seas which were worsening by the minute. 'Sometimes she rose high above us,' continued Ross, 'almost exposing her keel to view, and again descended as we in turn rose to the top of the wave, threatening to bury her beneath us, whilst the crashing of the breaking upperworks and boats increased the horror of the scene.'[19]

Eventually they wrenched apart, but *Erebus* was completely disabled. Moreover, the single berg had emerged as the forerunner of a chain of similar behemoths between whom there was only one clear route – that between the first berg and its neighbours. Tangled under a wreckage of spars, unable to make sail, and being driven ever closer to the bergs, the *Erebus*'s only hope was to use the dangerous and often ineffective remedy of a sternboard – going astern with a reversed helm and hoping that the bow swung around to circle them out of danger. Hazardous enough at the best of times, the manoeuvre was made even more fraught by the fact that Ross not only had to twirl the *Erebus* out of danger but time his movements so that it slipped bow-first through the one available passage in the chain of ice.

When Ross gave his order spray was already dashing over him from the frozen cliffs ahead. As he later wrote, 'nothing could justify [such a manoeuvre] during such a gale and with so high a sea running'. It was 'an expedient that perhaps had never before been resorted to by

seamen in such weather'.[20] But it was his only chance. The men mon-
keyed up the rigging and released the sails. Below them the lower
yard-arms brushed against ice.

It was three-quarters of an hour before they had everything ready,
during which time all that kept them from destruction was the under-
tow of water striking the berg and washing them those valuable few
feet out. By a miracle they scraped past the berg. But then came the
difficulty of forging the pass. They were heading, stern-first, for the
adjoining berg. Everyone feared that their move had been mistimed
and that they would be dashed against the ice. There was nothing that
could be done at this point. All they could do was wait while the
ship's bow swung slowly round. Abernethy the ice-master lay flat on
the ice-plank protruding from the bow, ready to shout directions. Ross
stood, arms folded, on the afterpart of the quarterdeck, the epitome of
fearlessness. The gap through which the *Erebus* must pass was only
three times the ship's own breadth. He was as petrified as a British
naval captain could be. 'His whole bearing,' wrote McCormick, 'whilst
lacking nothing in firmness, yet betrayed both in the expression of his
countenance and attitude, the all-but despair with which he anxiously
watched the result of this last and only expedient left to us in the
awful position we were placed in . . . But for the howling of the winds,
and the turmoil of the roaring waters, the falling of a pin might have
been heard on the *Erebus*'s deck, so silent and awestruck stood our
fine crew in groups around, awaiting the result.'[21]

Thanks to Ross's superb seamanship and Abernethy's desperate
signals they made it. They slipped between 'two perpendicular walls
of ice . . . and the next moment we were in smooth water'.[22] The
Terror, which had skirted the bergs undamaged, was waiting for them,
a lamp shining on its masthead.

It had been the most terrifying moment of any trip Ross had ever
made. In the lee of the bergs Ross inspected the damage, which was
worse than he had feared. Not only had his sails and masts been
destroyed but the *Erebus*'s bow anchor had been driven into its hull,
puncturing wood and copper sheathing alike.

During the emergency Ross had been amazed – and gratified – by 'the daring spirit of the British seaman'[23] as they rushed to obey his orders in the face of collision. Those same seamen now showed their worth by mending the masts and sails – there was nothing they could do about the anchor, whose fluke remained embedded for the rest of the voyage – and three days afterwards they were back on course. They navigated Cape Horn and by 6 April were at Port Louis on the Falkland Islands with only one casualty: the *Erebus*'s quartermaster, who fell off the main yard and was drowned on 2 April as they were approaching the Cape.

All in all, they had accomplished little. They had gone slightly further south, but had mapped only ten degrees of new Barrier; they had narrowly escaped death and had lost a man. When the Governor of the Falklands welcomed them ashore they were feeling the strain. Physically they were all well enough. As Crozier later boasted they only opened their medicine chests once in four years, and then only to treat a cut hand. Psychologically, however, the expedition was fracturing.

The fissures started at the top. Imperturbable as he may have appeared at the helm, and urbane as he was in normal society, Ross was still his uncle's nephew, with a quick temper and harsh words for any who disputed his judgement. At times McCormick had found him impossible to deal with, 'so strong were his prejudices, and . . . so difficult [was he] to reason with'.[24] Ross knew better than to let his stormy side interfere overmuch with the expedition's purpose, but in the relative tranquillity of the Falklands he allowed his anger to boil over. The Governor, a man named Moody, was at the receiving end. As Hooker recorded, 'they quarrelled most grievously, so that I was often unpleasantly situated'.[25] What on earth they can have found to quarrel about is a mystery. (Hooker himself got on well with Moody, who gave him the run of his library, and the two became 'great chums'.)[26] But quarrel they did.

Hooker himself fell foul of Ross over the question of whether or not the expedition's findings should be sent home ahead of them. Ross was against it. Hooker, the eager young man on the make, was all for it. He reasoned in a letter to his father: '[Ross] seems to wish all the news to come home with him, to astonish the world like a thunder clap; but will find himself much mistaken I fear; 'out of sight, out of mind', and if the knowledge of our proceedings be stifled it will beget indifference, instead of pent-up curiosity, ready to burst out on our firing one gun at Spithead. I do not believe he tells Sabine too much, or his own father.'[27]

Hooker was right. For all its accomplishments Ross's expedition had slipped from the public view. With no news and no clear indication of its objectives, which were no more than a boring set of magnetic observations as far as anyone was aware, the public had no reason to be concerned with the expedition's fate. Hooker had sent a few bulletins home to his father – against Ross's orders – but these had been shown only to Queen Victoria and the Prince Consort (who expressed polite interest). The popular feeling was that 'Ross will deserve a peerage if he gets to the Pole.'[28] But nobody knew if he had got anywhere near it.

There were other disagreements too. McCormick had taken a violent dislike to Lieutenant Sibbald of the *Erebus* who had roused his anger by not lowering a boat when McCormick wanted to go collecting – 'our automaton first lieutenant', he called him, 'whose prestige, if he has any at all, is more for holy-stoning decks in his morning watch'.[29] The general malaise that hung over the expedition was not improved when promotions arrived for Crozier and Bird but not for the other officers. Those who had not been promoted felt slighted. What reward was coming their way? (Hooker had been elected a member of the Linnaean Society in his absence but was unaware of the fact.) Many seamen were ready to jump ship. Rumours spread that the Falklands – which Hooker described as more dreadful than Kerguelen Island – had been chosen as a deliberately unpleasant revictualling station to prevent men deserting.

The Falklands were, indeed, very unpleasant and they stewed there for five months. The colony was pitifully neglected, with only seventy inhabitants, twenty of whom were government officials and four of whom were a stranded missionary family bound for Patagonia as soon as the means of getting there presented itself. In previous years it had enjoyed a community of South American gauchos, but they had long gone, leaving their cattle to roam wild across the tussocky countryside. Farming was conducted at subsistence level, and there were not enough fresh vegetables to supply Ross's mess with more than one serving per day. The listless populace depended on supplies sent out from Britain, but as these had been unaccountably delayed, they were short of most foods when Ross's ships dropped anchor. Ironically, Ross found himself having to provision his would-be provisioners from the stocks he had stowed at Hobart. The settlement, Ross wrote disappointedly, was 'rather retrograding'.[30]

A ship eventually reached Port Louis on 23 June, bringing as well as stores a new bowsprit for the *Erebus* and taking with it McMurdo, the first lieutenant of the *Terror*, who had fallen ill and was considered too weak to continue. By this time Ross had virtually taken over the colony. His men built a new pier and a small warehouse for ships' stores, which was used for the overhauling of the *Erebus*. He and Crozier surveyed the main island and reported that Port William rather than Port Louis was the better harbour – as testimony to their findings Port William later became Stanley, capital of the Falklands. Hooker roamed across the hills collecting as many specimens as he could. A temporary observatory was set up, in which the officers all took turns at recording magnetic measurements. And McCormick led hair-raising hunting parties into the interior, which left him with an abiding respect for feral cattle. They were vicious, with sharp horns, skin that was up to two inches thick, and displayed no fear of humans. One man who tripped and fell escaped goring by sheer chance, the earth on either side of him being ripped up by the horns of a bull who had misjudged his angle of attack.

The magnetic observations were completed on 4 September. Four days later Ross set out for Tierra del Fuego where the next set of measurements were to be taken. Everyone was relieved to be back at sea. 'Not one individual in either ship,' Ross wrote, felt 'the smallest regret on leaving the Falkland Islands.'[31] By the 19th they were at Hermite Island, being greeted by three Fuegans who watched with amusement as the sailors put up another observatory. When not

watching they did a bit of constructive pilfering. And when neither
watching nor pilfering they allowed the sailors to powder their hair
with flour and teach them to dance a hornpipe. 'The most degraded
savages that I ever set eyes upon,'[32] recorded Hooker.

On 17 December the two ships departed for what would be their
last stab at the Antarctic. This, their third attempt, was for once
uneventful. Sailing down the 55th meridian, through shoals of whales
so tame that they had to nudge them aside, they entered the South
Shetlands where they charted what is now called James Ross Island,
with its 7,000-foot hill, Mt. Haddington, and on 5 January claimed
Cockburn Island for Britain where the ever-eager Hooker 'procured
the ghosts of eighteen Cryptogamic plants'.[33] Here they were overtaken by the pack, which did not release them until 4 February by
which time they had lost much of the season and were only at 64° 0′
south. Ross turned to the east, following the pack, but did not
penetrate the Antarctic Circle until 29 February. By the time he
reached 71° 30′ south, 14° 51′ west on 5 March it was time to head
back.

The Antarctic saw them off with a gale which buffeted them from
all sides with changing winds for four days, save for a six-hour period
when they found themselves in the eye of the storm. On 4 April Ross
dropped anchor at Simon's Bay, South Africa, for a three-week rest
before he set off back to Britain. Here, with the end in sight, they
crumbled. Everyone fell ill. They felt the heat intensely, even though
it was the Cape winter. Ross and Crozier were nervous wrecks, quivering so badly that they could hardly hold a glass or cup. 'You see how
our hands shake?' Ross told the local admiral's daughter. 'One night in
the Antarctic did this for both of us.'[34]

By 13 May he was at St Helena, twelve days later he was at
Ascension Island and on 18 June he landed at Rio de Janeiro to complete his final magnetic observation. By 5 September he was at
Folkestone where he travelled immediately to London to be greeted
by 'my highly valued friends, Admiral Beaufort and Sir John Barrow'.[35]
When *Erebus* and *Terror* were paid off at Woolwich on 23 September
1843, their crews had been travelling for four and a half years.

For this, the last major voyage of exploration made solely under sail, Ross was duly rewarded. Awaiting his return were both the Founder's Medal of the Royal Geographical Society and the Gold Medal of the Royal Geographical Society of Paris. The following year he was given a knighthood and was awarded an honorary degree from Oxford University. But in his own mind he had failed. In his trunk, unpacked, lay the flag he had flown at the North Magnetic Pole. When he had set sail his intention had been to fly it at the South Magnetic Pole. He had not done so. Set against his astonishing achievements in leadership, planning and discovery lay this accusing scrap of ten-year-old cloth.

Ross was through. The journey had taken more out of him than he had expected. Now, with a knighthood and his new wife, Ann Coulman – her father had given permission for them to marry on the condition that Ross undertake no more polar voyages; a contract with which one suspects Ross did not quibble – he retired to a house near Aylesbury and became a country gentleman.

Interest in the Antarctic died with Ross's expedition. Britain had discovered all it needed to know about the continent, viz. that it was cold, useless and there – very much as Cook had predicted – and for more than half a century it was left in peace. In 1905, however, when Antarctica became once again the focus of international rivalry, Ross's expedition received an intriguing footnote.

In that year Hooker was still alive – just; he would die in 1911 aged ninety-four. His advice as the only man living who had journeyed so far south was sought by Captain Robert Falcon Scott, who was planning an expedition to the South Pole. 'I remember that it was quite news to me,' wrote Scott in reply to a letter from Hooker, 'to hear from you that Ross was coldly received on his return. At first it seems inexplicable when one considers how highly his work is now appreciated . . . I have always thought that Ross was neglected, and as you once said he is very far from doing himself justice in his book. I did not know that Barrow was the *bête noire* who did so much to discount Ross's results. It is an interesting sidelight on such a venture.'[36]

Perhaps Hooker was confusing uncle and nephew. He was eighty-eight at the time. Perhaps Barrow was confused. He was seventy-nine when Ross returned and, as the Rosses' biographer claims, 'might not have been able to tell one Ross from another'.[37] Perhaps Scott himself was confused. Whatever the answer, it provides a lingering echo of arguments long forgotten and in the ultimate failure of Scott's own venture a revisiting of Barrow's last gasp: the 'conquest' of the North-West Passage by Sir John Franklin.

23

THE LAST POST

While James Ross had been hurdling the Antarctic Circle, John Franklin had suffered grievously. His situation in Van Diemen's Land had deteriorated thanks to the machinations of John Montagu, his Colonial Secretary.

Montagu was a slithery character. After an inauspicious childhood, marked by 'a disregard for truthfulness which had for some time rendered his mother extremely anxious on his behalf',[1] he had joined the army, fought at Waterloo and then had made his way to Van Diemen's Land where he had found a job with the Colonial Office. By the time of Franklin's appointment he had acquired land, money and a great deal of influence.

Montagu disliked Franklin's liberal approach to life, and distrusted his interfering wife. When Franklin reinstated on the urging of others – his wife, mostly – an official whom Montagu had previously dismissed, matters came to a head. Montagu wrote a note to Franklin in which he all but called him a deceitful weakling. Franklin sacked him and wrote a report on Montagu's behaviour which he despatched on the next ship home. With it went Montagu, spitting and cursing. 'I'll *sweat* him,' swore the offended man. 'I'll persecute him as long as I live.'[2]

Behind him he left a vociferous body of supporters whose opinions coloured the Tasmanian press. 'The Imbecile Reign of the Polar Hero',[3] sneered the Cornwall *Chronicle*. The *Colonial Times* blamed Lady Jane. 'If ladies will mix in politics they throw from themselves the mantle of protection which as females they are fully entitled to.'[4] The knives were out and Franklin, quavering with the best will in the world from indecision to review, received them all.

The final stab came when Montagu caught the ear of Lord Stanley, the Secretary of State for the Colonies. Stanley not only supported Montagu but sent a ringing rebuke to Franklin and, in a terrible breach of etiquette, gave a copy to Montagu. Hardly able to believe his good fortune, Montagu sent it to Tasmania with a package of other material which would further his cause. The copy arrived in Tasmania before Stanley had even posted the original. Included in the package was a 300-page letter in Montagu's defence, which described Franklin among other things as 'a perfect imbecile'.[5] The evidence was stored in a Hobart bank where a select few were permitted to read it. Franklin, of course, was not among those few. But gossip ensured that he had no need to be. Before long anyone who mattered in Tasmania knew what Montagu's papers contained.

Franklin was doomed. On 18 June 1843 a ship arrived with an English newspaper. Tucked away in columns of print was the announcement that Franklin was to be replaced as governor. 'GLORIOUS NEWS!'[6] yelled a Hobart headline. It was another two months before Franklin received official confirmation of his dismissal. But by then he no longer needed confirmation. His replacement had landed three days before. When, on 12 January 1844, Sir John and Lady Franklin left Tasmania for ever, 2,000 people cheered them off. One would like to think some of them did so with regret.

During the journey home Franklin had time to review his prospects. They were bleak. Unlike Parry, who had sailed from Australia with his menagerie of parrots and kangaroos ten years previously, Franklin had no influential family to greet him, no guaranteed employment to which he could look forward. He had failed in his task and all that awaited him on his return was the half-pay of a naval captain.

Franklin was desperate for work. First, however, he had to clear his name. Whatever the merits of his dismissal, it had been handled in an outrageously insulting fashion and the entire naval establishment, including Barrow, backed him in his desire for justice. He demanded an apology from Lord Stanley. It was not forthcoming. He demanded an interview. It yielded nothing. He threatened to publish his account of events. Stanley remained silent. Franklin went ahead. Had he been a Ross we would probably still be reading about it today. But instead of a thunderous barrage of pamphlets, books and affidavits Franklin released a dry, reticent little balloon that floated away almost unnoticed.

Possibly Franklin might have dented Stanley's armour had he pressed his case. But he was not that kind of man. And besides, within four days of completing the preface he was once again on his way to the Arctic.

When Franklin returned from Tasmania, Barrow's reign was drawing to a close. He was now eighty, and although in excellent health he was beginning to feel the strain. It was time to retire. But before he did he wanted to finish the job he had started more than twenty-five years ago.

The North-West Passage was tantalizingly within reach. There remained a mere 200 or so miles of uncharted sea between Barrow Strait and the open water which Dease and Simpson had covered to the south. To give up now would not only be faint-hearted but embarrassing. 'If the completion of the passage be left to be performed by some other power,' Barrow wrote, 'England, by her neglect of it, after having opened the East and West doors, would be laughed at by all the world for having hesitated to cross the threshold.'[7]

The public were for it, Barrow claimed. There were officers who would kill for the privilege of leading it. There were seasoned Arctic sailors aplenty. And, above all, there were two ships, the *Erebus* and *Terror*, fully kitted out for the ice, so further expense in that department would be limited.

As before, Barrow's proposal was conduited through the Royal Geographical Society back to the Admiralty, and professional opinions were sought from experienced Arctic officers. But this time, to avoid interference from Ross and his ilk, the opinions were openly solicited rather than appearing under the cloak of a correspondence. Back, Beaufort, Beechey, Franklin, Parry and James Ross were all in favour of a renewed attempt. And to avoid the slightest dissent from the Admiralty, Barrow submitted their written statements to the Prime Minister, Sir Robert Peel.

The response was predictable. The mission having been approved, the next matter was finding a man to lead it. James Ross was the obvious choice, but he turned the offer down. At forty-four he felt he was too old; moreover, he had promised his wife he would never go on another expedition. Neither of these excuses quite stood up to examination, and he would discard them very happily a few years later, when the opportunity for Arctic sailing once again presented itself. The likely truth, as shown by the limited documentation available (Ross burned his papers before his death), was that he had a slight drink problem. It had first surfaced in South Africa with the shaking hands that he explained away as stress, and as time passed his condition became increasingly apparent.

John Murray, for one, noticed Ross's state. As the delivery of his Antarctic journal was delayed and delayed, Murray reminded him that it could only be published on sale or return and that the sale depended on the book coming out soon. James Ross cursed him roundly, and demanded proper royalties, whereupon Murray asked him to explain a letter, ominously dated 'Saturday Night',[8] in which Ross had not only agreed to sale or return but had also offered to buy fifty copies of his own journal plus other books from Murray's list to the value of £100. No more was heard on the subject.

With James Ross out of the running, who was left? Crozier was a possibility, having years of Arctic experience, but he turned it down – 'in truth I fear I am not equal to the hardship',[9] he told Ross self-deprecatingly. Rumour had it that the mighty Parry would come out of retirement. He had hinted as much to Beaufort. But as Sabine wrote to Ross, 'one can scarcely believe him serious – or that he can seriously meditate such a step . . . but I need scarcely say that that is the only case in which I would unreservedly rejoice in a N.W. expedition of which you are not the leader'.[10]

In the end Parry never did make a bid. So with him out, and with James Ross and Crozier out, that left Sir John Franklin as the most senior of Barrow's men – if one discounted Sir John Ross, as everybody did. Quivering with anticipation and desperate to restore his prestige, Franklin waited for the call. Lady Franklin pressed his cause. 'After being so unworthily treated by the Colonial Office,' she wrote to James Ross, 'I think he will be deeply sensitive if his own department should neglect him, and that such an appointment would do more perhaps to counteract the effect which Lord Stanley's injustice and tyranny have produced. I dread exceedingly the effect on his mind of being without honourable and immediate employment, and it is this which enables me to support the idea of parting with him on a service of difficulty and danger better than I otherwise should.'[11]

James Ross's arguments rolled back on him. Franklin was older than him; and although his wife put a good face on it, she was reluctant to let him go. On the other hand, Franklin was a popular man; he was also Ross's friend. Ross therefore suggested him as the best man for the job.

A shudder ran through the Admiralty. They did sincerely admire Franklin. They respected him and sympathized with him over his recent débâcle with Stanley. But he was plainly too old and too unfit for the job. Barrow was particularly shaken. The man he had in mind if Ross refused the job was an unknown thirty-three-year-old commander called James Fitzjames.

Back, inveigling maybe for his own appointment, asked Ross to reconsider. Ross sent him away with a flea in his ear. Later, Sabine arrived with the news that Beaufort too suggested a rethink. He was despatched forcibly with the message that if Beaufort had anything to say he could say it in person. When Beaufort did so, Ross stuck tetchily to his guns. Franklin was the fellow.

Frantic temptations were dangled in front of Ross. He was offered a baronetcy, a pension and a year's postponement of the mission to give him time to get over his problem. It was all in vain. Nothing could stop Franklin's progress. When Back pressed again, stating that Franklin could not withstand the cold, Dr Richardson came to his friend's defence. 'I shall have no hesitation in signing a certificate stating that I believe your constitution to be perfectly sound,' he told Franklin, 'and your bodily strength sufficient for all the calls that can be made upon it in conducting a squadron even through an icy sea.'[12] Parry, too, supported Franklin. 'If you don't let him go,' he told Lord Haddington, the current First Lord of the Admiralty, 'the man will die of disappointment.'[13] Finally, Franklin was called before Haddington for an interview.

Haddington, mustering all his tact, hinted that Franklin might not be fit enough. Franklin demanded a physical examination at once. The embarrassed First Lord waved his hands and said that he was thinking of mental fitness; Franklin might be too stressed by his recent experiences to go to the North-West Passage. Franklin told him that the stress of the North-West Passage would be nothing compared to life in Tasmania. In desperation, Haddington told him he was too old.

'You are sixty,' he said.

'No, my Lord,' Franklin replied, 'I am only fifty-nine.'

What could Haddington do? On 7 February 1845, Franklin was given command of the expedition.

His instructions were straightforward. He was to sail as far west as was possible, about 95° west. Then, 'from that point we desire that every effort be used to penetrate to the southward and westward in a course as direct towards Bering Strait, as the position and extent of the ice or the existence of land at present unknown, may permit'.[14] And if that didn't work, he was authorized to follow Richardson's hunch and go north up Wellington Channel.

The hammer and din was loud at Deptford when Sir John Ross came over from Stockholm to see what was going on. In a development that must have pleased him he noted that the *Erebus* and *Terror* were being fitted for steam. Although Barrow still distrusted steam power he could not deny its apparent usefulness in the Arctic, and therefore the two ships were kitted out in as up-to-date a fashion as possible. Instead of John Ross's gimcrack apparatus the *Erebus* and its consort were given tried and tested machinery that had already proved its worth – the *Erebus*'s engine was purchased second-hand from the Greenwich Railway – and were fitted not with cumbersome paddles but with innovative screw propellers that could be hoisted out of harm's way when they were in the ice. As well as powering the ships the engines also heated them via a network of twelve-inch-wide pipes that pumped hot air to every corner.

It looked to be a thorough, professional job. Nevertheless, Ross was dismayed by the whole thing. The ships were too large, he told Franklin: their nineteen-foot draught was too great; they carried too many men; and the massive steam machinery, with its coal, weighed them still lower in the water and took up space that could better be filled with food. Ross had struggled with the *Victory*'s nine-foot draught. What could Franklin's ships accomplish with a draught more than twice that?

Ross was so convinced that the expedition would be a failure that he made arrangements with Franklin for its salvage. He instructed him to leave cairns at regular intervals containing notes as to his progress and destination, and advised him to drop caches of food *en route* should he have to walk home as he himself had done. Finally, he offered to lead a rescue party should nothing be heard of the expedition by February 1847. 'Well, Ross,' said Franklin, amused at the older man's fears but not wanting to seem rude, 'you are the only person who has volunteered to search for me and I shall depend upon you.'[15] In private, he laughed it off as an absurdity.

Ross was not alone in slating the mission's odds. Barrow was attacked by at least two magazines, and was rounded upon viciously by Dr Richard King, who was still obsessed by overland travel. 'Had you advocated in favour of Polar Land Journeys with a tithe of the zeal you have the Polar Sea Expeditions the North-West Passage would have long since ceased to be a problem, and, instead of a Baronetcy you would deserve a Peerage, for the country would have been saved at least two hundred thousand pounds,'[16] King stormed. 'If you are really in earnest upon this subject, you have but one course to pursue; search for the truth, and value it when you find it. Another fruitless Polar Sea Expedition, and fruitless it will assuredly be . . . will be a lasting blot in the annals of our voyages of discovery.'[17]

King was absolutely right. And, as before when he had made similar proposals for a land expedition, he was ignored because the Hudson's Bay Company had launched its own. John Rae, a straightforward, practical Orkneyman whose forte was surviving long periods in the wilderness with no provisions at all, was charged with mapping the western coast of Melville Peninsula. Reading between the lines, this harmless task was to lead him, hopefully, to Boothia Felix. The men and women of the Hudson's Bay Company cheered Rae while scoffing at Barrow's laborious, heavyweight sea mission. '[Franklin] expects to meet him,' the Governor's wife wrote to her brother, 'but I believe no one expects such a thing but himself. The people here laugh at the Government part of the matter & think the officers & crew must have been "too hot at home".'[18]

Had King heard this he would have agreed wholeheartedly. But he did not hear it, and having been turned down by Barrow he appealed to Franklin's arch enemy, Lord Stanley, for help. 'Sir John,' he pleaded, 'will have to push through an ice-blocked sea in utter ignorance of the extent of his labours, and in case of difficulty with certainly no better prospects before him than that which befell Sir John Ross, whose escape from a perilous position of four years is admitted by all to have been almost miraculous.'[19] Stanley was as unforthcoming as Barrow. In despair, King published the correspondence, hoping to find support – any support – for his point of view. Franklin was 'being sent to form the nucleus of an iceberg',[20] he told the world.

The world was uninterested. People did not want to hear of their hero departing to inevitable failure. Let him be nipped, pinched, crushed, lifted, lowered, or whatever else went on in the ice. Let him face death, too – the vicarious tingle that had excited society after Franklin's boot-eating odyssey was never far from the surface. All these things could happen – but only when Franklin reached the

Arctic. Until then, King was spoiling things. People were much happier to hear Barrow's statement that 'There can be no objection with regard to any apprehension of loss of ships or men'[21] – or, better still, the rolling words of Sir Roderick Murchison, President of the Royal Geographical Society: 'I have the fullest confidence that everything will be done for the promotion of science, and for the honour of the British name and Navy, that human efforts can accomplish. The name of Franklin alone is, indeed, a national guarantee.'[22] Little did they imagine how gratifyingly Franklin would reward their insouciance.

Franklin's expedition was the last that Barrow would ever send out. He retired from the Admiralty in January 1845, in full confidence that his greatest dream would be realized. (In fact, according to Scoresby, his last act while in office had been to delay Franklin's expedition sufficiently to ruin its chances in the first year.) For almost thirty years he had played the Arctic like a game of patience, turning over chunks of geography, arranging them in orderly lines, and discarding discoveries that did not fit his plan. Now there was only one blank card on the table. When Franklin lifted it all would be revealed and the North-West Passage would fall neatly into place.

Barrow had set it all in motion and there was nothing more he need do. Unfortunately he had miscounted his pack.

24

EREBUS AND *TERROR*

When Franklin's expedition left the Thames on 19 May 1845 it would have cheered a bookie's heart. The ships looked clean and efficient, a wide yellow stripe painted across their black bodies so that they bobbed like chunky hornets on the Thames. The crews were keen and the ice-masters were experts in their trade. They carried three years' provisions which, augmented by hunting and fishing, they hoped might stretch to seven. And all this to cross just a few hundred miles of uncharted water.

Three years' provisions might have seemed excessive for so short a distance. But the food was not meant for the Arctic alone. It was to see them through the North-West Passage and down to the Sandwich Islands, Britain's nearest revictualling station. Barrow calculated that they might not even have to overwinter. The journey would take them a season – as he had predicted for Ross and Buchan in 1818.

The crews, now as in 1818, were hand-picked, according to Barrow – though hand-picked by whom and for what is hard to tell. The ice-masters, Thomas Reid and William Blanky, were good, experienced men. But only two officers other than Franklin had seen Arctic service: Graham Gore, lieutenant on the *Erebus*, who had sailed with Back to Repulse Bay; and Crozier, who had been given command of the *Terror*. The rest seemed to have been chosen at random or, as in the case of Fitzjames who sailed as Franklin's second-in-command on the *Erebus*, by force of patronage. This ran somewhat counter to Barrow's earlier assertion that trained Arctic hands were falling over themselves to enlist.

Their collective lack of experience, however, had no apparent effect on their morale. Indeed, by the time they reached Greenland they were in the highest of spirits, on which Franklin congratulated himself. 'I think perhaps,' he wrote a trifle smugly to his wife, 'that I have the tact of keeping officers and men happily together in a greater degree than [James] Ross, and for this reason: he is evidently ambitious and wishes to do everything himself.'[1]

Franklin was in his element. Like a charming, benevolent uncle, he won everyone's affections. He spun stories of his past experiences, surprising the youngsters with tales of legendary events that had occurred on the other side of the world before they were born. He opened the doors to his 1,700-volume library, dispensing Arctic reference books, novels by Dickens and bound editions of *Punch*. He conducted religious services with profound and regular devotion, and handed out slates to illiterate men who wished to join evening classes.

Twenty years before, he might have been seen as merely pleasant. Now he was viewed as an infallible deity. His officers lounged back with their copies of *Punch*, ate meals off fine porcelain with silver cutlery, and listened to heartening sermons regarding their success. Life was comfortable and failure was impossible. They trusted Franklin implicitly.

They liked him and he liked them. Ice-master Reid was one of Franklin's favourites, so was Fitzjames, and the busy little Gore, bustling about his natural history experiments, was 'a treasure'.[2] Franklin wrote to Parry telling him how envious he should be: 'It would do your heart good to see how zealously the officers and men in both ships are working and how amicably we all work together.'[3]

An unreal *Boy's Own* atmosphere reigned aboard the *Erebus*. 'We are very happy. Never was more so in my life,' Fitzjames wrote. 'You have no idea how happy we all feel – how determined we all are to be frozen and how anxious to be among the ice. I never left England with less regret.'[4] Charles Osmer, Franklin's purser, was almost overcome by the romance of the mission. 'Never, no never shall I forget the emotions called forth by the deafening cheering,' he wrote of their departure. 'The suffocating sob of delight mingled with the fearful anticipation of the dreary void . . . could not but impress on every mind the importance and magnitude of the voyage we have entered upon. There is something so thrilling in the true British cheer.'[5]

Here was the Victorian explorer *par excellence*: a brave, patriotic chap, steadfast but daring, manly but emotional, confident but modest, willing to carry the banner of queen and country to the furthest reaches of the world; ready not only to face the void but to stare it down, and to do so in blind, cheerful ignorance.

On the *Terror*, by contrast, conditions were more sombre. Crozier was still downcast at his rejection by Sophia Cracroft, and carried his gloom into his official duties. 'All goes smoothly,' he wrote to Ross in his ungrammatical fashion, 'but James dear I am sadly alone, not a soul have I in either ship that I can go and talk to "No congenial spirit as it were." I am generally busy but it is a very hermitlike life.'[6] Crozier lacked the other men's confidence in Franklin. The big man, he wrote, was 'very decided in his own views but has not good judgement'. He worried that the expedition would 'blunder into the ice and make a second 1824 out of it'.[7] He also feared, like Scoresby, that they had left too late in the season. 'James I wish you were here,' he wrote to Ross. 'I would then have no doubt as to our pursuing the proper course.'[8] He had a presentiment he would never come back alive.

Franklin had the same presentiment – though it would never be made public until many years later. While preparing for the trip, he had fallen asleep by the fire. In the chair opposite, Lady Jane was sewing a silk Union Jack in the by-now customary way. Playfully, she threw it over his feet. Franklin woke in horror, and warned her never to do it again. In the Royal Navy, the only time a man was wrapped in a Union Jack was when he was dead.

On 26 July 1845, Franklin's ships were spotted by two whalers, waiting for the ice to clear off Lancaster Sound. The whalers reported that they were cheerful, confident and had every expectation of success. Franklin said he could make his supplies spin out for at least five years if he had to.

Neither the *Erebus* nor the *Terror* nor the 133 men aboard them were ever seen again.

Within two years the expedition was destroyed – vaporized would be a better word – by an unknown calamity that sprayed human debris across the dark, unknown heart of the Arctic. In decades to come, explorers would pick wonderingly through the bundles of cloth, whitened bones, personal articles, stacks of supplies and scraps of wood that comprised the remains of the best-equipped Arctic fleet to have left England's shores. Two of Franklin's men were eventually found. They lay in a boat drawn up on the shore, with loaded muskets and a small supply of food by their sides. One, obviously an officer, wore a fur coat. Their skeletal grins gave no answer to a question that would burn for more than 150 years.

On 9 February 1847, true to his word, John Ross marched into Whitehall clutching a sheaf of maps and documents. He was ready, he announced, to rescue his friend Franklin. Word was passed to the Admiralty Board, which was then in session. A harried officer came out, took Ross's message, and went back inside. A few minutes later a head came round the door. No rescue expedition was being contemplated at the present. The head withdrew and the door closed behind it.

Ross was mortified. He tried again, incorporating into his outline the tempting idea of a sledge journey to the North Pole once the rescue had been accomplished. It was planned to the smallest detail, right down to the shop in Trondheim where the expedition should buy its winter clothes. The result was the same.

Dr King also proposed a rescue party, travelling overland down the Great Fish River to explore the western coast of Boothia where he was convinced Franklin would be. He never received a reply.

Throughout that spring and summer the Admiralty maintained its position. 'I do not think there is the smallest reason of apprehension or anxiety for the safety and success of the expedition under the command of Sir John Franklin,'[9] James Ross wrote on 2 March. He was supported by Barrow, Sabine, Back, Beechey, Parry, Richardson and all the other Arctic luminaries. Only Beaufort had a niggling suspicion that all might not be well. 'Though I would not let a whisper of anxiety escape from me,' he told James Ross, 'one must perceive that if he be not forthcoming by *next* winter, some substantive steps must be taken in 1848 – and for that step certain measures must be set on foot in 1847.'[10] Interestingly, this letter had been written in January, before John Ross had started agitating for a rescue. Apparently Beaufort's doubts were later soothed.

After all, what was the cause for worry? Franklin had been away only two winters and had supplies, as he had stated, for another three. If John Ross had survived four years in the Arctic Franklin could last as long if not longer.

John Ross was furious at his rejection. He was even angrier when Parry, Sabine, Richardson and James Ross voiced doubts that he had ever brought the subject of rescue to Franklin's attention. 'I am not surprised that the former (particularly Sir James Ross) whose hostility to me has long been notorious, should attempt to cast doubts on the veracity of my statements,'[11] he fumed in a letter to the Admiralty. 'These gentlemen would treat whatever emanated from me as an "absurdity".'[12] Behind it he saw the hand of his old enemy. 'I beg leave to state that it was *not* uncommon for Sir John Barrow to withhold from the Board to which he was secretary, any Communication creditable to me and if Sir John Franklin mentioned to him my suggestion, that was quite sufficient for its omission.'[13]

Undeterred, John Ross approached the Marquis of Nottingham, President of the Royal Society. 'You will go and get frozen in like Franklin, and we shall have to send after you!'[14] was Nottingham's retort. As a gesture, however, he agreed to consult experts on the matter. The experts, of course, were the Admiralty cabal who thought there was no need for a rescue expedition and so the door was again shut in Ross's face.

John Ross thrived on this kind of confrontation. He spent the rest of the year pestering every important organization in London, down to the British Association for the Advancement of Science. At the same time he was mustering affidavits for a resounding rebuttal of Barrow's derogatory *Voyages*, which had come out the year before. Meanwhile James Ross was putting in readiness the very mission which he had so publicly pooh-poohed. On 8 November he announced his willingness to 'take command of any expedition their Lordships may contemplate sending to the relief of . . . Captain Sir John Franklin'.[15] He was accepted a month later.

When John Ross heard how he had been outmanoeuvred, he congratulated the Admiralty on their choice. His nephew, he wrote with double-edged significance, 'was a very clever man'.[16] Privately, however, he thought James Ross's expedition was all wrong. His nephew wanted to take two heavy steam ships, like Franklin's, to scour the inlets off Barrow Strait. John Ross wanted him to take a flotilla of four smaller ships – if Franklin's ships had got bogged down, he reasoned, a similarly heavy expedition would suffer the same fate. Then, because he suspected Barrow's collusion in the enterprise, John Ross suggested it was not a rescue mission at all, merely an excuse to have another go at the North-West Passage.

Ross may have been right in his assertion. But in making it he was descending to the same level as Barrow. Had not Ross himself proposed a similar venture with the North Pole as its goal? His mean-spiritedness did him little credit.

In 1848, William Scoresby recorded the first display of electric street lighting. A large bulb was set up in the colonnades of the National Gallery, with a mirror behind and a lens before. The result was stupendous: by the light of this proto-searchlight, which flung the shadow of Nelson's Column across Trafalgar Square and beyond, it was possible to read the small print in a newspaper while standing as far away as Parliament Street.

It was fitting that Scoresby should record this event because it marked the end of an era that he had, partly, set in motion. When he had first agitated for a voyage to the North-West Passage, the world had been a completely different place. Back in 1817, London's streets had been lit by sputtering globes of whale oil – supplied by Scoresby; the swiftest means of public transport was the stagecoach; and the only way of communicating over long distances was by letter. In matters scientific Sir Joseph Banks ruled supreme and the globe was an untouched mystery.

Now, that was all gone. Gas lights were everywhere and electricity would soon be commonplace. Steam locomotives snaked across the country, belching steam and hot ashes as they carried Britons further and faster than ever before. The telegraph had been invented, allowing people to transmit instantaneous messages to anywhere in the realm – and soon to anywhere in the world. As for the mysterious globe – it was no more. The Niger had been discovered, so had Timbuctoo, Lake Chad, the Sahara, the North Magnetic Pole, most of the Arctic, segments of Antarctica, the north coast of Australia, and much else besides.

This new world was no place for Barrow. At eighty-three years of age he remained active and, remarkably, had no need of spectacles. He still wielded influence, and continued to heap scorn on the head of anyone who failed to see things his way. But the eager young man who had discussed the merits of hippopotamus meat with Britain's finest brains a quarter of a century before was fading. No longer was he the young, thrusting member of the Royal Society who sat eagerly by Sir Joseph Banks's side. Now he was the eldest, the 'Father' of the dining club.

The great names of his prime had vanished. Sir Humphrey Davy was gone, so were 'Phenomenon' Young, John Herschel, Nevil Maskeleyne and John Rennie. There were no more brilliant eccentrics such as Henry Cavendish who wore the same mildewed coat and tricorn hat come rain or shine, indoors or out, whose 'shrill, disagreeable voice'[17] had discussed astronomy in the most popular clubs, and whose aversion to women was so great that he would walk through a ploughed field to avoid meeting one. Gone was the society sculptor Sir Francis Chantrey, and gone too was Sir Charles Blagden who had persuaded him to spend two minutes in a 320° clay furnace just to see what happened. They were all dead, leaving only memories and – in the case of Henry Cavendish – a houseful of jewel-encrusted women's underwear.

Barrow joined their ranks at 1 p.m. on 23 November 1848. He ploughed his misdirected furrow to the end. In one of his last letters, written shortly before his death, he castigated a would-be explorer's achievements: 'I do not think there is a single line in these pages, which I herewith return, worthy of publishing in the Geographical or any other journal, nor do I think anything is to be expected from Capt. [?] – he is merely hashing up old matters and not discoveries, and has wholly laid aside the instructions of Lord Stanley, which were calculated to ascertain with safety, the direction of the ridges and the rivers which, like the bones and blood-vessels of animals, lead to the geographical outline of a country.'[18] This letter can be found in the Royal Geographical Society archives. The name of the unfortunate officer is illegible, but it reads suspiciously like Sturt, one of the great pioneers of Australian exploration.

25

THE ARCTIC COUNCIL

While Barrow was still alive, a semblance of order hung over the Franklin rescue expeditions. A tripartite thrust swung into action in the spring of 1848, involving a sea mission from the east under James Ross and Edward Bird in the *Enterprise* and *Investigator* respectively; another sea mission from the west under a Captain Henry Kellett; and an overland stab down the Mackenzie River led by Richardson and Rae.

They went, failed, and came back again, having made no progress towards the discovery of Franklin. This was deeply humiliating for James Ross, who had dragged himself out as the saviour angel, had been ill for most of the time he had been at sea and had gone no further than the head of Prince Regent Inlet before being driven back by adverse weather. Never again would he go to the Arctic.

With Barrow's death, however, everything changed. As far as the Admiralty was concerned, Franklin was a lost cause. Captain Baillie Hamilton, who had succeeded Barrow as Second Secretary on 24 January 1845, did his best to drum up interest but he was blocked by his superiors. Lord Dundas, the current First Lord, believed that Franklin had sunk in Baffin Bay and that the whole business

was a waste of time. The Lords wanted to 'give themselves no further trouble about it than public opinion and the pressure from
without compelled them',[1] McCormick, James Ross's old shipmate
from the Antarctic, was told. The Lords were distant, arrogant fools.
When McCormick offered to lead an overland attempt to rescue
Franklin, and made the mistake of asking for a promotion at the
same time – his last having been in 1827 following Parry's try for the
North Pole – he was rejected out of hand. 'I never before had an
interview with a more reserved, colder or more repulsive official,'[2]
he steamed.

But for all their Lordships' stonewalling, they could not ignore a
growing public demand that something be done. If Franklin had been
a hero before, he was now a superhero. Papers and magazines were
full of him, and interest in his expedition was so intense that Dr King
could fill lecture halls on an almost daily basis, delivering his opinions
to audiences several hundred strong. Even in America people were
advocating a rescue mission.

The Admiralty dithered and prevaricated. For forty years or so it
had been used to doing what Barrow told it. Now that its guiding light
had gone, it had no idea what to do. It was, after all, a mainly administrative body whose purpose was to facilitate the smooth running of
the world's largest navy. Had there been a war it would have known,
or would have been told, what to do. But in matters of exploration it
was lost without Barrow. It therefore offered a magnificent panoply of
prizes – £20,000 for anybody who rescued Franklin, £10,000 for anybody who simply found his ships, and another £10,000 for the first to
cross the North-West Passage – and turned the practicalities of
Franklin's rescue over to the Arctic Council.

The Arctic Council – or Committee – had been born in the mid-
1830s as an advisory group to filter proposals for attempts on the
North-West Passage. An influential but nebulous body, it comprised
all the big names in Barrow's arsenal. Members came and went,
according to circumstances, but its core remained solid: Parry, James
Ross, Beaufort, Back, Beechey, Bird, Sabine and Richardson. Franklin
had once sat on the panel, and Barrow had naturally been its leader.

Baillie Hamilton now took Franklin's place, and Barrow's son, John
Barrow Jnr., stepped into his father's shoes as coordinator.

John Barrow Jnr. was an excellent man. He had been seconded
into the Admiralty at an early age, had travelled reasonably widely,
and was a phenomenal archivist. He had inherited all his father's skills
but not his preconceptions. Everybody, without exception, liked him
and although he lacked any real power he was an ideal facilitator,
capable of handling both the Admiralty and the discordant personalities of his father's team. Under his direction, with Beaufort acting as
general foreman, the Arctic Council became a body to be reckoned
with. As McCormick was told, 'Could you point out the *very spot*
where you could put your hand on Franklin they would not listen to
it at the Admiralty, everything being left to the Arctic Council.'[3]

In 1851 the artist Samuel Pearce painted a picture of the Arctic
Council. There they all are, gathered around a table, Back with his
black mutton-chop whiskers, Bird with his receding hairline, Parry,
Ross and Sabine showing various degrees of grey, with Franklin,
Fitzjames and Sir John Barrow joining deliberations from portraits on
the wall behind. (Crozier, the untutored Irishman, was obviously considered unworthy of inclusion.) Pearce, however, omitted one of the
most influential figures on the Council: Lady Franklin.

If Lady Jane had been considered interfering by the inhabitants of
Van Diemen's Land she was considered even more so by the inmates
of Whitehall. For the next ten years she lobbied remorselessly for her
husband's rescue, spending all her money and time in unceasing efforts
to find him – or at least his remains. She had even tried to get a place
on Richardson's land expedition of 1848. When funds were low she
extorted them without mercy. McCormick recorded a cab ride with her
when she suddenly ordered the driver to pull up outside Dollond's in
St Paul's. Dollond, she explained, had been Franklin's optician. She
came back a few minutes later, eyes gleaming, and with another £100
in the kitty. Late at night, the Arctic Council gathered at her home,
working out new and propitious routes for Franklin's salvation.

Given its head, the Arctic Council moved with astonishing speed.
By 1850 the Arctic was crawling with rescue missions. The *Enterprise*

and the *Investigator* approached from the west under Captain Richard Collinson and Captain Robert McClure. Meanwhile, from the east no fewer than thirteen ships surged into Lancaster Sound, among them two separate Admiralty fleets under Captains Horatio Austin and William Penny, two American vessels, a ship financed by Lady Franklin and a tiny venture of one small schooner and a yacht, commanded and paid for by Sir John Ross, now seventy-three.

They were searching blind, their only clue being Franklin's instructions. Franklin had been told to go south-west from Melville Island and if that proved impossible to go north via Wellington Channel. They looked into the Peel Sound, the next opening along from Prince Regent Inlet which led down the west coast of Boothia Felix to King William's Land, saw that it was frozen over, and therefore devoted their attentions to Wellington Channel. It occurred to no one, despite repeated advice from all quarters concerning the volatility of Arctic ice, that Peel Sound might have been clear when Franklin saw it.

In late August they found the first signs of the expedition. On Beechey Island, at the mouth of Wellington Channel, they stumbled across the remains of Franklin's 1845 winter quarters. Signs of occupation were everywhere: fire sites, sledge tracks in the earth, rubbish heaps, a massive pyramid of 600 empty cans, and even a pair of gloves folded neatly on a rock. They also found three graves, their headstones helpfully inscribed with names and dates, and facing west in what had become an Arctic tradition.

Here, to the rescuers, was proof that they were looking in the right direction. Franklin had obviously found his way blocked to the south, as they had, and had turned north to fulfil the second part of his orders. The sledge tracks could be followed for forty miles up the east coast of Wellington Channel, suggesting that Franklin had scouted ahead for his next season's sailing. It was too late now for them to go after him, so they settled cosily into harbours on Cornwallis Island and prepared to follow the trail next year. In their enthusiasm they ignored the main clue Beechey Island had to offer – the graves. In their relief that there were only three instead of 133 they did not comment on the fact that this was a very high casualty rate indeed.

Most expeditions lost that many after several years, not in their first winter. Something had gone seriously wrong with the health of Franklin and his men.

There was another thing about Beechey Island – it lacked a cairn. Normally, at any stop, Arctic officers would leave a message under a pile of stones describing their current situation and their next intended move. But Franklin had not done so. Was this an oversight? Or was it because Franklin had nothing new to report and intended following his orders to go south? They all agreed it must be an oversight.

The rescuers spent that winter in more-or-less cheerful companionship at a spot that Austin named Union Harbour, visiting each other's ships and passing the time with the customary round of plays and entertainments. There were the usual personality clashes, occasioned mainly by John Ross, who bumbled merrily about reminding people of his past glories and bringing up yet again the business of Lancaster Sound. They, for their part, noted that Ross had come underprovisioned and was a drag on both their progress and food supplies. Ross blithely ignored any animosity. 'I found Penny an excellent and kind neighbour,' he wrote, 'he had luxuries which I could not afford and was liberal in sharing them out.'[4] Privately, Penny condemned Ross as 'an utterly selfish man'.[5]

Penny was a humourless, over-eager and slightly insecure forty-one-year-old whaler who was a favourite of Lady Franklin and had been given his command solely by virtue of her quick-footedness. He liked to exaggerate his past achievements and to expound on his future greatness. Ross and the others quickly picked up on this – 'a discovery which to us was very amusing'[6] – and promptly threw some pieces of plank onto the ice. Sure enough, when Penny discovered them, he was certain he had found the remains of Franklin's ships. Only when he caught his officers grinning behind his back did he realize he had been made a fool of. Hurrying back to his cabin he added to the accusation of selfishness that Ross was also 'proverbial for false statements'.[7]

'Dear old Sir John Ross!'[8] wrote one of Austin's midshipmen, Clements Markham.

The only absentees from this happy group were the crew of Lady Jane's ship, the *Prince Albert*, which had seen the way blocked by ice and had turned for home even before the discoveries at Beechey Island, and the two American ships that had become stuck in the ice fifty miles up Wellington Channel. Unlike the British, who were accustomed to the Arctic – and if not accustomed were too stiff-upper-lipped to mention it – the Americans were aghast at conditions. Coffee froze in their mugs. Butter had to be cut with a hammer and chisel. Cold metal burned their hands through two layers of mittens. They seared the skin off their lips by sucking icicles. When they put out their tongues they froze to their beards. Scurvy took hold, causing men to faint at the slightest exertion. And from all around came the sound of the ice, creaking, groaning and on occasion gristling against their bows like ground sugar. In the long gloom of the polar winter they turned white as cut potatoes. 'I long for the light,' wrote an appalled medical officer, Elisha Kane. 'Dear, dear sun, no wonder you are worshipped!'[9]

While the Americans were shivering in their icy anchorage, the British fanned out on sledges to find Franklin. Leading the onslaught was one of Austin's men, Lt. Leopold McClintock, a short-spoken but good-humoured Irishman who had travelled with James Ross aboard the *Enterprise* and had learned from him the rudiments of sledging. Off they went on cumbersome wooden barges that carried chivalric, medieval names – Resolute, Hotspur, Perseverance and the like – and bore fluttering pennants at their bows. The sledges were all man-hauled – James Ross had apparently not passed down the skills of dog-sledging – and covered little more than ten miles per day unless the teams ran, which then pushed the distance to almost twenty miles per day.

McClintock's sledges lumbered over the ice. They went west to Melville Island, where they found the block of sandstone on which Parry's men had carved their ships' names a quarter of a century ago and the red-painted wheels of the cart he had abandoned on his overland trip. They went south across the ice to Peel Sound and saw only an endless frozen sea. Of Franklin, nothing.

The rescuers returned to London in 1851, carrying a nasty rumour picked up by John Ross's interpreter to the effect that Franklin's men had been killed by Eskimos. It was quite untrue, and was disbelieved by all except Ross who stuck loyally by his man. However, it roused Lady Jane to anger, and she greeted it 'with a deep sense of gratitude to Sir John Ross for murdering her husband'.[10] It was an ungenerous comment, given Ross's unrivalled feat in leading an Arctic expedition at the age of seventy-three, and given the fact that he had gained nothing from it save a debt of £530. Ross probably did not mind – he had been called a lot worse in his lifetime. He was appointed a rear-admiral (retired) shortly after his return and never went to sea again, thus closing one of the most controversial careers in the history of Arctic exploration.

The Admiralty was by now even more unwilling to continue the Franklin search after the huge and profitless expenditure they had just incurred. However, Lady Jane and the Arctic Council had the public on their side.

Nobody cared a jot about the North-West Passage – 'we do not think the geographical importance of these expeditions commensurate with the cost or exposure of a single sloop's crew,' *The Times* stated frankly, 'but it does impinge most emphatically on our national honour that we should ascertain the fate of our missing countrymen and redeem them, if living, from the dangers to which they had been consigned'.[11] A hero in distress took on almost Christlike proportions: to ignore the call to rescue was an unforgivable sin, particularly when that hero's reputation had been inflated to such titanic proportions as had Franklin's. 'The blooming child lisps Franklin's name, as with glittering eye and greedy ear it hears of the wonders of the North, and the brave deeds done there,' wrote Captain Sherard Osborn, who had accompanied the last expedition. 'Youth's bosom glows with generous emotion to emulate the fame of him who has gone where none as yet have followed. And who amongst us does not feel his heart throb faster in recalling to recollection the calm heroism of the veteran leader, who . . .'[12] And so on and so on. Osborn's words may seem purple by today's standards, but they faded to a delicate mauve compared to the overblown language being used by others. People even went so far as to write poems about Franklin's birth-place.

Feeling ran so high that a parliamentary committee was formed to coordinate action and to investigate the merits of claims – if any – to the prize money. Advice promptly flooded in from all quarters, some of it ridiculous, some less so. Look for the 'Open Polar Sea', said one man, for Franklin was obviously trapped within it, sailing from point to point in search of a way out. Send only criminals in search of him, said another, for no other men were so resourceful. Use spotter bal-loons, said a third. A fourth recommended that the rescuers should release barrages of rockets so that Franklin's men would know where they were. A fifth advised the release of Arctic foxes with details of food caches tied around their necks. A sixth said that medals should be distributed to the Eskimos carrying information as to the searchers' whereabouts.

The last two ideas were, eventually, employed. And balloons were used too, although not for spotting but as wind-blown versions of the foxes and Eskimos. What was really needed, however, was a level-headed look at where the search should be directed. In this respect the Arctic Council seemed to have taken leave of its senses.

The main thrust of Franklin's orders had been that he go south-west from Barrow Strait, therefore that should have been the logical place to look for him. Yet almost everybody preferred to ignore this avenue in favour of Franklin's secondary option via Wellington Channel. Beechey murmured that it might be an idea to send a sledge party down Peel Sound to the mouth of the Great Fish River – 'nothing should be neglected [in that quarter]',[13] he advised. And of course there was Dr King, battering at the doors with his infuriating insistence that Franklin would be found off the west coast of Boothia, and that they were insane not to send him on a land journey to find him. Timidly, Parliament agreed that such an idea was not unreason-able. But the Arctic Council was having none of it.

'I *wholly* reject *all* and *every* idea of *any* attempts . . . to send boats or detachments over the ice to any point of the mainland eastward of the

Mackenzie River,' Back said, 'because I can say from experience that no toil-worn and exhausted party could have the least chance of existence by going there.'[14] James Ross was more outspoken, damning without a shred of evidence any suggestion that Franklin might have travelled so far south. McCormick, an erstwhile overland man but now, with promotion beckoning, a believer in the open polar sea, announced that an examination not only of Wellington Channel but of Smith Sound and Jones Sound was essential. Even Parry conceded that, although Franklin would certainly have prosecuted his primary instructions as far as was possible, he might have been forced north by default.

Thus another expedition, of five ships, was sent to Wellington Channel in 1852. It was commanded by the unsavoury figure of Captain – now Sir Edward – Belcher. Why Belcher was chosen is a mystery. He had a limited experience of the Arctic, having sailed as a lieutenant in the *Blossom* on Beechey's abortive link with Franklin's first overland venture. And he had taken part in the great magnetic survey of 1838–42. But he was generally known as a bad-tempered, dictatorial martinet, renowned for his intransigency and for his willingness to bring people to court martial for the most trivial offences. Even James Ross, himself a stern man, advised officers to make allowance for events (unnamed) in Belcher's past which had brought him to this state of temper. Belcher's entry in the *Dictionary of National Biography* sums him up very accurately: 'Perhaps no officer of equal ability has ever succeeded in inspiring so much personal dislike, and the customary exercise of his authority did not make Arctic service less trying.'[15]

In the long history of Arctic exploration, Belcher's expedition, the last all-out push by the Admiralty, stands proud as the most futile and ill-managed on record.

Belcher chose as his flagship the *Assistance*. Kellett was given the *Resolute*, McClintock the *Intrepid*, and Osborn the *Pioneer*. The *North Star* supply ship was given to a Commander Inglefield. Also, clinging like a limpet to the *North Star*, was McCormick who, having pestered everyone in sight, had been given permission to take whatever boat was available, manned by whatever six volunteers he could find, on a short voyage up Wellington Channel. Something, Beaufort reasoned, should be done to keep the man happy.

The fleet crept into Lancaster Sound and promptly became beset off Cornwallis Island. Belcher's worst side came out. Every minor detail, such as failing to report the sighting of a hare, or submitting a report on the wrong-sized paper, became an arrestable offence. Before long the crews were in a state of semi-mutiny and their officers gathered in the long nights to discuss ways of dealing with their commander. Should they roast him or strangle him?

Belcher was, actually, not that bad a leader. True, he was stupid and arrogant and bloody-minded and deserved all the opprobrium which was later heaped upon him. But he was trapped by a sense of his own importance, and the futility of following instructions in which he had no confidence. Belcher believed that Franklin would be found to the south – if he was still alive. But the rescue mission had been ordered north. What could he do? 'If I had commanded in 1848 I should have been there now,' Belcher wrote. 'It requires no Prophet to understand how inveterate some of their High Mightinesses feel towards me – because they were told "sans ceremonie", "If you had sent Belcher you would have had your work done in his own way. He would have acted upon his own judgement and considered instructions not binding." . . . In plain English, "They knew I would not have *thought* as they *wished*."'[16]

What exactly did they wish? In his letters Belcher referred darkly to '*Private Instructions*' to which his predecessors had '*promised obedience upon starting*'.[17] He spoke, too, of murky goings-on involving Austin, Penny and, of all people, John Ross. 'We are in expectation of a very warm discussion or possibly a Court of Enquiry,'[18] he said, regarding their activities of the previous year.

Here was something very odd. Why would an official naval court be interested in the actions of John Ross, whose expedition was not directly under the Admiralty's control? What had he done, or not done, to merit an inquiry? And what were the private instructions? Why the masonic secrecy? Belcher supplied no answers to these questions – or, if he did, they have since been destroyed – dropping only hints. 'I came here purely on public grounds – and urged to do something to satisfy the disappointed world,' he wrote, 'but I have been sadly deceived.'[19]

It seems likely that the Arctic Council was using the Franklin search as an excuse for a covert attempt on the North Pole. They urged, for example, the investigation not only of Wellington Channel but of Jones Sound and Smith Sound. Neither of the two last was remotely within Franklin's ambit, but they did represent potential avenues to the Polar Sea where, if conditions were as balmy and ice-free as Barrow had believed, the Pole would be within a few days' sailing. The Arctic Council started a global trend that would last for half a century. In later years, when a man said he was going to look for Franklin – whose legend was perpetuated for the purpose – it was understood that he was trying for the North Pole.

Belcher threw up his hands in despair: 'It is my firm belief that this is only the beginning of disaster . . . Another expedition is to start in the Spring – who will command it I know not but I will never again *volunteer*.'[20] Those words were written in October 1851, Belcher's first year out. Little wonder, then, that as time passed he lost interest in the search and reverted to the safety of the rule book. If he had to be fettered by instructions in which he did not believe, where else could he turn?

He freely acknowledged his faults. 'I never was a Nelson and never will be,' he wrote to his wife. 'To return before my duty is completed would subject me to scorn, derision and contempt. Better wait until ordered home . . .'[21] And so he did, shuttling nervously from ship to ship atop a supply-laden boat, to avoid the nip he was sure would come at any moment. Meanwhile, those of his officers not confined to quarters rushed out to find the missing vessels.

McCormick was the first to go, being slipped from his leash on 19 August 1852, just late enough to prevent him getting anywhere. He took his boat, the aptly named *Forlorn Hope*, some eighty miles up the east side of Wellington Channel and discovered nothing during three weeks of uninterrupted gales. He lingered aboard the *North Star* for another year, cursing Belcher's 'generally uncourteous line of conduct',[22] and caught the first available supply ship home.

He departed with two memories uppermost in his mind. The first was of a night during which he had wandered from the ship and had been forced to sleep in a shallow scrape while the thermometer stood at 64 °F below freezing – an event from which he emerged fresh as a daisy, so he said. The second was a more mundane occurrence in which he shot a polar bear. The animal was seven and a half feet long and weighed 1,000 pounds. McCormick was sixty yards away and armed only with a smooth-bore, double-barrelled gun. He fired as the bear was turning to run. The ball went through the bear's hip and travelled the length of its body, emerging with such force that it shattered its jawbone. A gruesome little vignette but interesting in its own way.

Behind him McCormick left an expedition that was rapidly disintegrating. Almost everybody who could had volunteered for sledging expeditions, preferring the discomfort of man-hauling to the prospect of life under Belcher. In fact, when McCormick departed on 24 August 1853 there were only five hands on board the *North Star*. 'This of itself indeed speaks volumes,'[23] he wrote.

26

INVESTIGATOR

Belcher's men did their best. As advised, they trapped Arctic foxes and sent them out with collars carrying details of the search; information-packed medals were distributed to the Eskimos; directions were daubed in huge letters on cliff faces and prominent rocks; balloons were released, to bobble over the Arctic landscape and finally die, their messages read by no one; and at the same time they dragged their sledges wearily across the snow and ice.

Belcher was not a sledging enthusiast. Having tried it once, he never went again, comparing it in a letter to a horse-riding friend to taking a good hunter on a forced march of 100 days. 'I can perceive the effect on all the long journey divisions,' he wrote on 1 September 1853. 'They are not fit for the heavy duty of this year which I have assigned to them.'[1] Later, maybe suffering from scurvy but probably drunk, Belcher ranted against the sledgers. Their efforts were worthless, 'a mere farce, a sporting trip'.[2] He blamed the men, who were mostly volunteers from whaling ships, and he blamed the officers too: 'double pay & promotion heroes',[3] he labelled them.

Belcher desperately wanted to go home. He was ready to abandon ship – 'but before the time arrives for such an alternative, decided orders from England will render this act one of obedience – although they may wish to place the odium on my shoulders by placing it at my discretion . . . You cannot conceive what degradation a man submits too in accepting such a command.'[4] While Belcher rotted slowly in his cabin – or in the cabin of whichever ship he thought least likely to be nipped – fresh instructions came in. He was to search not only for Franklin but also for the *Investigator* and the *Enterprise*.

Nothing had been heard of these two ships since they set out in 1850. They had not returned with the Austin–Penny mission and for all anybody knew they were as lost as Franklin.

The *Investigator* and the *Enterprise* were not exactly lost, but they were doing their best to become so. Their voyage from England had not been an easy one. Both captains were hard men, and Collinson in particular managed to outshine even Belcher in his severity. 'Discipline is essential for comfort' was his motto. Before he came home, most of his officers had been placed under arrest, some for as long as three years. McClure was as bad, if not worse. On one occasion he gave his cook forty-eight lashes for swearing.

Maybe Collinson and McClure had reasons for their heavyhandedness. Their crews were rough, very rough. McClure's Eskimo interpreter, a Moravian missionary from Labrador called Johann Miertsching, wrote that, 'I feel as if my lot had been cast among half a hundred devils. The harsh rules of naval discipline are barely enough to keep them under control.'[5] They were brazen sinners of a kind he had never met in a lifetime of proselytizing. 'A devil of discord seems to have found his abode amongst us,'[6] he wrote as early as 1850, when the ships had yet to reach their revictualling station at Hawaii.

McClure's temper was uncontrollable. When, on 15 May 1850, his first officer allowed the ship to hit a hurricane so that all the masts were broken, he erupted. 'The fury of the captain was terrible, positively inhuman,'[7] Miertsching wrote. The unfortunate first officer, one William Haswell, was arrested and sent to his cabin with two marines standing guard outside the door. He would be replaced at

Hawaii, McClure told him. At Hawaii, however, Haswell was peremptorily released.

The two ships had become separated on the journey over and, on
arriving at Hawaii, McClure was horrified to hear that Collinson had
left the previous morning for Bering Strait and intended to go ahead
without him, taking as his companion ship the *Plover*, a supply vessel
which had been sent ahead of the main expedition. McClure had to
catch up, and there was no time for finding replacement officers. He
made his repairs as speedily as possible and dashed north in pursuit of
the *Enterprise* while his crew were still suffering from the after-effects
of shore leave. (Hawaii must have been an extremely hospitable stop-
over; two men were on the sick list for a month, having indulged in
'frightful excesses'.)[8]

At this point McClure's ambition got the better of him. There were
two routes available: the planned, longer one that Collinson was
taking through the open Pacific, or a dodgy short-cut through the
shoal-ridden Aleutian Islands off Kamchatka. McClure chose the
Aleutian Islands. He would not only catch up with Collinson but he
would overtake him and 'take the ice' – as it was termed – on his own.
What he planned was strictly against orders. By now, no ship was
allowed to enter the Arctic alone. But McClure did not mind. He
sailed past the *Plover*, which was anchored off Bering Strait, and
lunged eastwards.

Just for a season, one of the rare seasons of which Scoresby had
spoken twenty-five years before, the Arctic laid itself bare. Bering
Strait was open – in its own way; McClure had to put forty men in five
boats to tow him round Point Barrow – and after much buffeting
through loose ice, with the impregnable mass of the permanent polar
pack glittering just ninety miles to port, he passed the Mackenzie
delta and reached Cape Bathurst. Banks Land, last seen by Parry in
1819, was above him. The sea was clear. The North-West Passage
beckoned. It was worth a try.

He reached the southern promontory of Banks Land, which he
named Nelson Head, then advanced along its southern coastline, now
sailing, now being carried by the ice. He found himself in a narrow

passage, Prince of Wales Strait, that separated Banks Land from another large land-mass to the south-east.

By 9 September 1850 he was within sixty miles of Melville Island and was beginning to wonder if his gamble might pay off. All that lay between him and the North-West Passage was that tiny distance. When he sent his ice-master up the mast he learned that open water was twenty miles away, separated from them only by a thin coating of ice. McClure had answered one of the overriding questions of Arctic exploration: a sea passage definitely did exist between the Atlantic and Pacific. All that remained was to sail through it. 'Can it be that so humble a creature as I am will be permitted to perform what has baffled the talented and wise for hundreds of years?'[9] he wrote in wonder.

The answer was no. Having lured McClure placidly into its depths the Arctic reverted to its vicious self. A gale blew up, tossing the *Investigator* hither and thither, driving the ship now north, now south. The storm was bad. It lasted a week, and before its conclusion McClure had made preparations for abandoning the ship. It flung the *Investigator* at steep cliffs, relented at the last moment, whirled it around, blew it about, drove it back, tipped it on its side and then righted it again. Amidst it all McClure strode back and forth, trying to keep order. The men – all sixty-six of them – took no notice and broached the rum barrels. They wanted to die happy. After a particularly bad seventeen-hour battering the storm suddenly vanished, leaving the *Investigator* locked in a sheet of solid ice some thirty miles down Prince of Wales Strait. The drunken crew lurched shamefaced on deck while an icily furious McClure read them the articles of war.

For the rest of that winter McClure peppered the area with sledge parties. They mapped the south coast of Banks Land and the north coast of its neighbour across Prince of Wales Strait, which McClure called Prince Albert Land. In fact, unknown to him, it was the massive Victoria Island whose southernmost tip pointed to King William Land. Had he sledged its length he would have come within a few miles of the Franklin expedition. But McClure was not terribly interested in Franklin by now. His heart was set on the Passage.

He drove himself furiously. He led several sledge parties and almost killed himself in the process. He returned from one outing looking like a frozen corpse and had to spend the next month in bed. His officers found they were expected to make similar sacrifices. One man who broke his chronometer a week out returned to get a new one, only to be driven back onto the ice – without the chronometer – by McClure's unreasoning rage. Another, who returned a week earlier than expected with his men suffering badly from frost-bite, suffered the same fate.

Neither McClure nor his men had any experience of sledging, with predictable results. McClure's provisioning was so poor that on the first night of his first journey he could offer his men nothing but a pint of tepid water mixed with a little oatmeal. The rough, grudging crews were hopelessly undisciplined and went on impromptu game shoots, only to become lost in the fog and snow. They slept uneasily at nights, terrified that their tents might be attacked by polar bears. In a chilling example of their inexperience, they were woken one stormy night by the cry that a bear's footsteps had been heard. They stuck their heads out, saw nothing in the maelstrom of flying snow, and yelled as loud as they could to frighten the creature off. The footsteps stopped. During a lull in the storm they opened the flaps to see whether the danger had passed and learned that the footsteps had not been those of a bear but those of a fellow seaman who had been lost the previous day while out hunting. He had struggled as far as the tent but had been overcome by cold even as the sledgers shouted at him. He had fallen to his knees less than a yard from safety. They found him there, kneeling on the ground, stiff as a board, his head thrown back, eyes staring at the sky and his mouth filling silently with snow.

The man – Whitefield – was amazingly still alive, and later made a full recovery. Bewildered as to what had happened, he could explain it only in terms of a 'fit'. McClure's men were finding out for themselves the paralysing effect which extreme cold had on the human frame, just as Parry had done in 1819.

In June 1851, the ice began to break up and by the middle of August McClure was back at the top of Prince of Wales Strait, searching for a way through the ice. None was forthcoming, leaving him with two options: to overwinter where he was and try again the next year; or to retrace his steps and search for a new route to the north of Banks Land. There was another option: to go home. McClure could have done this quite honourably, having sighted the North-West Passage and having made respectable efforts to find Franklin. But it was an option he never considered. To retreat now, when he stood on the cusp of success, would have been unthinkable. He chose the Banks Land route.

On 17 August he rounded Nelson Head and two days later was off the northern point of Banks Land at 73° 55', his furthest north of the voyage. To his north lay the polar pack, a rolling landscape of 100-foot-high ice-hills. To the south was Banks Land – or Banks Island as it obviously now was. In between the two was a channel of open water barely wider than the ship itself. Once in this channel McClure would never be able to retreat. There was no room to manoeuvre, let alone turn round. Without hesitation he sailed into it.

For the next month, day and night, he sailed along the coast of Banks Island, warping and hacking his way through the encroaching pack. When the ice was obdurate he blasted it with immense charges of gunpowder. Unlike previous explorers, McClure was not going to be put off by a few floes; he would break the Arctic.

By 24 September the *Investigator* found itself in a sheltered bay on the north-east flank of Banks Island, even closer to Melville Island than it had been the year before. A few days later McClure received a report that the sea was clear to the east as far as the eye could see. Had he gone on, McClure might well have been able to cross the short distance to Melville Island and connect with the eastern search parties. But the season was already far advanced, the ice was fickle and his nerve was failing. Although he remained as determined as before, the adrenalin rush that had carried him so far had burned out. To the north the polar pack ground together and cracked explosively as its ice-fields burst under the pressure. Peering out into the Arctic gloom, McClure could see huge blocks rearing and plunging in a ponderous, monochrome dance of light and shadow. He had no wish to become part of it.

He decided to stay where he was. Mercy Bay, as he called it, would be their wintering spot. Later, his medical officer, Alexander Armstrong, would write that it was an ideal name, 'from the fact it would have been a *mercy had we never entered it*'.[10]

In November 1851 the Arctic was almost empty. A month before it had been chock-a-block with the ships of Austin, Penny and the Americans, its landscape criss-crossed by the tracks of McCormick's sledging parties. Now they had gone, leaving the *Investigator* as one of only three ships remaining.

To the south, anchored off Victoria Land, was Collinson's *Enterprise*. Collinson had entered the Arctic a year behind McClure, had followed his track up Prince of Wales Strait, had seen the North-West Passage, had been similarly thwarted by it and had turned back. He had then, like McClure, decided to sail north around Banks Island. But when he reached Point Kellett on the west coast, he found McClure had beaten him there by thirteen days. Collinson was as intransigent as McClure. He wasn't going to be forestalled by anyone. So he left Banks Island and turned south for Victoria Island, hoping to reach the safe, discovered waters of the North American coast and thence, eventually, Back's Chantrey Inlet.

Meanwhile, tucked into Batty Bay in Prince Regent Inlet, was Lady Jane's latest venture, the tiny *Prince Albert*, commanded by Captain William Kennedy and Lieutenant Joseph-René Bellot. The two men were odd messfellows: the former was a stern, half-Cree Indian teetotaller from Canada; the latter was a stylish, fun-loving fop from France who had become Lady Jane's latest favourite and, from their correspondence, almost a surrogate son. The one grizzled and serious, the other smooth-skinned and frivolous, they reached an effective concord.

The *Investigator*, the *Enterprise* and the *Prince Albert* each sent off their own sledge teams. McClure went to Melville Island, where he learned from a note in a cairn that McClintock had been there the previous June. He fell down and wept. Had he dared to follow the open water the previous winter, or even had he dared to send a sledge party, he would have met the eastern division a year ago. He returned to his ship in despair.

As McClure was returning, Collinson was departing. He reached Melville Island just twenty days after McClure. He saw McClure's tracks and swore irritably. 'We had passed within sixty miles of the *Investigator* and had fallen upon the traces of her exploring parties [but] we again missed the opportunity of communication,'[11] Collinson wrote.

It was lucky they never met. McClure had disobeyed orders and, worst of all, had stolen a march on his commanding officer. Any communication would likely have been stormy.

While McClure and Collinson were avoiding each other in the west, Kennedy and Bellot were sledging happily around the east. No greater contrast could be imagined. As opposed to the slightly manic endeavours of Collinson and McClure, Kennedy and Bellot conducted their explorations in conditions of disparate harmony: Kennedy soldiering on in his thick furs while Bellot hopped about in a nice ensemble of salmon-pink tunic and tall sea-boots, showing with each bound just a hint of white leggings. Together they mapped the whole of Somerset Island and much of Boothia and discovered, importantly, the narrow, unnavigable passage from east to west that John Ross had missed and which was recorded on the charts as Bellot Strait. To the satisfaction of all, northern Boothia therefore became an island – but not an island around which one could sail. Bellot and Kennedy left for home that year and for a brief period in the middle of 1852 Collinson and McClure had the Arctic to themselves.

Conditions aboard the *Investigator* were bad. McClure had placed his men on two-thirds rations on reaching Mercy Bay. Now he reduced them to half rations. Going by the experiences of previous expeditions, this should have been no great hardship. Both Parry and John Ross had taken their men to this level. However, McClure's crew seemed unable to cope. They lost weight and strength. Had they wanted they could have gone hunting on Banks Island which, to Dr Armstrong's surprise, supported wildlife throughout the winter. But their inexperience and the long Arctic night counted against

them. For most of the time it was too dark to see their targets, and
when it was not too dark they proved useless shots. Only one man, a
marine sergeant called Woon, had any success and even he was far
from being a sharpshooter. Having missed a musk-ox, he was charged
by the outraged creature. When it was five yards away he still had the
ramrod in his musket. He took aim and fired. The ramrod ripped
through the musk-ox, killing it instantly.

Armstrong begged McClure to increase the rations but there was
nothing McClure could do at this stage. Even if they did not make the
Passage next year they would still need every scrap of food to take
them back the way they had come. To make matters worse still, by
July sixteen of McClure's men were ill with scurvy, which seemed to
be only slightly abated by the limited quantities of fresh food being
brought on board.

McClure hoped that summer would solve everything. But summer
did not happen that year – or, rather, it was so brief that it did not
reach Mercy Bay. By the end of August, when the ice should have
begun to melt, the surface was hard enough to permit skating. On 9
September, when new ice was forming and they were clearly destined to spend another winter in the ice, McClure called his men on
deck. There would be no more half rations, he announced. Instead
they would receive even less – one meal a day, consisting of half a
pound of meat and two ounces of vegetables per man. At the same
time their allowance of lemon juice was to be halved.

The winter deepened, and the ship creaked and groaned in temperatures of 99 °F below freezing – the coldest recorded by an Arctic
expedition thus far. McClure met hardship with hardship. He reduced
the coal consumption to eight pounds per day, and cut the oil
allowance so that for most of the time the ship was sunk in darkness.
The *Investigator* became an artificial pool of discomfort within the
wider misery of the Arctic night.

Trapped inside their cold, black tomb on rations which, as
Armstrong openly stated, were 'quite inadequate . . . to sustain life for
any lengthened period',[12] a seaman called Bradbury went mad and
started howling at night. A little later Lieutenant Robert Wynniat

also became demented. One man fell and broke his leg. By New Year almost everyone had scurvy and twenty men were on the sick list, two of them close to death.

Their meals defy modern belief. For breakfast they were issued a cup of hot water with a fraction of an ounce of cocoa, and a tiny piece of bread. They were given the rest of their rations in the morning and were told to cook and eat them throughout the day as they saw fit. Most people ate the food at once, and did not bother with cooking. When the bone had been removed, their meat weighed only six ounces. Cooked, this amount shrank visibly. They preferred to chew it raw. It lasted longer that way. In the evening they received a very weak cup of tea. On average each member of the crew now weighed thirty-five pounds less than when they had set out.

Soon, only the officers had the strength to go hunting. When they shot a deer they cut its throat and drank the blood on the spot, returning to the ship in gruesome triumph, their faces frozen over with gore. Often, however, they brought home nothing but a few Arctic mice – 'a tender morsel, of delicate flavour when slightly cooked, and very delicious when eaten raw'.[13]

A deputation approached McClure, pleading for more food to be given to the sick at least. McClure refused. He had already shared out his own private stock and there was nothing else to be had. When some men were caught stealing meat he had them flogged viciously. In his journal, McClure showed no sign of worry. 'The winter found us ready to combat its rigours as cheerfully as on previous occasions,'[14] he wrote. His own confidence was supreme and he painted a near-frenzied portrait of the crew's well-being: 'dancing, skylarking and singing were kept up on the lower deck with unflagging spirit, good humour and vitality'. All that was needed to see them through was 'cheerfulness, energetic exercise and regularity of habits'.[15] His journal, though, was written after the event and naturally showed no sign of despondency. It was left for Armstrong to record the dismay they felt as they heard the ship's bolts crack in the intense cold; and for Miertsching to recall their captain's despair as he hunched in his cabin, praying and muttering to himself.

McClure had every reason for despair. He was now in the position John Ross had been in save that, unlike Ross, McClure had to support a crew of sixty-six and had no providential Fury Beach lying to the north, nor any Eskimos to help him out. And unlike Ross, his hunting parties were unable to bring in sufficient fresh meat to feed the crew. As matters stood, his supplies could last no longer than the summer of 1853.

But he was not about to give up. On 2 March 1853 he announced his plan of action. Twenty-six men were to sledge east with forty-five days' supplies to Cape Spencer on the eastern side of Wellington Channel, where they might meet a whaler or a rescue ship. A second party of six was to go down Prince of Wales Strait and try to find a Hudson's Bay Company outpost on the North American coast. Meanwhile McClure would remain on board with a skeleton crew to extricate the ship if the weather allowed.

Armstrong was appalled. The larger party was being asked to travel 550 miles on provisions that required them to cover more than twelve miles a day. Setting aside the doubtful premise on which the plan was based – that there would be ships to greet them at the end of their journey – the rate of march was one that would have taxed even the fittest. As it was, McClure had asked Armstrong to hand-pick the weakest half of the crew for the journey. Trudging along on their black, swollen limbs, hauling the sledges of sick, crippled and demented patients behind them, Armstrong's chosen would be lucky to go 100 miles before they collapsed. Essentially, McClure was culling useless mouths in the hope that the food saved would give him and his cohorts a better chance at the North-West Passage. Armstrong wrote indignantly: 'Captain McClure had been fully informed by me on many occasions, of the state of the men . . . Nevertheless I felt called upon again to represent their condition and to express my opinion of their unfitness for the performance of this service, without entailing great and inevitable loss of life. *It had no result*.'[16] Finally, Armstrong put his feelings on paper, advising McClure officially 'of the absolute unfitness of the men for the performance of this journey'.[17]

McClure took no notice. Cruelly, he gave the travellers a few days on full rations to prime them for their trip. As their strength returned they became so confident of success that they thanked their captain for the opportunity he had given them. Miertsching, one of the fitter sledgers – of what use was an Eskimo-speaking missionary? – even gave McClure his fur coat. McClure and his officers did nothing to disabuse them, urging them to complete preparations in good time so that they did not miss their rendezvous. If anything, they gave the impression that the sledgers were getting the better part of the deal. 'If next year in Europe you neither see nor hear of me, then you may be sure that Captain McClure, along with his crew, has perished,'[18] McClure told Miertsching. And if he did die, he assured the missionary, the fur coat would tide him through snugly until the Day of Resurrection.

A month elapsed before the hollowness of McClure's plan became apparent. Among the sledgers was a man named John Boyle who, despite having scurvy himself, had been detailed to the sick bay to care for the worst cases. He went to bed on 4 April in good heart. Overnight, his disease galloped forward and by the morning of the 5th he was confined to bed and by nightfall he was dead. On 6 April the crew was in sombre mood. Boyle had been one of the healthier sledgers. If he could go so suddenly, and without any prompting, what would happen to the others on the march that lay ahead?

In the gloom, four grave-diggers hacked dismally at the granite-hard soil of Banks Island while McClure walked across the ice with one of his lieutenants – Haswell, as it happened, the man who had nearly been thrown off ship at Hawaii and was now wishing he had been – discussing funeral arrangements for the following day. As they walked they saw a solitary figure moving across the mouth of Mercy Bay. The light was too murky to be sure of anything, but he seemed to be dressed differently from the other 'Investigators'. Haswell commented on this. 'Yes, yes,' said McClure. 'It is some lad belonging to one of the travelling parties out trying his new travelling dress for the first time.'

Strolling along, they noticed that the novice traveller had started to run. 'He must be pursued by a bear!' McClure exclaimed. Too far away to help they waited for the tragedy to unfold. But no bear came in sight. And as the traveller drew nearer he began to jump up and down, waving his arms in typical Eskimo greeting, shouting gibberish that was carried away on the wind. McClure focused his attention. If Eskimos were in the region, then everything was changed – he could recharge his provisions and bring the *Investigator* and its crew home intact.

The man was 200 yards away. As he came nearer they could see that his face was coal black, tarred by living in the constant smoke and filth of an igloo. He had to be an Eskimo!

'In the name of God, who are you?' McClure shouted.

'I'm Lieutenant Pim of the *Resolute*, now at Dealy Island,' the man panted back, 'and I've come to relieve Captain McClure and the "Investigators".'[19]

From behind the outcrops that guarded the entrance to Mercy Bay, moving at the steady pace of long-distance travel, one of Belcher's sledge parties hove into view.

27

FRANKLIN'S FATE

The sensation aboard the *Investigator* was incredible. When the news of Pim's arrival broke the lower deck dismissed it as a joke. Then, as the realization dawned, they rushed for the stairs. Even sick men dragged themselves from their hammocks so that they could touch their rescuers and reassure themselves that they were not dreaming.

Pim and his two sledgers watched aghast as McClure's white, haggard men emerged from the hatch and crawled towards them like so many maggots. Pim distributed a large piece of bacon from his stores, which was devoured immediately. But the habits of starvation died hard. Come the evening, the crew lined up and began the customary process of drawing lots for who should dispense their evening 'meal' – a can of tea and a little piece of biscuit. Pim and his men broke down and cried.

McClure, who was obviously a little mad, could not believe his luck. For him, Pim's arrival meant not salvation but another chance at the Passage – and another chance, though he never said as much, to claim the £10,000 prize for its completion. However, the situation called for a finesse that was beyond his current state of mind.

On 8 April he sledged with Pim to the *Resolute* and told its captain, Henry Kellett, that all was fine. If Kellett would just take his weakest men on board, McClure could complete the Passage with the remainder. Before leaving he had instructed Armstrong to keep the crew on their existing regime. If anybody queried his ability to complete the passage McClure wanted to show that they could survive on their current food stocks.

He might have got away with it – Kellett was halfway to believing him – had he not made the mistake of ordering Armstrong to bring the weaker half of the crew in his wake. When the sad column completed the journey on 2 May, some blind, some insane, some lame, all of them scorbutic and several suffering from severe frostbite, having thrown aside their warm clothes to lighten their load, Kellett was appalled. Armstrong also brought the news that another two men had died shortly after McClure's departure. He laid their deaths squarely on the captain's decision to maintain starvation rations.

Kellett could not ignore the facts. Although sympathetic to McClure's situation, he was senior to him and therefore responsibility for the wrecked mission was his. He told McClure that the decision would be reached by independent medical advice. McClure sledged back to the *Investigator* with Armstrong and Kellett's surgeon, a man called Domville, on 19 May. The medical men reached a unanimous diagnosis – every single 'healthy' man on board the *Investigator* was suffering from scurvy. To continue would mean certain death. McClure fought to the end. Calling his men on deck he asked them to step forward if they wanted to continue the journey. Only four out of twenty did so.

The *Investigator* was scrubbed top to bottom prior to their departure. From stem to stern, everything was arranged in neat order, 'so as to be immediately available for any party whom adverse fate might compel to seek for succour in the Bay of Mercy'.[1] McClure called the men to order for a final speech – '*not at all complimentary*',[2] Armstrong wrote – and then they hoisted the colours and left.

On 17 June McClure arrived back at the *Resolute* with the residue of his crew, thereby traversing the Arctic, from the Pacific to the Atlantic, for the first time in the history of mankind.*

But McClure's troubles were not yet over. Having quit the deathtrap of Mercy Bay he was now in the equally hazardous position of belonging to Belcher's rescue squadron. The *Resolute* had anchored at Dealy Island, off Melville Island, in the company of the *Intrepid* under Commander McClintock. It had been McClintock who had sledged to Melville Island and had found there a letter left by McClure the previous year giving the *Investigator*'s position. While Pim had gone to find McClure, McClintock had sledged west with nine men to find Franklin. It was a superhuman effort, involving the man-haul of up to 280 pounds per man over a distance of 1,328 miles in 106 days. But it achieved nothing beyond the discovery of a small, barren island, at the cost of the near destruction of his team. When McClintock returned, shortly after McClure had shifted his crew across the ice, one man was dead, two others were on the point of death and the rest were so racked by the ordeal that they did not recover for another twelve months.

In August 1853 the two ships headed for home, by now carrying more sick men than healthy. They went only 100 miles east before the sea froze around them. Yet another winter beckoned for McClure and his crew. His second mate died of pneumonia on 14 September and in the absence of any nearby land was tipped through a square hole that had been cut 200 yards away in the ice. The wind was from the north-west and the temperature was 57 °F below freezing.

Only two men got away to safety that season: McClure's Lt. Cresswell and the deranged Lt. Wynniat, who were sledged to Belcher's depot ship, the *North Star* off Beechey Island, and caught a ride home on the *Phoenix*, a screw-driven steamer that had smashed its way through the ice to deliver fresh supplies.

---

* Intriguingly, among his men was a black seaman by the name of Anderson. Thus a black man was present not only at the discovery of the North Pole (Matthew Henson, 1909) but also at the first crossing of the North-West Passage.

Shortly after the *Phoenix* left, its accompanying transport, the *Breadalbane*, was nipped. It sank within fifteen minutes, giving its crew just time to reach safety. (The *Breadalbane* was found by Canadian divers in 1981, lying in 340 feet of water.)

Belcher's squadron now consisted of the *Resolute* and the *Intrepid*, stranded midway between Byam Martin Island and the west shore of Bathurst Land; his own two ships, the *Assistance* and the *Pioneer*, ice-bound in Wellington Channel; and the *North Star*, at Beechey Island. Sprinkled between them were the crews of the *Investigator* and the *Breadalbane*.

The Arctic demanded one more sacrifice before it was through with the expedition. It chose Bellot, the cheery French favourite of Lady Jane, who had returned the previous year on the *Prince Albert* and had promptly caught a passage back to the Arctic on the *Phoenix*. Disembarking at Beechey Island, Bellot had announced his willingness to carry messages to Belcher. He set off overland on 12 August in his salmon-pink outfit with four seamen and a gutta-percha boat. Six days into the journey, he went out to test the ice. One minute he was there, the next he was gone. Where he had been standing, a fifteen-foot fissure of water lapped inkily against the floes.

Shaky enough at the best of times, Belcher's command disintegrated completely during the winter of 1853–4. Transferring his flag at a moment's whim, he disconcerted his officers to the point of mutiny. Sherard Osborn, commanding the *Pioneer*, had previously supported his leader but now he withdrew his charity. So did Lt. Charles Richards of the *Assistance*, hitherto a soother of troubled waters.

Nobody knew what to do. Osborn's opinions were 'indirectly asked and invariably contradicted' which led him to declare that the crew were 'a body of men especially chosen to serve with one of the most diabolical creatures ever allowed to rule on earth'. They were 'half mad under the sting of unmerited abuse and brutal contumely'.[3] A few weeks later Osborn was stripped of his command and confined under arrest to his cabin.

The calm and mediatory Richards also gave up. 'I am obliged to own that there is something rotten in the state,' he wrote to Barrow

Jnr. Belcher was 'much broken down in health, and . . . his temper is *more* than proportionately affected by it . . . Support him *I must under any circumstances*, tho' I see and know he is acting most injudiciously. I only hope I can escape without discredit.'[4]

Even McClure was a little taken aback at Belcher's behaviour. 'Things are as bad as can be or as *you* might expect under B.,' he wrote to James Ross. 'Nothing but Courts Martial he, but as their Lordships will decide these matters, best it is kept quiet until it becomes public which it must very speedily.' As for the Arctic, it was a place 'which I hope to have done with forever'.[5]

The story of Belcher's mission could fill a book of its own. Suffice to say that he decided his ships were lost – quite unreasonably, according to Kellett – and ordered every single man on board the *North Star*. The ice broke in mid-August 1854, and Belcher fled for home. Had it not been for the providential arrival of two more supply ships, the *North Star* would have had no less than six ships' companies crammed aboard. Belcher's disgrace was complete. He had lost four ships, had found nothing of Franklin and, in his rush to save his skin, had neglected to explore the vicinity of King William Land, the only remaining place where Franklin might yet be found. He had also abandoned Collinson and the *Enterprise*.

Collinson, in fact, arrived home in 1855, having penetrated very creditably to within forty miles of King William Island. However, his crew was barely functioning. By the time he emerged from the Arctic, his first, second and third officers were all under arrest. So was his second ice-master, Francis Skead, who had been shut up in his cabin for thirty-two months. The only officers still at liberty were the surgeon and his assistant. Meanwhile the ship was being operated by one of the mates. Accusations flew: Collinson was a liar, a tyrant, a drunkard, a bully; he was a coward who had failed at every opportunity to press ahead; he was stupid, incompetent, careless – the list was endless. Collinson responded by calling for the whole lot to be court-martialled. They, in turn, swore that they would stake their very commissions to have Collinson brought to trial. And so it went on.

In the end it all fizzled out inconclusively. But there was one last

reminder of the Admiralty's Arctic débâcle. In 1855 the *Resolute* broke
free from the ice and floated down Lancaster Sound. It was picked up
by an American whaler who was so riddled with glee at salvaging one
of Her Majesty's indomitable ships that he left his own ship to be collected the next year and sailed home in triumph aboard the *Resolute*.
He sold it to the US Navy who, with equal glee, polished it until it
shone and returned it to Queen Victoria. (In an odd game of diplomatic pass-the-parcel it was later chopped up and made into a desk
which was handed back to the US President. The desk is still in the
Oval Office.)

The Admiralty was through with Barrow's Arctic business. It gave
McClure £10,000 for his trouble – Collinson was most put out – wrote
Franklin off as a loss, and called it a day. Not a moment too soon, as far
as England's fickle public was concerned. The *Hull Advertiser* spoke for
all when it said: 'We hope that our countrymen will all agree that the
mania of Arctic Expeditions has lasted long enough . . . We admit the
claim of science but not to the extent of repeated wholesale sacrifices
of human life.'[6] Franklin had been fun while he lasted. Now there was
something else to keep people interested: the Crimean War.

What *had* happened to Franklin? It was John Rae, the Hudson's Bay
Company overland man, who found out. Even as Belcher was planning his departure, Rae was zipping across the Arctic, his aim being to
explore the one blank space the Admiralty had left unfilled: King
William Land. Approaching overland from Repulse Bay he met a
group of Eskimos who told him, in gruesome detail, of an event that
had taken place four winters before in 1849–50.

To summarize Rae's account, the Eskimos had met a group of forty
men dragging a boat southwards down King William Land. They
were led by a tall, stout, middle-aged officer (possibly Crozier). They
were all very thin and indicated by sign language that their ships had
been crushed in the ice. They purchased a seal from the Eskimos.

Later in the season, when the ice was still firm, the Eskimos had
crossed to the North American mainland, and had discovered the
remains of the party lying a day's march from the Great Fish River.

Bodies were scattered all over the place, some in tents, others under the boat, which had been turned over to provide a shelter, and others simply lying in the open. The officer had a telescope over his shoulder and a double-barrelled gun beneath him. Many of the bodies had been hacked with sharp knives and the cooking pots contained human remains. The number of dead in that place was thirty. On a nearby island they discovered another five corpses. Not all the party had died, as became obvious later in the year when the Eskimos heard gunshots – presumably some time after May, when the game came north again.

In confirmation of their story the Eskimos sold Rae a number of articles they had picked up at the scene: a silver table-spoon with the initials 'F.R.M.C.' (Crozier), a silver fork with the initials 'H.D.S.G.' (Harry Goodsir, assistant surgeon on the *Erebus*), three more silver forks with the initials 'A.McD.' (Alexander McDonald, assistant surgeon on the *Terror*), 'G.A.M.' (Gillies A. McBean, second master on the *Terror*), and 'J.S.P.' (John S. Peddie, surgeon on the *Erebus*), a round silver plate inscribed 'Sir John Franklin, K.C.B.', and a star of the Royal Guelphic Order inscribed with the date 1835 and the ironic motto *Nec aspera terrent* – 'Difficulties do not terrify'.

The truth was out. Hurrying back to York Factory, Rae despatched his news to England on 1 September. It was greeted with relief by the Admiralty – they now had absolutely no reason to keep on searching – and with stunned horror by Lady Franklin and the Arctic Council. To return with a few relics was one thing but to accompany them with a story of cannibalism and wholesale death by starvation was beyond the pale.

Doubts were raised. Had Rae visited the spot where the deaths had occurred? No. Could he explain why Franklin's men had gone south to the Great Fish where they knew from previous expeditions that there would be no food at that time of the year? No. Had he anything to support his disgusting and most un-English tale other than the word of a few untutored natives who could count no higher than five? No.

While the dust was rising over Rae's report, the Hudson's Bay

Company sent another overland team under a chief factor called James Anderson to explore Montreal Island, the only island in the Great Fish estuary that might correspond to the one on which the Eskimos had found five bodies. He came across a site where a boat had obviously been repaired. Chunks of wood littered the ground, hacked by unskilled hands. A segment of straking bore the word 'Erebus' beneath its black paint. There were various tools, pieces of bunting, and one or two sections of snowshoe bearing the name Stanley, surgeon on the *Erebus*. But there were no graves, no corpses, no human remains. He went on to search a large stretch of mainland coastline. Again nothing, not a single bone.

Lady Jane and her supporters were overjoyed. Something had happened to the *Erebus* and *Terror*, that much was certain. Although it was now ten years since the expedition had sailed from England, some of its members might still be alive. Lady Jane had to admit that her husband was probably not one of them – by now he would be seventy years old – but some of the younger and fitter members might have survived with the help of the Eskimos. And if they had survived they might have with them diaries and logs containing details of the calamity which had befallen her husband. A new expedition was called for at once.

The Admiralty refused all Lady Jane's appeals. And in a vast, bureaucratic *faux pas* sent her a letter informing her that as they wished to wind up the year's accounts to 31 March 1854, they were assuming Franklin and his men to be dead and that she was, as of that date, entitled to a widow's pension. Lady Jane turned down the offer in a magnificently scathing twelve-page letter that she published for public consumption.

Within the twinkling of an eye she had £1,250 of subscriptions towards a new expedition and on 18 April 1857 she appointed McClintock to command the *Fox*, a 177-pound, screw-driven yacht, on which he was to sail to the Arctic and take one of his famous sledge parties to find her husband – or his remains. (Rae was clearly the better man for the job, but Lady Jane was having nothing to do with such a merchant of doom.)

After a frightful journey through Baffin Bay, during which his tiny vessel was almost 'knocked into lucifer matches',[7] McClintock sailed down Prince Regent Sound in 1858, spent a season trying to get through Bellot Strait, and in 1859 began his investigations. Interviews with Eskimos revealed that they had seen men travelling south, dropping dead as they walked – how many, and when, they could not say. They spoke of a ship that had been wrecked on the coast of King William Land. It had contained many books which were all now destroyed by the weather, and the body of a big man with long teeth. It had been there the year before and was presumably still there now – though when asked if the ship had masts they said no, mentioning the word 'fire' and laughing amongst themselves.

Had the ship been burned? McClintock was frantic to find out. First, however, he had to take on more supplies. Using dog sledges – he had at last abandoned man-hauling in favour of local customs – he went to Fury Beach. Much depleted by John Ross, this little Woolwich of the Arctic nevertheless provided him with a much-needed 1,200 pounds of sugar. Had he wanted, McClintock could have had his pick of tinned vegetables, soup, split peas, tobacco, flour and coal, all as good as when they had been deposited thirty-four years previously.

Having restocked, McClintock began his exploration of King William Island. He himself sledged down its eastern coast to explore Montreal Island before heading north up the west coast of King William Island. His second officer, William Hobson, was sent around the north and west. Montreal Island yielded nothing but a few shards of iron and the odd scrap of wood – much as Anderson had said. King William Island, however, was more profitable. Shortly after midnight on 25 May 1859, McClintock found his first skeleton. It was lying face down on a strip of high ground and belonged to a steward, as far as he could tell from the scraps of uniform. Alongside it was a brush, a comb and a pocket-book whose frozen pages might once have held valuable information but revealed nothing once thawed. The Eskimos had spoken truthfully – Franklin's men *had* fallen down and died as they walked.

Continuing, McClintock found the remains of a cairn. It had obviously been built by Franklin's crew but had since been demolished by animals or Eskimos. Any message it might have contained was lost. Twelve miles on, however, he found a message from Hobson. The lieutenant had found a cairn at Victory Point (James Ross's furthest point west), containing the first record of Franklin's expedition. It was a standard printed form, 'Whoever finds this paper is requested to foward it to the Secretary of the Admiralty, London . . .', with spaces left for dates and place-names. It was damp, and fringed with rust stains from the metal canister in which it had been stored. It contained the following message:

H.M. Ships 'Erebus' and 'Terror'
28th of May 1847, wintered in the ice in lat. 70° 5′ N., 98° 23′ W.
    Having wintered in 1846–7 [a mistake; the true date was 1845–6] at Beechey Island, in lat. 74° 43′ 28″ N., long. 91° 39′ 15″ W., after having ascended Wellington Channel to lat. 77°, and returned by the west side of Cornwallis Island.
    Sir John Franklin commanding the expedition.
    All well.
    Party, consisting of 2 officers and 6 men, left the ship on Monday, 24th May 1847.

It was signed, 'Gm. GORE, Lieut, CHAS. F. DES VOEUX, Mate.'[8]
Here it was, the news they had been looking for. Franklin had gone into Wellington Channel and he had sailed round Cornwallis Island, a feat which none of his rescuers had managed. The Admiralty had not been so stupid after all to concentrate their efforts in that direction. But if Franklin had managed to sail round Cornwallis Island the winter of 1845–6 must have been very mild – so mild that he had been able to press down the normally ice-clogged Peel Sound and reach the west coast of King William Island.
    This was where all Barrow's certainties rose up and hit Franklin on the head. He had not sailed east around King William Island because

Barrow had been convinced that King William Island was part of Boothia and that Boothia was separated from the mainland by a stretch of sea to the south through which the pent-up floes would be driven harmlessly into open water. In fact, the icy strait James Ross had crossed between Boothia and King William Island was the only possible way through the North-West Passage. To go west was to enter the most intransigent ice-trap in the Arctic, where the floes surged in from the northern oceans and, finding no escape, flung themselves ceaselessly against the shore of King William Island – as James Ross had noticed but had not been able to explain.

The ice had opened as wide as it ever would in the history of mankind, lured Franklin into its depths and then, when the weather reverted to normal, snapped around him. That much was clear from a second message scribbled around the margins of the first.

April 25th, 1848. H.M. Ships 'Erebus' and 'Terror' were deserted on the 22nd April, 5 leagues N.N.W. of this, having been beset since 12th September 1846. The officers and crews, consisting of 105 souls, under the command of F.R.M. Crozier, landed here, in lat. 69° 37' 42" N., long. 98° 41' W. Sir John Franklin died on the 11th June 1847; and the total loss by deaths in this expedition has been, to this date, 9 officers and 15 men.

And start on to-morrow, 26th, for Back's Fish River.

It was signed 'F.R.M. CROZIER, Captain and Senior Officer, JAMES FITZJAMES, Captain, H.M.S "Erebus".' Despite their losses and their entrapment of nineteen months, they were still alert, as a remarkably precise postscript showed:

This paper was found by Lt. Irving under the cairn supposed to have been built by Sir James Ross in 1831, 4 miles to the northward, where it had been deposited by the late Commander Gore in June 1847. Sir James Ross's pillar has not, however been found; and the paper has been transferred to this position, which is that in which Sir James Ross's pillar was erected.[9]

The disease that attacked Franklin's ships had been fast and ferocious. On 28 May 1847 all had been well. A fortnight later Franklin was dead and in the following months another twenty-four men died too. This was an unheard-of casualty rate. It could not have been scurvy; they knew by now how to combat it; and had it reared its head the first signs would have been apparent by the time the first message was written. So what was it?

McClintock's party never found the answer. But they did find clues as to what had happened after the ships had been abandoned. Having sledged along the coast of King William Island for seventy miles they encountered a boat containing two human skeletons. The boat was a cumbersome affair, that had been lightened by the substitution of thin fir planks for the upper seven oak strakes but even so weighed 700–800 pounds. It was mounted on a sledge of massive oak beams bound together with iron bolts that weighed as much if not more than the boat itself. The sledge, McCormick recorded, had a battered appearance as if it had been dragged many miles across rough country.

McClintock picked through the evidence like a forensic scientist. One of the skeletons belonged to a large, well-built, middle-aged man. It lay in the bow but had been so ravaged by wild animals that it was impossible to tell whether it had fallen there or had been dragged. Near it were the remains of a slipper – eleven inches long, white, with a black trim, and decorated in red and yellow. Its calfskin lining was intact as was its red-ribboned piping. Next to the slipper, neatly aligned, was a pair of sturdy walking boots.

The second skeleton lay under the boat's after-thwarts. Better preserved than the first, and smaller, it was wrapped in furs and thick cloth. Most likely this man had been the last to die. Next to him lay five watches and two double-barrelled guns propped, loaded, muzzle upwards, against the boat's side. Books were scattered about, among them *A Manual of Private Devotion* inscribed on the title-page, 'G. Back; to Graham Gore.' Others bore similar inscriptions to 'G.G.'.

Strewn throughout the boat was an improbable amount of equipment. There were cloth winter boots, sea-boots, heavy ankle boots and strong shoes. There were silk handkerchiefs – black, white and patterned – towels, soap, sponges, toothbrushes, and hair combs. There were gun-covers, twine, nails, saws, files, powder, bullets, a glove whose fingers were packed with shot, cartridges, wads, knives – dinner and clasp – needle-and-thread cases, boxes of gunners' slow matches, bayonet scabbards, knife sheaths and two rolls of sheet lead. There was also a small amount of tobacco, forty pounds of chocolate, twenty-six pieces of Sir John Franklin's silver, some sealing wax, and an empty tin that had once held twenty-two pounds of meat.

McClintock recorded it all with awe. But what amazed him the most was that the boat and its sledge were not pointing south, but north. Gore and his unknown companion had not been trying to escape; they had been heading back to their ships.

At Victory Point, the mystery deepened amidst a gallimaufry of discarded equipment. A huge pile of winter clothing rose almost to McClintock's shoulders. Next to it were four heavy stoves, a collection of iron hoops, a single wooden block from the ship's rigging, strips of lightning conductor, brass curtain rods, a complete medicine chest – 'the contents in a remarkable state of preservation'[10] – a scattering of scientific instruments and a sextant, leather-covered against frost but with its coloured eye-pieces removed – possibly for use as lenses against snow-blindness. Other rubbish was strewn around, from boot polish to bibles. The only item notably absent was food.

What did it all mean? Why had Crozier's refugees dragged so many inessentials ashore? And why had they left behind important items such as winter clothes, medicines and navigational gear? What had Gore been doing with his boatful of silk handkerchiefs, sponges and chocolate, returning to a place where there was every comfort known to Victorian life save food? And where was that food anyway? Where were the tins of meat and vegetables with which the expedition had been so lavishly stocked? They could not all have been consumed by 1848 – even had Franklin not brought aboard fresh game he would still have tons of provisions in reserve, far more than could be carried on sledges – and McClintock had found only the barest evidence of discarded tins as he retraced the survivors' route along King William Island. Possibly the tins had been filched by passing Eskimos but McClintock reckoned it unlikely; nothing else had been touched as would have been the case had the sites been disturbed.

Further north lay other mysterious remains. Three miles on from Victory Point was a cairn containing an empty canister. Beyond that was another cairn that yielded nothing. Further still, at the tip of King William Island, a third cairn was surrounded by the remains of three small tents, some scraps of clothing and a few blankets. A folded sheet of white paper had been tucked into the rocks but it yielded nothing, even under a microscope. Two corked bottles had maybe contained something of importance, but they were broken, their messages long since blown away by the same bitter north-west winds that had forced the ice onto Franklin's ships. The cairn was excavated and a trench dug around it to a distance of ten feet, but nothing more was found.

By August both McClintock and Hobson were back on board the *Fox*. Every man was exhausted and two were suffering from scurvy. They had no option but to sail home. On 6 August they got up steam, McClintock helping the weakened stokers, and two days later pushed north through mushy ice towards a watery sky, reaching the English Channel on the 20th. As far as Britain was concerned, the Franklin search was at an end.

In the last ten years stupendous sums had been expended on the errant captain and his crew. The Admiralty had disbursed approximately £675,000 in addition to which Lady Jane had spent £35,000 of her own and other's money. On top of this the US government had contributed $150,000, and a single American citizen, Henry Grinnell, had poured no less than $100,000 into the endeavour.

What had been achieved? Very little, at the cost of many lives and many ships. True, the Arctic had been given a thorough, cartographic enema. Ships had squeezed into every available crack of its intestines. More than 40,000 miles had been covered by sledge, more than 8,000 miles of coastline had been minutely examined, Wellington Channel had been explored and the archipelago that interposed itself between Parry's 1819 north and Franklin's 1822 south had been charted to within an inch of its life.

Beyond a catalogue of baffling and contradictory evidence, however, the Franklin mystery was unresolved. Where was he? What had happened to his officers and men? It was possible to draw a tentative track of his expedition's progress, but the track could be interpreted a thousand different ways. In the absence of his journals, all that could be said about Franklin was that he and his men had died. Why, where and how remained unknown.

Gulp by gulp the Arctic swallowed the remaining evidence. On King William Island ice turned to slush, slush to yielding bog, and bog to ice again, each successive season sucking the remains into a layer of earth and moss that was pressed down by new layers of fast-freezing snow and new layers of mystery. Whatever journals that remained to tell the tale of the expedition's end were drawn into the cycle. Nothing would ever be found.

In summer, the mosquitoes that Franklin had been reluctant to kill buzzed over King William Island. In winter, the ice that he had been unafraid to face broke against its shores. And the North-West Passage that he had sought so disastrously curled round its eastern coast, an eternal symbol of futility.

28

RIDING THE GLOBE

On 15 May 1850 – the same month in which Eskimos heard the last, sporadic gunfire of Franklin's survivors – the bells of St Mary's Church pealed, the Ulverston Brass Band huffed and trumped in the marketplace and the boys of Tower Bank School started on their march. Everybody turned out to watch as the children toiled up the Hill of Hoad, overlooking Morecambe Bay, towards a 100-foot-high tower in the shape of the Eddystone Lighthouse.

The tower was something special for the people of Ulverston. Eight thousand citizens had attended its foundation. King William IV's widow had contributed to its cost, so had Lord Palmerston and more admirals than you could cock a hat at. It was a monument to Sir John Barrow, erstwhile poor boy of the parish, who had done so well in the world.

At the front of the procession marched Sergeant-Major Bates of the Duke of Lancaster's Own Yeomanry Cavalry, keeping time as his team sang the song that had been drilled into them:

> *We'll sing the Tower Bank Scholar*
> *Who once was poor as we,*

And won his way by merit
To wealth and high degree.[1]

The children marched to the top of the hill, saluted the monument, and returned under the beady eye of Sgt-Major Bates to Ulverston where they had maybe their first taste of beer at a reception held in the local workhouse while local dignitaries gave interminable speeches about the virtues of Sir John Barrow.

John Barrow would have turned in his grave. He had not returned to his home town for fifty years. It was the very place he had spent his life trying to escape.

Barrow had done so many things in his career. He had visited China and South Africa. He had opened Africa to the world, had discovered Antarctica and had prized apart the mandibles of the Arctic. He had set in motion the largest and most expensive series of explorations in the history of mankind. Nothing similar would be attempted until the US and Soviet space programmes of more than a century later. And even then there was little comparison. Whereas the space programme involved bodies of scientists, hordes of advisers and squalls of technicians, engineers and press men, Barrow's programme had relied on nobody but himself. His memorial was not refreshments in the workhouse, speeches from the gentry, columns in the local newspaper and a shrill encomium from a group of school-children; it was the world – mapped, charted and set to rights by the men he had ordered to do so.

The ball Barrow had set rolling in 1816 did not stop at the Hill of Hoad. It trundled on until the Franklin searchers had completed their task and came finally to rest in London's Waterloo Place where, in 1866, the government erected a statue in memory of Sir John Franklin. The statue is still there today, a little pigeon-spattered, staring manfully towards a statue of Captain Scott, whose expedition was as disastrous as his own. It isn't a good likeness: Franklin is far too thin and bookish. And on its plinth it bears the inscription:

FRANKLIN

TO THE GREAT NAVIGATOR

AND HIS BRAVE COMPANIONS

WHO SACRIFICED THEIR LIVES IN

COMPLETING THE DISCOVERY OF

THE NORTH-WEST PASSAGE.

It was erected by the government by popular demand, partly as a reward for Lady Jane's persistence – refusing any monetary reimbursement she had asked only that McClintock and his crew be awarded £5,000 – and partly to shut her up, her name having become a by-word for aggravation in Admiralty circles. Like all governments, they would rather not have borne the expense but in this instance they had little choice. Whether rightly or wrongly, Franklin was now a national hero, an icon of the age, a symbol of British doughtiness and an exemplar of sacrifice to future generations.

Unfortunately the inscription is a lie. Franklin's sacrifice had been in vain; he did not discover the North-West Passage. Like so many others, he found only where it wasn't. McClure had walked the passage – a passage – but it was not until 1905 that a Norwegian named Roald Amundsen sailed east of King William Island through James Ross Strait, dodged the shoals off the North American coast, and finally crossed the 'vent' that had been sought for more than 400 years. He did it in a shallow-draught boat with a small crew and lived off the land. (John Ross would have been pleased.) It took him five years and he declared the Passage useless for anything.

Barrow's reign was finally over. It had started with one disaster – an expedition wiped out in Africa – and had wandered through tragedy and triumph to end with another – an expedition wiped out in the Arctic. Had it been a good reign? In the material balance of things, no, it had not.

Every single one of Barrow's goals had proved worthless in the finding: Timbuctoo was a mud town of no importance; the Niger had little practical application for trade; northern Australia was totally unworkable as the site of a 'second Singapore'; Antarctica was an inhospitable lump of ice; and the North-West Passage – as Scoresby and others had repeated so wearily – was an utter waste of time. The Open Polar Sea, meanwhile, was not only not worth finding but not even there to be found – although, in Barrow's defence, its absence was only proved in 1909.

Almost everything about Barrow's missions had been wrong – the orders, the ships, the supplies, the funding and the methods. Perhaps no man in the history of exploration has expended so much money and so many lives in pursuit of so desperately pointless a dream.

But what a reign it had been! It had encompassed surreal and unrepeatable events. In the future there would be no more cocked hats in the Arctic; no more blue serge uniforms and brass-buttoned waistcoats in the Sahara; no more sailing ships in the shadow of Mt. Erebus; never again would men struggle with reindeer and sledges to conquer the swirling north polar ice cap.

Never again, either, would such a disparate and entertaining band of explorers stalk the world – men such as the obstinate Rosses, the deranged Laing, the pious Parry, the debonair Lyon, the charmingly hopeless Franklin, the bluff Clapperton and his scheming nemesis Denham, the hard men McClure and Collinson, the dreadful Belcher, and the several hundred others, dead or alive, high or low, who made Barrow's dream possible.

Maybe Barrow had produced no great benefits for mankind – unless one counts such benefits as Lyon's ear-numbing conclusion that the aurora borealis made no noise. Maybe, too, his judgements might have been more accurate – although, to give him his due, it is hard to be accurate about the unknown. But he had filled so many gaps on the globe, had instigated so many dramatic events, and had stretched the known world to limits that would not be surpassed for half a century. Was that so bad?

Moreover, Barrow's dream inspired many others. On one of the Franklin search ships was an impressionable midshipman named Clements Markham. He was greatly taken by the ethos of Barrow's expeditions, the struggle to succeed, the pitting of human strength against the far greater forces of nature. He admired the man-hauled sledges which toiled out from his ship and spent his spare time compiling the ancestry of the men in each team. It left such an impression that he followed Barrow in becoming President of the Royal Geographical Society. He stepped precisely and disastrously in his footsteps. When he sent Scott and Shackleton to find the South Pole they went with man-hauled sledges from the Franklin age, complete with heraldic pennants. Their failures are now well-known.

Markham was not the only one to be moved by the endeavours of Barrow's men. Roald Amundsen, the twentieth century's compleat explorer who sailed the North-West Passage, who discovered the South Pole in 1912 and who, in 1926, was among the uncontested first to discover the North Pole – on an Italian Zeppelin – declared in his autobiography that he had been driven by stories of Barrow's men. They 'thrilled me as nothing I had ever read before. What appealed to me most was the sufferings that Sir John [Franklin] and his men had to endure. A strange ambition burned within me, to endure the same privations . . . I decided to be an explorer.'[2]

The theme was expanded upon by McClintock, one of Barrow's longest-lived explorers, in a speech to mark the half-centenary of Franklin's departure: 'In laying down their lives at the call of duty our countrymen bequeathed to us a rich gift – another of those noble examples not yet rare in our history, and of which we are all so justly proud, one more beacon light to guide our sons to deeds of heroism in the future. These examples of unflinching courage, devotion to duty, and endurance of hardships are as life-blood to naval enterprise.'[3]

Ultimately, for all his failures, Barrow had done something very important: he had set a benchmark for exploration. Throughout the nineteenth and twentieth centuries, scores of men – and women too – struggled in Barrowesque fashion to reach their pointless goals: Livingstone and Stanley battering away at Africa; Shackleton and Scott impaling themselves on the South Pole; Nansen drifting from Kamchatka to the North Sea on the polar ice that had thwarted Parry; Speke and Burton quarrelling over the source of the Nile;

Peary and Cook staking their rancorous claims to the North Pole; Fawcett vanishing into the Amazonian jungle in his doomed quest for Eldorado. They displayed all McClintock's qualifications of courage, devotion and hardship. But, to turn Barrow's words of 1816 back on him, 'to what purpose'?

John Ross had put this question as early as 1835. What use was there, he asked, in opening an area 'of which perhaps the only satisfaction that can ever be derived would be, that there is, on a piece of paper, a black line instead of a blank'? It was about as productive as drawing 'the anatomy of a fly's toe'.[4]

To find the answer one has to look not at results but at motives, and there is no better motive than the one supplied by William Edward Parry. When Parry was a small boy he had been taken by his parents to have lunch with some friends. Bored by proceedings, he had been given permission to leave the table. He wandered into the library. Books lined the walls. A table stood in the middle of the room. Near the window, on a stand, was a strange, round object that spun when touched – a globe.

The small boy climbed onto the globe and began to pedal it round. He was still doing so when the grown-ups found him.

'What, Edward! Are you riding on the globe?'

'Oh yes!' he said. '*How* I should like to go round it!'[5]

Riding the globe! There is the motive that propelled Barrow's expeditions and all the others that followed in their wake. They did not want to go round the globe – that had been done. They did not want to investigate the globe – that was left to others. What they wanted was to ride it. And, thanks to John Barrow, they did.

EPILOGUE

George Back

An invalid for six years following his dreadful voyage of 1836 on the *Terror*, Back managed nevertheless to promote himself with assiduity. Knighted in 1839, he became an admiral in 1857 and was elected President of the Royal Geographical Society in 1856, a post which he held for two decades, amassing the largest body of correspondence in the society's archives.

He remained unpopular amongst his fellow officers thanks to his sense of self-importance and his irritating habit of crossing the street to ask why they had not crossed the street to greet him first. Even in Italy, a country for which he had a fondness, he managed to spread discord. According to one old gentleman of Florence, 'if he was in love with himself he had no right to suppose every lady he met was the same'.[1] Lady Franklin and her niece Sophia found him particularly obnoxious.

He died on 23 June 1878. Nobody could question his achievements, but there was something about him that rankled. They could not put their fingers on it precisely, but people agreed that, in death as in life, he did not leave 'a very favourable impression behind him'.[2]

Francis Beaufort

Considering the personal troubles Beaufort faced, it is quite astounding that he took any part whatsoever in the Franklin search. His first wife died in 1836 and on remarrying in 1838 his second wife had a stroke two months after the wedding. Seven years later she had another stroke and broke her thigh. While nursing his wife, who eventually lost her mind, Beaufort also had to contend with his troublesome offspring, whose care would have been a career in itself: of his three daughters two were given to fits of hysterics, brought on in the case of one, apparently, by smoking too much cannabis; of his four sons, one was mentally disturbed, another disgraced himself as a clergyman with an unsuitable liaison and a third, having stolen his mother's jewellery, joined the East India Company where he was brought to trial for alleged embezzlement. On top of all this, Beaufort was plagued by ill-health, suffering from chronic gastritis, kidney stones, prostate trouble, dizzy spells and excruciating sciatica brought on by a slipped disc. The cure he was offered for his sciatica was a cold bath every morning followed by lengthy walks. On one of these walks, at the age of seventy-four, he was run over by a runaway Post Office cart. A little later he had a heart attack at his desk. And in 1854 he went deaf.

He retired on 24 January 1855 having spent sixty-seven years in naval service. His twenty-five-year tenure as Hydrographer remains the longest on record. He died on 17 December 1857, aged eighty-four, and was commemorated by a sour little obituary note from Back: 'And so poor Beaufort is gone! Well, peace be with him . . . He lived long enough for his fame – too long for many of his friendships, and probably for his happiness. His judgement was generally clear but he often acted from impulse and was susceptible to flattery.'[3]

A more generous monument was the construction of St Andrew's Waterside Church in Gravesend, its roof fashioned on the inside so that it looked like an upturned boat.

Frederick William Beechey

Beechey never fulfilled the promise he had shown in his early years. A sickly but well-connected officer, he attempted a survey of South America in 1835 but was forced to return the following year on grounds of ill-health. He pottered benignly on, surveying the coast of Ireland for ten years until 1847 when he was called to the Arctic Council.

He offered his sensible opinions on the Franklin search and was not dismayed when they were ignored. Intelligent and tolerant, he was liked by all. His friends found him an uncontroversial job as inspector at the Board of Trade which he held from 1850 until his death on 25 November 1856, doubling up for three years as aide-de-camp to Queen Victoria.

In the last year of his life he served as President of the Royal Geographical Society.

Edward Belcher

Belcher was court-martialled in the wake of his disastrous mission to the Arctic. Although acquitted, his sword was handed back to him in stony silence – the Admiralty's equivalent of a 'Not Proven' verdict. In private, he maintained that he had only been following orders when he abandoned his ships and that the court martial had been drummed up 'merely to please the malignant press'.[4]

He volunteered to serve in the Arctic again, but as he told a friend, 'I must freely say now that I see how miserably I should be supported in any gallant movement that I should be *very much disappointed* if they took me at my word.'[5] They didn't.

He was never offered another command, and devoted the rest of his life to writing. His first effort was a journal of his rescue mission, grandiosely titled *The Last of the Arctic Voyages*, which he followed with *A Treatise on Nautical Surveying* – a respected work that remained standard reading for many decades – and *Horatio Howard Brenton, a Naval Novel*, a three-volume saga that has been described as 'exceedingly stupid'.[6]

Shunted by the dead hand of the Navy List he was promoted to Vice-Admiral in 1861 and to Admiral in 1872. For some unknown reason he was also made a Knight Commander of the Bath in 1867. The most unsuccessful of Barrow's men, he conversely received more awards than most.

He died in 1877.

Edward Bird

Bird slipped gently into obscurity following the end of Barrow's Arctic programme. He eventually worked his way up the Admiralty ladder to reach the post of Admiral (on half-pay) in 1875 and died six years later aged eighty-three at his home in Kent – named, appropriately, 'The Wilderness'.

Richard Collinson

Collinson received no credit at all for the discovery of the North-West Passage, a fact which justifiably outraged him. Had he not covered as much of it from the west as Franklin had from the east? If Franklin was to be hailed as the discoverer, then it had to be remembered that the ice-clogged 'passage' Franklin had found led into ice-free waters that Collinson had found. That McClure, who had disobeyed orders, should be awarded £10,000 for becoming stuck and having to be evacuated incensed Collinson still further. Had McClure kept the rendezvous in Bering Strait, Collinson would have been able to take aboard Miertsching the interpreter, as had always been intended, and would then have been able to make sense of a garbled Eskimo message regarding ships stranded to the east. And had Collinson had McClure's ship at the tip of Victoria Island he would then have had the manpower to explore the west coast of King William Island and would therefore have found the Franklin expedition.

He never accepted another naval command and collected his dues grudgingly: the Royal Geographical Society tossed a Gold Medal his way, he was knighted in 1875 and was made an admiral on the retired list the same year. He died in Ealing on 12 September 1883.

Dixon Denham

The vile Denham became a favourite of Lord Bathurst and was given an experimental position as governor of liberated African slaves in Sierra Leone. He took up his position in January 1827 and at the end of the year received a letter from Richard Lander with the news of Clapperton's death. He transmitted it home, thereby scooping Lander completely.

He got his come-uppance, however. Having proved his aptitude for West African service he was sent there for life. He was promoted first to lieutenant colonel – the rank he had previously fled Africa to secure – and then to lieutenant-governor of Sierra Leone. He died there of yellow fever, after a short illness, on 8 May 1828.

Jane, Lady Franklin

Lady Jane was a woman who never gave up. From her home in Kensington Gore – next door to the scandalous saloniste Lady Blessington and her lover, the Comte D'Orsay, who had a preference for leaf-coloured gloves, whose gold dressing-case required two men to carry it and who appalled Macaulay almost as much as did Croker – she battered away with increasing feebleness at the doors of the Admiralty, demanding that something be done. They offered her nothing save a statue – what else could they do or offer; the man was dead, and that was that. But she was gratified when the Royal Geographical Society awarded her its Gold Medal in 1860.

She remained an important figure in Arctic circles, her advice being sought by youngsters such as Sherard Osborn in 1875 regarding the

North Polar expedition under Captain Nares, as well as the mad newspaper proprietor, James Gordon Bennett, who approached her in the same year regarding an attempt (doomed) at the North Pole which he hoped to pursue to the benefit of his *New York Herald*.

She died on 18 July 1875, from what her doctors diagnosed as a 'decay of nature'.[7] Her pall-bearers included Barrow Jnr., McClintock, Collinson and several other Arctic hands. Hooker was there, and the first-ever Bishop of Tasmania conducted the service.

A fortnight after her death, a memorial was unveiled in Westminster Abbey to Sir John Franklin. The inscription was written by Franklin's nephew by marriage, Alfred, Lord Tennyson:

> *Not here! the white North has thy bones; and thou,*
> *Heroic sailor-soul,*
> *Art passing on thine happier voyage now*
> *Toward no earthly pole.*

Underneath it the Dean of Westminster added a note of his own: 'This monument was erected by Jane, his widow, who, after long waiting, and sending in search of him, herself departed, to seek and to find him in the realms of light, July 18, 1875, aged 83 years.'

Her body was placed in the catacombs of Kensal Green Cemetery.

Her niece, Sophia Cracroft, attempted a biography but went blind in the process – anyone who has tried to decipher Lady Jane's cramped handwriting will sympathize – and in later years her descendants left her papers to the Scott Institute with instructions to 'take out whatever is of polar interest, and burn the rest'.[8] One wonders what was burned.

John Franklin

In the 1980s, two North American investigators unravelled a part of the Franklin mystery. They exhumed the three corpses buried on Beechey Island and performed a post-mortem. They found several things. First, that the bodies had been preserved so pristinely by the cold that they were as fresh as the day they died – publication of the very unsettling photographs is restricted to avoid sensationalism. Secondly, that they had been autopsied a century earlier by the Franklin searchers and had been reinterred with the comment that they had died of pneumonia-related diseases. And thirdly, that they contained massive quantities of lead.

Where did the lead come from? As far as can be ascertained it was in the tins of preserved food, which had been sealed with lead solder. The symptoms of lead poisoning are lethargy, an irrational state of mind, and a general debilitation. All of these, combined with the effects of scurvy, from which Franklin's expedition was probably suffering, could have brought the expedition to its knees.

Lead poisoning, however, offers no clue as to the whereabouts of Franklin's grave nor to the fate of his ships. Regarding the former, Eskimos told strange tales of a hole being dug on land and filled with a mysterious, soft mixture that later went hard. Could it have been a cement cap to a grave? If so, it has yet to be discovered. A yet more tantalizing tale was told of Franklin's ships. In 1851, a navy brig spotted a floe drifting down Baffin Bay. Perched on it were two ships. The brig followed the floe until it sank. They obtained a very clear sighting of the ships, which they described as being black with a yellow stripe along their sides. The only missing vessels that fitted this description were *Erebus* and *Terror*.

And Franklin's records? These would have undoubtedly survived to the last, and may well have been stored in a lead-lined casket to protect them from damp. To throw them away would have been unthinkable. Who knows where they might have ended up?

It is impossible at this distance to say anything about Franklin's death save that he was outlived by his ships, by most of his men and certainly by his records. The 1980s investigation proved that many of Franklin's men had died along the west coast of King William Island – and had resorted to cannibalism, as was demonstrated by tell-tale knife cuts on the longer bones of the skeletons they uncovered – but it answered none of the intimate questions.

That area of the Arctic is now well-known – there is even an airstrip on King William Island, and another on Boothia – but it is no Piccadilly and the northern part of Boothia, to which some of Franklin's men might have struggled, if Gore's boat-sledge is anything to go by, is relatively unexplored. Perhaps in future years, someone will stumble upon a flat piece of cement, half-covered with boulders, beneath which rest the bones of Sir John Franklin. Maybe, too, someone will scratch through the rocks of Boothia, or King William Land, or the North American coast and find a rotting, lead-lined casket, tucked out of harm's way, possibly surrounded by the toppled stones of a cairn, in which lie the last records of Franklin's expedition.

Fittingly, Barrow had picked up one mystery – Mungo Park and his missing journal – and put down another – Franklin and his missing journal.

John Hepburn

Franklin's and Richardson's old companion from the disastrous 1819–22 overland voyage was found a job in the rope yard at Woolwich. He later sailed on the *Prince Albert* in search of Franklin and regaled his fellow traveller, Bellot, with many insights into the expedition. He was particularly expressive about Back, whom he described as not very brave, but 'charming to those from whom he hopes to gain something'.[9] His subsequent fate is unknown.

Joseph Dalton Hooker

Ever since he sailed for the Antarctic with James Ross, Hooker had longed for recognition. In due course he found it. He became the most authoritative botanist of the century and travelled to New Zealand, India and the Himalayas in search of new specimens. He succeeded his father as Director of the Royal Botanic Gardens at Kew in 1865, and kept the post for twenty years before retiring to become Britain's elder statesman of botany.

The immature sprite who had bounded through the Antarctic ended his life as a bearded Victorian sage with an admirable 300 or more books and papers to his credit. He was buried in Kew on 17 December 1911 and is commemorated by a plaque in Westminster Abbey.

Along with McClintock he acted as adviser to Scott's Antarctic expeditions. His papers contain a letter that has eerie relevance to the climate trends of today. In 1911, he read a report of Scott's first expedition to the South Pole and told one member that 'the only serious omission . . . is that of the marvellous retrocession of the Barrier since Ross mapped it. To me this appears the most momentous change known to be brought about in the Antarctic in little more than half a century. I have seen doubts cast upon Ross's demarcation of the sea front of the Barrier – but that is ridiculous, he was a first-rate naval surveyor . . .'[10]

The Barrier had shrunk at the rate of approximately one mile per year. The clean white world that Hooker had visited so long ago was already starting to dissolve.

John Lander

John Lander died in 1839 of tuberculosis, in a house near Bryanston Square, London. He was thirty-two years old. He left a wife and three children who appealed for charity to the Royal Geographical Society but were turned down.

His family was eventually smiled upon by Queen Victoria, who gave them a pension of £75 per year from the Civil List. This lasted until 1881 when John's daughter Mary died. The pension's closure was fought by the oldest surviving Lander, John's eighty-one-year-old sister, Nannie, whose income was £10 per year. Her application was refused. She died in the workhouse.

Richard Lander

Richard Lander was buried in the Clarence cemetery on the island of
Fernando Po, off the West African coast. All attempts to commemor-
ate him were dogged by misfortune. His widow and daughter placed
a monument in the Savoy Hotel's chapel, but it was destroyed by fire
in 1864. It was replaced by a stained-glass window that was blown out
in the Second World War. A memorial column was erected in Lemon
Street, Truro, in 1835. It fell down the next year thanks to shoddy
workmanship. Re-erected it now carries his heroic image.

His widow was given a pension of £70 per year and his single
descendant, a daughter, received £80 until her death.

Gordon Laing

Laing's remains were discovered by a French expedition in 1910,
under a tree just as had been reported. His body, along with that of an
Arab boy who had been killed in the same attack, was exhumed and
later taken to Timbuctoo for reburial. In the same year the French
held an official inquiry into Laing's murder. Among the witnesses
was the eighty-two-year-old nephew of one of the assassins. His
family still possessed a piece of the booty – a brooch in the shape of a
golden cockerel, which had been Emma Laing's parting gift to her
husband.

Rousseau, the French Consul at Tripoli, who had been suspected
of stealing Laing's journal, never did publish his book on Timbuctoo –
wisely – despite having written the first half. The French inquiry
said that Laing's papers had been burned by his attackers. This is
open to question. If Laing's journal ever existed it is now probably
somewhere in America.

Emma Laing married one of her father's Vice-Consuls on 13 April
1829. She died six months later of tuberculosis, whose tell-tale pallor
had caused Laing such anxiety when he received her miniature portrait in the Sahara.

The African Society of London erected a plaque to Laing in 1930 one year after the last (official) slave caravan crossed the Sahara.

George Francis Lyon

On his return from the Arctic in 1824, Lyon put himself about in society. He married well and was one of the select few to dine at the celebration banquet given by Isambard Kingdom Brunel in his new tunnel under the Thames. But, dismissed by Barrow, he was never again given a naval command. For a while he fell into what he described as 'ruin and poverty'[11] until in 1826 he found himself a well-paid job as site-inspector for a Mexican mining company. The post was only for a few months, however, and Lyon lost his earnings, plus all his worldly possessions, when his homeward-bound ship foundered off Ireland. On reaching England he learned that his wife had died four months earlier, leaving him to bring up their only child, a girl, on his own. He earned a bit of money from a journal of his time in Mexico, then accepted a post in 1827 at £2,000 per annum to inspect the gold mines of the Real del Monte and Bolanos Mining Companies in Brazil.

In 1832 his eyesight began to fail – the result of opthalmia he had contracted in Africa – and he took a ship home for expert medical advice. He died *en route* on 8 October, from what his brother described as a particularly unpleasant 'complication of diseases'.[12] The man who had travelled so jauntily across Africa and the Arctic ended life as a blind, delirious wreck, his limbs swollen and his body wasted.

His mother took custody of his daughter.

Francis Leopold McClintock

The man who discovered Franklin's fate lived off his fame for the rest of his life. His journal of the voyage to find Franklin's remains has been described as 'the best and most interesting of all Arctic books'[13] – by his biographer, admittedly – and was a bestseller on its publication in 1860, subsequently going through seven editions.

McClintock later worked as surveyor for a submarine telegraph line between the Faroes and Labrador – a ghastly experience from which he returned with his ship half-wrecked – and saw service in the Mediterranean, the West Indies and the North Sea, often acting as unofficial naval nanny to the future King Edward VII.

He could turn on the charm when he wanted to – 'your sunny good temper is worth a thousand a year to you',[14] Lady Franklin assured him – and was drawn disastrously into the 1868 general election, when he was persuaded to enter his name as Tory candidate for the notoriously difficult Irish seat of Drogheda. The anti-British rioting was so violent, involving mobs, gunfire and at least one death, that McClintock had to be escorted by armed police from the polling station before he had received his 131st vote. Opposition having been removed, the voting continued cheerfully and to everyone's satisfaction. McClintock's last political act was to have the decision annulled. He left the re-election, with profound relief, to another.

From 1872 to 1877 he was Superintendent of Portsmouth Docks, during which time he oversaw the outfitting of the Nares expedition, Britain's last official stab at the Arctic. He then took the rank of Vice-Admiral and saw out his service in Bermuda as Commander-in-Chief of the North American station. He was pleased to find that Kellett was among his serving officers.

He died on 17 November 1907 and, like many of his Arctic fellows, was commemorated in Westminster Abbey.

Robert McClure

McClure carried on in his grim, combative fashion, commanding a battalion of marines at the capture of Canton in 1857. But the Arctic seemed to have drawn his teeth. He served no more after 1861 and was content to edge his way up the Navy List on half-pay until 1873

when he reached the rank of Vice-Admiral. He died the same year in
his home at 25 Duke Street, St James, and was buried in Kensal
Green Cemetery.

Richard McCormick

After his expedition with Belcher in 1852–3, McCormick never
went to sea again. He wasted his time and energy in a futile quest
for promotion before retiring in 1865 at the age of sixty-five with the
rank of Deputy-Inspector. McCormick was incensed by the fact
that fourteen out of his fifteen fellow Deputy-Inspectors were
junior to him, and that four of the six senior Inspectors were too. His
promotion to higher levels seems to have been blocked in part by
Sir James Ross, the two men having fallen out after their Antarctic
mission.

McCormick retired to Hecla House in Wimbledon, where he spent
his last years with a menagerie of stuffed animals that he had collected
on his journeys, an irritable Greenland husky called Erebus, and a
tame Aylesbury duck that slept on a cushion by the fire alongside a
pet sparrow. Dog, duck and sparrow followed McCormick wherever
he went until one day he walked from his sitting-room to the dining-
room and closed the door too hastily behind him. The sparrow flew
into it and broke its neck.

McCormick died on 28 October 1890.

Sherard Osborn

Osborn, he of the purple prose, who had been placed under cabin
arrest by Belcher and deprived of his command, devoted his literary
and exploratory ambitions to the Arctic. Both McClure and
McClintock gave him their journals to see to the press. In 1864, when
Osborn was agitating for a follow-up search, McClintock wrote to him
that, 'I am glad to know that you are poking up the embers so as to

keep the Arctic pot boiling. I wish I were now preparing for a trip to the North Pole, for I regard it as being within the reach of this generation.'[15] Osborn responded enthusiastically, being the driving force behind the 1875 Nares expedition of which he hoped to be a member. But on 6 May 1875, twenty-three days before Nares set out, Osborn died with 'awful suddenness'.[16] The likeable young man's funeral was attended by almost every man in Nares' contingent.

William Edward Parry

Parry, who had used his connections to gain an amazing clutch of posts – Hydrographer with no knowledge of surveying, Commissioner of the Poor Law while still in the navy, Comptroller of Steam Machinery with no knowledge of engineering, Superintendent of Haslar Hospital with no knowledge of medicine – died, probably of cancer, on 8 July 1855. Lady Isabella had preceded him, after a prolonged illness, on 12 May 1839.

The man who had gone further west and further north than anyone else in the history of Arctic exploration was desolate. He spent his final years writing a series of religious tracts, one of which he dedicated to his wife: 'the chief comforter of my earthly pilgrimage – the sharer of every joy, and the alleviator of every sorrow – but a faithful counsellor and friend, through many a rough and thorny path in our journey'.[17]

When Parry died, *The Times* lauded him with equal gush. 'No successor on the path of Arctic adventure has yet snatched the chaplet from the brow of this great navigator. Parry is still the champion of the North!'[18]

He was buried in Greenwich graveyard, and was redistributed by a German bomb that fell on the site during the Second World War. His name lived on, however, being given to an archipelago, four islands, five capes, a mountain, a crater on the moon, a type of kangaroo and a literary cat.

John Rae

Rae was awarded £10,000 for his part in ascertaining Franklin's fate. But somehow he was never accepted as a true explorer by the Arctic fraternity. His method of travel, involving small teams on dog sledges living off the land, went against the current ethos – even though it was extraordinarily successful. Besides, he was too blunt and too robust for London society. As Lady Franklin wrote, when rejecting him in favour of McCormick as a suitable man to find her husband, 'Dr. Rae cut off his odious beard but looks still very hairy & disagreeable.'[19]

He spent £2,000 of his prize money on kitting out a ship for further Arctic explorations only to see the vessel sink the same year on the Great Lakes. Undeterred, he plunged himself into further overland explorations of Canada and in the 1860s led several highly perilous missions as a surveyor for telegraph companies.

He was elected a Fellow of the Royal Society in 1880, was given honorary degrees by Edinburgh University and McGill College, Montreal, but he never quite gained the acceptance he felt was due to him.

He died on 22 July 1893 at his London home, 4 Addison Gardens, of an attack of flu that developed into pneumonia. Everyone agreed that he had been a very fit man – he had travelled some 23,000 miles across the Arctic during his lifetime, on one memorable occasion covering forty miles in seven hours wearing snowshoes to attend a dinner party in Toronto – but he was still too hairy.

He is buried outside St Magnus Cathedral in Kirkwall.

John Richardson

Richardson was a popular man and a robust one – he had three wives, two of whom he outlived. He also managed to endear himself to Barrow. His knighthood, which came in 1846, was one of only two favours that Barrow asked of his superiors on retirement – the other being the promotion of Fitzjames on the doomed Franklin expedition. When the approval came through, Richardson was ill-placed to receive it. 'It turned out,' Barrow wrote, 'that he was employing himself to plant flowers and ever-greens round the grave of his late wife, whom he had recently lost.'[20] Sadly, Richardson told Barrow that the intelligence would have been more welcome a few days earlier when his wife could have enjoyed it.

Although he had not visited the Arctic since his mission in 1825 with the man his children called 'Uncle Franklin', Richardson volunteered in 1848 to join an overland rescue attempt with Rae. By then sixty-two years old he took to the tundra with relish – 'I could almost fancy myself at times . . . that I have never been anything but an inhabitant of these wilds,'[21] he wrote to his wife. Alas, he discovered nothing about his old friend's whereabouts. His and Rae's solitary journeys by canoe along Canada's northern coastline were to no avail and they returned empty-handed in 1849.

The remainder of his life was spent in lecturing before various learned societies, in a belated Grand Tour of the continent and in doctoring the people who lived near his home in the Scottish Borders.

The Royal Society gave him a medal in 1856 and he was awarded a degree by Trinity College, Dublin, a year later. He was also elected a member of the Wernarian Natural History Society of Edinburgh, the Natural History Society of Montreal, the Literary and Philosophical Society of Quebec, the Geographical Society of Paris and the Academy of Natural Science of Philadelphia.

He remained immune to these honours, preferring to attend to his garden, of which he had become 'passionately fond'.[22] He saw his eldest daughter and his youngest son – his two favourite children – to their graves before following them on Monday 5 June 1865.

That Monday was a 'lovely, soft June day'.[23] Richardson pottered around his garden, visited a few friends, worked for a few hours and went to bed at ten o'clock with the Anglo-Saxon version of 'History of the World by Orosius'. At eleven o'clock his wife went up to say goodnight. He spoke of his plans for the next day. Then he gave a long sigh and died.

James Ross

James Ross never fully recovered from his experience in the Antarctic
and his subsequent travails in the Arctic only underlined his weakness. He spent the rest of his life in rural Buckinghamshire with his
wife, whose nickname was 'Thing'. When a memorial banquet was
proposed in honour of Barrow, Ross declined the presidency, stating
that 'my extreme abhorrence of public dinners, of which I have seen
so much, has occasioned me to entirely give up attending them'.[24]
Later, however, he regained a bit of his vim, to the extent that
Richardson recorded that Sir James and Lady 'Thing' Ross were both
'prompted by a love of notoriety'.[25]

He was very much in love with his wife, who perhaps shared the
fondness for drink to which he was prone. As William Jerdan, editor of
the *Literary Gazette*, wrote, 'I am bound to say that a more perfect state
of married felicity could not be imagined . . . enjoying what they
wished of neighbouring society, and entertaining friends at home,
surely their life was a pleasant one, and, above all, their tastes and
habits and opinions were ever in accord . . . if ever an observer could
affirm there were two human sympathies concentrated in one, it
might have been affirmed of Sir James and Lady Ross.'[26]

Ann, Lady Ross died in 1857, and her husband followed her five
years later. Both are buried in the churchyard of Aston Abbott,
Buckinghamshire. A stained-glass window above the altar reads: 'To
the glory of God and in memory of Rear-Admiral Sir James Ross and
of Ann his wife.'

John Ross

Old John Ross, active to the end in everything and anything that took
his fancy, continued to irritate the authorities from his 'castle' in
Stranraer. At one point he concluded the Admiralty's charts of the
Baltic were deficient and decided to remedy the matter, prompting a
weary response from Beaufort: 'I have to thank you for the 100th

copy of your Slitö Bay,' wrote the Hydrographer, 'and to satisfy you
that we are sufficiently supplied with them now, I send you one of
ours.'[27] Ross kept up his heckling with exceptional vigour – apart
from a brief interlude when he tried to cure his increasing deafness
with steam and burned himself so badly that he remained insensible
for four days – until September 1856, when he died during a visit to
London.

His personal life was, predictably, as controversial as his public life.
In 1847 his trophy wife, Maria, Lady Ross, left him for his lawyer –
Ross was a man who always had lawyers on call – and until his dying
day he never knew where she was. He did his best to find her, and
urged a reconciliation when he left, as he thought, for his death on the
1850 expedition to find Franklin. But Lady Maria stayed undercover.

The cause of their break-up was Ross's alleged molestation of two
servant girls, resulting in a pregnancy. Ross denied it all, stating that
he had only visited the first girl's room to fetch a towel and a bar of
soap that she had borrowed, and as for the second girl he had good
reason to believe that her brother had fathered the child. He ham-
mered away, gathering affidavits from all and sundry to prove his
innocence, but he never saw his wife again.

He was buried with full naval honours in Kensal Green Cemetery.

Edward Sabine

Sabine, who had probably been the primary agent behind John Ross's
disgrace of 1818 and was certainly the cause of Scoresby's compass
disappointments, rose to high and respectable rank as the most
knowledgeable magnetic expert in the world.

From being a man who knew nothing he became a man who knew
everything. By 1856 he was a major-general, a Fellow of the Royal
Society, and had several gold medals for this and that hanging round
his neck. He was even invited to join a three-man advisory committee
on magnetism of which the other two members were Faraday and
Young.

The transformation was not only from ignorance to wisdom. It was also from action to inaction. The longer Sabine lived the less he did and the more he opined. His opinions were not always correct, but nobody minded because 'his grace of manner and invincible cheerfulness rendered him universally popular'.[28] He was given honorary degrees by both Oxford and Cambridge in 1855, and was honoured by Prussia, Italy and Brazil.

He was supported in his academic career by his wife Elizabeth, a talented linguist who translated works by explorers such as Humboldt and Wrangel. Elizabeth died in 1879 and her husband lingered on, gradually losing his mind, until he too died on 26 June 1883. He was buried next to his wife in the family vault at Tewin, Hertfordshire.

William Scoresby

While John Barrow was alive, Scoresby remained an Admiralty pariah. His opinions were disregarded and the new compasses he offered them were dismissed as rubbish. It was with some pique, therefore, that he discovered on a visit to Canada in 1844 that Toronto University was displaying a compass that accorded exactly to one of his own designs. It had been donated by Sabine.

Following Barrow's death, however, he regained some of his status. His advice was actively sought by the Arctic Council, 'being aware of your great experience in all matters connected with the Polar Sea and of the value that consequently attaches to your opinions'.[29] In a later letter from Parry, it was made clear that he was considered one of 'us Arctic men'.[30]

Scoresby remained active to the last. As a man of the cloth he ministered to his various congregations – he set up a floating chapel in the East End docklands, a novelty that was very well attended – and as a man of science he kept in touch with all new developments. Amongst his correspondents was James Joule. In his later years he made several trips to America and even one to Australia; during the latter he amazed his fellow passengers by clambering up the rigging, aged sixty-six, to test yet another of his compasses.

He died in Truro on 21 March 1857.

Hanmer Warrington

Warrington lingered on in Tripoli, wrestling with the problems of an area that was increasingly of little interest to the rest of the world. In 1842 he tried to form the African Society, a company whose aim was to raise capital for developing legitimate Saharan commerce and thereby eliminating slavery. Investors were invited to buy a maximum of thirty shares and a minimum of fifteen at a cost of £200 apiece. The Pasha of Tripoli, to whom the rules did not apply, bought five. Nobody else bought any.

Left to his own devices, as he had been since 1814, Warrington understandably came to view himself as lord of his own domain. In London, however, his name was a by-word for insubordination. Officials became concerned by his disdain for bureaucracy and high-handed approach. In 1846 he sent a British subject to Malta to be tried for murder. The case was thrown out for a total lack of evidence. Warrington was reprimanded. That same year he insulted the Sardinian Consul so intolerably that another reprimand was issued. On 19 March two of his despatches were returned as being unpardonably imprecise. Three weeks later he was asked to resign. He did so with good grace, asking only that his son Herbert be allowed to take his place, having served as Vice-Consul for seven years. London replied that Herbert had only been appointed on condition that he not be paid. Moreover, on examination of the records, they could not help noticing that another son, Frederick, had been drawing unauthorized pay as an interpreter.

Warrington retired to Italy in ignominy, where he died in 1847. It was a sad end to fifty-two years' service, thirty-two of which had been spent in Tripoli. He left behind him a third son, Henry, who moved to Murzouk and lived as an Arab before being murdered in 1854.

SOURCES AND
REFERENCES

The following sources and references are cited by chapter, with each entry referring back to the author and his or her book within that particular chapter. Unless otherwise indicated entries refer to the author's most recently cited work. To save unnecessary repetition book titles have been condensed after their first appearance. All titles are given in full in the Bibliography. As regards archive material, the following abbreviations have been used:

BL	–	Bodleian Library, Oxford
DTC	–	Dawson Turner Collection, Natural History Museum, London
MHS	–	Museum of the History of Science, Oxford
PRO	–	Public Records Office, Kew
RBG	–	Royal Botanic Gardens Library and Archives, Kew
RGS	–	Royal Geographical Society Archives, London
RS	–	Royal Society Archives, London
SAR	–	Somerset Archive and Record Service, Taunton
SPRI	–	Scott Polar Research Institute, Cambridge.

1 The Man at the Admiralty

1 J. H. Tuckey, *Narrative of an Expedition to Explore the River Zaire* (John Murray, London, 1818), p. ii.
2 J. Barrow, *Autobiographical Memoir* (John Murray, London, 1847), p. 10.
3 C. Lloyd, *Mr. Barrow of the Admiralty* (Collins, London, 1970), cited p. 42.
4 Barrow, op. cit., p. 172.
5 Ibid., p. 261.
6 Ibid., p. 489.
7 Ibid., p. 490.
8 Ibid., p. 191.
9 Ibid., p. 504.
10 Ibid.
11 Ibid., p. 505.
12 Ibid., p. 504.
13 Ibid.
14 Ibid., p. 496.
15 Ibid., p. 504.
16 Lloyd, op. cit., cited p. 155.
17 J. Barrow, *Sketches of the Royal Society & Royal Society Club* (John Murray, London, 1849), cited p. 40.
18 *Fraser's Magazine*, March 1831.
19 Lloyd, op. cit., cited p. 87.
20 Ibid.
21 Ibid., cited p. 88.
22 Barrow, op. cit., p. 455.

2 Death on the Congo

1 J. G. Jackson, *An Account of the Empire of Marocco . . . and an Interesting Account of Timbuctoo, the Great Emporium of Central Africa* (Bulmer, London, 1814), p. 296.
2 Ibid., p. 303.
3 Ibid., p. 314.
4 M. Mackay, *The Indomitable Servant* (Rex Collings, London, 1978), cited p. 6.
5 M. Park, *Travels in the Interior Districts of Africa performed under the direction and patronage of the African Association in the years 1795, 1796 and 1797* (Bulmer, London, 1799), p. 195.
6 J. H. Tuckey, *Narrative . . .*, op. cit., p. xx.
7 Ibid., p. lvii.
8 J. Barrow, *Autobiographical Memoir*, op. cit., p. 395.
9 Ibid.
10 Tuckey, op. cit., p. v.
11 DTC – Banks to Barrow, 12 August 1815.
12 Ibid.
13 C. Lloyd, *Mr. Barrow of the Admiralty*, op. cit., cited p. 116.
14 Tuckey, op. cit., p. xxv.
15 Lloyd, op. cit., cited p. 117.

16 Ibid., cited p. 118.
17 Ibid.
18 Tuckey, op. cit., p. xxvii.
19 Ibid., p. xxvi.
20 Ibid., p. xxxii.
21 Ibid.
22 Ibid.
23 Ibid., p. xxxiii.
24 Ibid., p. xxxix.
25 Ibid., p. xxxvii.
26 Ibid., p. 229.
27 Ibid., p. lxxvi.
28 Lloyd, op. cit., cited p. 119.
29 Tuckey, op. cit., p. xxxi.
30 Ibid., p. 52.
31 Ibid., p. 18.
32 Ibid., p. 147.
33 Ibid., p. 139.
34 Ibid., p. 149.
35 Ibid., p. 214.
36 Ibid.
37 Ibid.
38 Ibid., p. 222.
39 Ibid., p. 223.
40 Ibid., p. lxii.
41 Ibid., p. xlii.
42 Ibid.
43 Ibid., p. 225.

3 The Mirage of Lancaster Sound

1 A. Parry, *Parry of the Arctic* (Chatto & Windus, London, 1963), cited p. 29.
2 Ibid.
3 DTC – Scoresby to Banks, 2 October 1817.
4 E. S. Dodge, *The Polar Rosses* (Faber and Faber, London, 1973), cited p. 35.
5 *Dictionary of National Biography*, Vol. XVII (Oxford University Press, 1917), p. 945.
6 DTC – Scoresby to Banks, 2 October 1817.
7 T. and C. Stamp, *William Scoresby, Arctic Scientist* (Caedmon, Whitby, 1976), cited p. 66.
8 Ibid., cited p. 67.
9 DTC – Scoresby to Banks, 25 November 1817.
10 Stamp, op. cit., cited p. 68.
11 Ibid.
12 Ibid.
13 Dodge, op. cit., cited p. 41.
14 John Ross, *A Voyage of Discovery . . . for the purpose of Exploring Baffin's Bay and inquiring into the probability of a North-West Passage* (John Murray, London, 1819), p. 1.

15 A. Parry, op. cit., cited p. 30.
16 Ibid., cited p. 9.
17 E. Parry, *Memoirs of Rear-Admiral Sir W. Edward Parry* (Longman, London, 1859), cited p. 52.
18 Ross, op. cit., p. iv.
19 E. Parry, op. cit., cited p. 83.
20 Ross, op. cit., p. 30.
21 Ibid., p. 58.
22 A. Parry, op. cit., cited p. 35.
23 Ross, op. cit., p. 70.
24 Ibid., p. 77.
25 Ibid., p. 80.
26 Ibid., p. 83.
27 Ibid., p. 89.
28 Ibid., p. 95.
29 Ibid., p. 110.
30 Ibid., p. 123.
31 D. Smith, *Arctic Expeditions, British and Foreign* (Fullarton, Edinburgh, 1880), p. 95.
32 Ross, op. cit., p. 157.
33 Ibid., pp. 172–5.
34 Smith, op. cit., p. 100.
35 RGS – Ross to Adams, 9 July 1818.
36 Ross, op. cit., p. 143.

4 Buchan's Retreat

1 F. Beechey, *A Voyage of Discovery towards the North Pole* (John Murray, London, 1843), p. 145.
2 E. Parry, *Memoirs . . . Sir W. Edward Parry*, op. cit., cited pp. 95–6.
3 Ibid.
4 J. Ross, *Observations on a work entitled 'Voyages of Discovery and Research within the Arctic Regions' written by Sir John Barrow* (William Blackwood, London, 1846), p. 9.
5 P. Berton, *The Arctic Grail* (Viking, New York, 1988), cited p. 32.
6 *Quarterly Review*, Vol. XXI, No. XLI, Article XI.
7 E. S. Dodge, *The Polar Rosses*, op. cit., cited p. 85.
8 Ibid., cited p. 86.
9 *Quarterly Review*, Vol. XXI, No. XLI, Article XI.
10 Dodge, op. cit., cited p. 77.
11 J. Ross, op. cit., p. 184.
12 Dodge, op. cit., cited p. 79.
13 Ibid., pp. 90–1.

5 Furthest West

1 J. Barrow, *Voyages of Discovery and Research within the Arctic Regions* (John Murray, London, 1846), p. 50.

2 Ibid., p. 77.
3 W. E. Parry, *Journal of a Voyage . . . in the years 1819–1820* (John Murray, London, 1821), p. iv.
4 A. Parry, *Parry of the Arctic*, op. cit., cited p. 47.
5 P. Berton, *The Arctic Grail*, op. cit., cited p. 36.
6 A. Parry, op. cit., p. 48.
7 Ibid., cited p. 46.
8 Ibid.
9 W. E. Parry, op. cit., p. 31.
10 Berton, op. cit., cited p. 38.
11 W. E. Parry, op. cit., p. 34.
12 A. Fisher, *A Journal of a Voyage of Discovery to the Arctic Regions . . . in the years 1819 and 1820* (Longman, London, 1821), p. 68.
13 Berton, op. cit., cited p. 39.
14 W. E. Parry, op. cit., p. 35.
15 Ibid., p. 38.
16 Ibid., p. 41.
17 Ibid., p. 51.
18 Ibid., p. 61.
19 Ibid., p. 38.
20 Fisher, op. cit., p. 114.
21 W. E. Parry, op. cit., p. 75.
22 Ibid., p. 162.
23 A. Parry, op. cit., cited p. 55.
24 W. E. Parry, op. cit., p. 97.
25 A. Parry, op. cit., cited p. 55.
26 W. E. Parry, op. cit., p. 52.
27 Ibid.

6 Winter at Melville Island

1 W. E. Parry, *Journal of a Voyage . . . in the years 1819–1820*, op. cit., p. 73.
2 Ibid., p. 101.
3 Ibid., p. 126.
4 Ibid., p. 105.
5 Ibid.
6 Ibid.
7 A. Parry, *Parry of the Arctic*, op. cit., cited p. 58.
8 Ibid.
9 W. E. Parry, op. cit., p. 110.
10 Ibid., p. 108.
11 Ibid., p. 109.
12 Ibid., p. 108.
13 Ibid., p. 145.
14 Ibid., p. 115.
15 Ibid., p. 106.
16 A. Parry, op. cit., cited p. 60.
17 W. E. Parry, op. cit., p. 124.

18 A. Parry, op. cit., cited p. 61.
19 W. E. Parry, op. cit., p. 134.
20 Ibid.
21 A. Parry, op. cit., cited p. 63.
22 Ibid., cited p. 62.
23 W. E. Parry, op. cit., p. 133.
24 A. Parry, op. cit., cited p. 63.
25 W. E. Parry, op. cit., p. 175.
26 Ibid., p. 179.
27 Ibid., p. 188.
28 Ibid., p. 199.
29 Ibid., p. 220.
30 A. Parry, op. cit., cited p. 67.
31 W. E. Parry, op. cit., p. 97.
32 Ibid., p. 255.
33 Ibid., p. 241.
34 A. Parry, op. cit., cited p. 68.
35 Ibid., cited p. 69.
36 E. Parry, *Memoirs* . . ., op. cit., cited p. 130.
37 A. Parry, op. cit., cited p. 74.
38 J. Barrow, *Voyages* . . ., op. cit., p. 119.
39 E. Parry, op. cit., cited p. 115.
40 W. E. Parry, op. cit., p. 296.
41 Ibid.
42 Ibid.
43 A. Parry, op. cit., cited p. 72.
44 Ibid., cited p. 73.
45 E. Parry, op. cit., cited p. 134.
46 A. Parry, op. cit., cited p. 72.
47 E. Sabine (ed.), *North Georgia Gazette and Winter Chronicle* (John Murray, London, 1821), p. 47, No. VIII, 20 December 1819.

7 Vice-Consuls of Murzouk

1 PRO – CO.9 Ritchie to Goulburn, 20 April 1818.
2 PRO – CO.9 Ritchie to Goulburn, 18 April 1818.
3 Ibid.
4 Ibid.
5 SAR – DD/H1/553 Lyon to Bayntum, 23 December 1815.
6 SAR – DD/H1/553 Lyon to Bayntum, 23 December 1829.
7 PRO – CO.9 Ritchie to Goulburn, 30 September 1818.
8 Ibid.
9 PRO – CO.9 Ritchie to Goulburn, 28 October 1818.
10 PRO – CO.9 Penrose to Warrington, 24 September 1818.
11 PRO – CO.9 Unknown to Goulburn, 15 July 1819.
12 PRO – CO.9 Ritchie to Bathurst, 28 October 1818.
13 Ibid.
14 Ibid.

15 PRO – CO.9 Ritchie to Bathurst, 24 March 1819.
16 Ibid.
17 Ibid.
18 G. Lyon, *A Narrative of Travels in Northern Africa in the years 1818, 19 and 20* (John Murray, London, 1821), p. 3.
19 Ibid., p. 90.
20 PRO – CO.9 Unsigned and undated memo.
21 Lyon, op. cit., p. 118.
22 Ibid., p. 117.
23 Ibid., p. 195.
24 PRO – CO.9 Lyon to Bathurst, 26 March 1820.
25 Lyon, op. cit., p. 347.
26 Ibid.
27 Ibid., p. 318.
28 PRO – CO.9 Lyon to Bathurst, 26 March 1820.
29 Lyon, op. cit., p. 148.
30 Ibid., pp. 199–200.
31 PRO – CO.9 Lyon Snr. to Bathurst, 5 September 1820.
32 Ibid.
33 Ibid.
34 Ibid.
35 Ibid. Note on reverse of the letter.
36 PRO – CO.9 Lyon to Bathurst, 6 November 1820.
37 Ibid.

8 Failure at Foxe Basin

1 E. Parry, *Memoirs of Sir W. Edward Parry*, op. cit., cited p. 122.
2 W. E. Parry, *Journal of a Voyage . . . in the years 1819–20*, op. cit., p. vi.
3 Ibid., p. viii.
4 Ibid., p. i.
5 Ibid., p. xxiii.
6 G. F. Lyon, *Private Journal During the Recent Voyage of Discovery Under Captain Parry* (John Murray, London, 1824), p. 3.
7 W. E. Parry, op. cit., p. 6.
8 Lyon, op. cit., p. 9.
9 W. E. Parry, op. cit., p. 15.
10 Ibid.
11 Lyon, op. cit., p. 26.
12 Ibid., p. 29.
13 Ibid., p. 55.
14 Ibid., p. 88.
15 Ibid., p. 98.
16 W. E. Parry, op. cit., p. xviii.
17 Ibid., p. 101.
18 Lyon, op. cit., p. 111.
19 Ibid., p. 119.
20 Ibid., p. 121.

21 Ibid., p. 149.
22 W. E. Parry, op. cit., p. 185.
23 Ibid., p. 187.
24 Lyon, op. cit., p. 168.
25 Ibid.
26 Lyon, op. cit., p. 179.
27 Ibid., p. 125.
28 Ibid., p. 242.
29 W. E. Parry, op. cit., p. 290.
30 Lyon, op. cit., p. 250.
31 W. E. Parry, op. cit., p. 290.
32 Ibid.
33 W. E. Parry, op. cit., p. 291.
34 Lyon, op. cit., p. 131.
35 SAR – Lyon to Bayntum, undated.
36 W. E. Parry, op. cit., p. 372.
37 Ibid., p. 371.
38 Ibid., p. 174.
39 Lyon, op. cit., p. 179.
40 Ibid., p. 397.
41 W. E. Parry, op. cit., p. 463.
42 Ibid., p. 470.
43 Ibid., p. 472.
44 Ibid., p. xvii.
45 SAR – DD/H1/553 Lyon to Bayntum, 31 October 1823.
46 P. Berton, *The Arctic Grail*, op. cit., cited p. 50.
47 Ibid.
48 SAR – DD/H1/553 Lyon to Bayntum, undated.
49 SAR – DD/H1/553 Lyon to Bayntum, 31 October 1823.

9 The Man Who Ate His Boots

1   G. Lamb, *Franklin, Happy Voyager* (Ernest Benn, London, 1956), cited p. 56.
2   J. McIlraith, *Life of Sir John Richardson* (Longman, London, 1868), p. 64.
3   Ibid.
4   J. Franklin, *Narrative of a Journey to the shores of the Polar Sea in the years 1819–22* (John Murray, London, 1823), p. 2.
5   Ibid., p. 3.
6   Ibid., p. 6.
7   R. Hood, *To the Arctic By Canoe, 1819–21* (McGill-Queen's University Press, Montreal, 1974), p. 61.
8   Franklin, op. cit., p. 140.
9   McIlraith, op. cit., p. 81.
10 E. Rich (ed.), *Colin Robertson's Correspondence Book* (The Champlain Society, Toronto, 1939), p. 116.
11 Franklin, op. cit., p. 201.
12 Ibid., p. 202.
13 Ibid., p. 251.

14 E. Rich (ed.), *Simpson's Athabasca Journal* (The Champlain Society, London, 1938), p. 261.
15 Franklin, op. cit., p. 217.
16 J. Richardson, *Arctic Ordeal. The Journal of John Richardson . . . 1820–1822* (McGill-Queen's University Press, Montreal, 1984), p. xxviii.
17 Rich, op. cit., p. 314.
18 Ibid., p. 243.
19 Ibid., p. 261.
20 Franklin, op. cit., p. 296.
21 Ibid., p. 346.
22 Ibid., p. 345.
23 Richardson, op. cit., p. 84.
24 Ibid., p. 83.
25 Franklin, op. cit., p. 384.
26 Richardson, op. cit., p. 129.
27 Ibid., p. 134.
28 Ibid., p. 146.
29 Ibid., p. 138.
30 Ibid., p. 141.
31 Ibid., p. 140.
32 Ibid.
33 Franklin, op. cit., p. 424.
34 Ibid.
35 Richardson, op. cit., p. 144.
36 Ibid.
37 Franklin, op. cit., p. 428.
38 Richardson, op. cit., p. 146.
39 Franklin, op. cit., p. 431.
40 Ibid., p. 436.
41 Ibid., p. 438.
42 Ibid., p. 439.
43 Ibid., p. 445.
44 Richardson, op. cit., p. 149.
45 Ibid., p. 154.
46 Ibid., p. 156.
47 Ibid.
48 Ibid., p. 157.
49 Franklin, op. cit., p. 461.
50 Ibid.
51 Ibid.
52 Richardson, op. cit., p. 197.
53 Ibid., p. 162.
54 Ibid., p. 163.
55 Franklin, op. cit., p. 466.
56 Ibid.
57 Richardson, op. cit., p. 165.
58 McIlraith, op. cit., p. 112.

59 Franklin, op. cit., p. 468.
60 L. Masson, *Les Bourgeois de la Compagnie de Nord-Ouest*, Vol. I (Quebec, 1889), pp. 148–9.
61 Ibid.
62 Franklin, op. cit., p. 474.
63 H. Fleming (ed.), *Minutes of Council, Northern Department of Rupert Land, 1821–31* (The Champlain Society, Toronto, 1940), p. 341.
64 P. Berton, *The Arctic Grail*, op. cit., cited p. 74.

10 Lyon's Departure

1 SPRI – MS 248/452 Parry to Franklin, 23 October 1823.
2 A. Parry, *Parry of the Arctic*, op. cit., cited p. 85.
3 Ibid., p. 83.
4 SAR – DD/H1/553 Lyon to Bayntum, 31 October 1823.
5 A. Parry, op. cit., cited p. 85.
6 Ibid., cited p. 84.
7 Ibid.
8 Ibid., cited p. 85.
9 W. E. Parry, *Journal of a Second Voyage for the Discovery of a North-West Passage . . . in the years 1821–23* (John Murray, London, 1824), p. 491.
10 Ibid., p. 489.
11 A. Parry, op. cit., cited p. 86.
12 F. Woodward, *Portrait of Jane: A Life of Lady Franklin* (Hodder & Stoughton, London, 1951), cited p. 155.
13 Ibid.
14 Ibid.
15 Ibid.
16 Ibid.
17 Ibid.
18 RGS – Eleanor Porden to Franklin's sister Betsy, 11 May 1824.
19 W. E. Parry, *Journal of a Third Voyage for the Discovery of a North-West Passage . . . in the years 1824–25* (John Murray, London, 1826), p. 50.
20 E. Parry, *Memoirs . . . W. Edward Parry*, op. cit., cited p. 192.
21 W. E. Parry, op. cit., p. 40.
22 A. Parry, op. cit., cited p. 91.
23 W. E. Parry, op. cit., p. 147.
24 P. Berton, *The Arctic Grail*, op. cit., cited p. 88.
25 Ibid.
26 A. Parry, op. cit., cited p. 94.
27 SAR – DD/H1/553 Lyon to Bayntum, 23 December 1829.
28 G. F. Lyon, *A Brief Narrative of an Unsuccessful Attempt to Reach Repulse Bay* (John Murray, London, 1825), p. 20.
29 Ibid., p. 11.
30 Ibid., p. 26.
31 Ibid., p. 27.
32 Ibid., p. 33.
33 Ibid., p. 34.

34 Ibid., p. 43.
35 Ibid., p. 69.
36 Ibid., p. 77.
37 Ibid., p. 78.
38 Ibid., p. 79.
39 Ibid.
40 Ibid.
41 Ibid., p. 81.
42 Ibid., p. 82.
43 Ibid., p. 99.
44 Ibid., p. 100.
45 Ibid., p. 101.
46 Ibid., p. 102.
47 Ibid., p. 104.
48 Ibid., p. 105.
49 Ibid., p. 136.
50 Ibid., p. 139.
51 Ibid., p. 143.
52 Ibid., p. 144.
53 A. Parry, op. cit., cited p. 95.
54 Ibid.
55 Berton, op. cit., cited p. 91.
56 A. Parry, op. cit., cited p. 86.
57 SAR – DD/H1/553 Lyon to Bayntum, 14 February (no year given).
58 Berton, op. cit., cited pp. 89–90.
59 G. Lamb, *Franklin, Happy Voyager* (Ernest Benn, London, 1956), cited p. 128.
60 Ibid., cited p. 129.
61 Woodward, op. cit., cited p. 157.
62 Lamb, op. cit., cited p. 134.
63 Ibid.
64 Ibid.
65 Ibid., cited p. 135.
66 Ibid., cited p. 137.
67 Ibid., cited p. 142.
68 J. Franklin, *Narrative of a Second Expedition to the shores of the Polar Sea in the years 1825, 1826 and 1827* (John Murray, London, 1828), p. 162.

11   Squabbles in the Sahara

1 DTC – Barrow to Banks, 8 October 1817.
2 PRO – CO.2/20 Laing to Warrington, 3 August 1825.
3 PRO – CO.2/14 Oudney to Barrow, 23 May 1821.
4 C. Lloyd, *The Search for the Niger* (Collins, London, 1973), cited p. 79.
5 RGS – Oudney to Barrow, 24 January 1822.
6 Ibid.
7 RGS – Beechey to Barrow, 4 November 1821.
8 Ibid.
9 Ibid.

10 Ibid.
11 D. Denham, H. Clapperton and W. Oudney, *A Narrative of Travels and Discoveries in northern and central Africa in the years 1822, 1823 and 1824*, Vol. I (John Murray, London, 1828), p. 14.
12 Ibid.
13 Ibid.
14 Ibid., p. 63.
15 RGS – Oudney to Barrow, 24 January 1822.
16 Lloyd, op. cit., cited pp. 80–1.
17 Denham, op. cit., p. 116.
18 RGS – Clapperton to Barrow, 4 June 1822.
19 RGS – Clapperton to Barrow, 19 September 1822.
20 Lloyd, op. cit., cited p. 82.
21 Denham, op. cit., p. 93.
22 Ibid., p. 111.
23 Ibid., p. 49.
24 Ibid., cited p. 81.
25 RGS – Oudney to Barrow, 4 November 1822.
26 Ibid.
27 Ibid.
28 Ibid.
29 Ibid.
30 Denham, op. cit., p. 131.
31 Ibid., p. 128.
32 Ibid., p. 131.
33 Ibid., p. 128.
34 Ibid., p. 52.
35 Ibid., p. 123.
36 PRO – CO.2/13 Denham to Bathurst, 20 February 1823.
37 PRO – CO.2/13 Clapperton to Denham, 1 January 1823.
38 Denham, op. cit., p. 36.
39 Lloyd, op. cit., cited p. 85.
40 Ibid.
41 RGS – Oudney to Barrow, 12 July 1823.
42 Denham, op. cit., p. 182.
43 Ibid.
44 Ibid., p. 183.
45 Ibid., p. 208.
46 Ibid.
47 Ibid., p. 212.
48 Ibid., p. 215
49 Ibid., p. 265.
50 Ibid., p. 280.
51 Ibid., p. 287.
52 Ibid., p. 279.
53 Ibid., p. 298.
54 Ibid., p. 286.

55 Ibid., p. 284.
56 Ibid., p. 218.
57 Ibid., p. 324.
58 PRO – CO.2/13 Warrington to Denham, 31 July 1823.
59 Denham, op. cit., p. 204.
60 *Quarterly Review*, Vol. XXIX, No. LVIII, Article XI.
61 Denham, op. cit., p. 401.
62 Denham, op. cit., Vol. II, p. 28.
63 Ibid., p. 76.
64 Denham, op. cit., Vol. I, p. 425.
65 Ibid., p. 471.
66 Denham, op. cit., Vol. II, p. 228.
67 Ibid., p. 256.
68 Ibid., p. 265.
69 Ibid., p. 266.
70 Ibid., p. 289.
71 Ibid., p. 318.
72 Ibid., p. 319.
73 Ibid., p. 340.
74 Ibid., p. 270.
75 Ibid., p. 360.
76 Ibid., p. 84.
77 *Edinburgh Review*, Vol. XLIV, No. LXXXVI, Article VI.
78 *Quarterly Review*, Vol. XXXII, No. LXVI, Article XI.
79 *Quarterly Review*, Vol. XXIX, No. LVIII, Article XI.
80 PRO – CO.2/14 Letter from Barrow, 11 November 1823.
81 J. Barrow, *The Mutiny and Piratical Seizure of HMS Bounty* (William Tegg, London, 1876), p. 292.
82 Ibid.
83 Denham, op. cit., Vol. II, p. 203.
84 C. Lloyd, *Mr. Barrow of the Admiralty* (Collins, London, 1970), cited p. 122.
85 Denham, op. cit., Vol. II, p. 203.
86 PRO – CO.392/1 Correspondents' names illegible, 21 June 1825.

12   The Madman of Timbuctoo

1 G. Gardner, *The Quest for Timbuctoo* (Cassell, London, 1969), cited p. 47.
2 C. Lloyd, *Mr. Barrow of the Admiralty*, op. cit., cited p. 122.
3 Ibid.
4 PRO – CO.2/15 Turner to Bathurst, 9 April 1825.
5 Ibid.
6 Ibid.
7 RS – 374 (La.) Undated draft letter from Laing.
8 Gardner, op. cit., cited p. 53.
9 PRO – CO.2/15 Laing to Bathurst, undated.
10 PRO – CO.2/20 Laing to Warrington, 29 March 1826.
11 RS – 374 (La.) Laing to Bandinell, 3 May 1825.

12 PRO – CO.2/20 Laing to Warrington, 5 October 1825.
13 PRO – CO.2/20 Laing to Warrington, 1 July 1826.
14 RS – 374 (La.) Laing to Bandinell, May 1825.
15 RS – 374 (La.) Laing to Bandinell, 24 May 1825.
16 Gardner, op. cit., cited p. 62.
17 PRO – CO.2/15 Laing to Bathurst, 24 May 1825.
18 Ibid.
19 PRO – CO.2/15 Laing to Bathurst, 18 July 1825.
20 Gardner, op. cit., cited p. 64.
21 RS – 374 (La.) Laing to Bandinell, 7 June 1825.
22 Gardner, op. cit., cited p. 64.
23 Ibid., cited p. 66.
24 PRO – CO.2/20 Laing to Warrington, 3 August 1825.
25 PRO – CO.2/20 Laing to Warrington, 5 October 1825.
26 PRO – CO.2/20 Laing to Warrington, 30 August 1825.
27 PRO – CO 2./20 Laing to Warrington, 24 July 1825.
28 RS – 374 (La.) Laing to Sabine, 29 July 1825.
29 PRO – CO 2./20 Laing to Warrington, 3 August 1825.
30 RS – 374 (La.) Laing to Bandinell, undated.
31 PRO – CO.2/20 Laing to Warrington, undated.
32 PRO – CO.2/20 Laing to Warrington, 5 October 1825.
33 PRO – CO.2/20 Laing to Warrington, 3 August 1825.
34 PRO – CO.2/20 Laing to Warrington, 29 September 1825.
35 PRO – CO.2/20 Laing to Warrington, 29 April 1825.
36 RS – 374 (La.) Warrington to Laing, 22 November 1825.
37 PRO – CO.2/20 Laing to Warrington, 27 September 1825.
38 RS – 374 (La.) Warrington to Laing, 22 November 1825.
39 PRO – CO.2/20 Laing to Warrington, 27 September 1825.
40 Ibid.
41 PRO – CO.2/20 Laing to Warrington, 29 September 1825.
42 PRO – CO.2/20 Laing to Warrington, 13 September 1825.
43 PRO – CO.2/15 Laing to Horton, 20 January 1826.
44 PRO – CO.2/20 Laing to Warrington, 10 May 1826.
45 PRO – CO.2/20 Laing to Warrington, 1 July 1826.
46 PRO – CO.2/20 Laing to Warrington, undated.
47 PRO – CO.2/20 Laing to Warrington, 10 May 1826.
48 PRO – CO.2/20 Laing to Warrington, 21 September 1826.
49 Ibid.
50 Ibid.
51 PRO – CO.2/14 Letter from Barrow, 11 November 1823.
52 Gardner, op. cit., cited p. 85.
53 *Quarterly Review*, Vol. XLII, No. LXXXIV, Article VI.
54 Ibid.
55 Ibid.
56 RS – 374 (La.) Warrington to Laing, 17 October 1825.

13   The Road from Badagry

1 H. Clapperton, *A Journal of a Second Expedition into the Interior of Africa* (John Murray, London, 1829), p. xiii.
2 Ibid.
3 PRO – CO.2/17 Barrow to Hay, 24 August 1825.
4 Ibid.
5 Clapperton, op. cit., p. xiv.
6 R. Lander, *Records of Captain Clapperton's last expedition to Africa*, Vol. I (Colburn & Bentley, London, 1830), p. 33.
7 Ibid., p. 34.
8 Clapperton, op. cit., p. 13.
9 Lander, op. cit., p. 70.
10 PRO – CO.2/17 Barrow to Hay, 27 June 1826.
11 Clapperton, op. cit., p. 36.
12 Lander, op. cit., p. 83.
13 Clapperton, op. cit., p. 80.
14 Lander, op. cit., p. 155.
15 Ibid., p. 153.
16 Clapperton, op. cit., p. 112.
17 Lander, op. cit., p. 149.
18 RS – 374 (La.) Laing to Bandinell, 9 January 1826.
19 Clapperton, op. cit., p. 104.
20 M. Mackay, *The Indomitable Servant* (Rex Collings, London, 1978), cited p. 56.
21 Clapperton, op. cit., p. 117.
22 Ibid., p. 238.
23 Ibid., p. 197.
24 Ibid., p. 176.
25 Lander, op. cit., Vol. II, p. 58.
26 Ibid.
27 Ibid., p. 225.
28 Clapperton, op. cit., p. 272.
29 Ibid., p. 275.
30 Ibid., p. 274.
31 Ibid., p. 276.
32 Ibid.
33 Ibid., p. 278.
34 Lander, op. cit., Vol. II, p. 107.
35 Clapperton, op. cit., p. 95.
36 Lander, op. cit., Vol. II, p. 154.
37 Ibid.
38 Ibid., p. 249.
39 Ibid., p. 268.
40 Ibid., p. 255.
41 Ibid., p. 257.
42 Clapperton, op. cit., p. 326.
43 Ibid.

44 Lander, op. cit., Vol. II, p. 284.
45 Clapperton, op. cit., p. xv.
46 Ibid., p. xviii.
47 Ibid.
48 Ibid.
49 Ibid., p. xvi.
50 Ibid., p. xvii.
51 Ibid.
52 Ibid., p. xix.
53 Ibid.
54 Ibid.
55 Ibid., p. xii.
56 Mackay, op. cit., cited pp. 115–16.
57 Ibid.
58 Ibid.

14 Parry to the Pole

1 *Quarterly Review*, Vol. XVIII, No. XXXVI, Article VIII.
2 W. E. Parry, *Narrative of an Attempt to reach the North Pole . . . in the year 1827* (John Murray, London, 1828), p. x.
3 P. Berton, *The Arctic Grail*, op. cit., cited p. 97.
4 A. Parry, *Parry of the Arctic*, op. cit., cited p. 105.
5 W. E. Parry, op. cit., p. 17.
6 R. McCormick, *Voyages of Discovery in the Arctic and Antarctic and Round the World* (Sampson, London, 1884), p. 390.
7 W. E. Parry, op. cit., p. 21.
8 Ibid., p. 74.
9 Ibid., p. 61.
10 Ibid., p. 56.
11 Ibid., pp. 56–7.
12 Ibid., p. 58.
13 Ibid., p. 71.
14 Ibid., p. 70.
15 A. Parry, op. cit., cited p. 115.
16 W. E. Parry, op. cit., p. 120.
17 W. Jerrold (ed.), *The Complete Poetical Works of Thomas Hood* (Oxford University Press, 1906), p. 24.

15 Ross Resurgent

1 P. Morrell (ed.), *Leaves from the Greville Diary* (Eveleigh Nash & Grayson, London, 1829), p. 98.
2 J. Barrow, *Autobiographical Memoir*, op. cit., p. 341.
3 A. Parry, *Parry of the Arctic*, op. cit., cited p. 127.
4 C. Lloyd, *Mr. Barrow of the Admiralty*, op. cit., cited p. 96.
5 M. Brightfield, *John Wilson Croker* (Allen and Unwin, London, 1885), diary entry 12 July 1828, cited p. 85.

6   Ibid., diary entry 19 September 1828, cited p. 87.
7   J. Barrow, *Voyages . . . within the Arctic regions*, op. cit., p. 311.
8   Ibid., p. 298.
9   A. Parry, op. cit., cited p. 47.
10 SPRI – Lady Jane Franklin's diary, 25 December 1833.
11 Lloyd, op. cit., cited p. 93.
12 Barrow, op. cit., p. 511.
13 Ibid., p. 512.
14 J. Ross, *Narrative of a Second Voyage in Search of a North-West Passage . . . during the years 1829, 1830, 1831, 1832, 1833* (Webster, London, 1835), p. 3.
15 J. Ross, *Observations on a work . . . by Sir John Barrow*, op. cit., p. 46.
16 E. S. Dodge, *The Polar Rosses*, op. cit., cited pp. 116–17.
17 Ibid.
18 Ibid., cited p. 119.
19 Ibid.
20 Ross, op. cit., p. xviii.
21 Ibid., p. 19.

16   The Riddle of the Niger

1   H. Clapperton, *Journal of a Second Expedition . . .*, op. cit., p. xv.
2   PRO – CO.2/18 Barrow to Hay, 19 September 1829.
3   P. Raby, *Bright Paradise* (Chatto & Windus, London, 1996), cited p. 56.
4   PRO – CO.2/18 Lander to Barrow, 16 October 1829.
5   R. and J. Lander, *Journal of an expedition to explore the course and termination of the Niger*, Vol. I (John Murray, London, 1833), p. lvi.
6   Ibid., p. 75.
7   Ibid., p. 39.
8   Ibid., p. 19.
9   R. Lander, *Records of Captain Clapperton . . .*, op. cit., Vol. II, p. 96.
10 R. and J. Lander, op. cit., p. 192.
11 R. Lander, op. cit., Vol. II, p. 12.
12 Ibid., p. 13.
13 Ibid., p. 38.
14 Lander, op. cit., Vol. III, p. 42.
15 Lander, op. cit., Vol. II, p. 42.
16 Ibid., p. 3.
17 Ibid., p. 108.
18 Ibid.
19 Ibid., p. 159.
20 Ibid., p. 200.
21 Ibid., p. 213.
22 Ibid., p. 242.
23 Lander, op. cit., Vol. III, p. 71.
24 Ibid., p. 93.
25 Ibid., p. 88.
26 M. Mackay, *The Indomitable Servant*, op. cit., cited p. 205.
27 Lander, op. cit., Vol. III, p. 177.

28 Ibid., p. 178.
29 Ibid., p. 198.
30 Ibid., p. 241.
31 Ibid., p. 219.
32 Ibid., p. 222.
33 Ibid., p. 233.
34 Ibid., p. 244.
35 Ibid., p. 246.
36 Ibid.
37 Ibid.
38 Ibid., p. 331.
39 *Edinburgh Review*.
40 Lander, op. cit., Vol. III, p. 313.
41 Lander, op. cit., Vol. I, p. lxiii.
42 PRO – CO.2/18 Lander to Bathurst, 27 July 1831.
43 Raby, op. cit., cited p. 64.

17   Second Singapores

1   W. Jerdan, *The Autobiography of William Jerdan*, Vol. 4 (Arthur Hall, Virtue, London, 1853), p. 271.
2   Ibid., p. 267.
3   *Journal of the Royal Geographical Society of London*, Vol. 1 (John Murray, London, 1831), p. v.
4   C. Lloyd, *Mr. Barrow of the Admiralty*, op. cit., cited p. 161.
5   Ibid.
6   *Journal of the Royal Geographic Society*, Vol. I, p. x.
7   Ibid., p. 1.
8   Lloyd, op. cit., cited p. 162.
9   Ibid., cited p. 163.
10 Ibid.
11 Ibid.
12 E. Parry, *Memoirs of Rear-Admiral Sir W. Edward Parry*, op. cit., cited p. 241.
13 A. Parry, *Parry of the Arctic*, op. cit., cited p. 135.
14 Ibid., p. 134.
15 Ibid., cited p. 137.
16 Ibid., cited p. 173.
17 Ibid., cited p. 175.
18 Lloyd, op. cit., p. 164.
19 L. Huxley, *Life and Letters of Thomas Henry Huxley*, Vol. I (Macmillan, London, 1913), Huxley to his mother, 1 February 1849, cited p. 63.
20 J. Huxley (ed.), *T. H. Huxley's Diary of the Voyage of HMS Rattlesnake* (Chatto & Windus, London, 1935), pp. 148–9.
21 Lloyd, op. cit., p. 164.
22 Ibid.

18 Ordeal of the *Victory*

1 P. Berton, *The Arctic Grail*, op. cit., cited p. 110.
2 J. Ross, *Narrative of a Second Voyage . . .*, op. cit., p. 205.
3 Ibid., p. 152.
4 Ibid.
5 Ibid., p. 186.
6 Ibid., p. 185.
7 Ibid., p. 191.
8 Ibid., p. 201.
9 A. Friendly, *Beaufort of the Admiralty* (Hutchinson, London, 1977), cited p. 307.
10 Ross, op. cit., p. 350.
11 Ibid., p. 199.
12 Ibid., p. 195.
13 Ibid., p. 246.
14 Ibid., p. 326.
15 R. Huish, *The Last Voyage of Captain John Ross by an officer attached to the Expedition* (Saunders, London, 1835), p. 329.
16 Ibid., p. 513.
17 Ross, op. cit., p. 458.
18 Ibid., p. 505.
19 Huish, op. cit., pp. 255, 510.
20 Ibid., p. 500.
21 Ibid., p. 509.
22 Ross, op. cit., p. 555.
23 Ibid., p. 557.
24 Ibid., p. 555.
25 Ibid., p. 604.
26 Ibid., pp. 597–8.
27 Ibid., p. 590.
28 Ibid., p. 619.
29 Ibid., p. 626.
30 Ibid., p. 632.
31 Ibid., p. 643.
32 Ibid.
33 Ibid.
34 RGS – Proposal by G. Ross.
35 RGS – Scoresby to G. Ross, 18 March 1833.
36 Ross, op. cit., p. 645.
37 Ibid., p. 651.
38 Ibid.
39 Ibid., p. 657.
40 Ibid., p. 670.
41 Ibid., p. 692.
42 Ibid.
43 Ibid., p. 714.
44 Ibid., p. 696.

45 Ibid., p. 717.
46 Ibid., p. 720.
47 Ibid., p. 721.
48 Ibid., p. 722.

19 'Any Animal Will Do for a Lion'

1 *Fraser's Magazine*, January 1834.
2 J. Barrow, *Voyages . . .*, op. cit., p. 46.
3 Ibid., p. 525.
4 E. S. Dodge, *The Polar Rosses*, op. cit., cited p. 168.
5 T. and C. Stamp, *William Scoresby, Arctic Scientist*, op. cit., Ross to Scoresby, 28 April 1835, cited p. 125.
6 Ibid.
7 Ibid.
8 Ibid.
9 W. Jerdan, *The Autobiography of William Jerdan*, op. cit., Vol. III, p. 83.
10 L. Jennings (ed.), *The Croker Papers* (John Murray, London, 1885), cited Vol. II, p. 258.
11 *Fraser's Magazine*, January 1834.
12 A. Parry, *Parry of the Arctic*, op. cit., cited p. 187.
13 Ibid.
14 J. Braithwaite, *A Supplement to Captain Sir John Ross's Narrative of a Second Voyage in the Victory . . .* (Chapman & Hale, London, 1835), pp. ii, 2.
15 J. Ross, *Explanation and Answer to Mr. John Braithwaite's Supplement . . .* (Webster, London, 1835), p. 5.
16 Ibid., p. 7.
17 Ibid.
18 *The Times*, 13 November 1835.
19 Ross, op. cit., p. 1.
20 *Quarterly Review*, Vol. LIV, No. CVII, Article I.
21 Ibid.
22 F. Woodward, *Portrait of Jane*, op. cit., cited p. 194.
23 Barrow, op. cit., p. 524.
24 *Quarterly Review*, Vol. LIV,. No. CVII, Article I.
25 Ibid.
26 Dodge, op. cit., cited p. 164.
27 Ibid.
28 SPRI – MS 246/467 J. C. Ross to Franklin, 29 March 1835.
29 Ibid.
30 Dodge, op. cit., cited p. 170.
31 Ibid.
32 J. Ross, *Narrative of a Second Voyage . . .*, op. cit., p. 568.
33 Ibid., p. 570.
34 P. Berton, *The Arctic Grail*, op. cit., cited p. 120.
35 MHS – MS Buxton 2 Ross to Jacob, undated.
36 Ibid.
37 J. Ross, *Observations . . .*, op. cit., p. 50.

20 The Overlanders

1 PRO – BJ.2/13 Sabine to J. C. Ross, 6 December 1833.
2 PRO – BJ.2/1 Richardson to J. C. Ross, 14 April 1834.
3 RGS – Letter from Back, 19 June 1833.
4 P. Berton, *The Arctic Grail*, op. cit., cited pp. 125–6.
5 G. Back, *Narrative of the Arctic Land Expedition to the mouth of the Great Fish River and along the shores of the Arctic Ocean in the years 1833, 1834 and 1835* (John Murray, London, 1836), p. 390.
6 G. Glazebrook, *The Letters of Letitia Hargrave* (The Champlain Society, Toronto, 1947), W. MacTavish to L. MacTavish, 16 July 1834, cited p. 145.
7 Ibid.
8 Ibid., cited p. 146.
9 J. Barrow, *Voyages . . .*, op. cit., p. 463.
10 Back, op. cit., p. 55.
11 Glazebrook, op. cit., T. Simpson to J. Hargrave, 25 September 1838, cited p. 266.
12 Berton, op. cit., cited p. 126.
13 RGS – G. Ross to Back, 7 August 1835.
14 C. Lloyd, *Mr. Barrow of the Admiralty*, op. cit., cited p. 97.
15 M. Brightfield, *John Wilson Croker*, op. cit., cited p. 207.
16 Lloyd, op. cit., cited p. 97.
17 PRO – BJ.2/1 Richardson to J. C. Ross, 14 April 1834.
18 Glazebrook, op. cit., T. Simpson to J. Hargrave, 17 January 1838, cited p. 261.
19 R. King, *A Narrative of a journey to the shores of the Arctic Ocean in the years 1833, 1834 and 1835* (Bentley, London, 1836), p. 309.
20 RGS – 'On Dr. King's N.W. Project April 1836'.
21 *Journal of the Royal Geographical Society*, Vol. VI, p. 48.
22 PRO – BJ.2/13 Sabine to J. C. Ross, 6 December 1833.
23 J. Barrow, *Voyages . . .*, op. cit., p. 487.
24 PRO – BJ.2/2 Belcher to J. C. Ross, undated.
25 RGS – J. Ross to G. Ross, 17 September 1835.
26 MHS – MS Buxton 2 Jacobs to J. Ross, 5 June 1836.
27 RGS – Franklin to Kay, 14 June 1832.
28 RGS – Beaufort to B. Franklin, 26 March 1836.
29 G. Lamb, *Franklin, Happy Voyager*, op. cit., cited p. 186.
30 Ibid., cited p. 187.
31 RGS – King to Dr Hodgkin re. address to Royal Geographical Society in 1836.
32 Ibid.
33 RGS – J. C. Ross proposal, February 1838.
34 Berton, op. cit., cited p. 133.
35 Glazebrook, op. cit., J. Rowand to J. Hargrave, 31 December 1838, cited p. 275.
36 Berton, op. cit., cited pp. 133, 134.
37 Ibid., cited pp. 136, 137.
38 Ibid., cited p. 136.
39 Barrow, op. cit., p. 525.

21   The Bottom of the World

1   PRO – BJ.2/3 Beaufort to J. C. Ross, 24 August 1838.
2   I. Cameron, *Antarctica: The Last Continent* (Cassell, London, 1974), Yves-Joseph de Kerguélen-Trémarc, cited p. 33.
3   Prof. G. E. Fogg and D. Smith, *The Explorations of Antarctica* (Cassell, London, 1990), cited p. 30.
4   Cameron, op. cit., cited p. 96.
5   Fogg and Smith, op. cit., cited p. 32.
6   J. C. Ross, *A Voyage of Discovery and Research in the Southern Antarctic Regions during the years 1839–43*, Vol. I (Sampson, London, 1884), p. xxi.
7   L. Huxley, *Life and Letters of Sir Joseph Dalton Hooker*, Vol. I (John Murray, London, 1918), Hooker to Hooker Snr., 27 April 1839, cited p. 41.
8   Ibid.
9   Ibid., cited p. 47.
10 Ibid., cited p. 45.
11 Ross, op. cit., p. 4.
12 T. and C. Stamp, *William Scoresby, Arctic Scientist*, op. cit., Scoresby to Beaufort, cited p. 133.
13 Ibid.
14 Ibid., Minutes of the Committee on Ship's Compasses, 9 March 1839, cited p. 138.
15 Ibid., Letter from Scoresby, 18 April 1839, cited p. 138.
16 Ross, op. cit., p. 94.
17 K. Fitzpatrick, *Sir John Franklin in Tasmania, 1837–43* (Melbourne University Press, Melbourne, 1949), *Colonial Times*, 18 April 1837, cited p. 110.
18 PRO – BJ.2/7 Kay to J. C. Ross, 10 September 1843.
19 P. Berton, *The Arctic Grail*, op. cit., cited p. 139.
20 Fitzpatrick, op. cit., cited p. 52.
21 Berton, op. cit., cited p. 138.
22 F. Woodward, *Portrait of Jane*, op. cit., cited p. 228.
23 Ibid., cited p. 229.
24 Ibid., cited p. 228.
25 Ibid., cited p. 229.
26 Ibid., cited p. 230.
27 Ibid., cited p. 224.
28 Huxley, op. cit., cited p. 106.
29 Ibid.
30 Ibid.
31 Ross, op. cit., pp. 116–17.
32 Ibid.
33 Cameron, op. cit., cited p. 108.
34 R. McCormick, *Voyages of Discovery . . . Round the World*, op. cit., Vol. I, p. 149.
35 Ibid., p. 158.
36 Cameron, op. cit., cited p. 108.
37 Ross, op. cit., p. 192.
38 McCormick, op. cit., p. 164.
39 RBG – Letter quoted in a lecture delivered at Swansea, 17 June 1846.

40 RBG – Narrative of James Savage written by C. J. Sullivan, Rio de Janeiro, 19 June 1843.
41 Ibid.
42 Ross, op. cit., pp. 218–21.
43 Ibid., p. 237.
44 Ibid., p. 191.

22   'You See How Our Hands Shake?'

1 J. C. Ross, *A Voyage of Discovery . . .*, op. cit., Vol. I, p. 281.
2 Ibid., p. 282.
3 RBG – Narrative of James Savage . . ., op. cit.
4 K. Fitzpatrick, *Sir John Franklin in Tasmania*, op. cit., cited p. 261.
5 F. Woodward, *Portrait of Jane*, op. cit., cited p. 230.
6 Ibid.
7 Ibid.
8 E. S. Dodge, *The Polar Rosses*, op. cit., cited p. 203.
9 Ibid., cited p. 205.
10 R. McCormick, *Voyages of Discovery*, op. cit., Vol. I, p. 253.
11 RBG – Letter from J. E. Davis to his sister, 1 April 1842.
12 Ross, op. cit., Vol. II, p. 168.
13 Ibid., p. 169.
14 Ibid.
15 Ibid., p. 198.
16 Ibid.
17 Ibid., p. 217.
18 McCormick, op. cit., p. 275.
19 Ross, op. cit., p. 218.
20 Ibid.
21 McCormick, op. cit., p. 276.
22 Ross, op. cit., p. 220.
23 Ibid., p. 219.
24 McCormick, op. cit., p. 163.
25 L. Huxley, *Life and Letters of Sir Joseph Dalton Hooker*, op. cit., Vol. I, Hooker to Hooker Snr., 29 April 1843, cited p. 130.
26 Ibid.
27 Ibid., Hooker to Hooker Snr., 7 March 1843, cited p. 145.
28 Ibid., Smith to Hooker, 3 August 1842, cited p. 146.
29 McCormick, op. cit., p. 265.
30 Ross, op. cit., p. 261.
31 Ibid., p. 321.
32 Huxley, op. cit., Hooker to his mother, 6 December 1842, cited p. 135.
33 Ibid., cited p. 139.
34 Mrs C. Bagot, *Links With the Past* (Edward Arnold, London, 1901), p. 77.
35 Ross, op. cit., p. 386
36 Huxley, op. cit., Vol. II, Scott to Hooker, 5 November 1905, cited p. 443.
37 Dodge, op. cit., p. 218.

23 The Last Post

1 K. Fitzpatrick, *Sir John Franklin in Tasmania*, op. cit., cited p. 107.
2 Ibid., Lady Franklin to Mrs Simpkinson, 7 February 1842, cited p. 280.
3 P. Berton, *The Arctic Grail*, op. cit., cited p. 139.
4 Fitzpatrick, op. cit., *Colonial Times*, 1 August 1843, cited p. 349.
5 Berton, op. cit., cited p. 140.
6 Fitzpatrick, op. cit., cited p. 360.
7 G. Lamb, *Franklin, Happy Voyager*, op. cit., cited p. 244.
8 PRO – BJ.2/8 J. C. Ross to Murray, undated.
9 SPRI – MS 248/364 Crozier to J. C. Ross, 30 December 1844.
10 PRO – BJ.2/13 Sabine to J. C. Ross, 13 June 1840.
11 Lamb, op. cit., cited p. 246.
12 Ibid., cited p. 247.
13 E. Parry, *Memoirs . . . W. Edward Parry*, op. cit., cited p. 329.
14 C. Lloyd, *Mr. Barrow of the Admiralty*, op. cit., cited p. 188.
15 MHS – MS Buxton 1 Ross to Hamilton, 17 November 1849.
16 R. King, *The Franklin Expedition from First to Last* (Churchill, London, 1855), p. 179.
17 Ibid., p. 180.
18 M. Macleod (ed.), *The Letters of Letitia Hargrave*, op. cit., L. Hargrave to D. Mactavish, 1 September 1845, cited p. 200.
19 King, op. cit., p. 8.
20 Ibid., p. 195.
21 Berton, op. cit., cited p. 145.
22 Ibid., p. 148.

24 *Erebus* and *Terror*

1 G. Lamb, *Franklin, Happy Voyager*, op. cit., cited p. 251.
2 Ibid., cited p. 250.
3 E. Parry, *Memoirs . . .*, op. cit., cited p. 311.
4 P. Berton, *The Arctic Grail*, op. cit., cited pp. 148–9.
5 Ibid.
6 SPRI – MS 284/364 Crozier to J. C. Ross, 19 July 1845.
7 Berton, op. cit., cited pp. 146, 150.
8 SPRI – MS 284/364 Crozier to J. C. Ross, 19 July 1845.
9 R. King, *The Franklin Expedition . . .* op. cit., cited p. 42.
10 PRO – BJ.2/3 Beaufort to Ross, 20 January 1847.
11 MHS – MS Buxton 1 Ross to Hamilton, 17 November 1849.
12 Ibid.
13 Ibid.
14 J. Ross, *Sir John Franklin, a Narrative* (Longman, London, 1855), p. 18.
15 Ibid., cited p. 49.
16 Ibid., p. 31.
17 J. Barrow, *Sketches of the Royal Society & Royal Society Club* (John Murray, London, 1849), p. 144.
18 RGS – Letter from Barrow, June 1845.

25   The Arctic Council

1 R. McCormick, *Voyages of Discovery* . . ., op. cit., Vol. II, p. 313.
2 Ibid., p. 293.
3 Ibid., p. 318.
4 J. Ross, *Sir John Franklin* . . ., op. cit., p. 61.
5 P. Berton, *The Arctic Grail*, op. cit., cited p. 181.
6 Ross, op. cit., p. 61.
7 Berton, op. cit., cited p. 181.
8 E. S. Dodge, *The Polar Rosses*, op. cit., cited p. 239.
9 Berton, op. cit., cited p. 184.
10 F. Woodward, *Portrait of Jane*, op. cit., cited p. 276.
11 Berton, op. cit., cited p. 203.
12 S. Osborn, *Stray Leaves from an Arctic Journal* (Longman, London, 1852), p. 283.
13 R. King, *The Franklin Expedition* . . ., op. cit., cited p. 89.
14 Ibid., cited p. 88.
15 *Dictionary of National Biography*, Vol. II, p. 143.
16 BL – MS Eng Lett d.239 Belcher to Napier, 1 March 1847.
17 Ibid.
18 Ibid.
19 BL – MS Eng Lett d.239 Belcher to Napier, 1 September 1853.
20 BL – MS Eng Lett d.239 Belcher to Napier, 1 March 1847.
21 C. Lloyd, *Mr. Barrow of the Admiralty*, op. cit., cited p. 199.
22 McCormick, op. cit., Vol. II, p. 53.
23 Ibid., p. 95.

26   *Investigator*

1 BL – MS Eng Lett d.239 Belcher to Napier, 1 September 1853.
2 Ibid.
3 Ibid.
4 Ibid.
5 J. Miertsching, *Frozen Ships – The Arctic Diary of Johann Miertsching 1850–1854* (Macmillan, Toronto, 1967), p. 13.
6 Ibid.
7 Ibid., p. 22.
8 Ibid., p. 34.
9 R. McClure, *The Discovery of the North-West Passage by H.M.S. Investigator* (Longman, London, 1856), p. 106.
10 A. Armstrong, *A Personal Narrative of the Discovery of the North-West Passage* (Hurst & Blackett, London, 1857), p. 465.
11 D. Smith, *Arctic Expeditions, British and Foreign* (Fullarton, Edinburgh, 1880), cited pp. 622–3.
12 Armstrong, op. cit., p. 545.
13 Smith, op. cit., p. 569.
14 McClure, op. cit., p. 242.
15 Ibid., pp. 223, 228.
16 Armstrong, op. cit., p. 544.

17 Ibid., p. 558.
18 Miertsching, op. cit., p. 187.
19 Smith, op. cit., p. 572.

27 Franklin's Fate

1 D. Smith, *Arctic Expeditions . . .*, op. cit., cited p. 575.
2 A. Armstrong, *A Personal Narrative of the Discovery of the North-West Passage*, op. cit., p. 576.
3 C. Lloyd, *Mr. Barrow of the Admiralty*, op. cit., cited p. 200.
4 Ibid., cited p. 199.
5 PRO – BJ.2/10 McClure to J. C. Ross, 3 October 1854.
6 *Hull Advertiser*, 28 October 1854.
7 Smith, op. cit., cited p. 662.
8 Ibid., p. 682.
9 Ibid.
10 Ibid., cited p. 688.

28 Riding the Globe

1 C. Lloyd, *Mr. Barrow of the Admiralty*, op. cit., cited p. 15.
2 I. Cameron, *Antarctica: The Last Continent*, op. cit., cited p. 160.
3 C. Markham, *The Life of Admiral Sir Leopold McClintock* (John Murray, London, 1909), cited p. 291.
4 J. Ross, *Narrative of a Second Voyage . . .*, op. cit., p. xxi.
5 E. Parry, *Memoirs . . .*, op. cit., cited p. 3.

Epilogue

1 SPRI – MS 248/364 Crozier to J. C. Ross, 10 January 1845.
2 Ibid.
3 A. Friendly, *Beaufort of the Admiralty* (Hutchinson, London, 1977), cited p. 323.
4 BL – MS Eng Lett d.239 Belcher to Napier, 5 October 1854.
5 Ibid.
6 *Dictionary of National Biography*, Vol. II, p. 143.
7 F. Woodward, *Portrait of Jane*, op. cit., cited p. 363.
8 Ibid., cited p. 7.
9 P. Berton, *The Arctic Grail*, op. cit., cited p. 90.
10 L. Huxley, *Life and Letters of Sir Joseph Dalton Hooker*, op. cit., Hooker to Bruce, 6 May 1911, cited p. 479.
11 SAR – DD/HI/553 Lyon to Bayntum, 23 December 1829.
12 SAR – DD/III/553 Lyon to Bayntum, 15 March 1835.
13 C. Markham, *Life of Admiral Sir Leopold McClintock*, op. cit., p. 240.
14 Ibid., cited p. 298.
15 Ibid., cited p. 276.
16 Ibid., p. 279.
17 W. E. Parry, *Thoughts on the Parental Character of God* (Harrison, London, 1841), p. iii.

18 *The Times*, 20 January 1856.
19 Woodward, op. cit., cited p. 291.
20 J. Barrow, *Autobiographical Memoir*, op. cit., p. 480.
21 J. McIlraith, *Life of Sir John Richardson*, op. cit., cited p. 231.
22 Ibid., p. 263.
23 Ibid., p. 264.
24 PRO – BJ.2/12 J. C. Ross to McClure, undated.
25 SPRI – MS 1503/34 Richardson to Fletcher, 23 June 1847.
26 E. S. Dodge, *The Polar Rosses*, op. cit., cited p. 247.
27 MHS – MS Buxton 2 Beaufort to Ross, 14 March 1854.
28 *Dictionary of National Biography*, Vol. XVII, p. 566.
29 T. and C. Stamp, *William Scoresby, Arctic Scientist*, op. cit., cited p. 217.
30 Ibid., Parry to Scoresby, cited p. 218.

Picture sources

Section 1

1. Sir John Barrow by John Jackson (1778–1831) by courtesy of National Portrait Gallery, London
2. 'An eskimo artist recorded the arrival of Ross and Parry in full dress uniform' © Royal Geographical Society, London
3. '*Hecla* and *Griper* in winter harbour' from William Parry, *Journal of a Voyage* (1819–20) © Scott Polar Research Institute, Cambridge
4. 'Cutting into Winter Island' (October 1821) from William Parry, *Journal of a Second Voyage for the discovery of a North-West Passage* © Royal Geographical Society, London
5. 'Situation of H.M. Ships *Fury* and *Hecla* at Igloolik' from William Parry, *Journal of a Second Voyage for the discovery of a North-West Passage* (1822–23) © Royal Geographical Society, London
6. 'Canoe broaching to in a Gale of Wind at Sunrise' (23 August 1821) from John Franklin, *Narrative of Journey* © Royal Geograhical Society, London
7. 'An Eskimaux watching a seal-hole' (c.1824) from William Parry, *Journal of a Second Voyage for the discovery of a North-West Passage* © Royal Geographical Society, London
8. 'Western Outlet of the Strait of the *Fury* and *Hecla*' (c. 1824) from William Parry, *Journal of a Second Voyage for the discovery of a North-West Passage* © Royal Geographical Society, London
9. Sir John Ross by James Green (1771–1834) by courtesy of National Portrait Gallery, London
10. William Edward Parry by Sir William Beechey © National Maritime Museum, London
11. Sir John Franklin by G.E Lewis © Scott Polar Research Institutute, Cambridge
12. Jane, Lady Franklin by Amelie Romilly (1788–1875) by courtesy of National Portrait Gallery, London

13. Admiral Sir George Back (1796–1878) by William Brockedon (1787–1854) ©
    Royal Geographical Society, London
14. Sir John Richardson by Negelen © Scott Polar Institute, Cambridge
15. 'Somerset House Plan' © Scott Polar Institute, Cambridge

Section 2

1. 'Boats on a Swell Amongst Ice' (c. 1826) © Scott Polar Institute, Cambridge
2. Captain Hugh Clapperton by George Manton © Scottish National Portrait
   Gallery, Edinburgh
3. Dixon Dehnam by Thomas Phillips (1770–1845) by courtesy of National
   Portrait Gallery, London
4. Captain G.F. Lyon by R.J. Lane © National Portait Gallery, London
5. Richard Lemon Lander by William Brockedon (1787–1854) by courtesy of
   National Portrait Gallery, London
6. James Clark Ross by John R. Wildman © National Maritime Museum,
   London
7. 'Christmas Harbour, Kerguelen Island' from J. C. Ross, *Voyage of Discovery*
   (1839–43) © Scott Polar Institute, Cambridge
8. 'Beaufort Island and Mt. Erebus' from J. C. Ross, *Voyage of Discovery*
   (1839–43) © Scott Polar Institute, Cambridge
9. '*Erebus* and *Terror*' from J.C. Ross, *Voyage of Discovery* (1839–43) © Scott Polar
   Institute, Cambridge
10. 'Gale in the Pack' from J.C. Ross, *Voyage of Discovery* (1839–43) © Scott Polar
    Institute, Cambridge
11. 'Critical Position of H.M.S *Investigator* on the North coast of Baring Island'
    (20 August 1851), Lieut. S. Gurney Cresswell lithograph © Royal
    Geographical Society, London
12. Sir Richard Collinson by Stephen Pearce (1819–1904) by courtesy of
    National Portrait Gallery, London
13. Sir Robert McClure by Stephen Pearce (1819–1904) by courtesy of National
    Portrait Gallery, London
14. John Barrow by John Lucas © National Maritime Museum, London

BIBLIOGRAPHY

Arctic

Armstrong, A., *A Personal Narrative of the Discovery of the North-West Passage* (Hurst & Blackett, London, 1857)

Back, G., *Narrative of the Arctic Land Expedition to the mouth of the Great Fish River and along the shores of the Arctic Ocean in the years 1833, 1834 and 1835* (John Murray, London, 1836)

Barrow, J., *Voyages of Discovery and Research within the Arctic Regions* (John Murray, London, 1846)

Beattie, O. and Geiger, J., *Frozen in Time: The Fate of the Franklin Expedition* (Bloomsbury, London, 1987)

Beechey, F., *A Voyage of Discovery towards the North Pole* (John Murray, London, 1843)

Berton, P., *The Arctic Grail* (Viking, New York, 1988)

Braithwaite, J., *A Supplement to Captain Sir John Ross's Narrative of a Second Voyage in the* Victory, *in search of a North-West Passage containing the Suppressed Facts necessary to a Proper Understanding of the causes of the failure of the steam machinery of the* Victory, *and a just appreciation of Captain Sir John Ross's character as an officer and a man of science* (Chapman & Hale, London, 1835)

Collinson, R., *Journal of HMS* Enterprise *on the expedition in search of Sir John Franklin's ships by Behring Strait 1850–55* (Sampson Low, Marston, Searle & Rivington, London, 1889)

Fisher, A., *A Journal of a Voyage of Discovery to the Arctic Regions . . . in the years 1819 and 1820* (Longman, London, 1821)

Fleming, H. (ed.), *Minutes of Council, Northern Department of Rupert Land, 1821–31* (The Champlain Society, Toronto, 1940)

Franklin, J., *Narrative of a journey to the shores of the Polar Sea in the years 1819–20––21–22* (John Murray, London, 1823)

—— Narrative of a Second Expedition to the shores of the Polar Sea in the years 1825, 1826 and 1827 (John Murray, London, 1828)

Glazebrook, G. (ed.), The Letters of Letitia Hargrave (The Champlain Society, Toronto, 1947)

Hood, Robert (ed. Houston, Stuart C.), To the Arctic by Canoe, 1819–1821 (McGill-Queen's University Press, Montreal, 1974)

Huish, Robert, The Last Voyage of Capt. John Ross . . . by an officer attached to the Expedition (John Saunders, London, 1835)

King, R., A Narrative of a journey to the shores of the Arctic Ocean in 1833, 1834 and 1835 (Bentley, London, 1836)

—— The Franklin Expedition from First to Last (Churchill, London, 1855)

Lopez, B., Arctic Dreams (Picador, London, 1987)

Lyon, G. F., Private Journal During the Recent Voyage of Discovery Under Captain Parry (John Murray, London, 1824)

—— A Brief Narrative of an Unsuccessful Attempt to Reach Repulse Bay (John Murray, London, 1825)

MacLeod, M. (ed.), The Letters of Letitia Hargrave (The Champlain Society, Toronto, 1947)

McClure, R. (ed. Sherard Osborn), The Discovery of the North-West Passage by H.M.S. Investigator (Longman, London, 1856)

Masson, L., Les Bourgeois de la Compagnie de Nord-Ouest (2 vols) (Quebec, 1889)

Miertsching, J. (trans. L. Neatby), Frozen Ships – The Arctic Diary of Johann Miertsching 1850–1854 (Macmillan, Toronto, 1967)

Osborn, S., Stray Leaves from an Arctic Journal (Longman, London, 1852)

Parry, W. E., Journal of a Voyage for the Discovery of a North-West Passage . . . in the years 1819–20 (John Murray, London, 1821)

—— Journal of a Second Voyage for the Discovery of a North-West Passage . . . in the years 1821–22–23 (John Murray, London, 1824)

—— Journal of a Third Voyage for the Discovery of a North-West Passage . . . in the years 1824–25 (John Murray, London, 1826)

—— Narrative of an Attempt to Reach the North Pole . . . in the year 1827 (John Murray, London, 1828)

Rich, E. (ed.), Simpson's Athabasca Journal (The Champlain Society, London, 1938)

—— The History of the Hudson's Bay Company, Vol. II, 1763–1870 (Hudson's Bay Record Society, London, 1959)

—— Colin Robertson's Correspondence Book, September 1817 to September 1822 (The Champlain Society, Toronto, 1939)

Richardson, J. (ed. Houston, C. Stuart), Arctic Ordeal. The Journal of John Richardson . . . 1820–1822 (McGill-Queen's University Press, Montreal, 1984)

Ross, John, A Voyage of Discovery . . . for the purpose of Exploring Baffin's Bay and inquiring into the probability of a North-West Passage (John Murray, London, 1819)

—— Narrative of a Second Voyage in Search of a North-West Passage . . . during the years 1829, 1830, 1831, 1832, 1833 (Webster, London, 1835)

—— Explanation and Answer to Mr. John Braithwaite's Supplement . . . (Webster, London, 1835)

—— Observations on a work entitled 'Voyages of Discovery and Research within the

Arctic Regions' written by Sir John Barrow Aetat 82: being a refutation of the numerous misrepresentations contained in that volume (William Blackwood, London, 1846)

—— *Sir John Franklin, a Narrative* (Longman, London, 1855)

Sabine, E. (ed.), *North Georgia Gazette and Winter Chronicle* (John Murray, London, 1821)

Smith, D., *Arctic Expeditions, British and Foreign* (Fullarton, Edinburgh, 1880)

Antarctica and Australia

Bagot, Mrs C., *Links With the Past* (Edward Arnold, London, 1901)

Cameron, I., *Antarctica: The Last Continent* (Cassell, London, 1974)

Fitzpatrick, K., *Sir John Franklin in Tasmania, 1837–43* (Melbourne University Press, Melbourne, 1949)

Fogg, Prof. G. E. and Smith, D., *The Explorations of Antarctica* (Cassell, London, 1990)

Franklin, John, *A Narrative of some passages in the history of Van Diemen's Land* (Taylor, London, 1845)

Huxley, L., *Life and Letters of Sir Joseph Dalton Hooker* (John Murray, London, 1918)

McCormick, R., *Voyages of Discovery in the Arctic and Antarctic and Round the World* (2 vols) (Sampson, London, 1884)

Ross, James, *A Voyage of Discovery and Research in the Southern Antarctic Regions during the years 1839–43* (2 vols) (John Murray, London, 1847)

Africa

Beechey, F. W. and H. W., *Proceedings of the expedition to explore the Northern Coast of Africa . . . in 1821 and 1822* (John Murray, London, 1828)

Boahen, A. Adu, *Britain, the Sahara and the Western Sudan, 1788–1861* (Oxford University Press, Oxford, 1964)

Clapperton, H., *A Journal of a Second Expedition into the Interior of Africa* (John Murray, London, 1829)

Denham, D., Clapperton, H. and Oudney, W., *A Narrative of Travels and Discoveries in northern and central Africa in the years 1822, 1823 and 1824* (2 vols) (John Murray, London, 1828)

Gardner, G., *The Quest for Timbuctoo* (Cassell, London, 1969)

Hibbert, C., *Africa Explored* (Penguin, London, 1984)

Huish, R. (ed.), *The Travels of Richard and John Lander into the Interior of Africa* (John Saunders, London, 1836)

Jackson, J. G., *An Account of the Empire of Marocco . . . and an Interesting Account of Timbuctoo, the Great Emporium of Central Africa* (Bulmer, London, 1814)

Lander, R., *Records of Captain Clapperton's last expedition to Africa* (2 vols) (Colburn & Bentley, London, 1830)

Lander, R. and J., *Journal of an expedition to explore the course and termination of the Niger* (3 vols) (John Murray, London, 1833)

Lloyd, C., *The Search for the Niger* (Collins, London, 1973)

—— *The Navy and the Slave Trade* (Longman, London, 1949)

Lyon, G. F., *A Narrative of Travels in Northern Africa in the years 1818, 19 and 20* (John Murray, London, 1821)

Mackay, M., *The Indomitable Servant* (Rex Collings, London, 1978)

Park, M., *Travels in the Interior Districts of Africa performed under the direction and patronage of the African Association in the years 1795, 1796 and 1797* (Bulmer, London, 1799)

Tuckey, J. H., *Narrative of an expedition to explore the River Zaire* (John Murray, London, 1818)

Biography and General

Barrow, Sir J., *Autobiographical Memoir* (John Murray, London, 1847)

—— *Sketches of the Royal Society & Royal Society Club* (John Murray, London, 1849)

—— *The Mutiny and Piratical Seizure of HMS* Bounty (William Tegg, London, 1876)

Brightfield, M. F., *John Wilson Croker* (Allen & Unwin, London, 1951)

Croker, J. W. (ed. Louis Jennings), *The Croker Papers* (John Murray, London, 1885)

Dawson, W. (ed.), *The Banks Letters* (British Museum, London, 1958)

Dictionary of National Biography (Oxford University Press, Oxford, 1917)

Dodge, E. S., *The Polar Rosses* (Faber and Faber, London, 1973)

Fleming, F. (ed.), *The Pulse of Enterprise* (Time-Life Books, Amsterdam, 1990)

Friendly, A., *Beaufort of the Admiralty* (Hutchinson, London, 1977)

Huxley, J. (ed.), *T. H. Huxley's Diary of the Voyage of HMS* Rattlesnake (Chatto & Windus, London, 1935)

Huxley, L., *Life and Letters of Thomas Henry Huxley* (3 vols) (Macmillan, London, 1913)

Jennings, L. (ed.), *The Croker Papers* (John Murray, London, 1885)

Jerdan, W., *The Autobiography of William Jerdan* (4 vols) (Arthur Hall, Virtue, London, 1853)

Jerrold, W. (ed.), *The Complete Poetical Works of Thomas Hood* (Oxford University Press, Oxford, 1906)

Lamb, G., *Franklin, Happy Voyager* (Ernest Benn, London, 1956)

Lloyd, C., *Mr. Barrow of the Admiralty* (Collins, London, 1970)

Lyon, G., *A Journal of a Residence and Tour in the Republic of Mexico in the year 1826* (John Murray, London, 1828)

McIlraith, J., *Life of Sir John Richardson* (Longman, London, 1868)

Markham, A. H., *The Life of Sir John Franklin* (George Philip, London, 1891)

Markham, C., *The Life of Admiral Sir Leopold McClintock* (John Murray, London, 1909)

Morrell, P. (ed.), *Leaves from the Greville Diary* (Eveleigh Nash & Grayson, London, 1829)

Parry, A., *Parry of the Arctic* (Chatto & Windus, London, 1963)

Parry, E., *Memoirs of Rear-Admiral Sir W. Edward Parry* (Longman, London, 1859)

Parry, W. E., *Thoughts on the Parental Character of God* (Harrison, London, 1841)

Raby, P., *Bright Paradise* (Chatto & Windus, London, 1996)

Royal Geographical Society Journal, Vols 1, 4, 6 and 8 (John Murray, London)

Spufford, F., *I May Be Some Time* (Faber and Faber, London, 1996)

Stamp, T. and C., *William Scoresby, Arctic Scientist* (Caedmon, Whitby, 1976)
Woodward, F., *Portrait of Jane: A Life of Lady Franklin* (Hodder and Stoughton, London, 1951)

Newspapers, Journals

Athenaeum
Beaver
Blackwood's
Edinburgh Review
Fraser's Magazine
Gentleman's Quarterly
Hull Advertiser
Illustrated London News
Musk-Ox
New York Times
Polar Record
Quarterly Review
The Times
Wigtown Free Press

Unpublished Sources

Manuscripts held by the:

Bodleian Library
British Library
Derbyshire Record Office
Dumfries Archive Centre
Museum of the History of Science, Oxford
National Library of Scotland
National Maritime Museum
Natural History Museum, Botanical Library
Public Records Office
Public Records Office of Northern Ireland
Royal Botanic Gardens Library and Archives, Kew
Royal Geographical Society
Royal Society
Scott Polar Research Institute
Somerset Archive and Record Service
West Devon Area Record Office

INDEX

Abernethy, Thomas, 248
Abernethy (ice-master), 356
Aboudah (slave), 226, 228, 229, 256
Achilles of Dundee, 168
Adam, Jean Baptiste, 135–6, 138, 144–5, 149, 151
Adare, Cape, 344
Adele, King of Badagry, 217, 227–8, 256–7
Adelie Land, 334
Admiralty Board, 2–3, 322, 375, 380–1
Admiralty Inlet, 68, 303
Admiralty Range, 344
African Association, 16, 22, 275
Akaitcho (Indian leader), 130–3, 135–6, 145, 150–2
Alaska, 322
Albert, Prince Consort, 358
Aleutian Islands, 394
Alexander, 35, 37, 41, 44, 47–8, 58–9, 75
Ali, Ben, 16
Amundsen, Roald, 422, 424
Anderson, James, 412, 413
Anderson (seaman), 407
Andrew Ross Island, 282, 283
Antarctica, 331–6, 342–7, 423
Arctic Council, 381–2, 386, 387–8, 390, 411
Armstrong, Alexander, 398, 399–400, 402, 406
Arnold, Thomas, 327
Asiatic Society, 274–5
Assistance, 388, 408

Aucklick, J. H., 352
Augustus (Eskimo voyageur), 136, 145, 174
Austin, Horatio, 159, 383, 384, 389, 398
Australia, 17, 126, 276–80, 378, 422–3
Australian Agricultural Company, 277–8
Ayre, Harry, 249

Back, Sir George: character, 127, 134, 319–21, 426, 433; Franklin's first expedition, 127, 128, 133–4, 143, 145–6, 150–2; Barrow's opinion of, 172, 175, 320, 321; Franklin's second expedition, 171–2, 173, 174–5; promotion, 175; John Ross's *Victory* expedition (1829), 247, 295; John Ross rescue mission (1833), 295–6, 318–22; expedition (1836), 324, 325, 326; knighthood, 324; view of Franklin's last expedition, 366, 367–8, 376, 388; Arctic Council, 381, 382; later career, 426
Back River, 322
Badagry, 215, 217, 227–8, 256–7, 262
Baffin, William, 27
Baffin Bay: mapping (1616), 27; existence questioned, 27, 34, 57; Ross's expedition (1818), 34, 39, 41–6, 50, 55, 57, ice, 41–2, 66, 159; mapping (1818), 55, 57; Parry's first expedition (1819), 65–6, 73, 88, 89–90; mapping (1820), 88; Parry's third expedition (1824), 159; John Ross's *Victory* expedition (1829), 252; McClintock's expedition, 413; Franklin's ships, 432

Banks, Sir Joseph: influence on Barrow, 8–9, 11, 378; career, 8–9; Timbuctoo project, 15; Niger project, 19, 177; climate observations, 29–30; North-West Passage project, 32–4; relationship with Parry, 36, 56

Banks Island/Land, 88, 394–5, 397, 399, 402

Barrier, the, 345–6, 354, 434

Barrow, Cape, 344

Barrow, George, 10, 321

Barrow, Sir John: appearance, 157; family background, 3; education, 3–4; travels, 4–5, 6–7; marriage, 5; writings, 5, 7–8, 176, 198, 212, 306, 377; Second Secretary to the Admiralty, 2–3, 5; lifestyle, 6; view of steam power, 11, 19–20, 369; Niger expedition planning, 17–23, 92–4, 177–9, 198, 199, 201–3, 215–16, 253–5; North-West Passage project, 34–7, 62–3, 107, 322, 365–6, 371, 372; relationship with John Ross, 55-8, 62, 63, 244, 248, 249, 306–7, 310, 313, 316–17; Parry's first expedition, 62–3, 89–90; Lyon's career, 105–6, 169; Parry's second expedition, 107–10; Franklin's second expedition, 124–5, 131; Parry's career, 154–5; Parry's third expedition, 157–8, 161; Lyon's expedition (1824), 163, 169; relationship with Back, 172, 175; opinion of Clapperton, 198–9, 216, 229–31; opinion of Lander, 229, 231, 253, 276; North Pole expedition, 233–4; relationship with Duke of Clarence, 242–4; Niger mouth discovery, 271; Geographical Society, 274–6, 280, 322; Arctic Council, 381, 382; opinion of Back, 320; baronetcy, 321; Repulse Bay expedition, 323–4; Antarctic project, 333, 360; Franklin's last expedition, 365–6, 371, 376; retirement, 371, 378, 440–1; death, 379, 380; monument, 420–1; achievements, 11, 422–5

Barrow, John (son of above), 382, 408–9, 431

Barrow, Nony (née Croker), 10, 321

Barrow Strait, 68–9, 72, 298, 323, 377

Bates, Sergeant-Major, 420–1

Bathurst, Cape, 394

Bathurst, Henry, 3rd Earl: Ritchie–Lyon expedition, 94; Lyon's complaints to, 105–6; Denham–Oudney–Clapperton expedition, 177, 184, 186–7; opinion of Barrow, 201; Laing Sahara expedition, 201, 204, 206; Lander's appeals to, 272; opinion of Denham, 430

Bathurst Land, 408

Batty Bay, 298, 300–2, 398

Beagle, 336

Beaufort, Francis: chart-making, 10, 18; relationship with Croker, 18; Geographical Society, 274; Hydrographical Department, 278; correspondence, 285; relationship with John Ross, 312, 314, 442–3; North-West Passage project, 322, 323, 366; Franklin's governorship, 326; work on compasses, 337; James Ross's return, 360; Arctic Council, 381; McCormick's posting, 389; later career, 427

Beaufort Island, 344

Beaufort Sea, 288

Beauparlant, Gabriel, 136, 144

Beechey, Frederick: appearance, 157; Parry's first expedition, 63, 68, 87–8; Blossom voyage, 175–6, 324, 328, 388; North Africa survey, 179–81; North-West Passage project, 366; opinion of Franklin's expedition, 376; Arctic Council, 381, 428; later career, 428

Beechey, William, 180

Beechey Island, 383–4, 385, 407, 408, 431

Belanger, Jean Baptiste, 136, 144, 146–8

Belanger, Solomon, 136, 139, 144, 145

Belcher, Sir Edward: character, 324, 388–9, 409, 423; career, 388; relationship with James Ross, 324, 388; expedition (1852–4), 388–91, 392–3, 407–9, 438; later career, 428–9

Belford (carpenter), 95–6, 99, 100, 101, 102

Bellingshausen, Fabian, Gottlieb Benjamin von, 62, 331

Bello, Sultan: relationship with Kanemi, 194, 223–4; Clapperton's arrival, 196–7; map, 196–7, 198, 202; Laing's arrival, 210–11; Clapperton's second expedition, 219–20, 223–5; Clapperton's funeral, 225

Bellot, Joseph-René, 398, 399, 408, 433

Bellot Strait, 282–3, 399, 413

Belzoni, Giovanni Battista, 202, 217

Benin, Gulf of, 17, 22, 202, 208, 230

Benoit Joseph, 136, 145, 151

Benue, River, 197, 260, 262, 272

Bering Strait, 90, 109, 175, 287, 368, 394

Beverley (surgeon), 44, 47

Beverly, Charles, 237

Bird, Edward: Parry's second expedition, 109, 115; tattoos, 115; Parry's third expedition, 159; Parry's fourth expedition, 237; Antarctic expedition, 335, 338, 358; promotion, 358; Investigator expedition, 380; Arctic Council, 381, 382; later career, 429

Black Joke, 270

Blackwood's Magazine, 58
Blagden, Sir Charles, 378–9
Blanky, William, 372
Bligh, William, 175–6, 198
Bloody Falls, 131, 136
Blossom, 157, 175, 179, 324
Bollman, Doctor, 64
Booth, Sir Felix, 246, 250, 282, 313, 325
Boothia Felix: naming, 282; John Ross's
    Victory expedition (1829), 282, 288, 301,
    314; Back's expedition (1833), 317, 318,
    320; King's expedition proposal, 323;
    Hudson's Bay Company expedition
    (1836), 329; Rae's expedition, 370;
    Franklin's last expedition, 383, 387, 415,
    433; Kennedy-Bellot expedition, 399;
    airstrip, 433
Bornu, 96, 177, 179, 222, 224
Boulton and Watt, 19
Bounty, 175–6
Bounty, Cape, 69
Boyle, John, 403
Boy, King, 265–9
Bradbury (seaman), 400
Braithwaite, John, 283, 310–11
Braithwaite and Erickson, 247, 250
Brass, 265–7
Breadalbane, 408
Bremer, Captain, 276, 279
British Association, 308
British Association for the Advancement of
    Science, 333, 377
Brooke, Sir Arthur de Capell, 274
Brown, Hannah, 312
Browne, Miss, 65, 155–6, 235
Brunel, Isambard Kingdom, 436
Brunswick of Hull, 66
Buchan, David, 35, 51, 52–5, 125–6, 171
Burton, Richard Francis, 424
Bushnan, John, 44, 60, 171
Bussa, 16, 196, 220–2, 233, 255, 258–61
Byam Martin Island, 408

Cabot, John, 27
Caillée, René, 211–12
Canning, George, 242
Cavendish, Henry, 378–9
Chad, Lake: Lyon's Niger theory, 104, 178;
    Oudney–Clapperton–Denham expedition,
    178, 185, 187–8, 191–2, 199, 378; Barrow's
    hopes, 230; Lander's expedition, 255, 260
Chantrey, Sir Francis, 378
Chantrey Inlet, 320, 328, 329, 398
Chatham Islands, 352
Christian's Monument, 282

Christmas Harbour, 338
Clapperton, Hugh: character, 177–8, 180,
    423; first expedition, 177–99; publication
    of first journal, 198–9, 230; advice to
    Laing, 205–6; second expedition, 203,
    209–11, 214, 215–26, 233, 257; death,
    224–5, 430; second journal, 229–31
Clarence Islands, 312, 317
Clavering, Douglas, 122, 153
Cobbett, William, 312
Cockburn Island, 360
Colburn and Bentley, 232
Collinson, Richard: character, 423; *Enterprise*
    expedition, 383, 393–4, 398–9, 409–10;
    Jane Franklin's funeral, 431; later career,
    429–30
Columbus (interpreter), 217–18
Congo, 19–20, 22–6
Congo, River, 17, 21–2, 23–6
Cook, Frederick, 425
Cook, James, 9, 115, 331–3, 361
Coppermine River: Hearne's expedition
    (1771), 124, 131; Franklin's first
    expedition (1819), 124, 131, 132, 135–8,
    141–3, 157; Hudson's Bay Company
    expedition, 328
Cornwallis Island, 69, 383, 389, 414
Cracroft, Sophia, 350, 351, 374, 426, 431
Cranch (collector), 21, 23, 25
Credit (voyageur), 136, 143–4
Cresswell, Lieutenant, 407
Cresswell Bay, 161, 282
Croker, John Wilson: character, 9–10;
    relationship with Barrow, 10, 321;
    relationship with Beaufort, 18;
    relationship with John Ross, 56, 249;
    Parry's promotion, 89; relationship with
    Duke of Clarence, 243, 321; view of
    Australian project, 277; relationship with
    Parry, 278; opinion of Maginn, 308
Croker, Nony, *see* Barrow
Crozier, Francis: Parry's second expedition,
    109; Parry's third expedition, 159–60;
    Parry's fourth expedition, 235, 237;
    Antarctic expedition, 335, 340, 343, 351–2,
    357, 358–9, 360; promotion, 358; Arctic
    Council, 382; declines expedition
    command, 366–7; Franklin's last
    expedition, 373, 374, 410, 411, 415, 417
Cumberland House, 128, 134, 173
Cumberland Sound, 50
Cumberland Strait, 90

Darling, Sir Ralph, 277
Darwin, Charles, 54, 335, 336

Davis, John, 331, 353
Davis Strait, 50–1, 324
Davy, Sir Humphry, 8, 9, 378
Dawson, George, 217–18
Dealy Island, 404
Dease, Peter, 129, 170–1, 174, 328–9, 365
Denham, Dixon: character, 178, 423; Niger
    expedition, 178, 179, 181–93, 197–8, 217;
    journal, 199; death, 199; correspondence,
    207; later career, 199, 270, 430; death, 199,
    430
Derwent River, 349
Des Voeux, Charles, 414
Devon Island, 67
D'Ghies, Hassuna, 213
Dickson, Dr (lawyer/surgeon), 215–16, 217,
    218
Disko Island, 40
Disraeli, Benjamin, 10
D'Israeli, Isaac, 158
Dixon, James, 293
Domville (surgeon), 406
Donkin & Gamble, 64, 108
Dorothea, 20, 23, 35, 39, 52–3
Drummond (naturalist), 171
Dundas, Francis, 5
Dundas, Lord, 380
Dupont (gardener), 94–5, 98
D'Urville, Jules Sébastien-César Dumont,
    333–4, 341, 343, 353

Edinburgh Review, 7, 198, 271
Edusi (historian), 13
Edward VII, King, 437
Elizabeth Harbour, 282
Encyclopedia Britannica, 8, 27
Enderby Brothers, 332
Enderby Land, 332
Enterprise, 380, 382–3, 393–4, 398, 409
Erebus: James Ross's Antarctic expedition,
    335–7, 340, 343, 351–60; Franklin's last
    expedition, 365, 368–9, 372–5, 412, 415,
    432
Erebus, Mount, 344, 346, 347, 423
Eyre (purser), 26

Falkland Islands, 357–9
Fanning, Edmund, 332
Fatima, Lilla, 99, 102
Fawcett, Percy Harrison, 425
Felix Harbour, 283, 289
Fernando Po, 270
Fife (master of the *Hecla*), 122
Fisher, Alexander, 58, 63, 67, 70
Fisher, George, 109

Fitzclarence Islands, 312, 317
Fitzjames, James, 367, 373–4, 382, 415,
    441
Fitzmaurice (mate), 26
Flinders, Matthew, 17, 18, 126
Flushe (governor of Whale Island), 40
Foggy Island, 174
Fontano, Antonio Vincenza, 136, 144, 147
Forday, King, 267
Forlorn Hope, 390
Fort Alexander, 318
Fort Chipewyan, 127, 128, 129, 130, 170
Fort Enterprise, 133–4, 136–8, 140–1, 143,
    144–5, 148–51
Fort Franklin, 174
Fort Providence, 130, 132–3, 151
Fort Resolution, 173
Foster, Henry, 159, 235, 237
Fox, 412, 418
Foxe, Luke, 27, 109
Foxe Basin, 109, 154, 155, 156
Franklin, Eleanor (*née* Porden), 126, 157,
    159, 172–3
Franklin, Eleanor (daughter of above), 173
Franklin, Jane, Lady (*née* Griffin): description
    of explorers, 157–8; relationship with
    Franklin, 172; story of the Clarence
    Islands, 312; Arctic Council, 382, 386;
    husband's career planning, 326–7, 367; life
    in Van Diemen's Land, 339–41, 350, 363–4;
    husband's last expedition, 374; organizing
    rescue missions, 382–3, 384, 386, 398, 412,
    418, 422, 440; reports of husband's end,
    411, 412, 415–16; husband's statue, 422;
    opinion of Back, 426; opinion of
    McClintock, 437; opinion of Rae, 440; life,
    430–1; funeral, 431
Franklin, Sir John: character, 125–6, 423;
    career, 126, 325–6, 364–5, 367; North Pole
    expedition, 35, 52–3; North Pole proposal,
    233, 234; first marriage, 126, 157, 159,
    172–3; first overland expedition (1819),
    63, 123, 124–53, 154; public reception,
    153, 159; second overland expedition
    (1825), 156–7, 170–6; knighthood, 175;
    opinion of John Ross, 245; Geographical
    Society, 275; Arctic Council, 381, 382;
    correspondence, 310, 314, 315–16; North-
    West Passage plans, 322–3; career plans,
    325–6; Governor of Van Diemen's Land,
    326–7, 339–41, 350–1, 363–4; dismissal,
    363–5; last expedition, 362, 366–71, 372–5;
    rescue missions, 375–7, 380–91; mystery
    of end, 410–19, 431–2; death, 415, 416;
    statue, 421–2, 430

Franklin Island, 344, 347
Fraser's Magazine, 308–9
Frobisher, Sir Martin, 27
Frozen Strait, 112, 164, 324
Fundah, 196–7
Fury: description, 108; Parry's second expedition (1821), 107–10, 113–14, 117, 119; Parry's third expedition (1824), 156, 159–61, 322; abandonment, 161, 298, 322; stores, 246, 247, 281, 293, 297–9, 322
Fury and Hecla Strait, 118, 119, 329
Fury Beach, 281, 284, 285, 293–4, 296–7, 413

Galwey (volunteer), 21, 25
Garden Island, 352
Gentleman's Quarterly, 161
Geographical Society, *see* Royal Geographical Society
George III, King, 85
George IV, King (Prince Regent), 35, 199–200, 259
Ghadames, 201, 208
Ghat, 183
Gifford, William, 7
Goderich, Viscount, 275
Goodsir, Harry, 411
Gore, Graham, 372, 373, 414, 415, 416–17
Goulbourne, Henry, 94
Great Bear Lake, 174
Great Fish River, 296, 318–19, 322, 375, 387, 410
Great Slave Lake, 124, 128, 129, 130, 296, 318
Greenacre, James, 312
Greenstockings (Indian girl), 134
Greville, Charles, 242
Griffin, Fanny, 158
Griffin, Jane, *see* Franklin
Grinnell, Henry, 418
Griper, 63, 65–71, 73–8, 122, 156, 162–70
Gustavus IV Adolphus, King, 36

Haddington, Mount, 360
Haddington, Thomas Hamilton, 9th Earl of, 368
Haig, James, 48
Hall, C. F., 122–3
Hamilton, Baillie, 380, 382
Haswell, William, 393–4, 403
Hawkey, Lieutenant, 26
Hay (at Colonial Office), 216, 254
Hearne, Samuel, 124, 131
Hecla: Parry's first expedition (1819), 63, 65–71, 73–8, 83–4, 86; Parry's second expedition (1821), 107–10, 113–14, 117,

119, 121–2; Parry's third expedition (1824), 156, 159–61; Parry's fourth expedition (1827), 234–40
Hecla Cove, 237
Henry the Navigator, 14
Henson, Matthew, 407
Hepburn, John: Franklin's overland expedition, 127, 128–9, 133–4, 143, 146–50, 152; later career, 433
Herodotus, 230
Herschel, John, 378
Hillman, William: Oudney–Denham–Clapperton expedition, 178, 182–3, 186; carpentry, 189, 191, 192, 197–8; return, 198
Hobson, William, 413–14, 418
Holsteinborg, 251
Hood, Robert: Franklin's overland expedition (1819), 127, 129, 130, 134, 140, 143, 146; death, 147–8, 152
Hood, Thomas, 241
Hood's River, 138
Hooker, Joseph Dalton: appearance, 341; Antarctic expedition, 336, 338, 341, 344–5, 353, 357–62; relationship with James Ross, 357–8; Jane Franklin's funeral, 431; advice to Scott, 361; later career, 433–4
Hooker, William, 240
Hooper, William, 63, 67, 109, 159
Hope, Sir George, 36
Hoppner, Henry, 44, 63, 68, 109, 159–61, 247
Houghton, Daniel, 16
Houtson (merchant), 217–18, 219
Hudson, Henry, 27
Hudson Bay, 90, 109, 110, 162, 163, 168
Hudson's Bay Company: history and activities, 111; Franklin's first expedition (1819), 124, 130, 135; Franklin's second expedition (1825), 170; King's attack on, 322; Dease-Simpson expedition (1836), 328–9; Rae's expedition, 370; Anderson's expedition, 411–12
Huish, Robert, 290–1, 311–12
Hull Advertiser, 410
Hunt, Henry, 312
Huskisson, William, 308
Huxley, T.H., 280

Icy Cape, 90, 175
Igloolik Island, 115, 117, 119, 122
Iligliuk, 115
Inglefield, Commander, 388
Intrepid, 388, 408
Investigator, 380, 383, 393–404, 405–8
Isabella, 35, 37, 40, 41–4, 58–9, 75

Isabella of Hull, 303–4

Jackson, James G., 14–15
James Ross Island, 360
James Ross Strait, 288, 422
Jenna, 216, 217
Jerdan, William, 274, 308, 442
John, 247, 251
John I, King of Portugal, 14
Jones Sound, 46, 50, 57, 63, 68, 388, 390
Joule, James, 444
Jowdie (slave), 226–7, 228, 229, 256
Jungavie, 225
Junius (Eskimo voyageur), 136, 143

Kaiami, 220
Kane, Elisha, 385
Kanemi, Sheikh Mohammed El, ruler of
    Bornu, 188–9, 191, 193–4, 219, 223–4
Kano, 194–5, 197
Kater, Henry, 38
Katunga, 219–20
Keats, John, 94
Kellett, Henry, 380, 388, 406, 409, 437
Kendall, E.N., 171
Kennedy, William, 398, 399
Kerguelen Island, 338, 358
Kesa, Mount, 262
King, Richard: Back's expedition (1833),
    318–19; publication of journal, 322;
    overland expedition proposal, 322–4, 327,
    370; attack on Barrow's plans, 369–71;
    rescue mission plan, 375, 387; lectures,
    381
King William Land: naming, 288; John
    Ross's *Victory* expedition (1829), 288, 415;
    Back's expedition (1833), 320; Hudson's
    Bay Company expedition (1836), 329;
    Franklin rescue missions, 383, 395, 409,
    413, 416–19, 432–3; Rae's expedition,
    410; Amundsen's expedition (1905), 422
Kreusenstern, 249, 294
Kuka, 187–9, 192, 197

Laing, Emma (*née* Warrington), 203–7, 435
Laing, Gordon: character, 201, 328, 423;
    Timbuctoo plans, 201–3; marriage, 203–4,
    435; expedition, 205–14, 223; wounds,
    208–9; arrival at Timbuctoo, 209–11;
    death, 211, 233, 435; journal, 211–14, 435;
    memorial, 436
Lake (Captain of the *Thomas*), 267–71
Lancaster Sound: John Ross's expedition
    (1818), 46–50, 55, 56, 58–9, 62, 66, 111,
    245, 306, 309; Parry's first expedition

(1819), 66–9, 71, 73; Parry's third
    expedition (1824), 159; whaling fleet
    (1824), 168; John Ross's *Victory* expedition
    (1829), 252; Franklin rescue missions, 383,
    389, 410
Lander, John, 231, 254–72, 276, 434
Lander, Richard: Clapperton expedition, 215,
    217–18, 220, 224–5; Clapperton's death,
    225, 430; Niger journey, 225–9; return, 229;
    journal, 229, 231–2; Niger expedition,
    253–71; Niger delta journey, 264–8; return
    to England, 268–71; publication of journal,
    271–2, 312; Gold Medal, 276; last Niger
    expedition, 272–3; death, 273; burial, 435;
    memorials, 435
Ledyard, John, 16
Leo Africanus, 13–14
Leviche, Captain, 352
Lewis, Benjamin, 48, 59
Liddon, Matthew, 63, 66, 74
Liddon Bay, 86
Light, William, 290, 311–12
Linnaean Society, 358
Literary Gazette, 274–5, 442
Little Table Island, 236, 240
Livingstone, David, 424
Lockhart (gardener), 21, 26
Longitude, Board of, 27–8, 119, 246
Louis Napoleon, 250
Louis Philippe, King of the French, 333
Lyon, George Francis: appearance, 157;
    character, 95, 157, 423; career, 95, 103,
    105–6, 169, 177; Ritchie's Sahara
    expedition, 95–103; Ritchie's death, 101;
    return, 92, 103, 177; reports on Niger,
    103–4, 179; journal, 106; Arctic expedition
    (1821), 107, 110–23; support for Parry, 155;
    Sahara expedition project (1823), 201;
    Arctic expedition (1824), 156–7, 162–70,
    324; later career, 436; death, 436
Lyon Inlet, 112

Macartney, George, 1st Earl, 4–5, 6
Macaulay, Thomas Babington, 10
McBean, Gillies A., 411
McClintock, Francis Leopold: character, 385,
    425, 437; search for Franklin, 388, 398,
    407, 413; finds remains of Franklin
    expedition, 413–14, 416–18, 422; return,
    418; journal, 438; Jane Franklin's funeral,
    431; speech on Franklin, 424; advice to
    Scott, 434; later career, 436–7
McClure, Robert: character, 393, 423; search
    for Franklin, 383, 393–404; search for
    North-West Passage, 395–8, 405, 422, 429;

starvation in Mercy Bay, 399–403; Belcher's rescue, 403–4, 405–7; return, 407; opinion of Belcher, 409; Admiralty award, 410, 429; journal, 438; later career, 437–8

McCormick, Robert: Parry's fourth expedition (1827), 235, 236; Antarctic expedition, 335–6, 338, 343, 352, 355–9; search for Franklin, 381, 382, 388–91, 398, 416; later career, 438

McDiarmid, George, 248

McDonald, Alexander, 411

Macintosh, Charles, 171

Mackenzie, Alexander, 124

Mackenzie River: Mackenzie's expedition (1789), 124; Franklin's second overland expedition (1825), 157, 170, 173; Hudson's Bay Company's expedition (1836), 328; Franklin rescue missions, 380, 388

Maclise, Daniel, 309

McMurdo, Archibald, 335, 359

Macquarie Island, 352

MacTavish (of Hudson's Bay Company), 319, 320

Magdalena Bay, 52–3

Maginn, William, 308–9

Mandara, 190, 197

Mansa Musa, Emperor of Mali, 14

Markham, Clements, 385, 423–4

Marryat, Frederick, 94

Martin, Sir Thomas Byam, 39

Maskeleyne, Nevil, 8, 378

Melville, 338

Melville, Henry Dundas, 1st Viscount, 5

Melville, Robert Saunders Dundas, 2nd Viscount: first Arctic expedition (1818), 34, 35, 39; conversation with Parry, 55–6; Ross's appeal to, 61; Parry's return, 89; Lyon's promotion, 95; Parry's hydrographic post, 154, 278; Parry's expedition (1827), 234, 244; opinion of steam power, 245

Melville Bay, 41, 65–6

Melville Island (Australia), 276–7

Melville Island (Northwest Territories): naming, 69; Parry's first expedition (1819), 70–1, 73–87, 88; North-West Passage routes, 322, 395, 397; Franklin rescue missions, 383, 385; McClure's expedition, 395, 397, 398–9

Melville Peninsula, 370

Mercy Bay, 398, 399, 400, 403–4, 406–7

Michel, *see* Teroahauté

Middleton, Christopher, 109

Miertsching, Johann, 393, 401, 403, 429

Montagu, John, 339, 350, 363–4

Montreal Island, 412, 413

Moody (Governor of the Falklands), 357

Mora, 190

Morrison, Dr (surgeon), 215, 218

Mukni, Mohammed el, Bey of Fazzan, 96, 98, 99, 100

Murchison, Sir Roderick, 174, 371

Murdoch ('engine man'), 19

Murray, John: *Quarterly Review*, 8; Admiralty publications, 8, 307; expedition journals, 12, 123, 199; Lander's work, 231, 253, 271; travel guides, 275; John Ross's work, 306–7; James Ross's work, 366

Murzouk, 100–2, 177, 181–4

Nansen, Fridtjof, 424

Napoleon, Emperor, 6, 338

Napoleonic Wars, 1, 2, 6–7

Nares, George Strong, 431, 437, 439

Nautical Review, 271

Naval Chronicle, 26

Navy Board Institute, 68, 303

Nelson, Horatio, Viscount, 6, 248

Nelson Head, 394, 396

New Holland, 280

Niger, River, 13–14; Mungo Park's expeditions, 16–17; Banks' proposal, 15–16; Barrow's project, 12, 17; Tuckey's expedition, 18–27; Peddie's expedition, 92–3; Ritchie's expedition, 94–106; Oudney–Clapperton– Denham expedition, 178, 197–8; Beechey's expedition, 179–80; Laing's expedition, 201–3; Clapperton's second expedition, 215–31; Clapperton's arrival, 222, 230; Lander's journey, 225–6; Lander's second expedition, 253–73; discovery of mouth, 271, 378; value of discovery, 197, 422

Nile, River, 178, 192

North Georgia Gazette, 80, 91

North Georgia Islands, 69

North Magnetic Pole, 291–2, 306, 314, 315, 334, 378

North Pole, 33–5, 233–4, 239–40, 244, 390, 424

North Star, 388, 391, 407, 408, 409

North West Company, 111, 124, 130, 131, 134

North-West Passage: search for, 27–8; Banks' project, 32–4; Scoresby's ideas, 32–3, 63, 289, 423; Barrow's project, 34–7, 62–3, 107, 322, 365–6, 371, 372; John Ross expedition (1818), 62–3; Parry's expeditions, 89–91, 122; Franklin's expedition, 131; John Ross's *Victory* expedition, 244–52, 280, 318;

North-West Passage – *contd*
    John Ross's opinion (1835), 425; Barrow's
      plans (1836), 322; Hudson's Bay Company
      expedition, 328; Admiralty prize, 381;
      Franklin rescue missions, 381, 386, 419;
      McClure's expedition, 395–8, 405, 422,
      429; Amundsen's expedition (1905), 422,
      424
Nottingham, George William Finch-Hatton,
    5th Earl of, 376
Nutland (Admiralty messenger), 307
Nyffee, 220

Obie, King, 263–6
O'Connell, Daniel, 312
Open Polar Sea, 34, 244, 423
Osborn, Sherard, 386–7, 388, 408, 430–1,
    438–9
Osmer, Charles, 374
Oudney, Walter, 177–94
Owen, Captain, 278

Park, Mungo: expeditions, 16–17; journal,
    17, 222, 231, 256, 258, 261–2, 433; mystery
    of end, 17, 433; Clapperton's search, 196,
    220–2, 233; Sultan Bello's information,
    196; Laing's search, 205, 222n; stories of
    murder, 221–2; Lander's search, 256,
    258–62
Parry, Charles, 155, 156, 169
Parry, Isabella (*née* Stanley), 159, 235–6,
    278–9, 439
Parry, Sir William Edward: appearance,
    157; character, 36, 423; childhood, 425;
    career, 36–7; John Ross's expedition
    (1818), 35–50; relationship with John
    Ross, 55–6, 58, 60, 245, 249, 282, 309–10,
    376; first expedition (1819), 56, 61,
    63–72, 73–88; provisions, 63–4, 76;
    entertainments, 64, 75, 79–80, 113, 160;
    relationship with Miss Browne, 65,
    155–6, 158, 235; overwintering on
    Melville Island, 73–87; return, 88;
    reception, 99; journal, 89–90; opinion of
    North-West Passage, 89–91, 366; second
    expedition (1821), 107–22, 324;
    overwintering on Winter Island, 112–17;
    land exploration 117–19; overwintering
    on Igloolik, 119–22; return, 122; rumours
    of disgrace, 122–3; post as hydrographer,
    154–5, 243; third expedition (1824),
    156–62, 322; ball (1824) 159;
    overwintering at Port Bowen, 160;
    abandonment of *Fury*, 161–2; court
    martial, 161–2; opinion of Lyon's

    treatment 169–70; fourth expedition
    (1827), 233–41, 244; marriage, 235–6;
    Australian post, 277–9; view of Franklin's
    expedition, 368, 376; Arctic Council, 381,
    382; later career, 439; death, 439
Parry Mountains, 349
Pasko (interpreter), 217, 228, 229, 256,
    259
Pearce, Captain, 215, 218, 229
Pearce, Samuel, 382
Pearson, John, 78
Peary, Robert Edwin, 425
Peddie, John S., 411
Peddie, Major, 92–3
Peel, Sir Robert, 321, 366
Peel Sound, 383, 386, 414
Peltier, Joseph, 136, 145, 149
Penny, William, 383, 384, 389, 398
Penrose, Sir Charles, 95–6
Perrault, Ignace, 136, 144, 147
Phipps, Constantine, 234, 237
Phoenix, 407–8
Pim, Lieutenant, 404, 405–6, 407
Pioneer, 388, 408
Pitcairn Island, 175
Pliny, 230
Plover, 394
Point Barrow, 328, 394
Point Kellett, 398
Point Turnagain, 138, 156, 288, 296, 328
Polo, Marco, 198
Popham, Rear-Admiral Sir Home, 19–20
Porden, Eleanor, *see* Franklin
Porpoise, 334
Port Bowen, 160, 162
Port Essington, 279–80
Possession Island, 343
Prince Albert, 385, 398, 408, 408, 433
Prince Albert Land, 395
Prince of Wales Strait, 395, 396, 398, 402
Prince Regent Inlet: Parry's first expedition
    (1819), 68; North Magnetic Pole theories,
    119; Parry's second expedition (1821), 119;
    Parry's third expedition (1824), 156,
    159–60; John Ross's *Victory* expedition
    (1829), 282–3, 294, 303, 316; John Ross
    rescue plan, 296; Barrow's map, 316;
    Franklin rescue missions, 380, 383, 398,
    413
Providence, Cape, 70
Ptolemy, 13, 230

Quarterly Review, 7–8, 10, 35, 57, 58, 59, 161,
    198, 212, 233, 310, 313
Quorra, River, 196–7, 221, 231

Rabba, 272
Rae, John, 370, 380, 410–11, 412, 440, 441
Raleigh Club, 274–5
Reichard (geographer), 17
Reid, Thomas, 372, 373
Rennie, John, 8, 378
Repulse Bay: Parry's second expedition (1821), 109; Franklin's first overland expedition, 125, 132, 138; Lyon's expedition (1824), 156, 162, 324; Back's expedition (1836), 323–4
Resolute, 404, 406–8, 410
Resolution Island, 110, 111, 127, 164
Richards, Charles, 408
Richardson, Sir John: appearance, 157; Franklin's overland expedition (1819), 127, 130, 135–52; Franklin's second overland expedition (1825), 171, 174–5; knighthood, 175; John Ross rescue proposal, 295–6; on North-West Passage, 318, 322; South Pole proposal, 331; Franklin's last expedition, 368, 376; Franklin rescue mission, 380; Arctic Council, 381; later career, 440–1; death, 441
Ritchie, Joseph, 94–102, 181
Robertson, Colin, 130
Robertson, Doctor, 354
Robertson, William, 59
Rockwood, 251
Roes Welcome Sound, 112, 164
Ross, Andrew, 282
Ross, Ann, Lady (*née* Coulman), 361, 366, 442
Ross, George, 295–6, 320–1, 325
Ross, Sir James: appearance, 37; character, 37, 291, 357, 423; relationship with uncle, 58, 59–60, 291, 312, 313–16, 325; career, 37; uncle's first expedition (1818), 37, 38, 41, 58, 59–60; Parry's first expedition (1819), 63, 79; Parry's second expedition (1821), 109, 122; Parry's third expedition (1824), 159–60; Parry's fourth expedition (1827), 235, 237–40; uncle's *Victory* expedition (1829), 248, 282, 284–8, 291–2, 299, 303, 415; accounts of expedition, 306, 312, 315–16; Special Parliamentary Committee, 313–15, overland expedition project, 322; Davis Strait rescue mission, 324–5; expedition proposal, 327–8; compass tests, 337–8; Antarctic expedition, 331, 334–9, 342–9, 351–7, 359–60, 361–2, 434; in Van Diemen's Land, 339–42, 349–51; in Falklands, 357–9; knighthood, 361; marriage, 361;
refuses expedition command (1844–5), 366–8; Franklin rescue mission, 376–7, 380, 388; relationship with McCormick, 438; Arctic Council, 381, 382; later career, 442; death, 442
Ross, Sir John: appearance, 36; character, 36, 50, 290–1, 423; career, 36, 325; expedition (1818), 35–51, 55–61, 237; Lancaster Sound decision, 46–50, 55–61, 111; controversy on return, 55–61; relationship with nephew, 58, 59–60, 291, 312, 313–16, 325; expedition (1829), 244–52, 280, 281–304, 422; overwintering in Felix Harbour, 283–9; overwintering in Sheriff Harbour, 289; third winter, 292–4; abandonment of *Victory*, 294–5; arrival at Fury Beach, 296–8; overwintering at Somerset House, 299–301; arrival at Batty Bay, 301–2; sailing to Navy Board Inlet, 302–3; rescue, 303–4; responses to expedition, 305–17; marriage, 306, 325, 443; publications, 306–17, 325; expedition proposal, 323; opinion of North-West Passage, 425; British Consul in Stockholm, 325; Franklin's last expedition, 367, 368–9; Franklin rescue mission, 369, 375–7, 383, 384–6, 389; later career, 442–3
Ross, Maria, Lady (*née* Rymer), 306, 325, 443
Ross Ice Shelf, 345
Ross Island, 240
Rousseau, Baron, 213, 435
Royal Arctic Theatre, 79, 113
Royal Geographical Journal, 323
Royal Geographical Society: foundation, 274–5; New Holland exploration, 280; North-West Passage project, 322, 323; James Ross's proposal, 327; Gold Medal award, 329–30; Founder's Medal award, 361; Franklin's last expedition, 366
Royal Society: membership, 8; presidency, 274; lectures, 126; Barrow's election, 8; John Ross's expedition (1818), 38; Parry's election, 89; Parry's expedition (1821), 110; Parry's expedition (1827), 234; James Ross's lecture (1834), 315; North-West Passage project, 322; treatment of Hooker, 336
Rymer, Thomas, 306

Sabine, Edward: on John Ross's expedition (1818), 38; criticisms of John Ross, 56, 57–60; Parry's first expedition (1819), 63, 64, 68, 74, 80, 82–3, 122; niece, 65, 156; Greenland survey, 122; Laing friendship, 201, 205, 211; on North-West Passage, 318;

Sabine, Edward – *contd*
    letters to James Ross, 324, 366–7; on study
    of magnetism, 333; work on compasses,
    337; Franklin rescue question, 376; Arctic
    Council, 381, 382; later career, 443–4
Sabine, Elizabeth, 444
Sabine, Mount, 344
Sackheuse, John, 38, 43
Sahara crossing, 93–4, 99–103, 378
St Germain, Pierre, 135–6, 138, 143, 144
Samandré, François, 136, 145, 149
Savage, Isaac, 345, 349
Savage Islands, 111–12
Scallon (gunnery officer), 81–2
Schi, Prince, 25
Scoresby, Frederick, 308
Scoresby, William: appearance, 31; character,
    32; career, 30–2; North-West Passage
    expedition proposal, 32–4, 63, 289, 423;
    North Pole expedition proposal, 233–5;
    John Ross friendship, 245, 296, 307–8;
    work on compasses, 337–8, 443; on
    Franklin's last expedition, 371, 374; on
    electric lighting, 377–8; on Arctic climate,
    394; later career, 444–5
Scott, Robert Falcon, 239, 361–2, 421, 424,
    434
Scott, Sir Walter, 8
Scott (buried in Winter Harbour), 87
Shackleton, Sir Ernest, 424
Shaka, King of the Zulus, 5
Shari, River, 192–3
Sheriff Harbour, 289
Sibbald, Lieutenant, 358
Sidi el Muktar, 208
Simpkins, A.A., 217
Simpson, George: Franklin's first expedition,
    126, 132, 134–5, 153; Franklin's second
    expedition, 170; opinion of Back, 319, 320
Simpson, Thomas, 319, 320, 322, 328–30, 365
Skead, Francis, 409
Skene, Midshipman, 44
Smith, Christian, 20, 23, 26
Smith Sound: John Ross's expedition (1818),
    46, 50, 57, 310; Parry's expedition (1819),
    63; Franklin rescue plans, 388, 390
Smyth, Captain, 93, 96–7, 179, 181
Snap, 162
Sokoto, 194, 210–11, 214–15, 219, 222–3
Somerset House, 298–302
Somerset Island, 68–9, 281, 399
Sotheby, William, 274
South Magnetic Pole, 343, 344, 349
South Pole, 239, 331, 424
Southampton Island, 164, 166–7, 169, 324

Spackman, Sergeant, 116
Speke, John Hanning, 424
Spencer, Cape, 402
Spink (sailor), 54–5
Spitsbergen, 4, 52–3, 54, 234, 236–7, 244, 316
Spittle (mate of the *Thomas*), 269–70
Stanley, Edward George Smith Stanley,
    Lord, 364–5, 367, 370, 379
Stanley, Sir Henry Morton, 424
Stanley, Isabella, *see* Parry
Stanley (surgeon), 412
Staunton, Thomas, 4
Stockwell (commander of marines), 270
Stuart, Sir Charles, 94
Sturt, Charles, 379
Sullivan, C.J., 345
Sylvester (stove designer), 108, 112

Talbot, William Henry Fox, 335n
Tasmania, *see* Van Diemen's Land
Tennyson, Alfred, Lord, 431
Teroahauté, Michel, 136, 144, 146–8
Terror: Back's expedition (1836), 324; James
    Ross's Antarctic expedition, 324, 334–7,
    351–60; Franklin's last expedition, 365,
    368–9, 372–5, 412, 415, 432
Terror, Mount, 344
Thom, William, 59, 248, 296
Thomas, Chimham, 300
Thomas of Liverpool, 264, 267–70
Thornton (London merchant), 246
Three Brothers of Hull, 40
Tierra del Fuego, 359–60
Timbuctoo: reports of, 13, 14–15, 98, 196;
    Banks' project, 15; Ritchie's expedition
    (1818), 93, 96, 98; Oudney–Denham–
    Clapperton expedition, 196; Laing's
    expedition, 201, 203, 205, 208–12; Laing's
    arrival, 209–12, 378, 422
Times, The, 311, 386, 439
Toole, Ernest, 192
Trent, 35, 39, 52, 54, 127
Treurenberg Bay, 237
Tripoli, 180, 203–4, 213, 233
Tshadda, River, 260
Tuckey, James Kingston: appearance, 21;
    career, 17–18, 21; health, 17, 21, 23;
    marriage, 21; Niger expedition, 18–20;
    mission, 21–3; Congo voyage, 23–6; death,
    26
Tudor (Comparative Anatomist), 21, 25
Tulluahin (Eskimo), 286
Tyrwhitt (in Kuka), 192

Union Harbour, 384

Vaillant, Registe, 136, 143–4
Valentine (whaling captain), 168
Van Diemen's Land (Tasmania), 326–7, 339–41, 349–51, 363–4
Victoria, Queen, 343, 358, 410, 428, 434
Victoria Island, 395, 398
Victory, 247–52, 281–95, 314
Victory Point, 288, 292, 414, 417
Viscount Melville Sound, 69

Wager Bay, 323
Walden Island, 236
Walnut Shell, 171, 172
Warrington, Emma, *see* Laing
Warrington, Frederick, 445
Warrington, Hanmer: character, 97; career, 97; Ritchie's expedition, 97; Oudney's expedition, 179, 181–4, 187; Laing's expedition, 203–7, 209–13, 233; daughter's marriage, 203–7, 435; later career, 445
Warrington, Henry, 445
Warrington, Herbert, 445
Watt, James Jnr., 19
Wawa, 220–1, 226, 260
Weddell, James, 332
Weddell Sea, 332
Weeks (clerk), 134–5
Wellington, Arthur Wellesley, 1st Duke of, 243, 246
Wellington Channel: naming, 69; Parry's first expedition (1819), 69; Franklin's last expedition, 368, 383, 414; Franklin rescue missions, 383, 385, 388–90, 414; exploration, 418–19

Wentzel (interpreter), 130, 135–7, 152
Whitefield (seaman), 396
Wilkes, Charles, 334, 341–2, 349, 352
Wilkes Land, 349, 352
Wilks, Samuel, 127
William IV, King (Duke of Clarence): John Ross's expedition (1818), 39; Lord High Admiral, 242–4; relationship with Croker, 243–4, 321; John Ross's expedition (1829), 250; Lander's expedition, 271; John Ross's knighthood, 305, 313; Clarence Islands, 312–13
William Harris, 271
Winter Harbour, 71, 86–7
Winter Island, 112
Woon (marine sergeant), 400
Wynniat, Robert, 400–1, 407

Yauri, 222, 258–60
Yeou, River, 191–2, 194, 198, 198
York Factory, 127, 153, 411
Yorktown, 352
Young, Thomas ('Phenomenon'), 8, 378
Yussuf Karamanli, Pasha of Tripoli: character, 97; offers of help to British expeditions, 93, 96–7, 177; Ritchie–Lyon expedition, 96–8; Oudney–Denham–Clapperton expedition, 177, 179–80, 184, 188–9; Laing's expedition, 204, 213

Zuma, 220–1, 226, 229, 231